TOWARD
HUMANISTIC
TEACHING
IN HIGH SCHOOL

Aurelius

WEEMS A. SAUCIER
Northern Illinois University

ROBERT L. WENDEL
Miami University, Ohio

RICHARD J. MUELLER
Northern Illinois University

TOWARD HUMANISTIC TEACHING IN HIGH SCHOOL

D. C. HEATH AND COMPANY
Lexington, Massachusetts   Toronto   London

PREFACE

This book was written for use in a course of general methods for high school teaching. It can also be used effectively for supplementary reading in special methods courses and in educational foundation courses.

As indicated by the book's title, its central purpose is to provide both the beginning and the experienced high-school teacher with help toward humanistic teaching. This kind of teaching is focused on meeting the present and future needs of every kind of student for life in the modern world. In a humanistic atmosphere, both the teacher and the student cooperatively and reflectively identify the students' educational needs. In the process, the teacher involves the student in learning through choosing, investigating, discovering, creating, generalizing, evaluating, applying, and performing. This teaching-learning process also requires extensive sharing between teacher and student and student and student. Thus humanistic teaching is democratic teaching. It has been found to produce not only satisfactory academic achievement, but also to develop in students democratic traits they need to become useful citizens in an interdependent social order. Descriptions and examples of this kind of teaching are presented throughout the book.

The writing is forward looking, suggesting adjustments in teaching in accord with the requirements of a rapidly changing world. It repeatedly comes to grips with current educational thought and classroom procedure in high-school teaching, focusing on learning that develops the whole student. There is recognition of the difference between mere change and real progress—change chiefly for ease, convenience, display, or novelty and change for meeting the actual needs of young people in education directed toward worthwhile goals.

The book aids the teacher who wishes to appraise the "old" and the "new" of theory and practice. It does not accept or reject thought or procedure chiefly because of its period of origin. Instead it subjects all educational beliefs and practices to four points of reference: (1) various problems of youth in present-day society, (2) a sound view of learning, (3) the democratic ideal, and (4) educational research.

Part I presents basic ideas and educational objectives, which are of value in the rational evaluation of specific methods and techniques in classroom procedures. Parts II and III explain and illustrate how a teacher may use the fundamental concepts of education in the selection and application of particular methods and techniques in different teaching-learning situations. The practices recommended, whether traditional or innovational, are

v

supported by modern educational theory and by documented experimentation.

The concluding chapters, which comprise Part IV, are designed to focus attention on special means and processes, materials, guidance, discipline, and evaluation of results. These chapters provide further evidence that means of instruction do not have inherent values but are valuable only as contributors to acceptable ends and that innovations (or so-called innovations) may be new in form but old or even unsound in view of educational theory and research. They show also how special aspects of the educational process may be improved in effectiveness as they are considered integral parts of the process.

There is implicit and explicit recognition in all chapters that the teacher is the most important factor in the student's school environment. This is essential, because some teachers assert that an educational concept will not work, when inquiry reveals that they are unqualified or disinclined to make it work. Accordingly, there is repeated effort to help the teacher realize that in the provision of relevant, high quality learning for different students, the role of a particular form or technique of instruction is less important than the strong commitment of a skillful teacher to psychologically and philosophically sound objectives for all classroom procedures.

A feature of the book that is especially helpful to the beginning teacher is the frequent reference to sources of teaching-learning materials. These sources are given at several points, particularly in Chapters 7–10 and 13. Another desirable characteristic is the many reports of experiments showing how teachers have improved both quality and quantity of learning, by focusing on involvement of students in learning through a process of goal-seeking, inquiring, reflecting, and discovering. Finally, there are explanations and examples of how this teaching-learning process may be used effectively in teaching any subject of the high-school curriculum.

In the presentation of sound, effective classroom practices, the authors received help from experiences in visiting student teachers in several modern high schools, some within and some near Chicago, and they drew extensively on professional books and magazines. Our thanks are due to publishers who graciously granted permission to quote from their books or periodicals. The writers are particularly indebted to Ollie Rauls for her diligence in copying the manuscript and to Ernest E. Bayles, University of Kansas, for his suggestions and assistance in the process of writing the book.

Weems A. Saucier
Robert L. Wendel
Richard J. Mueller

CONTENTS

PART II MAJOR STEPS OF TEACHING

Chapter 4 THE TEACHER-STUDENT ASSIGNMENT 61

Chapter 5 THE STUDY PERIOD 83

Chapter 6 THE CULMINATING PERIOD 102

PART I

FUNDAMENTAL
CONCEPTS
FOR TEACHING

CHAPTER 1

The inclusive function of the high school is to meet the actual educational needs of all students for democratic living in modern society. This reason for the existence of the secondary school constitutes the point of reference for evaluation of every teaching procedure. To make proper use of this point of reference, teachers first must have realistic conceptions about the students' concerns and needs. This is basic to the study of methods of teaching in junior and senior high schools.

SOCIAL FORCES AFFECTING STUDENTS

The Home

There is consensus among psychologists and sociologists that the home is the greatest single social force affecting adolescents. High-school students who experience no strong emotional conflicts, extreme anxieties, or serious difficulties in social adjustment have had, in most cases, parents who guided them toward the development of sound personalities. On the other hand, students who have developed conflicts within themselves and with society usually have had unwise parents who coddled, nagged, or suppressed them. Students who have had irritable and dictatorial parents can be expected to reflect the treatment received from such parents. If they have not been given suitable experiences in the choice and pursuit of beneficial group activities under the guidance of sympathetic parents, they probably will be deficient in mental health and social responsibility. The typical delinquent's family is likely to be hostile, nonconforming, unstable, and anxiety-ridden. Discipline alternates between laxity and autocratic, cruel treatment.

Family influence is obvious also in the case of those who remain

UNDERSTANDING STUDENTS

in school and succeed. Havighurst reported a five-city study which showed that homes of stayins typically were happy in contrast to homes of drop-outs and that the former homes surpassed the latter homes in encouraging children to graduate from high school and attend college.[1] Brembeck drew similar conclusions from reports of other investigations. He added that family status evidently has a direct bearing on the child's self-concept, which in turn affects his success in school.[2] The conclusion seems to be that, in addition to having normal or superior intelligence, those who do well in high school usually come from families that stimulate them and help them succeed.[3]

The Peer Group

Another social group affecting the student is the peer group, clique, or gang. In some instances this group may have an even stronger influence on high-school students than the family group. Writers on juvenile gangs have agreed that members tend to lose their individualities and become submerged in the group. The individual is very loyal to the gang and will not take any step that he or she knows will bring condemnation from it. Although delinquent gangs interfere with the proper social development of adolescents, other kinds of gangs and youth groups in fact may facilitate this development. Youngsters may organize themselves into groups that satisfy commendable desires—to gain security, to raise self-esteem, and to obtain social approval. Such groups constitute strong socializing forces, which a high-school teacher needs to recognize to study students. If a student acts foolishly or antisocially, often it is with the belief that the peer group approves such action. Further, confusion and frustration on the part of the student may be the result of having to choose between loyalty to the adolescent group and a desire to meet the demands of adults inside and outside the school.[4]

Adult Groups

As just indicated, adult groups are also very effective in determining student character and conduct. All the organizations of youth are patterned after or are part of the organizations of adults. Many of these are very commendable. However, others function in ways that do not make them models for children or adolescents. Consider, for example, the violence of

1 R. J. Havighurst and others, eds., *Society and Education: A Book of Readings*, Allyn and Bacon, Boston, 1967, pp. 96-101.
2 C. S. Brembeck, *Social Foundations of Education: Environmental Influences in Teaching and Learning*, 2nd ed., John Wiley, New York, 1971, pp. 123-132.
3 Ibid., Chaps. 5-6, 19.
4 J. E. Horrocks, *The Psychology of Adolescence*, 3rd ed., Houghton Mifflin, Boston, 1969, Chap. 14; G. Graham, *The Public School in the New Society: The Social Foundations of Education*, Harper and Row, New York, 1969. Chap. 15; and H. Wagner, "The Increasing Importance of the Peer Group During Adolescence," *Adolescence* (Spring, 1971), 6, pp. 53-58.

racist groups, the emotional demonstrations of political conventions, both the prejudice and blind loyalty to political parties, the economic warfare between capital and labor, and the economic as well as military warfare among nations. In view of some adult group behaviors, members of delinquent gangs or other such youth groups may sincerely believe that their organizations should not be condemned. Understandably, many young persons are likely to be disillusioned as they learn that there is a wide gap between the way they are expected to act and the way many adults act.

The Community

Finally, it should be noted that students are products of their whole community. This is an observable fact; and it has been shown by studies of areas of cities where juvenile delinquency is and is not prevalent. Of significance here is the fact that some of the responsibilities for the development of adolescents, formerly considered as belonging to the home, have been assumed increasingly by governmental and private agencies of the community. Of particular value are the youth-serving agencies created by schools, churches, government agencies, and independently formed associations. Examples are Hi-Y Clubs, Y-Teens, Girl Scouts, and Boy Scouts. Unfortunately, all such agencies of the community are likely to be unavailable to teen-agers in communities of low socioeconomic classification. This may partially explain why a high percent of delinquents and dropouts live in depressed areas of our cities. Those youths, lacking adequate help from socially beneficial groups, are inclined to form delinquent groups or gangs as a means of seeking collective solutions to their problems of growing up.[5]

The typical community stimulates and directs students toward both social and antisocial conduct. It is obvious that nearly all young persons receive from their communities cultural and educational advantages not experienced by most of their parents. On the other hand, these youngsters as well as adults are confronted with large and somewhat impersonal organizations, which are often in conflict with one another and are adept in the use of modern means of spreading propaganda. The individual in such a community is likely to have difficulty in deciding intelligently whether a particular group is shortsighted and selfish or has a broad social outlook. This suggests the need for extended, cooperative effort between community and school to assist young people in dealing with the problems of living.

[5] W. B. Brookover and E. L. Erickson, *Society, Schools, and Learning,* paper, Allyn and Bacon, Boston, 1969, Chap. 3; and G. Unks, "The School in the Social Order," *High School Journal* (January, 1971), 54, pp. 217-231.

Suggestions for Teaching

Recognition of the role of the social environment in the development of high-school students brings with it the need for studying each student's particular environment—past and present. Knowledge thus gained may aid the teacher in understanding why students engage in certain kinds of behavior. It may show good personal adjustment in some social groups but maladjustment in others. Some students who are in harmony with the social ideals of their peer groups may be in conflict with those of the school staff. Others may be adaptable, vocationally and socially, to life on the farm or in the shop but be misfits and failures in the traditional academic atmosphere of the high school. Indeed, this may also be true of the teacher, who may have difficulty in fitting into some of the social and economic groups of the students. It behooves the teacher to understand and to be charitable toward each student and to go as far as possible toward providing a school environment that will assist everyone in preparation for life outside of school.

This suggests that the prospective secondary teacher should extend study of the nature and needs of high-school students beyond courses in educational psychology and educational sociology and include courses in methods and student teaching. In fact, since our changing society continuously produces changes in the concerns and needs of high-school students, all teachers must keep up by studying and adjusting instruction to those concerns and needs. The authors' observations and some of the educational research they have reported indicate that the current dissatisfaction and unrest of students have been, at least to some extent, of many teachers' failures to comprehend their social backgrounds and to provide them with suitable guidance and instruction.[6]

If teachers assume that the student's inherited condition completely explains peculiar or undesirable conduct, they may react as though they are helpless or may apply only repressive measures. On the other hand, if they view the student's attitudes and habits as stemming chiefly from past environments, they may conclude that one way to improve attitudes and habits is to improve the present environment in the school. Precepts and corrections will not suffice. Even the example of the teacher's own conduct may be a weak social force in comparison with that of the student's contemporaries.

CONCERNS OF STUDENTS

Further understanding of students requires an understanding of their major concerns or problems. There has been sufficient investigation of

6 For instructions about how to study and guide students, see Chap. 13.

students' problems for teachers to know with considerable certainty their interests, anxieties, and difficulties.[7] Such investigation, reveals that the problems may be grouped under a few major headings such as the following:

1. Education—inefficiency in basic skills, ineffective study habits, low motivation, too many outside activities, and inappropriate instruction.
2. Health and physical condition—poor habits of eating, sleeping, and exercise; reactions to physical handicaps and blemishes and to unsatisfactory height and weight; and avoidance of the harmful health habits of many adults.
3. Home and family—unhappy relationships with parents and siblings, parental domination or rejection, moral or financial problems, and neglect or abandonment by one or both parents.
4. Sex and boy-girl relationships—the conflict between their sexual behavior and the demands of adult society, the changing beliefs and attitudes of some people about sex, and proper conduct in dating.
5. Vocation—the frequent gap between ambitions and abilities, difficulties toward preparation for a chosen vocation, the probability that one's occupation will be discontinued, and the securing of helpful guidance in school.
6. Religion and ethics—questions about existence and nature of God, religions of the world, and rightness or wrongness of individual and of group conduct.
7. Nation and world—urban conditions, rights and responsibilities among races and among nations, and causes and preventions of wars.[8]

Obviously, some of the problems do not apply to some youths or are not recognized as such by them. An obligation of counselors and teachers is to assist students in recognizing and dealing with their real personal and social problems in a changing and perplexing social order.

Educational Problems

The characteristics of those having special educational problems are suggested in the studies of underachievers, including those with high IQ's. Their underachievements can be viewed as resulting from their nonintellectual behavior characteristics. Beginning in elementary school, they have developed feelings of inadequacy, rejection by their peer groups,

[7] A valuable means of studying the problems of youth is provided by questionnaires and inventories. These may be purchased from companies listed in Footnote 10 in Chap. 13.
[8] J. F. Adams, "Adolescents' Identification of Personal and National Problems," *Adolescence* (Fall, 1966), 1, pp. 240-250; E. B. Hurlock, *Adolescent Development*, 3rd ed., McGraw-Hill, New York, 1967, pp. 13-18; W. H. Lowry and R. R. Reilley, "Life Problems and Interests of Adolescents," *Clearing House* (November, 1970), 45, pp. 164-168.

poor mental health, vague educational and vocational goals, insufficient motivation, and generally negative attitudes toward schoolwork and authority figures. Indeed, such characteristics are rather common among most underachievers, and they reduce or block efforts of those students to learn. In addition, investigations reveal that many students who are otherwise quite capable of normal achievement in school are underachievers because of deficiencies in reading skills.

The extent of students' educational problems is underscored in the study of those who leave high school before graduation. About 22 percent of those who enter senior high school leave before graduation. Of these dropouts, about three times as many quit school during the last two years as during the first two.[9] The chief reason is their lack of interest in an instructional program that has little relevance to their needs. Success in school is a key factor in a student's continuing there.

Additional findings about students who quit school reveal that some of them have IQ's of 110 and above. It also has been found that fewer boys than girls continue in high school until graduation, the ratio being about 2 to 3. Further analysis of the dropouts indicates that they belong to underprivileged groups, are overage for their grade, are frequently absent, are failing in one or more courses, and participate very little in extracurricular activities. Obviously, the secondary school must improve the adjustment of its instructional programs to the abilities, interests, and needs of students, particularly boys, so that it will not only educate them well but also increase its holding power over them.[10]

The point of emphasis here is that if the school provides an educational program for all kinds of students, many who ordinarily would drop out will remain. Typically, these young people have experienced in their homes and elsewhere meager language facilities, a poor educational tradition, restricted mental stimulation, and low motivation; and they have been retarded one or more years in reading. These students need help in raising their self-esteem after they have experienced years of failure in reading and other school activities and their peers, parents, and teachers have indicated low expectation for their future academic attainments.[11] Certainly, it is better for these young people to be engaged in some kind of worthwhile school activity than to be out of school, vocationally and socially unprepared for life. Indeed, providing for the student's success in school is essential both for effective learning and continuing in school. A

9 R. H. Barr and B. J. Foster, *Fall 1968 Statistics of Public Elementary and Secondary Schools*, U.S. Government Printing Office, Washington, D.C., 1969, p. 17.

10 R. L. Abrell and C. C. Hanna, "High School Student Unrest Reconsidered," *High School Journal* (March, 1971), 54, pp. 396-404; J. L. French, "Characteristics of High Ability Dropouts," *National Association of Secondary School Principals Bulletin* (February, 1969), 53, pp. 67-79.

11 R. J. Havighurst, "Unrealized Potentials of Adolescents," *National Association of Secondary School Principals Bulletin* (May, 1966), 50, pp. 75-96; and R. J. Havighurst and D. U. Levine, *Education in Metropolitan Areas*, 2nd ed., Allyn and Bacon, Boston, 1971, Chap. 3.

combination of proper guidance, good teaching methods, and relevant subject matter will assist students in attacking their present and future life problems. The teacher who cannot help students in dealing with their life problems, will not help them very well toward success in school. Personal and social problems and educational problems are intertwined. This points to the need for personalized instruction.[12]

Problems of Health and Physical Condition

Personal problems of students requiring special attention are their health and physical condition. Adolescence is not marked by unusual illnesses or physical disorders. Yet investigations indicate that the attitudes and habits of health developed by many teen-agers cause about 25 percent of young people in their twenties to begin adult life with physical handicaps that interfere with their usefulness and happiness. Significantly, many of this group have health habits and physical defects of which they are unaware or which they are unable or unwilling to correct. These facts suggest that health education in the secondary schools must include a clinical program to meet the special physical needs of large numbers of students.

Health education at the secondary school level is urgently needed to help teen-agers confront the following health problems of society:

1. Alcohol, tobacco, and drugs
2. Venereal disease and illegitimacy
3. Malnutrition
4. Quackery
5. Early prevention and detection of disease
6. Accident prevention
7. Environmental pollution[13]

In an effort to improve students' attitudes and habits toward their health and physical condition, the teacher needs to recognize that those attitudes and habits have been produced largely by culture, particularly that in the home and in the peer group. It is also helpful to note that, typically, teenagers from low-income families have more health problems than

[12] B. H. Hackney, Jr., and C. A. Reavis, "Poor Instruction—The Real Cause of Dropouts," *Journal of Secondary Education* (January, 1968), 43, pp. 18-25; E. G. Dauw, "Individual Instruction for Potential Dropouts," *National Association of Secondary School Principals Bulletin* (September, 1970), 54, pp. 9-21; W. H. Miller and E. Windhauser, "Reading Disability Tending toward Delinquency?" *Clearing House* (November, 1971), 46, pp. 183-187.
[13] Adapted from J. C. Reynolds, Jr., and L. R. Wooton, "Health Education: Golden Opportunity for the Middle School," *Clearing House* (December, 1972), 47, p. 220. See also H. L. Munson, *Foundations of Developmental Guidance*, Allyn and Bacon, Boston, 1971, Chap. 10; L. Cole and I. N. Hall, *Psychology of Adolescence*, 7th ed., Holt, Rinehart and Winston, New York, 1970, Chaps. 6-7; D. J. Huberty, "Drug Abuse: A Frame of Reference for Teachers," *High School Journal* (February, 1972), 55, pp. 234-240.

those from other income brackets. Then the teacher may be instrumental in providing counsel and instruction as the means of meeting the physical needs of particular individuals and groups who may have harmful and deeply ingrained attitudes and habits.

Health instruction must be vitalized by all possible means, and an adequate program of physical exercise must be provided. Courses such as general science, home economics, and health may well include functional instruction on nutrition and diet. In teaching these courses, there can be effective use of such aids as paperbacks, periodicals, pictures, film strips, statistics, graphs, and talks by specialists. Further, as far as possible, the instruction should be organized around students' problems and their need to be directed toward attacking these problems. Such instruction may assist them to see how improvement of health can promote improvement in complexion, how an intelligent conception of physical appearance may be developed better in a world of reality than in the make-believe of television, and how some adults have succeeded in adjusting to unavoidably defective physiques. Of supreme importance is that teachers, counselors, and administrators do all they can to assist boys and girls to have good health as a basis for being good students and citizens.

Problems of Home and Family

That many students have anxieties arising from conflicts and difficulties in the home has been indicated in preceding paragraphs. We have noted that delinquents, for example, usually come from homes that fail to make proper provision for children's all-round development—emotional, social, vocational, and cultural. In fact, some home environments actually train children for delinquency. The home in which one or both parents neglect or reject the child is certainly developing the aggressive, antisocial behavior of the delinquent. Likewise, the extremely withdrawn, unresourceful, and emotionally immature child ordinarily comes from a home in which parents are so emotional and solicitous about their children that they pamper and overly protect them. Such children may become so passive, emotionally unstable, and dependent that they are unable to face the realities of the modern world. In extreme cases, they may become subjects for a mental hospital.[14]

Teachers in high school would do well to learn about the kind of home each student has. They can modify, or at least arrest, the aggressive, antisocial conduct of those who are neglected or rejected in the home by providing them with evidence of acceptance, recognition, and security. What teachers may not have recognized clearly is that they may help those who have been pampered or dominated in their homes by giving them experiences in assuming responsibility and in thinking and acting for them-

14 P. A. Clarke, *Child-Adolescent Psychology*, Merrill, Columbus, Ohio, 1968, pp. 179-199.

selves. Freedom to plan and to carry out plans under the thoughtful guidance of the teacher is what they need. Furthermore, all should have opportunities to concentrate on the study of significant problems which today's youth must face. These must be built-in objectives of all courses in the secondary school curriculum.

Problems of Sex and Boy-Girl Relationships

Other personal-social problems of major concern to students involve their sex instincts and the achievement of satisfactory boy-girl relationships. That more than 50 percent of adolescent boys do not develop attitudes and habits of sex in accordance with the expressed standards and laws of society is indicated by the well-known Kinsey study. Apparently, millions of the male population of this country experience a conflict between sexual behavior and legal, social, and moral demands, with the concomitant effects of intellectual dishonesty, inner conflict, lowered self-respect, and a demoralizing sex life. In investigations, many girls likewise reveal that they experience perplexities and anxieties in their sex life that interfere with emotional and social maturity. Furthermore, many boys and girls state that their chief source of information about sex is their peer group rather than their home, church, or school. They also express a strong desire for adequate, dependable information bearing on their sex problems.[15]

If we are to judge from the actions of some parents, administrators, and teachers, it would seem that youngsters receive the best information about sex from one another and offering them any kind of sex instruction in school will do little except increase the preoccupation with sex that they already have. Those who hold such views should note that sex offenders as a group are notoriously ignorant and distorted in sexual matters. The obviously sound conclusion is that the school, along with the home and the church, must assume its responsibility to provide young people with suitable sex education.[16]

It is encouraging to note that a Gallup Poll revealed that 72 percent of parents favor sex education in public schools and only 22 percent express opposition.[17] Moreover, in localities where a positive program has been adopted there has been little active opposition. In some communities it has been necessary to deal with opposing forces by introducing the instruction quietly, gradually, and incidentally. Among the subjects most suitable as a vehicle for instruction have been science, the social studies,

15 A. C. Kinsey and others, *Sexual Behavior in the Human Male*, W. B. Saunders, Philadelphia, 1948; A. M. Juhasz, "Student Evaluation of a High School Sex Education Program," *California Journal of Educational Research* (September, 1971), 22; pp. 144-155.
16 M. L. Thompson, R. H. Nelson, and G. H. Farwell, "Sex Education: A Ball Nobody Carries," *Clearing House* (February, 1965), 39, pp. 353-358.
17 G. Gallup, "Second Annual Survey of the Public's Attitude toward the Public Schools," *Phi Delta Kappan* (October, 1970), 52, p. 103.

physical education, and home economics. However, only teachers who have the necessary preparation for sex instruction should provide it.

Sex education must be aimed toward not only supplying sound information, but also improving social relationships. Unless a young person has a wholesome attitude toward contemporaries of both sexes, including regard for their persons, any information about sex will be of little value. The point is that the sex life of an individual is an integral part of his or her whole life and must be considered as such in the whole educational program of the high school.[18]

An example of effective sex education in high school was reported from San Diego, California. The program there was initiated through extensive use of group discussion, demonstration lectures, and questionnaires involving teachers, administrators, doctors, nurses, the council of churches, civic clubs, and the community welfare council. This resulted in community-wide acceptance of the undertaking. Then followed formation of a committee consisting of representatives from the schools and leading groups of the city. This committee assisted in preparing and promoting the program.

Beginning with the sixth grade, the program included study of family life, adolescent development, boy-girl relationships, manners, morals, human reproduction, venereal disease, social-sexual attitudes, dating, marriage, and the like. Instruction was provided chiefly by teachers of health. One special feature was extensive, systematic group and individual counseling by well-prepared counselors. Students attended the meetings voluntarily and expressed interest and satisfaction with the instruction and counseling. The parents gave their approval almost without exception.[19]

Vocational Problems

Studies of students' anxieties indicate further that among their chief problems or needs are choosing and preparing for a vocation. Their concern about their vocational success and happiness shows up also in most case studies of adolescents.

The occupational problems confronting students are by-products of a technological society characterized by complexity and change. It has been estimated that at least 60 percent of the occupations in which college graduates will work did not exist when they were born. Moreover, automation and the increased demand for high-level technical skills have been reducing jobs for young people. There has been rising unemployment of teen-agers because of their age and immaturity and their deficiency in

18 S. R. Sacks, "Widening the Perspectives on Adolescent Sex Problems," *Adolescence* (Spring, 1966), 1, pp. 79-90.
19 G. G. Wetherill, "Sex Education in the Public Schools," *Journal of School Health* (September, 1961), 31, pp. 235-239; see also H. F. Kilander, *Sex Education in the Schools: A Study of Objectives, Content, Methods, Materials, and Evaluation*, Macmillan, New York, 1970.

education and experience.[20] In addition, many of them lack sufficient knowledge for the intelligent selection of a vocation. They need guidance toward available, suitable occupations and assistance toward recognition of the inconsistency between their vocational aims and their abilties. Although there has been considerable provision for guidance in high school, many students evidently have not received effective vocational guidance from teachers and counselors.[21]

The foregoing vocational problems suggest the need for more emphasis on vocational education than on vocational training. Vocational education concentrates on comprehension and insight rather than on specific, automatic responses. In home economics, business, and industrial arts, for example, good instruction is not restricted to individual projects designed merely to develop manipulative skills. Instead, considerable amounts of time are devoted to group discussion stemming from and leading to use of suitable reading and audio-visual materials. In the process there is drawing on mathematics, science, English, and other "nonvocational" courses. Thus, in vocational education, teachers may assist students to develop ideas, concepts, or generalizations such as are developed in liberal, academic education. There is integration of vocational and general education.[22]

Vocational education is desirable also for vocational adjustment. In our modern economic order it is unrealistic for a high school to train a student in only one particular vocation. A person may be required to shift from one vocation to another. In specializing too soon, a young person runs the risk of preparing for an occupational specialty that might completely change or be eliminated. Counselors, using various means of aiding unemployed youths, have concluded that the majority of them need a well-rounded, generalized experience in an area of occupations. Satisfactory adjustment of workers on jobs does not, in the majority of instances, call for specialized vocational training in schools. Moreover, a vocation that is not followed may become a hobby, and the development of skills and understanding in more than one vocation adds to enrichment of one's outlook on life.

Of significance here is the recent movement toward adoption of "career education" in public schools. In view of the more than two million young people who leave school each year without marketable vocational skills, the federal government in 1972 initiated a focus on career

[20] H. Folk, "Youth Unemployment: An Economic Analysis," *National Association of Secondary School Principals Bulletin* (February, 1969), 53, pp. 41-56.

[21] R. R. DeBlaissie, "Occupational Information in the Junior High School Curriculum," *Journal of Secondary Education* (October, 1970), 45, pp. 269-274.

[22] For further discussion of the theory and practice of effective vocational education, see Chap. 9. Also see J. J. Kaufman and M. V. Lewis, "The Potential of Vocational Education," *National Association of Secondary School Principals Bulletin* (February, 1969), 53, pp. 1-22; and Irving Pinkney, "Work-Study for Potential Dropouts," *National Association of Secondary School Principals Bulletin* (April, 1971), 55, pp. 46-54.

education within a few school districts of different parts of our country. The goal of the program, which is provided for both elementary and secondary students, is to have every student equipped, when leaving high school, with suitable skills for immediate employment or for entrance to college.

Important features of the program include work-study procedure, vocational content in all school subjects, and the fusion of vocational and academic education. Through extensive integration of counseling and instruction, the student is led to a *better self-understanding, an improved self-image, and, thereby, to an increased understanding and regard for others.* In addition, opportunities are given to explore various current occupations, to assist in making an intelligent vocational choice.[23]

Those features of the program are commendable. Before the career education project was initiated, they had been used successfully in some high schools to meet both the academic and the vocational needs of different students. Further appraisal of the program requires consideration of the idea that marketable skills developed in high-school students must include academic skills as well as skills relating to a particular career. To be specific, a student's development in personality traits and in reading, writing, and mathematics is very important for acquisition and retention of jobs.[24]

In adopting the program, schools have confronted problems and some have had reason to modify it. They decided they could better serve their students' needs by concentrating on specific aspects of the project rather than trying to launch the entire program. They found the whole project to be quite costly, and they feared the result would be a reduction in the quality of education.[25]

Religious Problems

The problems of young people extend further to include religion. A significant percent of youth reveal concern about religion, even though the nature of their concern may be different from that of some youths of the preceding generation.

Whatever the present interest of youth may be in religion, it continues to be a very strong force for good or evil. It may promote either bigotry and persecution or love and service. This suggests that the high school should contribute toward the development of socially desirable religious concepts and ideals. In fact, young people cannot adequately comprehend

23 W. Riles, "California and Career Education," *Thrust* (April, 1972), 1, pp. 4-5; R. A. Sampieri, "Comprehensive Career Education Model," *Thrust* (April, 1972), 1, pp. 10-12.

24 For further consideration of the integration of academic education and vocational education, see the section on industrial arts in Chap. 9.

25 W. L. Deegan and others, "Career Education: Progress, Proposals, and Problems," *Thrust* (January, 1973), 2, p. 7.

the culture in which they are being reared unless they consider how religion has affected that culture. Some of them, moreover, have received little in religious instruction beyond denominationalism. Accordingly, they may depend largely on the high school for development of a rational as well as an emotional commitment to religious values. They need to view religion in the light of democracy as they study history, science, literature, and other subjects.

It is commonly recognized that the public high school must refrain from teaching denominationalism. Instead, there should be a democratic, intellectual approach to religious questions, similar to the approach to other controversial matters in school subjects. This involves providing study of several religions instead of just one, with the aim of promoting investigation rather than indoctrination. As in all other instruction in the modern high school, the method of instruction should emphasize comprehension, inquiry, and discovery.[26]

Problems of Broad Social Relationship

Personal problems of the immediate environment in home and school are viewed in a large setting by some students. That adolescents are increasingly concerned about national and international problems is evident not only from research but also the news media. Many adolescents recognize two major problems confronting both themselves and adults—how to provide peaceful, mutually beneficial relationships among races and among nations. Furthermore, it is commonly recognized that some young people are inclined to be more idealistic about improving society than are their elders. This is obvious to adults engaged in organization and direction of youth groups in religion or politics. Teachers must perceive this inclination of some youths to reform society and must direct them toward wise action in such an endeavor. They are obligated further to meet the needs of the many young people who view their problems within quite a restricted social horizon. Through suitable readings, audio-visual aids, class discussion, and other vital means, all boys and girls in high school may be helped to realize that the extensive interdependence of groups has bearing on both the production and the solution of personal problems.

In assisting students to enlarge and intellectualize their social outlook, teachers may lead them to see the role of science in the modern world. That society today is largely a product of science is obvious in spiritual as well as material values. As science has advanced, it has furnished means by which democracy could be accelerated. Concurrently, science, through

26 T. S. Warshaw, "Teaching about Religion in Public School: 8 Questions," *Phi Delta Kappan* (November, 1967), 49, pp. 127-133. See also K. C. Garrison, *Psychology of Adolescence*, 6th ed., Prentice-Hall, Englewood Cliffs, New Jersey, 1965, pp. 186-188.

technology, has been changing society, making it increasingly interdependent and complex. In doing this it has both added new social problems and increased the difficulty of dealing with some of the old ones.

In today's society many adults as well as adolescents have difficulty making intelligent, democratic adjustments. Instead, they act blindly, inclining toward either autocracy or anarchy. Too often they have not used science as a way of thinking and democracy as a way of living in dealing with their personal and social problems. This suggests that to prepare young people for life today, teachers must aim to educate them toward scientific and social awareness. Many adults do not have the facts bearing on domestic and foreign problems or are unwilling to use pertinent facts in thinking and acting on those problems. This requires that teachers relate instruction to the community, the nation, and the world. The teacher can use the community somewhat as a laboratory to direct adolescents in recognizing and attacking real life problems. Also, the teacher may provide students with various books and periodicals for extensive reading. This may help broaden their social outlook as well as develop their desire and ability to think.[27]

It seems evident that the high-school teacher has an inclusive function to assist all students to deal wisely with their major anxieties or problems in a world of change, complexity, and confusion. These problems are societal as well as personal. Young people need assistance in recognizing as well as solving persistent problems. As teachers adopt the functional approach, they may expect to be more effective in the development of intelligent and socially minded citizens. Otherwise, the public school can indirectly contribute to delinquency, or other antisocial conduct, among our teen-agers. This is indicated by a study of delinquency and the school.[28]

IMPLICATIONS OF STUDENTS' PROBLEMS FOR TEACHING IN URBAN SCHOOLS

The Situation Confronting Urban Schools

The use of students' concerns and needs toward the improvement of humanistic teaching in high school is especially urgent within our cities. It is here that students have often demonstrated their restlessness and rebellion in protest against what they have considered to be irrelevant instruction. The negative attitude of these students is so strong that a large percentage of them become troublemakers and ultimately dropouts. Many teachers spend so much time "policing" the class that they accomplish

---

27 Graham, *The Public School,* Chaps. 6-7.
28 F. I. Closson, "Delinquency: Its Prevention Rests on the Academic Community," *Clearing House* (January, 1971) 45, pp. 290-293. See also E. L. Herr, "Student Activism: Perspectives and Responses," *High School Journal* (February, 1972) 55, pp. 219-233.

little effective teaching. The final result has been extensive low-level learning in all areas of the school program, notably within the basic skills.

The urban student is the product of a fluid, frustrating environment. Cities are the centers of racial conflict, drug abuse, violence, and crime, with which the student is in close and continuous contact. Many homes are very deficient in promoting the student's physical and mental health and in providing encouragement and help to remain and succeed in school. Furthermore, in a typical urban high school, several students have moved to the city from communities with poor schools. Also, because of extensive movement of families within a city, the majority of a typical school's students may be transferees during a given school year. In addition, some students are handicapped by being in an antiquated school building and excessively large classes, without adequate facilities and learning materials. They suffer further from a rigid, uninspiring school program, which ignores the existence of individual interests, abilities, and needs.[29]

Further comprehension of the educational situation confronting urban schools may be gained from a report of the situation in an area of a large midwestern city. In this area of two and one-half square miles were living 75,000 people. One-third of the children did not have a father in the home, and many of the families had an income of $3,000 or less. Seventy-seven percent of the high school's dropouts were unemployed and unemployable, and 66 percent of the graduates were in the same category. This is understandable since 7 percent of all those in high school were reading below the fourth-grade level, and 40 percent of the tenth-grade students were reading below the seventh-grade level. Even more significant is the fact that during every semester more than one-third of the students failed in at least one course.[30]

Conditions inside and outside of urban schools indicate to some educators that these schools constitute the leading educational problem in the United States. They believe that the main battleground in the fight to save our democratic way of life is within our cities and that the schools are the front line of battle.

Suggestions for Improvement of Teaching

A basic requirement in providing suitable instruction for different students within urban schools is adequate financial support from national and state government. Also, of fundamental importance are school administrators who will lead and support teachers in the very difficult task of inspiring and guiding teen-agers toward becoming strongly motivated,

[29] C. H. Smith and W. R. Hazard, "On Decentralized School Systems," *Illinois School Journal* (Spring, 1971), 51, p. 21.
[30] P. G. Kontos and J. J. Murphy, *Teaching Urban Youth: A Source Book for Urban Education*, John Wiley, New York, 1967, p. 4.

quite competent students. The principal of a school should have freedom to work with the staff of teachers to construct the school's program. Then every teacher must be free to refrain from using any part of the curriculum that he or she deems ineffective for suitable, personalized instruction of students in the class.

A first essential step toward improvement of instruction in an urban classroom is to change many students' attitudes toward school from negative to positive. This is not easy, because several of the students will have had very unpleasant experiences with former teachers and will have been so unsuccessful in school that they feel discouraged and hopeless. That there is a close causal relationship between student attitude *toward* school and behavior and achievement *in* school is evident from casual observation; moreover, this relationship has been verified in studies of students' attitudes toward school. In one investigation a questionnaire was used in an inner-city vocational high school to discover the attitudes of approximately a thousand students. It was found that usually the attitudes of high-attending and good-achieving students are positive, and the attitudes of the poor-achieving and low-attending students are negative. Of significance also is the finding that several students who had a negative attitude toward school indicated that it stemmed from their belief that the teacher disliked them. Could it be that these students had reason to believe this about their teachers?[31]

Apparently many urban teachers must improve their attitudes toward their students before they can function effectively in assistance of students toward improvement of their attitudes toward school. Some teachers seem to hold the erroneous view that the low-achieving student could improve in schoolwork but for an ingrained obstinacy or "laziness." Unfortunately, these frustrated teachers tend to rely on scolding, humiliating, and punishing in a desperate effort to force the student to learn. Other teachers apparently believe that the poor student is hopeless, lacking the natural ability to achieve a higher level of learning and, accordingly, that it is futile for the teacher to provide special, individualized help. Obviously, these two views of poor students contribute to the number who become failures, troublemakers, and dropouts.

In addition, the necessary drastic changes in the urban school require that teachers develop special skills. This became quite evident in the strong and comprehensive effort to reform education in the schools of Louisville, Kentucky. In this city progress toward providing suitable education for the different students was being restricted by the teachers' inability to organize and manage their classes for implementation of the new program.[32]

31 C. A. Clark, "Student Attitudes and Success," *Illinois School Journal* (Summer, 1972), 52, pp. 38-40.
32 See R. C. Doll and others, "Systems Renewal in a Big-City School District: The Lessons of Louisville," *Phi Delta Kappan* (April, 1973), 54, pp. 524-534.

To improve both attitudes and skills of teachers, some teacher-education institutions—notably in Kansas, Missouri, Nebraska, and Oklahoma—provide prospective urban teachers with field experiences within city schools. Unless teachers understand the special problems of urban students and are willing to assist them in solving those problems, they should not be employed in city schools.[33]

Of course, in many urban high schools a few teachers and sometimes the entire teaching staff believe that the poor student's achievement can be significantly improved with suitable instruction tailored to individual concerns, abilities, and needs. Like a dedicated physician, this type of teacher accepts the discouraged and frustrated student as a challenge, beginning in the first class period, to provide students with experiences that will lead them to consider worthwhile goals. The teacher raises questions, provides appropriate learning materials, stimulates and directs class discussion, holds individual conferences, learns about the nature and needs of each student, avoids "spoon-feeding," and focuses on student investigation and discovery. By word and action the teacher reveals interest and confidence in every student providing each, especially the poor one, with experiences which taste of success and thereby improve self-esteem.

This personalized type of teaching has been demonstrated well in the reading program of Marshall High School in Chicago. This is a comprehensive program designed for efficient readers as well as those reading near the fourth-grade level. As we have seen, this latter group of readers is a special, major challenge to urban teachers. How the teaching staff of Marshall High School has met that challenge is vividly described as follows:

It is the belief of the teachers involved in the Reading Workshops and tutorial phase of the program that true mental retardation is almost nonexistent in these students. Their inability to acquire the early basic skills because of such factors as transiency, chronic absenteeism, and a lack of experiential background has caused them to experience failure in their academic pursuits; and this failure has convinced them that they are inferior to their contemporaries. Once this occurs, the students slide further down the academic ladder and into a very real, albeit bogus, retardation. This failure owing to a lack of basic skills results finally in a failure for which a low estimate of their capacities is responsible.

The first job of the teachers, then, is to improve the students' self-image and confidence. No academic advancement can be hoped for until they can be made to understand that they are not naturally and permanently inferior. This is no easy task because they are extremely sensitive to any open discussion of their past failure.

The teacher must gain the personal trust of the students before any academic work can begin. This process is difficult to explain because of its very personal nature. An outside observer might think that no education is taking place during

[33] G. M. Clothier, "The Cooperative Urban Teacher-Education Program," Phi Delta Kappan (June, 1973), 54, pp. 664-667.

the first few weeks of school, but to the experienced teacher periods of discussion, joking, and probing are as important to the student's success as all of the academic work which will be accomplished for the rest of the year. Without this early rapport between the students and their personal teacher-friend, the same habit of failure is inevitable.

. . . The reading advance of most of the students seems to be in direct ratio to their emotional maturity: once the mute student begins to grow more verbal, his reading score will rise; and by the same token, once the hysterically vocal or nervous student settles down, his score will advance. The really wonderful part of all of this is that the success itself tends to accelerate the learning process. We often fail to understand that the psychology behind the maxim, nothing breeds success like success, is only the obverse of the equally valid principle of failure breeding failure. What has started as a remedial reading class will often become an accelerated reading class. . . .

The taste of success, often the student's first, can work wonders in his estimate of himself; and this increased self-esteem necessitates a more conscious attempt to appear in a favorable light to others, especially the teacher. The sense of competition can become so intense that the teacher often finds himself hard pressed to keep up with his own assignment schedule.[34]

Like Marshall High School, other high schools have been developing programs to assist different students to attack their problems in modern society. These schools should be commended. In the chapters that follow there will be incidental references to practices in some of these schools in an effort to show teachers of other schools how they may go and do likewise. Progress toward meeting the real needs of all students in some schools can be duplicated successfully in other schools.

QUESTIONS AND ACTIVITIES

1. Some people have viewed adolescence as a kind of disease, something which afflicts young people at a particular stage in life; others view adolescence as a continuation of life during childhood. Evaluate these conflicting views.

2. Prepare a short questionnaire based on the social forces that seem to affect youth. Administer it to a sample of students in a nearby school. Tally the responses and check to see if the students you sampled are as affected by these pressures as implied by research literature. If

34 J. Woods and R. Kittridge, "The Marshall High School Reading Program," *Illinois School Journal* (Summer, 1967), 47, pp. 110-111. For an explanation of how other subjects may be taught through student involvement in investigative, creative learning, see Kontos and Murphy, *Teaching Urban Youth*, Parts Two and Three. For an explanation of the special teacher-education program required for that type of teaching, see G. M. Clothier, "The Cooperative Urban Teacher-Education Program," *Phi Delta Kappan* (June, 1973), 54, pp. 664-667.

there are large differences in results, what do you think accounts for these differences? What other generalizations can you make from your survey?

3. Combining the information of this chapter with the results of your survey, suggest some ways in which a high-school teacher might understand and interact better with prospective dropouts and delinquents.

4. Have a panel of students freely discuss the pressures they feel, the aspirations they have, and their views of what an education should do for them.

5. Compare the problems of adolescents with those of adult society. One way of doing this is to interview your parents, relatives, or adults in the neighborhood and compare their reactions to the responses you received from students on the questionnaire in question 2. Did you find much overlap or are the problems different?

6. Weigh the possibility of building the educational program of a high school around the interests, anxieties, or problems of adolescents in the modern world. What new courses would you offer? How would you teach these courses?

SELECTED REFERENCES

Aldridge, J. W., *In the Country of the Young,* paper, Harper and Row, New York, 1971.

Alexander, T., *Children and Adolescents: A Biocultural Approach to Psychological Development,* Atherton, New York, 1969.

Bigge, M. L., and M. P. Hunt, *Psychological Foundations of Education,* 2nd ed., Harper and Row, New York, 1968, Chaps. 2-4.

Brody, E. B., and others, *Minority Group Adolescents in the United States,* Williams and Wilkins, Baltimore, 1968.

Cain, A. H., *Young People and Revolution,* John Day, New York, 1970.

Caplan, Gerald, and Serge Lebovici, eds., *Adolescence: Psychological Perspectives,* Basic Books, New York, 1969.

Clarke, P. A., *Child-Adolescent Psychology,* Charles E. Merrill, Columbus, Ohio, 1968.

Cole, L., and I. N. Hall, *Psychology of Adolescence,* 7th ed., paper, Holt, Rinehart and Winston, 1970.

Cottle, T. J., *Time's Children: Impressions of Youth,* paper, Little, Brown, Boston, 1971.

Cusick, P. A., *Inside High Schools: The Student's World,* Holt, Rinehart and Winston, New York, 1973.

Fleming, C. M., *Adolescence: Its Social Psychology*, paper, International Universities, New York, 1969.

Gordon, I. J., *Human Development: From Birth through Adolescence*, 2nd ed., Harper and Row, New York, 1969.

Grinder, R. E., *Studies in Adolescence*, 2nd ed., paper, *Macmillan*, New York, 1969.

Havighurst, R. J., and D. U. Levine, *Education in Metropolitan Areas*, 2nd ed., Allyn and Bacon, Boston, 1971.

Havighurst, R. J., and others, eds., *Society and Education: A Book of Readings*, 2nd ed., Allyn and Bacon, Boston, 1971.

Horrocks, J. E., *The Psychology of Adolescence*, 3rd ed., Houghton Mifflin, Boston, 1969.

Hummel, R. C., and J. M. Nagle, *Urban Education in America: Problems and Prospects*, Oxford University Press, New York, 1973.

Kontos, P. G., and J. J. Murphy, *Teaching Urban Youth: A Source Book for Urban Education*, John Wiley, New York, 1967.

McCandless, B. R., *Adolescents: Behavior and Development*, Holt, Rinehart and Winston, New York, 1970.

Medinnus, G. R., and R. C. Johnson, *Child and Adolescent Psychology: Behavior and Development*, John Wiley, New York, 1969.

Medinnus, G. R., and R. C. Johnson, *Child and Adolescent Psychology: A Book of Readings*, John Wiley, New York, 1970.

National Society for the Study of Education, *The Educationally Retarded and Disadvantaged*, Sixty-sixth Yearbook, Part I, University of Chicago, Chicago, 1967, Chaps. 2-6, 9-10.

National Society for the Study of Education, *Metropolitanism: Its Challenge to Education*, Sixty-seventh Yearbook, Part I, University of Chicago, Chicago, 1968, Section 1.

National Society for the Study of Education, *Social Deviancy Among Youth*, Sixty-fifth Yearbook, Part I, University of Chicago, Chicago, 1966.

Offer, D., and others, *The Psychological World of the Teen-ager: A Study of Normal Adolescent Boys*, Basic Books, New York, 1969.

Powell, M., and A. H. Frerichs, *Adolescent Psychology: Selected Readings*, Burgess, Minneapolis, 1971.

Rogers, D., *Issues in Adolescent Psychology*, Appleton-Century-Crofts, New York, 1969.

Sebald, Hans, *Adolescence: A Sociological Analysis*, Appleton-Century-Crofts, New York, 1968.

Smith, F. R., and R. B. McQuigg, *Secondary Schools Today: Readings for Educators*, 2nd ed., paper, Houghton Mifflin, Boston, 1969, Chaps. 13, 15-19.

Stewart, C. W., *Adolescent Religion: A Developmental Study of the Religion of Youth*, Abingdon, Nashville, 1967.

Stone, L. J., and J. Church, *Childhood and Adolescence,* 2nd ed., Random House, New York, 1968.

Strom, R. D., *Psychology for the Classroom,* Prentice-Hall, Englewood Cliffs, New Jersey, 1969, Chap. 2.

Thayer, V. T., and M. Levit, *Role of the School in American Society,* 2nd ed., Dodd, Mead, New York, 1966, Chaps. 12-15.

Thornburg, H. D., *Contemporary Adolescence: Readings,* Wadsworth, Belmont, California, 1971.

Walberg, H. J., and A. T. Kopan, eds., *Rethinking Urban Education: A Sourcebook of Contemporary Issues,* Jossey-Bass, San Francisco, 1972.

Weinberg, Carl, *Education and Social Problems,* Free Press, New York, 1969.

Winder, A. E., and D. L. Angus, *Adolescence: Contemporary Studies,* American Book, New York, 1968.

CHAPTER 2

We have seen that the teacher's understanding of the concerns and needs of students is basic to good teaching. Secondary education should center on assisting adolescent boys and girls toward the solution of their individual and group problems in the present-day world of complexity and change. To meet this challenge teachers need an understanding of the learning process. Recognition of this has led authors of textbooks in educational psychology to devote as much as 50 percent of such texts to views of learning. However, the authors of this book have observed that some experienced as well as beginning teachers are deficient in their conception of high quality learning. Our immediate task, therefore, is to present what constitutes satisfactory learning and how the secondary school teacher can promote it.[1]

ESSENTIAL FEATURES OF LEARNING

Learning occurs as the individual interacts with the environment. In the process, both are changed. Change in the individual involves learning to the extent that one purposes, perceives, discovers, creates, and reflects. In the learning process, the individual has an objective, takes a backward as well as a forward look, perceives what happens, and acts according to what is seen. Learning is a dynamic, interactive process, whereby the learner experiences changes in intellectual structure—knowledge, aims, understandings, and skills. It is goal-directed or purposive, occurring through acquisition of insight or meaning.[2]

[1] For a brief challenge to teachers to promote effective learning, see H. V. Price, "Whence Cometh the Spark?" *School Science and Mathematics* (February, 1967), 67, pp. 162-174.
[2] M. L. Bigge, *Learning Theories for Teachers*, 2nd ed., paper, Harper and Row, New York, 1971, pp. 198-199, 204-212.

EFFECTIVE LEARNING

Goal and insight exist in all forms of learning—in the acquisition of *skills* and *attitudes* as well as ideas. Blind repetition is not the way to learn to swim or to play a game. A person develops skills by clarifying personal goals and discovering ways of reaching them. One rises above the plateaus of performance through devising improved patterns of performance. Likewise, one forms a certain concept and attitude toward a political party or any other such organization from experiences that lead to a perception of the organization's possible contribution to personal goals. Changes in attitude toward the organization come about as the concept of its usefulness in carrying out purposes changes.

It is important to recognize here that the goal may be either intrinsic or extrinsic to the learning activity. An intrinsic goal may be found by the learner in the activity itself, and what is learned is the reward. In contrast, an extrinsic goal lies outside the activity and provides an external reward. For example, a student studying bees in biology has an intrinsic goal to find out how bees live and work—for satisfaction of curiosity or for use in a vocation or avocation. However, if the student studies about bees just as an assignment or to stay out of trouble or make a passing grade, the objective and reward are outside, or extrinsic to, the learning activity.[3]

Learning becomes effective as the goals, interests, or objectives of the learner become *intrinsic*. This is obvious, particularly in learning through problem solving and thinking. Many students in algebra, for example, reveal little interest or understanding of their work on lists of word problems, for they lack perception of the *why* and *how* of solving the problems. A chief function of a teacher of any subject is to use various means to provide learning situations in which each student is helped to recognize and find means of solving various problems that occur in the pursuit of goals both in and out of the classroom.

EXAMPLES OF EFFECTIVE LEARNING

The roles of goal and insight, intrinsic to the learning task, may be illustrated in the way one learns to spell. That repetition or drill is not the key to improvement in spelling is shown by the fact that students who have had about the same amount of drill in the subject and have about the same ability as measured by intelligence tests vary extensively in their spelling efficiency. Those who are weak in spelling usually lack strong determination to master spelling in general and "spelling demons" in particular. Those who have challenging goals in spelling, immediate and ultimate, apply themselves to discovering ways of reaching the goals. A good speller who misspells a word once or twice, realizes the word must be analyzed to

3 Ibid., pp. 279-284.

form a lasting picture of it. Such a word might be *making*. Believing that the only thing needed to spell this word correctly is to add *ing* to *make*, the student promptly misspells the word. Recognizing the error, the student may look to see whether or not *take, shake,* and other words of this form require dropping the final e when *ing* is added. As a result, the learner may construct a generalization or pattern for use in this spelling situation. Thus the student may improve in spelling through goal seeking and insight. This suggests that in teaching spelling the teacher should concentrate on assisting students to sense their individual needs and to acquire the necessary interests and understandings to meet those needs.

These features of learning are experienced by the teacher during the first year in the classroom. Facing the new and challenging work for the year, the novice begins to gain a comprehensive view of it by conferring with the department head or principal and other teachers and by meeting some of the patrons and students of the school. Learning continues as the beginning teacher attacks the problems of planning the schoolwork for the year, the first semester, the first month, and the first day. The first several weeks of school are an especially impressive and challenging series of new and varied experiences. The new teacher studies the individual students in order to gear teaching as close as possible to their abilities, needs, and interests as well as to develop their respect. Furthermore, as learning activities are developed in order to meet the objectives of the course content, the teacher is likely to experience a strong need for additional knowledge of the subject matter. As a result probably more information and background in the subject field will be acquired in the first year of teaching than had been gleaned in any one year of study in school or college. In addition, through continuous experiences in working and playing with young people and in dealing with school officials and parents, the teacher is likely to gain more insight into human nature and behavior than had been gathered from reading courses in psychology and education during any one school year. Too, there may be an awareness that adolescents in a secondary school classroom react differently from what he or she has come to expect from adults. It is all these experiences that make beginning teachers remark: "I learned more the first year I taught than in any one year at college."

A brief analysis of the experiences of the beginning teacher explains why this new learning is very effective. One important reason is that the experiences of the year are relatively untried. Hence, curiosity and the desire to prove to oneself as well as to others that new demands can be met motivate the teacher to work rather diligently. Another causal factor is the strong need for application to the tasks involved in the position. Very likely, while in high school and college, this person neglected many opportunities to acquire facts and skills necessary for successful teaching. Suddenly, it is clear that they must be obtained at once; so the teacher concentrates on their acquisition, solving problems and acquiring facts and skills as needed. The new teacher learns well because of the intrinsic motivation and meaning that the teaching situations now hold. Many of the facts, principles, and generalizations in English or history once learned more or less by rote may now be seen in a new and clearer light as the teacher attempts to assist students to acquire them. Some will be quickly discarded as it is realized that they lack relevance to objectives of learning in the secondary school classroom. The teacher also may begin to draw from former courses in education and psychology and to formulate tentative solutions to problems of instruction and classroom control.

We will see additional examples of situations conducive to effective learning in this and succeeding chapters. Some of the examples appear in discussion of trends or innovations in secondary education. For instance, leading writers on the new mathematics, the new sciences, and the new social studies provide illustrations of how to teach those subjects so that students learn through discovering. The discovery method of learning, they insist, is the important result of the "new" procedures in the teaching of those subjects. This kind of learning occurs in settings in which students develop challenging objectives. It involves goal setting, investigating, experimenting, and reflecting. It is not learning through memorization and application of ready-made generalizations or rules, but through a variety of concrete experiences which lead to purposing, inquiring, catching on, generalizing, and applying.

Examples of provisions for such learning also may be found in discussions of teaching other subjects, including the practical arts. In typewriting, for instance, present writers on the subject explain how learning may be improved by assisting the student in acquisition of wholes or patterns, with reference to both the keyboard and the material typed. They also insist that the student continuously have in mind remote and immediate objectives to challenge and direct in the learning process. Similarly, in industrial arts several recent writers have been contributing to the trend away from narrow concentration on manipulation of tools and acquisition of motor skills. Instead they advocate learning involving broad perspective and perception of relationships. They would assist the student to perceive both a possible role in industrial arts and the role of industrial arts in modern society. Moreover, much of the learning would result from projects or problems individualized to meet the differing needs of students. In all such situations learning is likely to be goal-directed, significant, and useful.

REPRESENTATIVE EXPERIMENTATION IN SCHOOLS ON
EFFECTIVE LEARNING

Beginning in the second quarter of this century there has been extensive research on the essentials for production of high quality learning.[4] Wrightstone, for example, studied learning in some experimental high schools in which emphasis was on organization of subject matter around units and problems and on direction of instructional procedure toward learning through student purposing, planning, investigating, and reflecting. Schools not concentrating on such a teaching-learning process were matched as control schools with the experimental schools. The results of learning in the two types of schools were considered within three categories: (1) intellectual—acquisition, recall, interpretation, organization, and application of facts; (2) dynamic—attitudes, beliefs, and values; and (3) performance—self-initiated, cooperative, intelligent, and responsible actions.[5] The findings of results in all three categories of learning indicated significant superiority of the experimental schools.[6]

Additional experimentation on purposive, reflective learning was reported by Bayles. Six experiments on learning through provision of many experiences in reflective thinking were conducted in connection with master's theses at the University of Kansas under his direction. Four were in social studies classes in high school, grades 11 and 12; the fifth included classes in a self-contained sixth-grade classroom; and the sixth, classes in a fifth-grade classroom of the same type. The purpose of each experiment was to compare the achievement of students taught reflectively with the achievement of those taught in conventional classes.

Each teacher endeavored to organize the subject matter as far as possible around problems and to direct students in following the steps of reflective thinking in their work toward solving the problems. In such teaching, he or she led pupils to set up objectives inherent in the activity and to learn with intrinsic interest and meaning.

Bayles reported that the achievement of the experimental classes, both in acquisition of facts and in development of reflective thinking, surpassed the achievement of conventional classes to a marked degree. The superiority in achievement included students of low IQ's of the two groups. Incidentally, Bayles also found that teachers in their second year of teaching reflectively had improved in their ability to teach. Moreover, if they followed democratic procedure quietly and efficiently in their teaching,

[4] To understand how well research has supported this concept of learning for high-school teaching we must realize that the research has extended over decades and that currently it exists impressively in all areas of the curriculum, including the "new" subjects.

[5] J. W. Wrightstone, *Appraisal of Experimental High School Practices,* Teachers College, Columbia University, New York, 1936, pp. 120-121.

[6] Ibid., pp. 190-191.

they were unlikely to experience troublesome opposition in the school or the community.[7]

More recently, the Salt Lake City school district experimented with 432 fifth- and sixth-grade pupils in a study of the comparative effectiveness of the discovery method versus the expository presentation of arithmetic. The pupils were equally divided among sixteen classes, and again equally divided among eight elementary schools. In each of the eight schools, two classes were taught arithmetic by the same teacher. One class, designated as D, functioned by the discovery method; the other class, designated as E, by the expository method. The expository method consisted of the well-known conventional rule-demonstration approach, in which the teacher first presents the rule and then shows the students how to apply it to the solution of a problem. In contrast, the discovery procedure involves the students in seeking and finding how to work a problem and then in the formulation of the rule. In the learning process the teacher assists by providing the students with suitable visual aids, with simple illustrative problems, and with stimulating, suggestive thought questions. Accordingly, the students acquire challenging goals and use reflection to advance toward the goals.

The reporter of the experiment explained in detail that there was extended effort to control all the variables of the experiment. For example, the teachers were carefully selected and trained and the same amount of time was given to the teaching of the two groups.

Tests were given at the end of the experiment, and five and eleven weeks later. On the first test group E was distinctly superior, but on the two subsequent tests group D showed significant superiority. The reporter of the experiment concluded that discovery learning causes the student to integrate the learning conceptually, in a manner that assists in retaining it better than could be done if expository learning had been experienced. His other conclusion was that learning by discovery techniques significantly increases a pupil's ability to use problem-solving approaches in new situations.[8] Thus both in retention of concepts and in transfer of problem-solving procedures, the discovery method significantly surpassed the other method.

In a similar experiment, two college teachers studied the inquiry-discovery method of laboratory instruction in freshman chemistry. The experiment was conducted over a period of three years, during only one semester of each year. Three experimental groups were provided with experiences in the acquisition of chemical concepts through the laboratory approach. Three control groups were taught the concepts through the conventional

---

[7] E. E. Bayles, *Democratic Educational Theory*, Harper and Row, New York, 1960, Chap. 1.
[8] B. R. Worthen, "A Study of Discovery and Expository Presentations: Implications for Teaching," *Journal of Experimental Education* (Summer, 1968), 19, p. 237.

textbook-lecture approach. The experimenters stated that in the first two experiments there was almost complete control of the variables, but in the third experiment there was complete control.

For a thorough, reliable check on the results from the two approaches, tests were administered during and at the end of each semester. From the findings, the experimenters concluded: "If a comparison is made of the experimental and control groups involved during the three experiments, the facts show that the experimental groups achieved statistically significantly better (scores) than the control groups in a majority of instances."[9]

As in all other examples of discovery learning, the students of this experiment were placed in situations that involved them in the setting up of objectives and the choosing of ways to advance toward the objectives. Thus the learning activity possessed for them inherent motivation and meaning. Furthermore, the laboratory approach provided the students with sensory experiences at the beginning of their study of a concept. The importance of this is clear in view of the fact that sensory experiences are basic for the formation of percepts, which are essential for the development of concepts.

SUPPORT FROM EDUCATIONAL PSYCHOLOGY

The Nearness to Consensus on the Essentials in Learning

Emphasis on the kind of learning thus far presented has strong support from several writers in educational psychology. Drawing on many investigations of learning situations, these writers have concluded that the two essentials for effective learning are the learner's attitude and insight. Research, they say, has shown conclusively that the student's involvement, set, or goal, and his or her comprehension, perception, or understanding, are basic factors in acquisition, retention, and transfer of learning.[10]

Cronbach demonstrated his belief in the same essentials of learning while discussing the results of several investigations of the discovery method.

Pupils who apply a generalization given by the teacher may learn the mechanics of application without understanding and retaining the principle. If the generalization is given ready-made, the pupil may think he understands it when he does not, hence he may misapply it. When one detail fades from memory his knowledge tends to fall apart. But if he has constructed the principle for himself, he can reconstruct it fairly rapidly by recalling the underlying experiences.

9 V. Richardson and J. W. Renner, "A Study of Inquiry-Discovery Method of Laboratory Instruction," *Journal of Chemical Education* (January, 1970), 47, p. 78.
10 K. C. Garrison and others, *Educational Psychology*, 2nd ed., Appleton-Century-Crofts, New York, 1964, pp. 183-219.

Pupils are challenged when asked to discover a solution. This motivates them to pay attention and to think about the material outside of class. The solution, when achieved, contributes to a sense of competence and to interest in further learning.[11]

He and other writers of books on educational psychology devote impressive space to the support and application of motivation and comprehension in learning. Significantly, this closeness to agreement on two essentials for efficiency in learning is not confined to educational psychologists who express belief in a particular theory of learning.

The Two Contemporary Theories of Learning

One theory is basically the *stimulus-response (S-R) theory* formulated by Edward L. Thorndike in the first part of this century. This theory views human beings as a system of numerous connections. Ideas and purposes are mechanical, and learning is purely associative and behavioristic. Except in degree of complexity, learning in a human is the same as in a fish. The learning process consists of making connections between stimuli and responses. The required instruction centers on providing the necessary stimuli and rewards to produce the desired responses. The emphasis is on external control directed toward conditioning the learner. In the classroom the result is that often the student is rather passive and learning is deficient in purpose and meaning.

The other theory is the *Gestalt, organismic, or field theory*. It was originated in Germany by Max Wertheimer in the second decade of this century and was introduced into the United States by Kurt Koffka and Wolfgang Köhler in the 1920s. This theory emphasizes a dynamic interaction of the learner with the environment, wherein the person perceives the learning situation as a pattern and each part in relation to it. The learner is also an active person, having desire, ability, and freedom to set up objectives and to perceive and test possible ways of reaching the objectives. This theory specifically provides for learning characterized by perspective, comprehension, purposefulness, investigation, perception, reflection, and evaluation.

Significantly, the effect of Gestalt theory on educational psychology has been strong enough to cause some S-R theorists to broaden their theory by including purposive, cognitive interpretations. Some of them have included those interpretations without using the terms common to Gestaltists. Even Thorndike, near 1930, recognized goal and insight as important factors in a learning theory, as he devoted a chapter to each, explaining that he had expressed them in terms of readiness and connecting.[12] There

11 L. J. Cronbach, *Educational Psychology*, 2nd ed., Harcourt, Brace and World, 1963, pp. 379-380. Also see Bigge, *Learning Theories*, pp. 266-275.
12 See E. L. Thorndike, *Human Learning*, Appleton-Century-Crofts, New York, 1931, Chaps. 8-9.

are some S-R theorists, however, who continue to adhere closely to the original emphases of the theory, notably some of those promoting programed instruction and machine teaching. An appraisal of their learning theory is reserved for discussion of programed instruction in Chapter 11.[18]

Which of the two theories of learning is preferable to meet the educational needs of teen-agers for democratic living in a changing, chaotic, and confused world? The Gestalt theory seems to answer the need best. An additional look at the essentials of this theory, therefore, may be helpful.

Field or Setting

Gestalt psychology emphasizes that in a learning situation a person does not respond to only one element in the environment and then isolate it from its setting; one does not learn just one distinct thing at a time. Instead, a learner is affected by the functional unity, or relationship, of the parts of the environment. The field or background of the learning situation gives meaning to any of its elements on which the learner may be concentrating. (This is why this psychology is sometimes called the *field theory*.) The experiences of a person occur in patterns, also called "configurations" or Gestalts. Things and events are understood when they are perceived as constituting patterns or parts of a pattern. Nothing having meaning exists in isolation; its meaning derives from its relationships in accordance with a pattern or whole.

As an example, consider a geometric figure such as a square. The person constructing a square has the form in mind before beginning to draw the four lines. Also, a square consists of not only four lines but lines drawn in a particular relationship. It is the *wholeness* of the lines that gives the figure its distinct quality of being square.

A musical composition is an excellent example of an organization, through the elements of which meaning emerges from the total configuration. The composer does not select notes at random but according to the planned-in-advance organization of the musical concepts. To produce harmony and melody, it is essential that each note be placed in the required relationship to other notes. The quality of the original vision (or Gestalt) determines the musical excellence of the composition. A similar illustration can be seen in the work of the painter. Almost literally, the artist combines many elements of color and form to achieve an artistic Gestalt that vividly transcends the sum of the individual parts. In viewing the picture, too, the mind's eye must successfully combine all the elements of the painting in order to realize the overall idea of the picture.

---

18 For further appraisal of the two theories, see M. L. Bigge and M. P. Hunt, *Psychological Foundations of Education*, 2nd ed., Harper and Row, New York, 1968, Chaps. 13-14; National Society for the Study of Education, *Theories of Learning and Instruction*, Sixty-third Yearbook, Part I, University of Chicago, Chicago, 1964, Chap. 2; R. D. Strom, *Psychology for the Classroom*, Prentice-Hall, Englewood Cliffs, New Jersey, 1969, pp. 167-208.

More prosaic, perhaps, is the example of a person making a coat. It is the pattern that provides direction in the purchase of cloth, thread, buttons, and other necessary items. Each part of the coat is significant to the tailor because it fits into the pattern.[14]

Insight or Meaning

From preceding paragraphs, it can be seen that another essential characteristic of Gestalt psychology is its strong stress on insight. Appropriate synonymous expressions are catching on, seeing through, knowing what it is about, understanding, significance, and meaning. A person experiences insight when confronting a situation and seeing it in a "new light" creates a new pattern of thought. One gains insight into a drawing, picture, or scene when one's perception of the whole reveals the nature and relationship of all its parts. Similarly, in the solution of a problem, insight occurs when the individual discovers through testing hypotheses the one that furnishes the correct solution to the problem. In participation in any activity, insight is the participant's awareness of the means toward reaching the goal. Something new suddenly dawns on the learner, who is likely to say, "Ah, I see it now."

This emphasis on insight is based on the psychologically sound assumption that meaning in learning does not occur merely as an absorption or as a reflection of objects and events from the environment. Instead, the learner is involved in observing, reflecting, inquiring, finding, and creating —all in search of meaning. Through direct and indirect experiences with objects and processes the learner develops what psychologists call percepts and concepts. A percept consists of one's perception of a particular object or process. A concept is an abstract, generalized idea, resulting from one's extended experiences with the object or process. From a variety of rich experiences in any area in or outside the school, the person increasingly senses new relationships and forms new patterns thereby gaining both in the quantity and quality of insights. This way of learning involves the use of past experiences in new situations. Psychologists have found that one perceives what one's background of experiences inclines and enables one to perceive. That is, the perceptual field determines learning and conduct.[15]

This explains, to a large extent, why there are differences among students in their ability and inclination to learn certain subject matter and why the teacher must always take into account the different backgrounds of students. It suggests further that the teacher should deal with various

---

14 Emphasis on wholeness of the learner's environment is accompanied by emphasis on wholeness of the learner, who reacts—physically, mentally, emotionally, and socially—as a dynamic unity.

15 R. B. Sund and L. W. Trowbridge, *Teaching Science by Inquiry in the Secondary School,* Charles E. Merrill, Columbus, Ohio, 1967, Chap. 3; Bigge, *Learning Theories,* pp. 207-210.

aspects of the student's environment, in school, home, and community, in order to provide maximal understanding in learning. Specifically, the teacher needs to take steps toward improvement of social and cultural backgrounds of the deprived student.

The Goal

Gestalt psychology considers the goal of learning to include more than receipt of an external reward or avoidance of punishment. The effectual goal is not entirely outside a purposeful, useful activity, but is an integral part of the activity, impelling and directing the participant. The goal of a person in an activity that is useful and significant is to accomplish the task, to succeed in doing the job. Thus the teacher provides for effective learning by assisting students to recognize and work toward suitable and worthwhile goals and thereby to gain intrinsic motivation for the work.

It is through goal seeking that students best perceive relationships and meanings in learning. In working toward a goal, they view every step and hurdle of the path in relation to the goal. The students recognize, use, and learn facts and skills not in isolation as ends in themselves but as means toward reaching the goal. Such integration and meaning in the learning of facts and skills is obvious in the writing of a report of a vital experience by a student. The objective is not primarily to please the teacher or obtain a high grade but to write a good report. Toward this end are directed the spelling of every word and the construction of every sentence and paragraph. These specific or minor goals are useful to the students because they are essential to reaching their dominant goal of effectively conveying ideas. Moreover, as students thus work toward objectives, they may be led to discover and attack other objectives, both immediate and remote. The new objectives produce tensions, and these tensions in turn produce other objectives. Consequently, this kind of learning is a continuous, on-going affair, in which the learner experiences expanding meanings.

As will be seen in Chapter 5, investigations show that students' motives or purposes largely determine their habits of study. The conclusion reached by investigators is that when there is goal seeking or intrinsic motivation in the learning situation, effective learning is likely to occur. Strong and worthwhile objectives of learning drive and direct a person toward forming efficient habits of study. To improve the students' learning, therefore, the teacher may well concentrate on improving their goals.[16]

Of special significance at this point are the findings from several investigations reported by Bruner and his colleagues from the Center for Cognitive Studies at Harvard University. In a statement of an overview of the

16 See G. M. Gabor, "Teaching Methods and Incentives in Relation to Junior High Mathematics Achievement," *California Journal of Educational Research* (March, 1972), 23, pp. 56-70; and Bigge and Hunt, *Psychological Foundations*, Chap. 17.

findings of those investigations, Bruner reached the conclusion that intellectual growth involves learning through "instrumental conceptualism." In the process of learning, the learner uses culture to gain "intrinsic motivation" to acquire percepts, facts, and skills in the development of concepts. Likewise, the individual is an instrument affecting the culture. Thus "cognitive growth . . . occurs as much from the outside in as from the inside out." Consequently, the teacher promotes purposive-cognitive learning by providing each student with a rich, motivating environment that improves perceptions and goals and assists the student in finding rational means of reaching those goals.[17]

The Essentials of Learning Demonstrated in Remedial Reading

The essentials of effective learning may be seen in the modern remedial reading program, as it concentrates on (1) study of the whole person in the whole environment, (2) individualized, intrinsically motivated, reading, (3) understanding and success in reading, and (4) extensive provision for suitable reading materials. In remedial reading, teachers are increasingly dealing with the student's physical, emotional, social, and mental development and with traits, interests, abilities, attitudes, and habits, as all these are affected by the total environment in the school, the home, and the community. Their tendency is to look beyond the student's IQ to discover reasons for poor reading and to use more than drill on lists of words to improve reading. They see that there are many interrelated causes of poor reading and many interrelated remedial procedures. Further, the efficient teacher often uses individual guidance and instruction to assist the student in choosing and reading suitable materials. Toward this end, teacher and students may work cooperatively in the selection of adequate and appropriate reading materials for the classroom library. As a result of such procedures, the students are likely both to have real and strong goals for reading and to read with comprehension and meaning. They are thereby reading to learn, not just "learning to read."

According to a relatively recent publication on reading instruction, current innovations in remedial reading indicate application of a comprehensive view of instruction. Two emphases are on raising the students' levels of thought and on adapting instruction to their individual needs. In instruction of learners in upper grades of the elementary school and in junior and senior high school, the focus is on improvement in reading purposefully, understandingly, reflectively, and creatively. The teacher uses aspects of the students' physical and social environments to develop their concepts and interests. In trying to provide adequate, suitable reading materials,

[17] J. S. Bruner and others, *Studies in Cognitive Growth*, John Wiley, New York, 1966, Chaps. 1, 14. See also J. S. Bruner, *The Relevance of Education*, W. W. Norton, New York, 1971, Chaps. 2-4.

probing thought questions are employed before and after the students read. As bases for individualizing the instruction, the teacher considers the socio-cultural background and the mental hygiene of each student. Such procedures are necessary for present and future development of poor readers toward becoming self-dependent and thoughtful readers.[18]

A report of experimentation on improvement of students in reading through their involvement in significant, useful reading was given by Witty. In a Chicago high school four ninth-grade classes, each enrolling about thirty retarded readers, were formed to receive remedial instruction. In the first meeting of each class, attractive reading materials were presented and so discussed that their contents were related to the abilities and interests of the young people. During the first week each student was encouraged to examine and read materials displayed on tables and racks in the room. Meanwhile, the teacher had individual conferences, questioning the students about their favorite leisure pursuits and reading preferences. The teacher thus acquired some understanding of dominant individual and group interests and found that these teen-agers had read few books. For them, reading usually ended soon in frustration and disappointment.

The nucleus of a classroom library was assembled by the teacher. The students, the librarian, and the teachers suggested additional books. The classroom was equipped with open bookshelves, racks, tables, and pictures. There were introduction and evaluation of reading materials in group discussion. The students talked about the books they enjoyed and indicated the kind of stories they would like to read. Then different assignments were made to individuals or small groups. Each assignment was according to students' interests and abilities. On some days there was voluntary reading of books and periodicals in the classroom. Occasionally, the class was taken to the school library, where they were assisted in finding information bearing on group or individual interests.

In the evaluation of results, large gains were shown on standardized tests of reading. In addition, the students reported that they had learned to enjoy reading at school and at home. Improvement was also evident in their ability to organize acquired information into comprehensive thought patterns.[19]

In this experiment on improvement in reading skill, the teacher placed readers in situations leading to intrinsic goals for reading and to comprehensive reading to attain those goals. The teacher developed the students' vocabularies through extensive, varied, and suitable reading, depending little or not at all on a basic text. By individual conferences and other means, the teacher assisted the students to rid themselves of emotional

[18] National Society for the Study of Education, *Innovation and Change in Reading Instruction*, Sixty-seventh Yearbook, Part II, University of Chicago, Chicago, 1968, Chaps. 4-5.
[19] P. A. Witty and others, *The Teaching of Reading: A Developmental Process*, D. C. Heath, Boston, 1966, pp. 314-317.

strains, to adjust themselves socially, and to raise their beliefs in themselves. Above all, the teacher helped them to change their unfavorable attitudes toward reading, through directing them in reading with success and satisfaction.[20]

General Implications for the High-School Teacher

The view of learning presented in this chapter has strong implications for humanistic teaching in the high school. The principle that the individual develops as an integrated whole in the complete environment suggests that the teacher should consider aspects of the student's development in the home, the clique, the gang, and the community. The student's physical, emotional, and social, as well as intellectual, development are basically important. Every phase of the individual's all-round development occurs in relation to every other phase. Specifically, a problem case, academic or disciplinary, cannot be handled properly unless there is intelligent consideration of the individual's whole life, in and outside the school. Indeed, the school may contribute to the production of problem cases, through unsuitable subject matter and teaching procedure, inadequate teaching aids, the teacher's poor personality, and either autocratic or laissez-faire classroom management.

The principle of wholeness in learning also supports certain practices toward integration in subject matter and teaching procedure in the modern high school. These practices include organization of subject matter around units and problems designed for development of concepts and generalizations. They also require that every course, including the specialized ones such as physics and geometry, be related to other courses and to life outside of school. Further, in the arts, for example, the students need to develop skills through use of the skills in purposeful, significant activities or settings. All such efforts to relate or integrate instruction are based upon a sound psychology of learning.

In addition, this concept of learning has made insight, not repetitious drill, the key to effective learning in any subject. Insight largely determines the degree, the permanence, and the usefulness of learning. The rationale for this position is shown extensively in subsequent chapters, especially Chapters 4-11. Efficient, successful teachers provide students with many direct, concrete, and functional experiences that enable them to discover, generalize, and apply. This is the opposite of teaching and learning that consists of unquestioning acceptance and application of ready-made generalizations found in the textbook. Furthermore, in all subjects of the high-school curriculum, teachers are increasingly organizing courses around the personal and educational problems of young people in modern society.

---

[20] For a further discussion and reports of research on teaching reading, see the section on reading in Chap. 7.

They assist students to recognize, choose, and study their problems. As will be seen, experiments indicate that learning in such courses is quite relevant to the student.

Finally, this view of learning indicates that the high school can best improve students' learning by taking into account their purposes, motives, or goals. In Chapter 1 we considered the interests, anxieties, or problems that adolescents state as their chief concerns. The high school is obligated to assist students to deal with their individual and group needs, which constitute for them the vital goals of their education. The teacher may use these life goals of adolescents to develop in them an urge to learn, which is the force that produces both the successful learner in school and con-tinued, effective learning after graduation. In any course, it is much more important to develop in the student a lasting desire to learn than to "drill" in a few fleeting facts and skills. Hence the teacher may well concentrate on directing youths in discovering and working understandingly toward worthwhile educational goals. More, he or she may provide students with valuable experiences in problem solving and reflective thinking.

QUESTIONS AND ACTIVITIES

1. Drawing on your reading from more than one source, state what you consider to be a sound, adequate theory of learning.
2. Carefully observe the teaching style of one or more of your instructors for a period of time. From these observations, generalize about which theory of learning that instructor seems to be employing most. What methods appear most successful? Discuss your observations and con-clusions with the instructor.
3. Apply the point of view of this chapter to the teaching of one or more subjects of the high-school curriculum. Consider, through applying this point of view, how you may teach the subject so that the students learn in situations containing the factors essential for effective learning.
4. How does this view of learning help the student to develop in an all-around manner—in personality traits as well as in academic achieve-ment?
5. Through a panel discussion or a debate among students, consider the belief that teachers have been inconsistent in teaching due mainly to their failure to apply a theory of learning to their instruction. A panel of teachers may also wish to express their views on this topic.
6. How does Gestalt psychology support a program of education suitable for the education of youth for life in modern society? How does this program differ from that based on behaviorist principles?

7. In a mini-teaching episode, present a lesson in which you contrast the Gestalt and the neobehavioristic principles of learning applied to teaching. Have the class discuss the accuracy of the presentation in relation to the theories and suggest needed improvements.
8. View the films entitled "Critical Moments in Teaching." Appraise each for consistent use of a psychology of teaching and evaluate how the main teacher in each film could improve instruction by becoming more aware of the principles of learning.

SELECTED REFERENCES

Ausubel, D. P., *Educational Psychology: A Cognitive View*, Holt, Rinehart and Winston, New York, 1968, Chaps. 2-5.

Bigge, M. L., *Learning Theories for Teachers*, 2nd ed., paper, Harper and Row, New York, 1971.

Bigge, M. L., *Positive Relativism: An Emergent Educational Philosophy*, paper, Harper and Row, New York, 1971, Chap. 2.

Bigge, M. L., and M. P. Hunt, *Psychological Foundations of Education*, 2nd ed., Harper and Row, New York, 1968, Chaps. 13-14, 16-17, 21-22.

Blair, G. M., and others, *Educational Psychology*, 3rd ed., Macmillan, New York, 1968.

Brembreck, C. S., *Social Foundations of Education: Environmental Influences in Teaching and Learning*, 2nd ed., John Wiley, New York, 1971, Chap. 2.

Bruner, J. S., *Beyond the Information Given: Studies in the Psychology of Knowing*, W. W. Norton, New York, 1973.

Bruner, J. S., *The Process of Education*, Vintage Books, Random House, New York, 1970.

Bruner, J. S., *Toward a Theory of Instruction*, paper, Harvard University Press, Cambridge, Massachusetts, 1968.

Combs, A. W., and others, *Helping Relationships: Basic Concepts for the Helping Professions*, paper, Allyn and Bacon, Boston, 1971, especially Chaps. 4-6, 9-11.

Eson, M. E., *Psychological Foundations of Education*, 2nd ed., Holt, Rinehart and Winston, New York, 1972, Chap. 2.

Frey, S. H., and E. S. Haugen, eds., *Readings in Classroom Learning*, Van Nostrand Reinhold, New York, 1969.

Gnagey, W. J., and others, *Learning Environments: Readings in Educational Psychology*, paper, Holt, Rinehart and Winston, New York, 1972.

Hamachek, D. E., *Human Dynamics in Psychology and Education: Selected Readings*, paper, Allyn and Bacon, 1968, Chaps. 1-2.

Hilgard, E. R., and G. H. Bower, *Theories of Learning,* 3rd ed., Appleton-Century-Crofts, New York, 1966.

Klausmeier, H. J., and R. E. Ripple, *Learning and Human Abilities: Educational Psychology,* 3rd ed., Harper and Row, New York, 1971.

Loree, M. R., *Psychology of Education,* 2nd ed., Ronald, New York, 1970.

MacMillan, Donald L., *Behavior Modification in Education,* Macmillan, New York, 1973.

Marx, M. H., ed., *Learning: Processes,* Macmillan, New York, 1969.

Michael, W. B., ed., *Teaching for Creative Endeavor: Bold New Adventure,* Indiana University, Bloomington, 1968.

Mouly, George J., *Psychology for Effective Teaching,* 3rd ed., Holt, Rinehart and Winston, New York, 1973, Chap. 9.

National Society for the Study of Education, *Theories of Learning and Instruction,* Sixty-third Yearbook, Part I, University of Chicago, Chicago, 1964, Chap. 2.

Noll, V. H., and Rachael P., *Readings in Educational Psychology,* 2nd ed., paper, Macmillan, New York, 1968.

Perkins, H. V., *Human Development and Learning,* Wadsworth, Belmont, California, 1969.

Rich, J. M., *Humanistic Foundations of Education,* Charles A. Jones, Worthington, Ohio, 1971, Chap. 2.

Rogers, Carl, *Freedom to Learn: A View of What Education Might Become,* Charles E. Merrill, Columbus, Ohio, 1969.

Strom, R. D., *Psychology for the Classroom,* Prentice-Hall, Englewood Cliffs, New Jersey, 1969, Chaps. 4-5.

Strom, R. D., ed., *Teachers and the Learning Process,* Prentice-Hall, Englewood Cliffs, New Jersey, 1971, Chap. 4.

Travers, J. F., *Fundamentals of Educational Psychology,* International Textbook, Scranton, Pennsylvania, 1970, Part III.

Wilson, J. A. R., and others, *Psychological Foundations of Learning and Teaching,* McGraw-Hill, New York, 1969, Chaps. 4-5.

CHAPTER 3

The preceding chapters presented, in relation to the concerns and needs of students and the essentials of effective learning, basic suggestions for teaching in high school. However, those two fundamental points of reference are not enough for determining teaching procedures. Youths as well as adults deal well with their problems when they use democratic means for democratic ends. Likewise, their learning in school subjects is of high quality when its direction is in line with democratic points of reference. Accordingly, the teacher needs a sense of the principles of democracy and of the objectives of education which stem from it for a complete sense of direction in classroom procedure.

THE MEANING OF DEMOCRACY

Some Current Views of Democracy

Many have conceived of democracy only in the political area—in the relationship between the government and the people—but have disregarded the relationship of the people to one another. While they have advocated government of the people, by the people, and for the people, majority rule, and the franchise, they have expressed approval of a society that involves class and sex privilege, race prejudice, religious intolerance, and economic oppression. Democracy thus placed in a compartment is an inadequate concept. Indeed, can we expect political democracy to function well, apart from religious, social, and economic democracy? Democracy must not be restricted to the political area but rather viewed as a way of life, applicable to all areas of human activity.

Further, democracy has been seen by many as being absolute or unhampered freedom for the individual, as allowing the individual to act

TEACHING TOWARD
DEMOCRATIC OBJECTIVES

without concern for the interests and welfare of the group. A person with such a view may say, "This is a free country; I can do as I please." He sees democracy as akin to anarchy.

In viewing democracy as solely an individualistic concept, many people have not considered it to be also a social concept. Certainly, democracy involves regard for the welfare and optimal development of the individual but it is always the individual in relation to other individuals and as a member of the group. Strictly speaking, the self-made person does not exist. Each person is developed by and for life in the group and, hence, is obligated to society; one's freedom, rights, and privileges are affected by the freedoms, rights, and privileges of other members of society. The individual develops well only as he or she shares freedom with others. If individualism in a democracy consisted of disregard for other individuals, the hermit or the criminal would be a democratic person.

The Democratic Ideal

Leading educators have given positive expression to the essentials of democracy to help teachers avoid both autocratic and anarchistic classroom procedures and to promote intrinsically interesting and meaningful learning. They have analyzed the democratic ideal into at least three essential elements: (1) the freedom, welfare, and optimal development of all individuals, regardless of class, creed, sex, or color; (2) the sharing of interests among individuals and groups, resulting in continuous enlargement of social outlook and sensitivity; and (3) the free use of intelligence, through reflective thinking, involving continuous intellectual growth of all persons.[1]

The democratic ideal recognizes the importance of both aims (or ends) and processes (or means) in human behavior. That the end is essential in determination of a democratic activity can be illustrated easily in the political area. For example, a majority vote in favor of withholding economic, educational, or other rights of minority groups is clearly undemocratic in aim and result, whatever may be said about exercise of the franchise. On the other hand, the democratic process is necessary for advancement toward a democratic end. The temptation is ever present to teachers as well as laymen to adopt the short-cut method of the dictator. Also, some teachers have resorted to extreme permissiveness, claiming that they are promoting democratic behavior. What all teachers must re-

---

1 For similar statements of the democratic ideal see H. B. Alberty and E. J. Alberty, *Reorganizing the High School Curriculum*, 3rd ed., Macmillan, New York, 1962, pp. 49-55; H. Gordon Hullfish, *Toward a Democratic Education*, Publications Office, Ohio State University, Columbus, 1960, pp. 8-15; P. G. Smith, *Philosophy of Education: Introductory Studies*, Harper and Row, New York, 1965, pp. 240-252; R. K. Bent and A. Unruh, *Secondary School Curriculum*, D. C. Heath, Boston, 1969, Chap. 10; G. Graham, *The Public School in the New Society: The Social Foundations of Education*, Harper and Row, New York, 1969, Chap. 4; and T. Anderson, "A Broader View of Democracy," *Phi Delta Kappan* (January, 1973), 54, pp. 319-320.

member is that students acquire democratic attitudes and habits by experiencing democratic classroom procedure.

We will improve our comprehension of the importance and mutual dependence of ends and means in democracy further when we see how each of those factors may shift to the category of the other. We consider a means as an end until it has been reached; we view an end as a means as soon as it is attained. For example, a diploma is an end to a student before he or she graduates, but a means after graduation. Thus only as we view democracy as both an aim and a method do we have an adequate concept of it.

This leads to a definition of democracy as an ideal way of life. *The democratic ideal envisions a society in which individuals progressively possess aims stemming from a spirit of good will and use of the reflective method to determine adequate and suitable methods for reaching those aims.*

Of course, this ideal of democracy has never been attained fully in any "democratic" or "free" country. Furthermore, it has been practiced to some degree in dictatorships or in "class" societies. That some societies have moved further toward democracy than others is the point of importance. Thus the democratic ideal can well be used to examine progress toward democracy in different social orders. Its immediate use for us is in providing a frame of reference for the evaluation of educational objectives for the high school.

OBJECTIVES FORMULATED BY EDUCATIONAL ORGANIZATIONS

In an effort to direct teachers toward educating students according to their everyday needs, the National Education Association appointed the Commission on Reorganization of Secondary Education to present a list of objectives for the high school. In 1918 the Commission set forth as objectives what were commonly called the Seven Cardinal Principles of Secondary Education. They are (1) health, (2) command of fundamental processes, (3) worthy home membership, (4) vocation, (5) citizenship, (6) worthy use of leisure, and (7) ethical character.[2]

In this statement of objectives there is no direct reference to educating toward democratic ends. The list of objectives is so formulated that a teacher could use them in following any kind of an educational philosophy. In fact, these objectives are not really objectives. They merely designate areas of human interest in which all students should be educated. Education of students democratically or undemocratically depends on whether the teacher's objectives are democratic or undemocratic.

This is not to say that these objectives did not make a contribution to

---

[2] C. D. Kingsley, *Cardinal Principles of Secondary Education*, Bulletin 35, U.S. Government Printing Office, Washington, D.C., 1918.

secondary education. Their chief value was in directing the minds of some teachers away from an abstract curriculum to areas of the student's life where education is needed. Nevertheless, this does not change the fact that they were inadequate for the direction of education toward democratic ends.

The National Education Association seemed to recognize the inadequacy of the Seven Cardinal Principles as educational objectives for a democratic society. In the fall of 1932 the Association appointed a committee of six leading educators to formulate objectives growing out of the social and economic needs of all the people. In an introductory statement to the presentation of the first report of this committee in 1934, Morgan mentioned that, in order to attain the seven "social" objectives set forth by the Commission on the Reorganization of Secondary Education in 1918, "the schools have been seeking an answer to a prior question: 'What kind of society is it into which the educated person is to fit?' "[3] The Committee of Six considered this primary question as it constructed a list of ten social, economic goals of education for a democratic society.[4] In 1938 the Committee published ten general objectives, some of which stemmed from the democratic ideal. Functioning in a time of economic depression and social unrest, the Committee reflected the belief that education should promote democracy in the economic and the social areas.[5] In the same year the Educational Policies Commission published four groups of objectives, designated as (1) self-realization, (2) human relationships, (3) economic efficiency, and (4) civic responsibility.[6]

Following publication of those groups of educational objectives, the Educational Policies Commission produced a list in terms of the needs of youth for democratic citizenship.

Youth have specific needs they recognize; society makes certain requirements of all youth; together these form a pattern of common educational needs, which may be expressed as follows:

1. All youth need to develop salable skills.
2. All youth need to develop and maintain good health and physical fitness.
3. All youth need to understand the rights and duties of the citizen of a democratic society.
4. All youth need to understand the rights and duties of the family for the individual and society.
5. All youth need to know how to purchase and use goods and services intelligently.

3 J. E. Morgan, "Restating Our National Goals," NEA Journal (January, 1934), 23, p. 5.
4 Committee on Social-Economic Goals of America, "What Are Desirable Social-Economic Goals for America?" NEA Journal (January, 1934), 23, pp. 6-12.
5 Committee on Social-Economic Goals of America, "The Future of Our Country," NEA Journal (January, 1938), 27, p. 9.
6 Educational Policies Commission, The Purposes of Education in American Democracy, National Education Association, Washington, D.C., 1938.

6. All youth need to understand the influence of science on human life.
7. All youth need an appreciation of literature, art, music, and nature.
8. All youth need to be able to use their leisure time well and to budget it wisely.
9. All youth need to develop respect for other persons.
10. All youth need to grow in their ability to think rationally.[7]

A more recent similar list of educational objectives was designed by a California group of school administrators. As reported by McGowan:

A committee of the California Association of Secondary School Administrators, after a two-year study, has just published a list of fifteen "responsibilities" of education that illustrates the broadening scope of the public school program. The list says that a modern school needs to fulfill these responsibilities:

1. To provide opportunities for understanding and appreciation of the need for individual flexibility in an atmosphere of change.
2. To develop in youth an attitude of inquiry; to teach the process of problem solving and decision making as distinguished from the storing of facts.
3. To continue training in the basic tools of learning.
4. To develop a curriculum where the criterion for priorities is based upon relevance of contemporary and future needs of youth.
5. To prepare youth for a changing world of work.
6. To prepare youth for responsible, participating citizenship.
7. To provide preparation for productive use of leisure time.
8. To extend and emphasize the teaching of the fine arts.
9. To teach civilized human relations.
10. To build bridges to an understanding of all the peoples of the world.
11. To assist youth in developing moral and ethical guidelines.
12. To prepare youth to understand and deal constructively with psychological tensions.
13. To assist youth in developing ways of insuring individual privacy and worth in a world of increasing group activity and social supervision.
14. To provide opportunities for study and understanding of urban life and problems.
15. To develop an instructional program in school that fully utilizes information sources and agencies outside of the classroom.

A school that is successfully fulfilling the responsibilities listed above is successfully coping with problems of student unrest. The unfortunate truth is that not many schools are successfully filling all of the listed responsibilities.[8]

The objectives listed by diverse educational organizations reveal a significant common trend. The lists have been formulated less in terms of areas of subject matter than in terms of the individual's traits, attitudes, and habits. The trend also seems to be toward basing the objectives on the

[7] Educational Policies Commission, *Planning for American Youth*, National Education Association, Washington, D.C., 1944, p. 10. See also Educational Policies Commission, *Social Responsibility in a Free Society*, 1963, and *The Central Purpose of American Education*, 1961, National Education Association, Washington, D.C.
[8] W. N. McGowan, "About Student Unrest," *Journal of Secondary Education* (October, 1968), 43, pp. 258-259.

ideal of the all-round education of every young person for democratic living in the modern world. These lists of objectives provide teachers in high school with useful suggestions for meeting the real educational needs of youth through pursuit of democratic ends through democratic means.

A STATEMENT OF DEMOCRATIC OBJECTIVES

Using the preceding lists of objectives, along with the democratic ideal as the all-inclusive aim of education in the United States, we can derive three general objectives. The education of every student in high school should be directed toward (1) continuous enlargement and refinement of shared interests or goals which are of benefit to society as well as the individual; (2) progressive expansion of social outlook and sensitivity to include different ethnic, economic, religious, and cultural groups; and (3) free use of intelligence, involving the desire and ability to think reflectively.

These three general educational objectives are designed particularly for a democratic society. They would not be completely acceptable in a social order characterized by rigid group barriers and by dictation and domination. They offer teachers in the United States a sense of direction and points of concentration in the teaching of any subject. If they are followed, students may be expected to progress well not only in democratic attitudes and habits but also in physical and mental health and in "mastery" of school subjects.

Shared Interests

The development of shared interests as a major objective in the education of every young person in high school is seen to be important when we consider how any kind of interest functions. An interest is more than excitation, amusement, or entertainment. Interest is involved in a purpose, aim, goal, or end. It is a drawing force, leading and directing a person in conduct and learning. The most effective way to say *no* to a detrimental interest is to say *yes* to a beneficial one. Likewise, a wide range of worthwhile interests is the best insurance that a person will be continuously occupied in worthwhile activities. Certainly the students' interests in vocations, avocations, sports, civic activities, clubs, home living, and other such areas of life will definitely affect their interests and consequent application in school subjects. Thus conceived, interests are basic in the individual's development—mental, social, and physical, as well as educational.

The important point here, however, is that each individual high-school student should develop not just interests but also shared interests. There are individual, personal interests for which the school program must provide. These interests may be recognized in specialized courses and in individualized instruction. Regard for individual interests in teaching reading and literature, for instance, has produced marked results. However, the interests of the individual are best served by sharing them with others. Moreover, the student has much to learn from schoolmates as well as from the teacher when attacking personal problems. That no person is self-made—socially, economically, politically, or educationally—the students should be led to see. With the development of every boy or girl in personal-social interests as a goal, the teacher may so direct cooperative work and play that the student learns the value and method of group action for individual as well as group ends.

One of the chief hindrances to following this objective in high school is the traditional view of will, duty, and discipline as being in opposition to interests. It has often been said that regard for the learner's interests in the modern school inevitably results in the elimination of discipline from the school, hindering students from gaining a sense of duty and from reaching full intellectual and moral stature. Clearly, this belief is based on the old theory of faculty psychology and formal discipline, which modern psychologists have discovered through experimentation to be baseless. It views what is called the "will" as a faculty of the person, which is best developed apart from interest, through exercise on unpleasant tasks. It holds that after the "will" has been thus developed, it functions equally well in all situations, for example, writing stories, reading foreign languages, painting pictures, and solving mathematical problems.

This something called the "will" is not opposed to interest but includes interests, desires, motives, or purposes. A person follows a course of action when impelled to do so by a dominating interest. Even teachers who believe to have developed within themselves a strong general faculty of the will, which is expected to function well in all areas of life, may find that they have no will to engage in the work of a salesperson or a politician.

Likewise, there is a possible reconciliation between interest and duty and discipline. Duty does not exist in the abstract, apart from due consideration of all the competing interests in the moral situation. We read and hear about our obligation to be loyal, cooperative, peaceful, prompt, persistent, and the like. Yet cooperativeness or promptness, for example, is not always a virtue but is sometimes the opposite. Duty is merely the obligation of a person to give intelligent consideration to all rival interests and to act in accordance with the best interests of society as well as oneself. A person who has learned to do his or her duty is well disciplined and is not a victim of whims or fleeting fancies, as some educators seem to believe. On the contrary, that person chooses and follows interests with foresight and social awareness.

Obviously, this objective involves no support of soft pedagogy. Instead, it is advanced because at present often there is not a reasonable amount of serious, hard work in high school. The attempt to force useless, meaningless, and uninteresting work upon students has been largely the cause of their not applying themselves diligently to their studies. Having little background for the items taught or seeing no present or future need of them, the students are either unable or unwilling to apply themselves sufficiently to profit from their courses. Hence many have low standing and some fail and are held back. Facing the problem of whether to fail or pass a large number of weak, unchallenged, and uninterested youngsters, the teacher often resorts to coddling them, pushing many through the courses. Thus, whether these youths are passed or failed, they work carelessly and form faulty habits of study. In either case, many boys and girls drop out of school in disgust as soon as the compulsory education law permits. We conclude that teachers should first discover suitable work for all adolescents and then insist on persistent and intelligent application from each one of them.

It is important to recognize here that interests can be made to play an essential role in the development of reflective thinking. They furnish the drives and the rewards for thinking in different areas of living. Desire, as well as the ability to think, determines the nature of thinking in various problematic situations. Hence the teacher needs to use interests to improve attitudes toward thinking as well as skills in thinking.

The foregoing discussion suggests that one principal aim of the high-school teacher in any subject should be to promote lasting interest in the work itself. If interest in school subjects is sufficiently genuine, it will be likely to ensure the learner's continued growth in the subjects once the actual course study is over. Also important is the relationship between the student's attitude toward the subjects and the student's conduct in school. Absorbed in schoolwork, he or she is not apt to become a behavior problem. Moreover, the adolescent's conduct in school, may indicate how it is likely to be outside the school, now and later. Specifically, the young person's desire to surpass a previous record, to stick to a task until it is well completed, to be self-dependent as well as cooperative, and so on, tend to be quite general and permanent in their functioning. The same is true of the opposite kinds of desires. Thus the development of interests is not just to increase the acquisition of subject matter but also to enrich lives and to advance democratic conduct. The larger the number of worthy interests the adolescent has, the greater is the likelihood that that person will be continuously well balanced, efficient, and happy, both as a student and as a citizen.

Broad Social Outlook and Sensitivity

The first of the three objectives of education—shared interests—suggests the second one, the continuous expansion of social outlook and sensitivity. Significantly, this objective not only has been implied by leaders in democratic education but also has been expressed explicitly by them. They have seen an acceptable program of education not merely as student centered but also as society centered. According to them, education is social with respect to both means and ends. Moreover, they have always stressed the social concept of education, some critics to the contrary notwithstanding. Near the beginning of this century, Dewey wrote a book showing the need of viewing education in relation to the march of events in society.[9] Later he described in another book the kind of society required as a frame of reference for education. The following statement is representative of his repeated emphasis on the social:

Since education is a social process, and there are many kinds of societies, a criterion for educational criticism and construction implies a *particular* social ideal. The two points selected by which to measure the worth of a form of social life are the extent in which the interests of a group are shared by all its members, and the fullness and freedom with which it interacts with other groups. . . . Such a society must have a type of education which gives individuals a personal interest in social relationships and control, and the habits of mind which secure social changes without introducing disorder.[10]

Bode, who was second to no one but Dewey as an expositor of democratic education, always placed a similar emphasis on the social concept of education. Commenting on Dewey's central point in education, he said: "For Dewey all educational thinking leads back to the meaning of 'social,' just as all roads lead to Rome. Education from this standpoint becomes a process of initiating the child into spiritual membership in society." Consequently, Bode believed that a major function of the school is to provide an educational program according to the needs of youngsters in their social environments of school, home, community, and nation. Curriculum, classroom procedure, counseling, and all other aspects of the program should be related to life in an interdependent and fluid social order. Thus, direction of education in school toward the social objective is not left to natural enfoldment of human nature or to chance in instruction. Rather it requires continuous concentration on development of the student in social spirit and action for living democratically in the present-day world.[11]

More recently, Harl R. Douglass, a prominent writer on democracy in secondary education during the four preceding decades, referred to the social function of secondary education as a current trend. He pointed out that since a democratic society is not static, schools must not lag behind the rapidly changing conditions. He added that some educators believe the school is obligated to go beyond mere adjustment of young people to recent changes. Teachers, therefore, should initiate goals and procedures conducive to development of students for the *improvement* of

9 Dewey, *The School and Society*, rev. ed., University of Chicago, Chicago, 1915, pp. 4-5.
10 J. Dewey, *Democracy and Education*, Macmillan, New York, 1916, p. 115.
11 B. H. Bode, *Modern Educational Theories*, Macmillan, New York, 1927, pp. 29-30.

current social, economic, and political conditions.[12] Gorman adds: "Rare is the school whose educational philosophy does not list near the top of its aims 'preparation for responsible citizenship in a free society.' Its wording varies, but it is always there."[13]

An analysis of this second objective of education reveals that its two essentials are social interest and social intelligence. The objective is composed of social sensitivity (attitudes, concern for the other person, or a sense of obligation to the group) and of social understanding, or insight—the recognition of social problems and the habits of thinking necessary for the solution of these problems. Thus both social spirit and social ability are included in the objective. Obviously, it is based on the sum and substance of the democratic ideal and is interwoven with the other two democratic objectives—the development of shared interests and of reflective thinking.

This objective also includes recognition of the flexibility of social ideals and the relativity of social conduct. Such a conception of this objective is especially important in view of the change and interdependence of modern society. Moreover, since competing ideals always exist in problems of human relationships, right and wrong can be intelligently determined only when there is due consideration to all the factors in a moral situation that are to the best interests of all the people involved. For instance, the rightness of tolerance or loyalty depends on the object of tolerance or loyalty. Certainly, it does not require tolerance of or loyalty to murderers or others engaged in antisocial conduct. This recognition of the flexibility of ideals and the relativity of social conduct makes the individual's social development more than the acquisition of social information or training in set ways of behaving. An adequate view of the social objective includes the goal of so developing young persons in social attitude and intelligence that they will be willing and able to shift personal conduct wisely toward democratic ends.

The social aim applies to teaching every secondary school subject. It is not restricted to the social studies. Incidentally, it has not always been properly stressed in this subject matter area. The facts of history, for example, are best taught not in isolation but as they throw light on the solution of current life problems. As to the place of this aim in teaching other high-school subjects, science accords an illustration. Courses in this subject may be organized partially around the economic and social problems of today's world. They may be taught so that they lead students to apply scientific thinking to social as well as practical problems and to see the work of science in remaking the ideals and practices of society. Like-

---

12 H. R. Douglass, *The High School Curriculum*, 3rd ed., Ronald, New York, 1964, p. 140. See also Graham, *The Public School*, Chap. 15.

13 B. W. Gorman, *Secondary Education: The High School America Needs*, Random House, New York, 1971, p. 267.

wise, teachers of English literature need to refrain from teaching the classics merely in an attempt to provide all students with a common fund of information contained in those books. In this course a book is not completely suitable for a particular student unless it is the best one possible for helping him or her to gain social insight and sensitivity toward meeting problems in modern society. In like manner, any specialized courses offered primarily to provide for individual differences may best meet the individual's needs when learning is made social in aim, content, and procedure.

In following the social objective, the teacher consistently considers methods as well as subject matter. The weakness of much social education has been its dependence on social information alone, to the neglect of socialized procedure. The teacher should aim to teach young people so that they will have many opportunities in groups to participate in questioning, judging, choosing, planning, and carrying out plans. In the assignment, directed study, and what is commonly called the "recitation period," an extensive exchange of ideas in cooperative activities is essential. In short, the social atmosphere of the classroom is of fundamental importance both for the successful acquisition of knowledge and the development of desirable social ideals and habits.

This emphasis on the social objective involves *due regard for the uniqueness and the self-realization of the individual.* Proper socialized procedure does not crush or absorb the individuality of the student. Instead it provides a social environment that is conducive to the satisfactory development of different kinds of individuals. It was pointed out in Chapter 2 that the individual learns in interaction with the environment. In the democratic classroom, each student's personal needs may be met while experiencing an environment of give-and-take or sharing with others. Even when the student takes a specialized course and engages in individualized activities in such a course, common aptitudes and interests may create shared experiences. Furthermore, proper development of the individual in self-realization does not involve development in self-centeredness but in social responsibility. The individual is likely to develop the desire and the ability to use his or her unique self for the welfare of the group, at the same time enlarging self-growth through active group membership.

Free Use of Intelligence in Reflective Thinking

Progress toward attainment of the first two major objectives requires the third one, the development of free and effective use of intelligence in reflective thinking. This objective is of secondary importance for schools in a society having set class barriers and an autocratic government, where the individual is frequently compelled to follow custom and authority without question. In this kind of society, there is relatively little demand for many persons to act reflectively on many major issues and to share their thoughts with others. In contrast, a society aiming to be democratic is in constant need of change in its effort to move continuously toward the democratic ideal. This requires that all the people adjust themselves to change and recognizes that all have the obligation as well as the right to act and speak wisely in common efforts to move toward democratic goals. The result to be expected is that the people will improve in reflective conduct as they contribute to the improvement of democracy.

Recognition of intelligent action as an essential of democracy does not imply that a particular democratic procedure must be considered as undemocratic just because an error of judgment occurs, for example, in casting a ballot or in making a judicial decision. However, democracy cannot be expected to progress or even remain in a society unless the people show more wisdom in political, economic, and social affairs than that shown by the people in countries where democracy is sadly lacking.

The importance of improvement in thinking as a major objective of the high school is indicated further by the difficulty that adults as well as young people have in reasoning soundly when they are confronted with the complicated and novel problems of today. Tradition or custom has become very inadequate as a substitute for thinking in the direction of conduct in a society of change, complexity, and confusion. More than ever before, training in set ways of behaving does not suffice.

In our society youngsters are growing up in an environment which is best characterized by schisms, diversities, and a plethora of cultural alternatives. . . . In addition to the problem that is created by the existence of relatively numerous ethical norms and cosmologies, the person who is brought up in an industrial society where change and innovation are key terms descriptive of the age is continually confronted with surprises necessitating courses of action never before considered to be within the realm of the possible and real. . . . The young can no longer be expected to find ready made answers to their dilemmas.[14]

In promoting reflective thinking in high school, difficulties arise. This is particularly evident to teachers who really undertake to follow this objective. The difficulties result partly from the failure of many elementary school teachers to make this objective a dominating aim of instruction in all the subjects and grades of the school. Observation of teaching procedure in the elementary school reveals that adequate provision for the development of thinking is lacking. Much of the work of the pupils consists of simply memorizing items in the text and filling out blanks in workbooks. Since all habits established in childhood tend to persist in ado-

---

[14] B. G. Massialas, *The Indiana Experiments in Inquiry: Social Studies,* Bureau of Educational Studies and Testing, Indiana University, Bloomington, 1963, pp. xi-xii.

lescence, the habits of thinking formed in elementary school affect those in high school. Accordingly, the high-school teacher has the double task of breaking bad habits and forming good ones.

Some traditional beliefs of secondary school teachers are likewise a hindrance to their contributing to thinking in the high school. There is an old notion that students must first be given facts before they can begin to think. The typical remark is: "A person cannot think without facts, so I concentrate on teaching them." The unreasonableness of this conclusion is obvious to the thinking teacher. It is true that people cannot think well unless they have the facts, but it is also true that many people have facts but are unable or unwilling to use them in thinking. Evidently the only way for the teacher to be certain of providing both facts and thinking ability is to concentrate on the latter. A related erroneous belief is that the high school cannot or should not undertake to teach students to think. This view was expressed by one teacher as follows: "I leave it to God and to nature to develop young people in thinking; my task is to give them the facts." Finally, there is the traditional, unsound theory of the formal disciplinarians that certain subjects are valuable for the development of thinking and others for furnishing only practical facts and skills. This old theory was repudiated long ago by experimentation in psychology.

Every secondary school subject can and should be taught so that the students improve in thinking. Theoretically, one of the principal objectives proposed for teaching science has been the development of the scientific mind or scientific habits of thinking. In practice, however, some teachers of science have neglected this objective. Apparently they have viewed the subject primarily as a body of matter to be memorized rather than as a method of discovering truth. Worse still, some teachers of English and of the social studies do not even have the promotion of thinking as one of their chief goals of instruction. Certainly, their infrequent use of purposeful activities in teaching procedure and their extensive reliance on factual examinations for the discovery of results reveal that they are not consciously and persistently aiming at the development of thinking. Some teachers of the practical arts, home economics and industrial arts, for example, may be doing a better job of teaching young people to think than some teachers of the old-line, academic subjects. This is not because all teachers of the practical arts have aimed at the objective of thinking. Rather it is that these subjects usually surpass the other subjects in the inclusion of problems and projects that are useful, meaningful, and interesting to the learner. No subject has inherent value for thinking; it is the type of teaching and the reaction of the learner that count.

Practice is as necessary in thinking as in any other act. The act of thinking occurs in a perplexing situation—in a creative activity or a search for truth. In the confronting situation, the person devises ways and means of reaching a goal. One thinks as one recognizes and defines a problem, sets up and tests hypotheses, and draws logical conclusions. In the process, the person has an open mind, suspends judgment, searches for as many as possible of the pertinent facts, goes to reliable sources, and is persistent, careful, and accurate.

The proper practice of thinking results in the development of both the inclination and the ability to think. A student improves interests and skills in problem solving by involvement in various experiences with meaningful problems of school, home, and community. The stock of meanings necessary for thinking in certain areas of life are built up by attacking useful and meaningful problems in these areas. Concepts or meanings constitute the materials of thinking, without which habits of thinking could not function. Since girls traditionally have had a larger stock of meanings in home economics than boys, they may seem to surpass them in thinking in this field. For the same reason, in shop work boys may seem superior to girls in thinking. (This situation is changing now as both boys and girls are moving into nonsex-role stereotyped curricula.) This is saying that the development of thinking depends, not on a magical effect of a few "disciplinary subjects" upon the mind, but on a wide range of challenging experiences in thinking in several areas of human activity.[15]

Reports of extensive research appear in succeeding chapters. They reveal that some teachers have provided learning situations in which students have improved perceptively in social and academic interests and in habits of thinking. Moreover, obtainment of these basically important results has been accompanied by normal or above normal "mastery" of subject matter, as indicated by standardized achievement tests. What those teachers have done constitutes a challenge to other teachers.

This challenge is not only to autocratic, dictatorial teachers but also to extremely permissive teachers. It has been found that teachers in some experimental "open" schools have given students so much freedom that they do not develop well in self-discipline and in a sense of responsibility to others. Extreme autonomy has produced unnecessary noise and confusion in the place of study. "Some students flit restlessly from one attraction to another, sampling a smorgasbord of interests and activities. . . . Few students master the steadiness of purpose to pursue a problem as far as it may lead."[16] From a study of open schools, Wilson concluded that students may be expected to demonstrate obvious self-discipline, maturity, and absorption in their activities in only those open schools having above-

---

15 For further discussion of the nature and the development of reflective thinking as a major objective in the classroom, see E. E. Bayles, "Thinking: A Pivotal Goal of Secondary Schools," *High School Journal* (March, 1972), 55, pp. 243-255.

16 B. Leondar, "English in Experimental Schools," *English Journal* (September, 1971), 60, p. 750. See also the section on flexible scheduling in Chap. 12.

average teachers, who provide the students with necessary guidance along with freedom.[17]

It is helpful to realize that the teacher who teaches democratically is likely to be seen as an excellent teacher. This is indicated by an investigation of the characteristics of excellent teachers.[18] In some Northern Illinois public senior high schools, students, teachers, and administrators were requested to rate 236 teachers. Thirty-three of those teachers were identified as being excellent. It was found that they could be distinguished from other teachers by the following performances:

1. Initiation of learning activities, requiring students to use higher mental processes, such as problem solving, thinking, and conceptualizing.
2. Expression of confidence and skill in verbal performance, making good use of student questions, comments, and information to advance the class goals.
3. Extensive use of class discussion and active student participation, showing concern about what they stimulate the student to do in learning.
4. Indication of genuine interest in the progress of each student and provision of individual guidance.
5. Serious planning, indicating belief that plans should be flexible and should focus on ways to improve student activities.

Teachers who demonstrate these and similar practices are quite unlike either autocratic, dictatorial teachers or laissez-faire, extremely permissive teachers. Instead, they continuously assume their responsibility of leadership, sharing their ideas with the class and helping students to recognize and attack relevant personal and social problems. Accordingly, they recognize the necessity of planning carefully out of class so that they will be well prepared to plan intelligently with the students and render them assistance when it is needed.

Thus we see that the three general objectives for democratic education constitute the points of reference for the evaluation of all methods of teaching in high school. If the teacher's practice is in harmony with such objectives, it is good. All teaching should contribute ultimately and at least indirectly to the promotion of shared interests, the extension of social insights and concerns, and the improvement of meaning and thinking in conduct.[19]

---

[17] F. S. Wilson, "Are Pupils in Open Schools Different?" *Journal of Educational Research* (November, 1972), 66, p. 118.

[18] B. F. Radebaugh and J. A. Johnson, "Phase II. Excellent Teachers: What Makes Them Outstanding," *Clearing House* (March, 1971), 45, pp. 410-418.

[19] For an additional plea for adoption of the democratic ideal as the point of reference in appraisal of innovational as well as traditional teaching, see W. G. Williams, "The Forgotten Innovation: Democracy," *Clearing House* (September, 1972), 47, pp. 3-7.

QUESTIONS AND ACTIVITIES

1. Secure a copy of a high-school curriculum guide or the document stating the educational goals of that school or district. Evaluate these goal statements with the democratic ideas suggested in this chapter. How democratic are these goals? To what degree do you think the school is accomplishing these objectives? To find out, you may want to interview some students.
2. It has often been stated that the high school of today does not show concern for the teaching of facts. Point out the truth in this accusation.
3. Some democratic values are trust, respect, self-initiative, and responsibility. Design a role-playing activity that will give the participants an opportunity to experience how it feels to have these values denied them. Try to involve everyone; discuss freely this experience and how teachers unconsciously *do* this in their teaching.
4. In small group discussions, identify the changes that are necessary for implementing democratic values and goals in high schools. How would this implementation affect teaching, course offerings, the principal, the students, the parents, and the community?
5. From the democratic objectives discussed in this chapter, suggest several teaching-learning techniques that a democratic teacher might use. What are the principles from learning theory that support these techniques? Can you demonstrate some of these methods, either before the class or on a TV video tape for playback to the class.
6. During the decade of the 1960's and early 1970's there appeared a "new morality." This phenomenon was demonstrated by such overt acts as freedom marches, peace marches, passive resistance, a return to nature, and a reconsideration of war, politics, natural resources, and the environment. How consistent are these activities with the democratic values discussed in Chapter 3? What is the school's role in making high-school students aware of changing values and attitudes?
7. Attend a meeting of some club or organization (for example, City Council, PTA, School Board, or a teacher's meeting) and observe to what degree the procedures, the attitudes of the participants, and the conclusions they arrive at are extensions of democratic principles.

SELECTED REFERENCES

Alberty, H. B., and E. Alberty, *Reorganizing the High School Curriculum,* 3rd ed., Macmillan, New York, 1962.

Bayles, E. E., *Democratic Educational Theory*, Harper and Row, New York, 1960.

Bayles, E. E., *Pragmatism in Education*, Harper and Row, New York, 1966.

Becker, Weldon, and W. Dumas, eds., *American Education: Foundations and Superstructure*, paper, International Textbook, Scranton, Pennsylvania, 1970, Sections 2, 4, 6.

Bent, R. K., and A. Unruh, *Secondary School Curriculum*, D. C. Heath, Boston, 1969, Chap. 10.

Bigge, M. L., *Positive Relativism: An Emergent Educational Philosophy*, Harper and Row, New York, 1971, Chap. 6.

Education Policies Commission, *The Central Purpose of American Education*, National Education Association, Washington, D.C., 1961.

Education Policies Commission, *Social Responsibility in a Free Society*, National Education Association, Washington, D.C., 1963.

Fenton, E., *Teaching the New Social Studies in Secondary Schools*, Holt, Rinehart and Winston, New York, 1966, Chaps. 2-5.

Gorman, B. W., *Secondary Education: The High School America Needs*, Random House, New York, 1971, Chaps. 2, 11.

Graham, G., *The Public School in the New Society: The Social Foundations of Education*, Harper and Row, New York, 1969, Chap. 4.

Hullfish, H. G., *Toward a Democratic Education*, Publications Office, Ohio State University, Columbus, 1960.

National Education Association, *Schools for the 70's and Beyond: A Call to Action*, National Education Association, Washington, D.C., 1971.

National Society for the Study of Education, *The Changing American School*, Sixty-fifth Yearbook, Part II, University of Chicago, Chicago, 1966, Chaps. 1, 11.

National Society for the Study of Education, *Educational Evaluation: New Roles, New Means*, Sixty-eighth Yearbook, Part II, University of Chicago, Chicago, 1969, Chaps. 7-10.

Ortman, E. J., *Challenges of Democracy*, Philosophical Library, New York, 1968.

Silberman, C., *Crises in the Classroom*, Random House, New York, 1970.

Smith, F. R., and R. B. McQuigg, eds., *Secondary Schools Today: Readings for Educators*, 2nd ed., Houghton Mifflin, Boston, 1969, Part I.

Smith, P. G., ed., *Theories of Value and Problems of Education*, University of Illinois Press, Urbana, 1970.

Strain, J. P., ed., *Modern Philosophies of Education: A Book of Readings*, Random House, New York, 1970.

Strom, R. D., ed., *Teachers and the Learning Process*, Prentice-Hall, Englewood Cliffs, New Jersey, 1971, Chap. 7.

Trump, J. L., and D. F. Miller, *Secondary School Curriculum Improvement: Proposals and Procedures*, Allyn and Bacon, Boston, 1968, Chap. 2.

Venable, T., *Philosophical Foundation of the Curriculum*, Rand McNally, Chicago, 1967.

Weigand, J. E., ed., *Developing Teacher Competencies*, paper, Prentice-Hall, Englewood Cliffs, New Jersey, 1971, Chap. 2.

Wilson, J. A. R., and others, *Psychological Foundations of Learning and Teaching*, McGraw-Hill, New York, 1969, Chap. 6.

PART II

MAJOR STEPS
OF TEACHING

CHAPTER 4

We have considered the needs of young people, the purposive-cognitive view of learning, and the democratic ideal as fundamental points of reference for teaching in high school. These are basic and interrelated guideposts in secondary education. They suggest three general objectives for secondary schools: increase and refinement of the student's interests or goals; enlargement of social outlook and sensitivity; and development of inclination and ability to think reflectively. These objectives give comprehensive direction to the whole educative process as it transpires in the three major stages of teaching—teacher-student planning, the study period, and culminating activities. The purpose of this and the next two chapters is to indicate how these objectives can be implemented effectively. The assignment, being of primary importance, receives first attention.

SOME ESSENTIAL CHARACTERISTICS

The Provision for Active Student Involvement

As indicated in the preceding chapter, students need to share with the teacher in the planning of learning activities. This need has been recognized often by leading educators and expressed convincingly in many classrooms. Despite all the evidence from educational theory and practice showing that the teacher-student assignment is superior to the teacher assignment, most of the student's work in high school continues to be a series of tasks assigned without active learner involvement. After fifty years of attacks on the conventional assignment by competent critics who have been armed with valid evidence, student participation in developing the assignment continues to be rare. The prevailing practice in high school

THE TEACHER-STUDENT ASSIGNMENT

consists of a ground-to-be-covered assignment, given by the teacher in terms of pages or chapters and through telling and directing, with the students being passive recipients. Visits in classrooms indicate that many teachers have not yet grasped fully the educational values deriving from student participation in the assignment. Teachers need to understand that the student who shares thoughtfully in the development of learning activities thereby improves insight into, and attitude toward, the objectives of the assignment. Furthermore, it would help them to realize that the active participation of different students assists the teacher in understanding their different abilities, interests, and needs.

Student participation in the assignment need not be limited to courses in a few subjects such as art, home economics, and the social studies but may be promoted in such rigidly organized courses as algebra and geometry. As we will see later, some mathematics teachers have been initiating learning by means of drawing on the students' experiences through using a series of thought questions to lead the students to discovery. They also have provided students with a variety of additional experiences, using concrete and graphic aids in the process. This approach to learning in mathematics is not through rules and formulas or by just telling and showing. Instead, it is through pertinent experiences and thought questions that direct students toward acquiring concepts and toward gaining insights into the solutions of problems. Encouragingly, research reveals that this type of assignment is superior to the conventional dictated assignment.[1]

Thus teachers can promote useful, active involvement of students in any assignment. Such involvement certainly can be increased and improved beyond what is found in many classrooms without involving the teacher in expecting adolescents to make decisions beyond their level of maturity or in abdicating the position of final judge. Also it will not require that every youngster in the class be vocal during every assignment. However, the teacher may reduce control by motivating students to begin discovering the nature, the need, and the proper procedures of the new work. He or she may provide the students with some immediate experiences and ask them to draw on these, along with their past experiences, as a way of beginning to understand the purpose, meaning, and usefulness of the confronting activity. We will see all of this more clearly in the examples of teacher-student assignments given later in this chapter.

This student-identified involvement in the content of any subject can best be accomplished when the teacher recognizes that each student enters the classroom possessing questions about his perceived reality. Drawing on these questions, the teacher can create an atmosphere in which the students and the teachers mutually identify the most relevant issues and proceed cooperatively to plan how best to

1 B. C. Mathis and others, *Psychological Foundations of Education: Learning and Teaching,* Academic Press, New York, 1970, pp. 692-693.

investigate the topic. A student-centered approach to learning, as such, should not lead to a laissez-faire attitude on the part of the teacher, for the success of this approach relies heavily on carefully guided student participation in the learning situation. If we agree that man is interactive, not just reactive, the teacher must actively lead, guide, or facilitate structuring of the learning; however, the student's interests within the structure of the course, as well as those of the teacher, become the center of the class. Thus, when the classroom environment allows students to inquire into their perplexities and when students have a significant part to play in the selection and planning of learning experiences, conditions present should allow more meaningful learning to take place.[2]

The Contribution to Sharing of Interests

Student participation both requires and promotes development of mutual interests, goals, or objectives. Moreover, as we saw in the preceding chapter, enlargement and refinement of the individual's interests is fundamental for growth in valuable personal qualities and improvement in academic achievement. In Chapter 1 there is evidence that the dropout typically has limited interests and that those few interests are usually self-centered or antisocial. Experiencing pursuit of few, if any, shared objectives, the dropout does not feel part of the group. Further, it is well known that the underachiever lacks the interests or goals necessary for reaching his or her potential level of achievement. This suggests that every teacher ought to use the assignment to begin improving the shared interests of all individuals in the group.

In enlisting students' interests in the formulation of appropriate learning activities, it is necessary first to know their present interests. This information may be gained through observations, individual conferences, and interest inventories. Then a teacher of reading or literature, for example, may begin helping the retarded and uninterested reader through providing reading in a present field of interest. However, as soon as this student begins to improve in reading in this area, the teacher wisely introduces attractive reading in related areas. Moreover, as the student is directed in working with others toward common objectives, individualized reading may be a natural outcome of sharing findings with other members of the group. Thus the teacher helps the student to expand and refine interests in reading.

Improvement of Social Qualities

Students who become involved in sharing interests as they approach common tasks tend to develop in social attitudes and habits. Specifically, discussion of the assignment, under the direction of a wise, sympathetic teacher, can be expected to improve desire and ability to exchange

2 R. L. Wendel, "Developing Climates for Learning," *Journal of Secondary Education* (November, 1970), 45, pp. 330-331. See also S. A. Taylor, "New Directions in Teaching Political Science," *Social Studies* (April, 1971), 62, pp. 147-154.

ideas with others. Such guided discussion may help the withdrawn students to share their thoughts with others and the forward ones to refrain from too eager expression. All participants, of course, are requested to support their own statements. Thus each one may gain an intelligent evaluation of his or her own opinions as well as the opinions of others. Through such participation of different members of the class in choosing and planning together, a group spirit tends to evolve. Expressions of mutual interests contribute to oneness within the class. Furthermore, individuals assume responsibilities as they assign tasks to themselves as well as to other members of the class. The result is that individuals and groups acquire a sense of responsibility to the whole group, that there is strong commitment to group goals and to positive group discipline. As a member of a cohesive group, a student is affected by the words and actions of other members.[3] Understanding this, some teachers see assignment making as an opportunity not only to initiate the study of subject matter meaningfully and interestingly but also to improve the social traits of boys and girls. They realize also that unless there is a group spirit in the assignment, it is unlikely to occur in the subsequent teaching periods.

These propositions project a social-psychological framework for the analysis of the educational process by emphasizing the importance of the social environment in which the student lives and his interaction with others in his social world. Such a conception of human learning has been identified as a *social interaction* theory because the individual acquires both the perceptions of appropriate behavior and his ability to learn in interaction with others who are important or significant to him. Not all members of groups or a society are equally significant. For each of us, certain persons and groups influence our perceptions of ourselves and our world more than others. We refer to these *significant others* and *reference groups*. Interaction with reference groups and significant others accounts for much of the variation in student performances.[4]

As the assignment is made social through such procedure, it should be made social also in its content. Since many teachers depend on only the textbook, many assignments are unnecessarily isolated from the students' lives outside the classroom. Some of these teachers, however, do question students about their past experiences in the course and help them to relate these experiences to the work at hand so that they gain intrinsic goals and insights. Other teachers go further as they question students about problems in the community and sometimes in the nation and the world. Then they help the students to go from such a discussion to a discussion of the new work. In general science, for example, some teachers approach study of the lever not through first looking at a principle or law and then ap-

---

[3] F. P. Bazeli, "Creating Group Cohesion in Inner City Classrooms," *Clearing House* (May, 1971), 45, pp. 547-550.
[4] W. B. Brookover and E. L. Erickson, *Society, Schools, and Learning*, paper, Allyn and Bacon, Boston, 1969, p. 16.

plying it but through questioning students about their experiences involving uses of a lever. Such a teacher also provides them with additional experiences, all the while asking them what they see. Similarly, teachers of literature are using assignments not only to improve students' reading and writing but also to enable them to gain an understanding of possible solutions to the problems of living in a modern society.

Initiation of Reflective Thinking

The fourth criterion of the assignment is provision for the stimulation and direction of reflective thinking. By providing students with concrete experiences and by questioning them skillfully, the teacher may lead them to look back at their experiences and reflect on those that bear on the confronting work. They may be helped to exchange ideas so that they are led to perceive worthwhile goals and to reflect on effective ways of moving toward the goals. Further, the teacher may challenge them to find support for assertions they make during the assignment.

This suggests that both in planning and making the assignment the teacher should endeavor to provide situations conducive to reflective learning. In doing this the teacher needs to have as one continuous point of reference the steps in a complete act of thought, as presented by Dewey at the first of this century:

1. Confronting a "forked road," perplexing situation, resulting in recognition of a problem
2. Limiting or defining the problem
3. Searching for possible solutions or hypotheses and weighing their implications, sometimes eliminating one or more hypotheses without further consideration
4. Gathering of data and testing the hypotheses
5. Further testing of hypotheses, leading to formulation and verification of conclusions

In using these steps of thinking, it is necessary to recognize that they are not to be followed rigidly. For instance, Steps 1 and 2 are sometimes taken simultaneously. Also, before one of the last steps is taken, there may be need to reconsider one or more of the preceding steps.[5]

Use of the assignment to involve the class in problem solving requires the utilization of thought questions. Unfortunately, these questions are not included in many assignments, which consist of merely telling students what to do and how and when to do it. Problem-solving questions not

[5] For further discussion of these steps of reflective thinking, see: John Dewey, *How We Think,* D. C. Heath, Boston, 1910, Chap. 6; M. P. Hunt and L. E. Metcalf, *Teaching High School Social Studies,* 2nd ed., Harper and Row, New York, 1968, pp. 67-69; M. R. Loree, *Psychology of Education,* 2nd ed., Ronald, New York, 1970, pp. 436-461.

only initiate thinking in the assignment but also provide the incentive and guidance for continuation of thinking in subsequent periods of study and discussion. Some examples are:

1. Compare the Monroe Doctrine with the Truman Doctrine.
2. Point out any similarities or differences between the actions of those in the Boston Tea Party and the actions of some civil rights workers in their disobedience of some laws.
3. Why does it take longer to cook cereal on a mountain than on a beach?
4. How is salt beneficial to animals in view of the fact that more than 50 percent of it consists of chlorine, a poison?
5. Show how there is lack of meaning in the rule of finding the area of a rectangle stated as "multiply the length by the breadth."

Special attention to thinking during the assignment is particularly important in that the assignment is the first step, or period, in the teaching process. The teacher who really is concerned about improving the way young people think will not miss the opportunity to improve them in any of the steps of teaching, including the assignment. Except by using the assignment to help students discover real problems and set up guesses or hypotheses toward the solution of those problems, the teacher is not preparing them to engage in thoughtful investigation during the study period and to state sound conclusions and generalizations during the culminating activities. If the assignment is restricted to prescribing ground to be covered and procedures for covering it, the teacher alone is to blame if students subsequently learn by rote instead of by thinking. Psychologists today emphasize the principle that learning is a continuous process. This principle implies that unless students engage in thinking during the assignment, they will be disinclined or unable to engage in it during the periods that follow.

Teacher Planning Before the Assignment

In advance of the assignment, it is necessary that every teacher do some out-of-class planning. This includes planning how the teacher and the students may act cooperatively and reflectively during the assignment. Furthermore, the teacher anticipates the probability of needing to make some changes in plans during that period. Too often a teacher decides to follow only the textbook to determine what the next lesson will be and how it will be assigned. Moreover, assignment time frequently is spent solely in giving specific directions about what is to be done. Routine and rigid textbook teaching requires relatively little planning. In contrast, enabling students to discover for themselves the need for the work and how to do it requires extensive, thoughtful planning.

The form of the plan is determined by the teacher's objectives. The writers have heard supervisors of student teachers complain that the students were not instructed in the technique of constructing a lesson plan while they were studying methods. The fact is that there is no reason for the student teacher to acquire any particular technique of writing a lesson plan. What is of importance is that the plan provide for learning in accordance with modern educational theory, which aims to provide for individual needs, shared interests, associated living, and reflective thinking. Consequently, a good plan includes ways to have free and thoughtful student participation in the assignment and the subsequent steps of teaching. The beginning teacher who is intelligent, well informed, and democratic can write appropriate plans without special training in any particular form. It is the nature of the students, the teacher, and the latter's educational objectives that determines the nature of the lesson plan.

Essential to an effectual lesson plan are the following:

1. Statements of the objective or objectives of the learning activity, stemming from the general objectives and the nature and needs of different learners
2. Realistic, problematic experiences for the students in the assignment, the directed study, and the discussion periods
3. Teaching materials, including audio-visual aids and books and periodicals
4. Pivotal thought questions, which may be used to stimulate and direct reflective learning in the assignment period and in the subsequent periods of study, instruction, and evaluation
5. Designations of how these essentials of the plan will be used in accordance with the criteria of making a good assignment

Proper planning by the teacher outside the classroom should include ideas to start the students in purposeful and meaningful learning during the assignment. The teacher should be ready to raise stimulating questions, conduct reflective discussion, recommend and provide audio-visual and reading materials and employ any useful means toward helping students join as a group in planning the next suitable learning activity for the class.

ILLUSTRATIONS OF THE TEACHER-STUDENT ASSIGNMENT IN FOUR SUBJECTS

An Illustration in the Teaching of English

The teacher-student assignment can be demonstrated in teaching grammatical understandings, concepts, or generalizations. A teacher, who depends on the actual self-expression of students as the chief means of improving their organization of thoughts and use of grammatical forms, may notice that some of them are misusing the verbs *lie* and *lay*. Rightly assuming that several others in the class also may need instruction on those verbs, he decides to take time at once for a special assignment to meet this particular need. Another teacher may observe that several students are making the same errors but may wait until the class reaches the lesson on verbs in the textbook. In either case, the teacher can avoid the conventional, rule approach assignment for one of student involvement and discovery. The objective of the assignment exists in the problem of differentiating between correct and incorrect uses of verbs *lie* and *lay*.

The teacher may attack the problem by presenting some uses of the two verbs taken from the students' speaking and writing and from reports of interviews by news media. Examples of some expressions are:

---

1. I saw him laying on the street.
2. I made him lay there until help came.
3. He laid there a long time.
4. I watched them lay him on the stretcher.
5. He lay still all the way.
6. He was lying on his back.
7. I will lay down for an hour.

The teacher has two reasons for providing such examples. One is to help the students to see that the two verbs are frequently misused even by some college graduates; the other, to provide expressions that may aid the students in gaining insights into the proper ways of using the verbs. Of course, the teacher will present additional examples and call on students to add several of their own.

As the teacher and students supply various examples, the teacher questions one student after another, asking for evaluations of the answers given. In the question-and-answer procedure, the teacher often postpones approving or disapproving an answer until one or more students have stated, and given reasons for, their answers to the question. The teacher also may use the answer of a student to direct further questioning. Rarely, of course, is an answer repeated. In using examples and questions, the teacher's aim is to lead each member of the class toward finding out individually.

A pertinent question, as the class is considering the fifth example above, may be: "How is *lay* used correctly in this expression, if *to lay* means *to place?*" More than one student may be required to reply to this question, to clarify and emphasize the correct answer, and to show the degree to which members of the class have gained a functional understanding of the uses of *lay*. A companion question may be added: "If *lie* means to recline and *lay* is used to express the past of *lie,* why is it incorrect to say, 'He was laying on the street'?" By such use of questions, demonstrations, and other means, a teacher may assist students to follow steps in a complete act of thought.

Similarly, a teacher of English may observe that, in conversation and writing, the students are misusing the nominative and the objective case of the first personal pronoun. This is particularly true when the pronoun is used in conjunction with a noun or a second pronoun. The same errors are commonly made by uneducated adults and even by some public speakers. Hence the teacher employs inductive procedure to involve students in a concerted, purposive effort to discover proper uses of these two cases of the personal pronoun. As in teaching the uses of *lie* and *lay,* the teacher relies on expressions in oral and written usage to enable students to see the nature and prevalence of the errors. It is hoped thereby to stimulate them to set as their problem finding out how these cases of the personal pronoun may be used correctly. Some common expressions are:

---

1. Us boys will do the work.
2. Jane and him saw Mary and I.
3. Henry will sit between you and I.
4. Our teacher and us are going.
5. It was Daddy and me.

When the students are confronted with such erroneous expressions, they may be asked to remove the noun or second pronoun and see how the expression sounds. Of course, they also should be helped to consider reflectively the function and the grammatical correctness of the form. For instance, if a student happens to recall and merely state the rule that the objective case of a pronoun is always used to express the object of a transitive verb, the teacher may ask that student to show functional understanding of what the transitive verb and object of a verb mean. Assistance in doing this may come through use of oral and written expressions, drawings on the chalkboard, and the give and take of class discussion.

Likewise, if a student gives the patent answer that the object of a preposition is always in the objective case, it may help to ask some students to consider their conception of a preposition in relation to its object. They need to understand the functional relationship of a preposition and a pronoun to each other and to the rest of the sentence. Their attention may be called to the two parts of the word *preposition, pre* and *position.* Then, through analysis of various prepositional phrases, they may be led to discover that a preposition functions with its object to express a literal or figurative relationship of position.

In such an assignment—featuring problem raising, demonstration, discussion, and discovery—the aim is to initiate development of concepts or generalizations. Accordingly, the teacher does not press students for final answers. These they may find for themselves in the subsequent periods of study and expression. Especially in the assignment, the teacher does not insist on premature verbalization of insights or concepts. To do so would encourage students to express symbols of thought in advance of thought. The result would be that students would tend to accept words as substitutes for understandings and to learn by rote instead of reflection.

Toward the end of such a goal seeking and insightful assignment period, the students are assigned experiences for study. These may include having the students bring to class one or more illustrations of various uses of all the forms of *lie* and *lay* or of the nominative and the objective case of the personal pronoun. The experiences may even include filling out blanks in the ordinary workbook, provided the students in a discussion period are called on to explain why a particular form is correct or incorrect.

Demonstration in the New Social Studies

The value of intrinsic goals and understandings in the approach to development of concepts in English has been recognized also in the new social studies. Some educators in this area conceive of an assignment as focused on helping students to recognize, define, and formulate possible solutions of a problem. The learning process is characterized by goal seeking, discovering, and generalizing.

Toward those ends the teacher enlists students in confrontation with personal and societal problems. In the process the teacher and the class recognize the increasing complexity and interdependence of the modern world. There is an effort to help young people perceive the confusion of today in a broad perspective of time and place. They are provided experiences in perceiving the immediate in relation to the remote and in using the democratic ideal and the scientific method.

In planning and making assignments, the teacher is aware of objectives toward meeting the students' real needs in a changing, complicated society. This is basic, but according to investigations many teachers of social studies indicate by their practices that their dominant objectives are covering ground of the textbook and preparing students for factual examinations. The two major aims of teachers in the new social studies are development of the individual (1) in socially desirable values and (2) in investigative, critical decision making. These aims begin to function in the teaching-learning process as students become positively involved in the initiation of learning activities.

Questions bearing on current problems are another essential feature of such an assignment. These questions are about conditions in homes, the community, the nation, and the world. Examples are:

---

1. What are some needs for improvement of our community?
2. What are some hindrances to provision of those needs?
3. How is life in my home affected by conditions in my community and through-out the world?
4. What do facts in the history of Vietnam in recent decades lead us to conclude about how the United States became involved in the Vietnam War?
5. How have science and technology been instrumental in the production of conditions difficult for, but demanding, reflective decisions?
6. How may we differentiate between prejudice and propaganda and scientific procedure?

Such questions are presented and discussed in any assignment of the new social studies. If a class in United States history is about to study the formation of the federal Constitution, suitable questions could pertain to application of the Bill of Rights. Examples are "Should government of-ficials have the power to ban or censor certain books and movies in a city?" "What is your attitude toward heckling a political speaker?" These questions can contribute to a problematic approach to a study of the Constitution, and they can stimulate and direct discussion and study.

In discussions, the students are encouraged to express freely their understandings and attitudes. Yet they are led tactfully and considerately toward precision in their selection of words and structure of thoughts and toward recognition of implicit assumptions and irrelevant or unsupported statements. It has been found that such teaching during and following assignments contributes to student improvement in critical study and thinking.

Reflective learning is initiated not only through verbal questioning. Some provision for adequate, suitable learning materials and activities is also essential. Problem-raising can be accomplished by confronting stu-dents directly with situations witnessed during a field trip or by a movie shown in the classroom. Newspaper clippings, tape recordings of events, and visiting speakers also are means of encouraging students to explore a topic deeply. Frequently, these initial motivating activities are followed by the involvement of students in field-centered research. In small groups or individually, students may interview news makers, submit question-naires to other people, and investigate and gather "facts" through visits to city offices, museums, businesses, and the like. These experiences are appropriate for use in each major step of teaching, but they are of special importance in the assignment period to supply concrete information as a basis for the development of concepts.

For work during the study period, a list of suitable reading materials is provided. For reflective reading and decision making on the perplexing, changing problems of today, the textbook alone does not suffice. Students are referred, therefore, to periodicals, paperbacks, and other reference materials for use in classroom study or the central library. These references are used by them to find answers to questions acquired in and outside the classroom.

This kind of assignment period may provide for individual, along with group, work. In group discussion of questions and materials leading to an assignment, the teacher often discovers individual as well as group needs which may form a basis for initiation of some individual projects. Additional individual activities are initiated as the teacher observes and assists students in the directed study period.[6]

Demonstrations in Conventional Mathematics

An assignment that starts students toward discovering a concept or generalization has been demonstrated in some conventional courses of mathematics. These courses relate mathematics to other subjects and to life in the modern world. For example, some teachers of geometry draw on algebra and trigonometry and as far as possible on science and other subjects. Even more significant is their use of propositions and basic assumptions in editorials and political speeches as bases for introducing learners to the propositions and basic assumptions in geometry. As the course is thus broadened and made somewhat flexible, the students have opportunities to share in the initiation of learning activities. Furthermore, the work on nongeometric materials improves learning in geometry and in the transfer of the learning to areas outside the subject. The result is that students develop in thinking in the nongeometric as well as the geometric area.

This way of approaching learning activities in the teaching of geometry was used by Aten in the University High School at Oakland, California. Realizing that the content and the form of Euclid's geometry had long been in need of change, Aten undertook to accomplish some necessary changes through teaching geometry as a method of thinking and through providing parallel situations in life for transference of thinking. Eighty-five tenth-grade students constituted the experimental group. There was much student involvement. In the procedures, the learner was assisted

---

[6] Further consideration of selection and application of methods and materials in the social studies can be found in Chaps. 7 and 10. See also E. Fenton, *Teaching the New Social Studies in Secondary Schools: An Inductive Approach*, Holt, Rinehart, and Winston, New York, 1966, Chaps. 2-8; B. G. Massialas and C. B. Cox, *Inquiry in Social Studies*, McGraw-Hill, New York, 1966, Chaps. 5-7.

in discovering as much as possible and the geometry learned was used at once in nongeometric situations. The common theorems were taught in a psychological order instead of textbook order. Noteworthy changes made in the teaching process were:

1. The displacement of superposition proofs
2. The discovery of assumptions and theorems by pupils from assigned given data
3. The discovery of the proof by the students, with a few appropirate models and flexible suggestions
4. The assignment of originals without a "to prove," the pupil to find and prove what he can from the given data
5. The evolution of figures with proofs
6. The organization of units about aspects of thinking. The theorems studied in each unit then become assimilative material directed at the mastery of a specific phase of straight thinking
7. The incorporation into this assimilation material of parallel life situations using the same principles
8. The evaluation of learning in nongeometric as well as in geometric situations
9. The introduction and use of inductive proof
10. The use of notebooks in lieu of a text[7]

According to Aten, there was observable evidence of very satisfactory learning among the students of the experimental group. They showed spontaneous enthusiasm, individual responsibility, and unusual accomplishment. This was true especially of those considered to be slow learners. "It is at least some reassurance to find groups studying geometry at this age, and enjoying it, trying to improve their statements of discovered relationships, eager to hear or explain an original proof."[8]

In this method of teaching geometry, the assignment is used to assist students in the perception of assumptions, theorems, and proofs of originals. The teacher concentrates on what may be called "inductive proof," providing the students with experiences in and outside of geometry, leading them to recognize problems and raise questions, and to set possible solutions to the problems and answers to the questions.

A similar type of assignment in geometry was reported by Ulmer.[9] In offering suggestions for teaching geometry to improve thinking, he stated that the teacher may direct students in approaching the subject through

---

[7] H. D. Aten, "A Reorganization of Geometry for Carryover," *Mathematics Teacher* (April, 1941), 34, p. 153.
[8] Ibid., p. 154.
[9] G. Ulmer, *Some Suggestions for Teaching Geometry to Develop Clear Thinking,* Kansas Studies in Education, Vol. 2, No. 7, University of Kansas Press, Lawrence, 1942.

helping them to see that one of the most important needs in the world today is clear thinking. Then the teacher may say to the class that, to start at the beginning in this matter of logical thinking, the first step to take is to learn how certain statements necessarily imply others. To assist the learners to discover this truth for themselves, the teacher may write on the board several pairs of statements such as the following:

---

1. All Chinese are yellow.
2. Wing Toy is Chinese.
1. All new pupils in our school are required to take an examination.
2. Bob is a new pupil.
1. All 90° angles are right angles.
2. This angle is a 90° angle.

As the teacher writes each two statements on the board, the students are asked to express the third statement that logically follows the first two. To help them further toward finding out how basic assumptions produce conclusions, several pairs of propositions that lead logically to conclusions may be given. In addition, they may be directed in giving some unsupportable basic assumptions and conclusions. An example is:

---

1. All red-haired people have bad tempers.
2. William has red hair.
3. William has a bad temper.

At this point it may be helpful for the class to consider further the function of basic assumptions in government, industry, and other areas. The first part of the Declaration of Independence provides such assumptions. Examples of assumptions that may be obtained from life today are (1) every form and degree of socialistic practice is unnecessary and undesirable in the United States and (2) individual freedom always increases as governmental regulation of industry decreases.

After the students have thus found out for themselves the nature and function of basic assumptions in thinking, they may be expected to approach understandingly the study of these assumptions in geometry. The usual way of having them "learn" assumptions in geometry is to have them read and study them from the textbook. As an alternative, Ulmer proposed that they be directed in constructing and expressing some assumptions at least so that they may adequately understand their nature and function in the science of geometry.

In proceeding beyond the study of assumptions, the youngsters need to discover for themselves the relationships and implications of the assumptions. Too much of the thinking done in geometry develops young people more in rationalization than in scientific thinking. People often spend time and energy trying to justify positions already taken rather than trying to follow scientific thinking to whatever positions it may lead them. Yet, according to Ulmer, "this is precisely the kind of thinking we have been emphasizing in our geometry classes. The student is told what position to take. He is handed a statement and asked to defend it."[10] Instead, the teacher should spend much time assisting students to take positions in the light of their assumptions.

Thus, in the approach to learning activities, Ulmer advocated and practiced leading students to suspect and investigate, focusing more on seeking than on demonstrating or proving. He believed that if the learner is actively involved in the search for a conclusion, satisfactory insight is likely to come from a demonstration of the activity by the learner or a classmate.[11]

Earnestly desiring to teach geometry so that the subject contributes not only to the students' mathematical thinking but also to their economic, social, and political thinking, the teacher steadfastly helps them to watch all such essential points relative to sound thinking in the nongeometric as well as in the geometric area. Fortunately, the class that spends considerable time on problems of life learns as much geometry as the ordinary class does. The fact is that teachers who have adopted this way of teaching geometry report that "pupils gain in their understanding of geometric relationships, because pupils use in geometry those principles of clear thinking which they have learned. Their thinking improves in geometry as it improves elsewhere."[12]

Reemphasis in the New Mathematics

The experience-question-discovery approach to the assignment in experiments in conventional mathematics has been reemphasized in the new mathematics. Beginning in the early 1950's, the new mathematics has evolved chiefly through the work of two groups: the School Mathematics Study Group and the University of Illinois Committee on School Mathematics (UICSM). It has become a remodeled program of mathematics, including reorganized courses, textbooks, and manuals. Much old subject matter has been retained, and some new subject matter, demanded by modern society, has been added. The central aim, especially of the UICSM program, has been to help students to develop concepts or generalizations. This requires initiation of learning activities through student involvement in discovering.

An appraisal of the new mathematics should hinge not on a comparison

---

10 Ibid., p. 18.
11 Ibid., pp. 18-19.
12 Ibid., p. 20.

of new subject matter with old, but on whether students should learn mathematical skills through purpose, meaning, and inquiry in either conventional or new programs. Beginning in the assignment, the students are provided a variety of experiences directed toward their developing a concept or generalization. This is the inductive process in which the learners are contributors, not just recipients.

In the process of leading students to discover, especially during the assignment period, the teacher is warned against insistence on their verbalizing prematurely, which has been found to be harmful. Hence the teacher should continue providing them with appropriate experiences and thought questions that will assist them in grasping the why as well as the how of the mathematical operation. First the group, and then the individual, practices in working some simple, representative problems. Ultimately each individual needs to develop enough understanding to assimilate the generalization.

To use the teaching procedure of the new mathematics, many teachers have had to engage in special study. This has been particularly true of those who did not practice the procedure when they taught conventional courses. Instead, they used the rule-telling-showing approach. To acquire workable knowledge of the "new" procedure, some teachers have attended workshops outside or within their schools. Others have taught themselves through studying and trying out some of the published materials.[13]

The results from this "new approach" of learning in the study of mathematics have been encouraging. Teachers have enjoyed stimulation from the use of reflection and discovery in the teaching procedure. Parents have asked what has happened to improve their children's attitudes toward mathematics, and even the poor students have come alive as they increasingly experience goal seeking, insightful learnings.[14] Furthermore, satisfactory "mastery" of the subject matter has been indicated by standardized achievement tests, which were devised for conventional courses in mathematics.[15]

An Example in the New Sciences

As in the new mathematics, the assignment in the new sciences consists of initiating the process of investigation and discovery. Students are given an "invitation to inquiry." They are provided with concrete, realistic experiences, thought questions, and inquisitive discussions. These are used to

13 For a list of these materials write to School Mathematics Study Group, School of Education, Stanford University, Stanford, California, and Director of UICSM Project, University of Illinois, Urbana.
14 W. E. Ferguson, "Current Reforms in Mathematics Curricula—A Passing Phase or Progress?" *Mathematics Teacher* (March, 1964), 57, pp. 143-145.
15 For further description and evaluation of this inductive approach to instruction in mathematics, see the section on teaching mathematics in Chap. 8. See also National Council of Teachers of Mathematics, *The Continuing Revolution in Mathematics*, National Council of Teachers of Mathematics, Washington, D.C., 1968.

pose, and begin an attack on, one or more problems. Textbooks and manuals of the new sciences present problems and list questions and audio-visual aids for use in work on the problems in the laboratory and library. Neither the textbook nor the manual is of the old cookbook type. The students are not given a law of science and then told to verify it in the laboratory. With the assistance of the textbook, the manual, and the teacher, they are prepared in the assignment period to go to the laboratory and, in some instances, to the library, to find out for themselves.

For example, in an approach to the study of light, a teacher of physics may question students about the operation of a camera or an overhead projector or may ask them to explain the cause of a rainbow or of a seemingly broken stick that is half submerged in water. Then they are called on to submit hypotheses bearing on explanation of the phenomena of refraction and reflection of light. A question asked may be: "Why do the right and the left side of your body seem to be in reverse when you view yourself in a mirror?" In the discussion the aim is not to supply final answers to questions but to promote the desire and ability to search for the answers during the work period in the laboratory or library.[16]

Beginning in the assignment, and continuing through the second and third stages of the teaching cycle, the new sciences and the other new subjects focus on the following points:

1. Active involvement of students in initiation and continuation of each learning activity
2. Students learning the "why" of scientific phenomena
3. Students solving problems that are real to them
4. Extensive promotion of student projects
5. Student development in the discovery of concepts and generalizations
6. Development of students in scientific attitudes and reflective thinking
7. Extensive use of questions in the teaching-learning process
8. Frequent use of a variety of learning materials
9. Employment of problem solving not only in instruction but also in evaluation[17]

This type of instruction, conducted by a science teacher or any other teacher, requires that some ground rules be formulated cooperatively by teachers and students. Here is a list of rules used by a class:

1. The teacher will allow thinking time when a student is asked a question.
2. If the student is getting off the track, or if the answer seems too involved, the teacher reserves only the option of polite interruption.

[16] For further information about the new sciences, see the section on the teaching of science in Chap. 8. For illustrations of the teacher-student assignment in the practical arts, see the section on industrial arts and on home economics in Chap. 9.
[17] See P. B. Hounshell and E. L. West, Jr., "Trends in the Teaching of Science," *High School Journal* (January, 1970), 53, pp. 207-215.

3. All students are expected to participate in the discussion.
4. Students may challenge or disagree with one another and with the teacher as long as they are courteous and able to support their positions.
5. The students may ask for clarification of the question if it is not clear.
6. The teacher may request clarification if the response is unclear.
7. A prearranged signal will be used to indicate inaudibility.
8. Discussion participants may feel free to modify their views if other positions seem more reasonable, more feasible, or better, in the light of further information. The modification is permissible, not mandatory.
9. The teacher will evaluate pupil response on the basis of quality and quantity.
10. If other limitations are to be placed, such as textbook-only answers, time limit, brief answers only, the teacher will indicate this before beginning the discussion.

Ground rules have a way of binding the teacher as well as the students to a consistent mode of behavior. They are effective only if both parties respect them.

Students get a feeling of worth when they know that their opinions as well as their memories are respected. They admire a well-phrased question. Clarity is equally important. No matter how brilliant a student may be, he cannot respond effectively unless he understands the question. Some teachers are guilty of ambiguity, or of couching a question in obscure or advanced vocabulary to impress students with their profundity. The answer of the student depends on the clarity of the question as well as on the listening ability of the teacher.

Too often teachers accept ridiculous, vague, or even erroneous statements of students without challenge. When the teacher fails to listen and/or fails to pursue the discussion, students are tempted to engage in the double-talk game. They never really answer the question at hand but they employ appropriate vocabulary, receiving the absent-minded nod of approval from the teacher. Some of the more adroit students seem able to time their answers to suit the teacher's interest span or the time set aside for discussion.[18]

Use of Questions in the Assignment

We have seen that the use of questions is essential in the effective assignment. In too many assignments the teacher does not make a sufficient number of interrogative statements but rather concentrates on stating and explaining ideas. What should be done is to question students about their former experiences and provide them with new and meaningful experiences about which they are also questioned. Concrete, realistic experiences and skillful questioning should be used to assist students to find out what many teachers merely would tell them. In all this procedure the teacher encourages them to ask questions and to give answers to those asked by their classmates.

The teacher must be careful to distribute the questions among as many as possible of the class. Too many teachers, following the line of least resistance, allow volunteers to monopolize question answering while the reticent students sit idly by. Usually the teacher will do well to direct the

18 M. R. Lindman, "Improving Oral Response," *High School Journal* (December, 1970), 54, p. 214.

first questions to those who are disinclined to participate and be attentive. In so doing their active attention may be gained to find out where and how they need help. If the teacher permits the weak and inattentive to refrain from active participation during the first minutes of the discussion, a poor response may be expected from them when they are called on later. Of course, during all the questioning, the teacher should alternate between the weak or reticent and the strong or talkative. Often the teacher could effectively use the answers of the best to assist the others in learning. These suggestions about how the teacher may improve the distribution of questions do not imply that the teacher should aim to question every member of a class in each assignment. This, of course, is usually both impossible and undesirable.

The use of questions to promote real discussion of issues in the assignment requires that the teacher often have one youngster comment on the answer of another. Many teachers express approval or disapproval of answers at once, passing to students only the unacceptable ones. The result is that many students often pay little or no attention to the answers of their classmates, waiting for the comments of the teacher. Thus the teacher has a series of dialogues with one student after another while there is scarcely any give and take of discussion among the others. What the teacher should do frequently is pass the respondent's answer to classmates, asking them to supplement, evaluate, or support the answer. In this way the teacher can provide some with additional experiences in class discussion and may gain further information about their abilities, interests, and needs at the initiation of a learning activity.[19]

Time for the Assignment

Ideally, the assignment should be made when the teaching-learning process leads to it. Then the students are most likely to see the need for it and to recognize and accept its objective. This may be at any juncture during a learning activity. Accordingly, an assignment may be made near the beginning, the middle, or the end of a class period. It may also extend over the entire period.

Many teachers have a set time for the assignment. Too often it is immediately before or at the signal for dismissal. Some teachers, of course, need little time for their type of assignment which consists only of a brief list of directions. Others plan to reserve sufficient time, but they become so absorbed in teaching the lesson for the day that they are unaware of the approaching end of the period. These teachers may also feel that their instruction on the present learning task is more important than their instruction on the assignment for the next day. All of them may need full

[19] For additional information on questioning strategies, see Chaps. 6 and 15; also see N. M. Sanders, *Classroom Questions: What Kinds?* Harper and Row, New York, 1966.

realization that the assignment is not a "necessary evil" to be given as quickly as possible so that students may have additional time for study and recitation. The fact is, of course, that the most valuable instruction is often provided in a good assignment.

Some teachers, having found it almost impossible to save sufficient time for an effective assignment toward the end of the class period, have set aside the first part of the period for that purpose. If they find during the remaining part of the period that the assignment should be altered, they can usually do this briefly and adequately. These teachers thus give themselves sufficient time to make an assignment that may help students enter the study period with enough interest and insight in the task to work with considerable self-directed reflection.

Obviously the assignment described in this chapter requires an "open" classroom in which both the teacher and the student are actively and cooperatively involved. Unfortunately, some experimental schools, in an effort to eliminate the teacher-dictated assignment, have turned to the opposite extreme of giving the student almost unlimited freedom to decide what to do and where and when to do it. As seen in Chapter 3, that practice has been indicated in reports of some "open" or "free" schools. For democratically oriented assignments, the classroom must be neither autocratic nor anarchistic. Instead the teacher and the students need to raise and tentatively answer questions and jointly plan learning activities. The teacher functions through discovering the students' interests and needs and furnishing the guidance necessary for meeting these interests and needs. Thus in the assignment the students may receive guidance toward development in self-directed learning, which will continue in the ongoing major steps or periods of learning experiences. In this type of open classroom there is sharing in the decision making process, with the teacher and the students jointly choosing the learning activities.[20]

QUESTIONS AND ACTIVITIES

1. Outline and then discuss in small groups or with the entire class the characteristics of a good assignment as suggested by Gestalt psychology. How democratic are these characteristics?

[20] See the concluding paragraphs of Chap. 3 and the section on independent study in Chap. 12. See also H. C. Sun, "The Open Classroom: A Critique," *High School Journal* (December, 1972), 56, pp. 134-141; C. A. Hardy, "Societal Change and the Open Classroom," *Clearing House* (November, 1972), 47, pp. 139-141; and G. R. Weldy, "Building Democratic Values Through Student Participation," *National Association of Secondary School Principals Bulletin* (May, 1970), 54, pp. 72-79.

2. State differences between the teacher assignment and the teacher-student assignment.

3. Give an example of an assignment, showing how the assignment may be used not only to improve academic learning but also to promote democratic behavior.

4. First, prepare a short, sample introductory lesson patterned after Dewey's reflective thinking process described in this chapter. It might be best to use some familiar content from your subject area in planning this mini-lesson. Now present it to the class, a small group of fellow students, or make a video tape of your demonstration. Invite a critique of your efforts.

5. Interview several teachers to find out how they go about involving students in the selection and planning of learning activities. Are the teacher's suggestions democratic? Can they always be? Are their ideas consistent with learning theory?

6. As a class, brainstorm how the teacher may question individuals during the assignment so that pertinent information about their abilities, interests, and needs are discovered and their work may be planned according to that information.

7. Invite an experienced high-school teacher into your class as a guest to discuss and answer questions about the characteristics of planning a learning experience.

8. Illustrate ways of approaching even the workbook assignment through questioning pupils on their experiences and providing them with some additional experiences.

SELECTED REFERENCES

Alberty, H. B., and E. Alberty, *Reorganizing the High School Curriculum,* 3rd ed., Macmillan, New York, 1962, Chaps. 1, 10.

Alcorn, M. D., and others, *Better Teaching in Secondary Schools,* 3rd ed., Holt, Rinehart and Winston, New York, 1970, Chaps. 4-5.

Bayles, E. E., *Pragmatism in Education,* Harper and Row, New York, 1966, Chap. 6.

Bigge, M. L., and M. P. Hunt, *Psychological Foundations of Education,* 2nd ed., Harper and Row, New York, 1968, Chaps. 21-22 and Epilogue.

Blount, N. S., and H. J. Klausmeier, *Teaching in the Secondary School,* 3rd ed., Harper and Row, New York, 1968, Chaps. 6-7.

Carin, A. A., and R. B. Sund, *Teaching Science Through Discovery,* 2nd ed., Charles E. Merrill, Columbus, Ohio, 1970.

Dale, Edgar, *Building a Learning Environment*, Phi Delta Kappa, International Headquarters, Bloomington, Indiana, 1972.

Emmer, E. T., and G. B. Millett, *Improving Teaching Experimentation: A Laboratory Approach*, Prentice-Hall, Englewood Cliffs, New Jersey, 1970.

Gorman, B. W., *Secondary Education: The High School America Needs*, Random House, New York, 1971, Chap. 6.

Home Economics Association, *Reaching Out to Those We Teach*, paper, National Education Association, Washington, D. C., 1969.

Loree, M. R., *Psychology of Education*, 2nd ed., Ronald, New York, 1970, Chap. 12.

Loretan, J. O., and S. Umans, *Teaching the Disadvantaged: New Curriculum Approaches*, Teachers College Press, Columbia University, New York, 1966.

Lutz, F. W., ed., *Toward Improved Urban Education*, Charles A. Jones, Worthington, Ohio, 1970.

Massialas, B. G., and J. Zevin, *Creative Encounters in the Classroom: Teaching and Learning Through Discovery*, John Wiley, New York, 1967, Chaps. 1-2.

Morine, Harold, and Greta Morine, *Discovery: A Challenge to Teachers*, Prentice-Hall, Englewood Cliffs, N. J., 1973.

Mouly, George J., *Psychology for Effective Teaching*, 3rd ed., Holt, Rinehart and Winston, New York, 1973, Chap. 13.

National Society for the Study of Education, *The Educationally Retarded and Disadvantaged*, Sixty-sixth Yearbook, Part I, University of Chicago, Chicago, 1967, Chaps. 9-10.

Overly, D. E., and others, *The Middle School: Humanizing Education for Youth*, Charles A. Jones, Worthington, Ohio, 1972, Chaps. 1, 16.

Rich, J. M., *Humanistic Foundations of Education*, Charles A. Jones, Worthington, Ohio, 1971, Chap. 3.

Shulman, L. S., and E. R. Keislar, eds., *Learning by Discovery: A Critical Appraisal*, Rand McNally, Chicago, 1966.

Strom, R. D., ed., *Teachers and the Learning Process*, Prentice-Hall, Englewood Cliffs, New Jersey, 1971, Chaps. 1, 2, 5.

Tyson, J. C., and M. A. Carroll, *Conceptual Tools for Teaching in Secondary Schools*, Houghton Mifflin, Boston, 1970.

Von Haden, H. I., and J. M. King, *Innovations in Education: Their Pros and Cons*, paper, Charles A. Jones, Worthington, Ohio, 1971, Chap. 12.

Washton, N. S., *Teaching Science Creatively in the Secondary Schools*, W. B. Saunders, Philadelphia, 1967, Chap. 11.

Weigand, J. E., ed., *Developing Teaching Competencies*, paper, Prentice-Hall, Englewood Cliffs, New Jersey, 1971, Chaps. 3, 6.

CHAPTER 5

The assignment prepares students for, and extends into, the second period or step of teaching commonly called the "study period." In fact, students' experiences in any assignment unavoidably affect their experiences in the period of study. This is because learning is a continuous process in each individual, always occurring through past as well as present experiences. Accordingly, the teacher should not view the study period as a step or period entirely different from the assignment. During the assignment the teacher may provide for some study and, during study, for some revisions of and additions to the previous assignment. This is noticeably true when students learn reflectively through extended work on a common problem.

POSSIBILITY AND DESIRABILITY OF SOME GROUP ACTIVITIES

Some cooperative, or shared, activities of the assignment need to be extended into the study period. Of course individual work, in which the student engages in activities with reference to particular abilities and needs, *is especially appropriate* in this second step of teaching. We will see later in this chapter how this very important type of work may be rightly emphasized. Our immediate concern is with group activities which do not compete with but can be made to involve and produce individual activities.

Work considered and planned by a group in the assignment sometimes can be done by group action during study. For example, a class in general science may be studying a problem on sanitation and health. During the assignment the teacher may decide in planning with the class on a field trip. So in the study period the group takes the trip, on which individuals assume different responsibilities for carrying out the group plans. Likewise, this class may discuss in the assignment how to secure data on a problem

THE STUDY PERIOD

through viewing a particular picture and then reading different references in the class or central library. During study the students, in viewing the picture and in reading the references, will be inclined to relate their learnings to group as well as individual goals.

In a group activity during the study period, a class usually divides into individuals and small groups joined by common interests and needs. These small groups are not necessarily committees, formally organized and assigned specific activities during a teacher-student assignment. Instead, they may be formed in a workshop environment when a few individuals, in the process of studying, unite to exchange ideas and assist one another, all under the guidance of the teacher.

As individuals and small groups study to meet their particular interests and needs, they also may be studying to meet their obligation to share in the activity of the whole class. The teacher focuses on the direction of all the students as they work according to their individual needs but aims also to help each student view his or her work in relation to group interests. This may be expected to add both to interest and understanding in learning.

An outcome of such group undertakings that deserves special attention is the students' intellectual development. The old conception of development of mind or intelligence is quite individualistic. A person was expected always to be best in learning when separated from the other people and working completely alone. This notion has been questioned by many educational psychologists and sociologists. They hold that the give and take of individuals and groups may contribute much to the quantity and quality of learning. The nature and function of a person's mind is social. Exchange of ideas is as important in education as exchange of goods in business. The educational miser suffers with the educational pauper when each individual tends to act alone in a learning situation. In study, as in everything else, learning often occurs best as the mind of the individual interacts with the minds of other members of the class.

This is particularly true of a student's development in thinking. The group activity may provide an individual with goals and means of thinking. The student may acquire from classmates and the teacher a recognition of important problems, suggestions for the solutions of the problems, and facts bearing on the solutions. No individual, especially the inexperienced learner, can improve significantly in reflective thinking without stimulation and assistance from others. One's mind develops and functions in social environments. The exchange of ideas in group activities develops the individual's stock of meanings and process of thinking. Moreover, modern society is so complex and is changing so rapidly that no individual, not even an adult, is wise enough to grapple successfully with personal and social problems without drawing on the intelligence of other people. In attacks on problems, the individual working alone cannot know all the pertinent facts even in one single field of specialization and cannot always perceive what personal motives and prejudices may be determining seemingly objective conclusions.

An Illustration in English Composition

Some teachers of English composition have recognized the value of common experiences in the students' environments as bases for writing through thinking. Among the sources of these common experiences are radio, television, athletic events, school programs, field trips, and books and periodicals. From such sources students may draw shared experiences which provide the best situations for group writing through thinking.

Under the direction of the teacher, the students may write a report of a shared or common experience, by following steps of thinking as stated in Chapter 4. They may begin by free discussion of an experience such as attending a convocation or watching a ball game or a motion picture. They may list on the chalkboard expressions of various ideas, rejecting vague statements for concrete and definite ones, and use this list for construction of a title for their report. Then they may draw on both the ideas and the title to discuss and determine the organization of the paper, following this by different expressions of an introductory paragraph. After these expressions have been evaluated and a paragraph has been approved, the next step may be to state and tentatively choose a topic sentence for the second paragraph and even some succeeding paragraphs. All of these first steps in making an effective report on a common experience may require a whole class period. They consist of recognition and definition of the problem and setting up and testing suggestions for valid conclusions.

In the next period the teacher may continue directing the class in writing a group report or may shift to having each student complete the report individually. Choosing further group action, the teacher may question the class about what it did in the previous period and then invite suggestions for improvement. Then the class should be ready to suggest the content and form of the second paragraph and to work toward completion of the report. As each paragraph is constructed the teacher questions the students about its structure and its role in developing a line of thought in the report. After the report has been completed, the students are directed in revising and polishing it.

As a student thus participates in writing various group reports of common experiences, improvement in interest, understanding, and writing skill is likely to come about. The student may be expected to develop an inclination and ability to write through thinking. Indeed, the student may gain more from observing teacher and classmates in the process of writing than from receiving and applying rules and instructions from the teacher and the textbook.

The primary aim of group writing, of course, is to improve the student in individual writing. The teacher, therefore, encourages and helps students to write individually, requiring them to do the work in class. In fact, some teachers refrain from requesting students to write out of class and then hand in the papers. Like teachers of home economics, these teachers of English composition want students to do their work in class under their observation and direction. As each student writes alone, the teacher usually walks about the room to observe, assist, and offer encouragement and suggestions when the student needs them. In such directed work the teacher may render effective help and discover needs of the student not revealed by a paper written out of class.

After, or even before, the student has completed a paper in class, letting a classmate read it may be helpful. Writing for a classmate as well as for the teacher should increase the incentive of the writer to do a good job of communicating. Also comments and suggestions from a peer may help the writer to comprehend objectively the nature of the writing and to develop an interest in improving it.

The individual conference also has been found to be helpful. This conference may be held before, during, and after the writing. In it the teacher may encourage free expression about the student's particular interests and needs and may point out strong and weak points, specifying how improvements may be made. The rapport between teacher and student also may be improved. Moreover, unnecessary time and energy are required for a teacher, in the reading of written work, to write on each paper comments sufficiently adequate and definite to be of much help to the student. Some teachers have discovered that the individual conference contributes more toward improvement of writing than marginal comments on the papers or lectures to the group. An experimental group, which had individual conferences, improved significantly in comparison with a control group, which had only comments on the papers.[1]

In the process of directing students in writing, it is necessary at some point to assist each one in revising his or her paper. Too often themes are accepted and handed back without definite provision for any revision. As in art, industrial arts, and home economics, the student in writing needs the experience of altering a production toward the goal of perfection. It may help at this point of the learning to explain that revision is normal procedure, even among expert writers.

Students and teachers like this workshop teaching-learning situation. It provides a group-individual procedure, in which members of the class have reasons to communicate, share interests and ideas, and help one another to improve their written compositions in both content and form. It promotes learning through cooperation, reflection, and self-direction.

1 See the section on written composition in Chap. 7.

A Demonstration in the New Chemistry[2]

How the study period can be used for group-individual instruction, con-centrated on investigating and discovering, has been demonstrated in the laboratory procedure of the new chemistry. There has been discontent with the conventional course in chemistry in high school. This course too often emphasizes memorization of valence tables and balancing of equations more than development of scientific concepts, attitudes, and habits. Nearly all entries in notebooks require only perusal of textbook material, with little or no reference to laboratory work. As a reaction against such teach-ing, in 1960 or so, groups of scientists and educators began construction of new chemistry courses, one group being the Chemical Education Material Study (CHEM). Using a grant from the National Science Foundation, this group produced a new chemistry course, including a textbook, a laboratory manual, a teacher's guide, and other teaching aids. These were tried out in several high schools and were revised in accordance with suggestions from teachers.

In the CHEM course, students begin work in the laboratory and the laboratory continues to be the point of departure for their study throughout the course. Nearly all of the first ten days may be spent in the laboratory, and about a week may go by before the textbook is used at all. Through directed work in the laboratory, the student is assisted, not in demon-strating or verifying what he has studied in the text, but in experimenting as a scientist toward discovering new ideas. During the entire year students observe and experiment before they read in the textbook about the ma-terial involved or discuss it in class. The teacher's guide helps the teacher to find and use experiments that the students may perform in advance of studying the generalization or principle in the textbook. This approach to study of phenomena and problems in chemistry leads students to see that the subject is really an experimental science and to become intrigued with their experiences in scientific investigation.

The textbook *Chemistry—An Experimental Science* (W. H. Freeman, San Francisco and London, 1963), makes the students aware of the impor-tance of the experimental approach, particularly in the first six chapters. These and subsequent chapters help the learners to develop concepts or principles based on laboratory experiences. Some films have been pro-duced to show experiments too difficult or expensive to be performed in the classroom.

Thus the teacher in new chemistry spends a large percentage of time directing learning in laboratory situations. This includes directing the per-formance of experiments and study of the textbook. There is evidence to

2 The writers are aware that courses in science and other subjects called "new" are only relatively new, but we use the word to differentiate the course or subject from the conven-tional course or subject.

warrant belief that time thus spent results in stimulating students of low as well as of high ability. This evidence is similar to what has been found about results from directing learning through discovery in other subjects.[3]

In all such use of directed discovering during study, and during the assignment and the culminating period, learning is effective when there is provision for the two essentials in a learning situation: intrinsic interest and meaning. The value of these two essentials for improvement of quality as well as quantity of learning is shown in previous chapters, particularly Chapters 2 and 4. Their value in retention and transfer of learning has been expressed by some educational psychologists.[4] The good results from the discovery method, however, depend on recognition that the discovery method does not of itself assure satisfactory learning. This method does not function automatically, and a teacher may bungle in using it, for example, by giving too much or too little direction or by giving it at the wrong time. This method, like any other produces effective learning as learners become so involved in the activity that they perceive the goal and contrive a way or ways of reaching it.

INDIVIDUALIZED INSTRUCTION

As the teacher directs the class in either group or individual activities, the different abilities, interests, and needs of the students may emerge and require individual attention. As already indicated, *there is a prominent place in directed study for distinct individual instruction, which may or may not be closely related to the group instruction.*

The necessity of emphasis on individualized, personalized instruction during the study period is shown by the nature and extent of individual differences among students of any grade level. Psychologists have revealed that in intelligence a range of about six years is likely to be found in any unselected class. Thus a teacher at one moment may be looking at an individual who seems to comprehend everything but, the next moment, at one who does not understand what is taking place. Furthermore, as can be seen by an analysis of the constituent elements of the intelligence test, intelligence as measured by that test differs in quality as well as quantity. That is, two students having the same intelligence score may be quite different in the nature of intelligence.

As we saw in Chapter 1, differences among students extend beyond intelligence to include physical development, emotional stability, social maturity, vocational interests, home background, and other variables. If an

3 See the section on teaching science in Chap. 8.
4 M. L. Bigge and M. P. Hunt, *Psychological Foundations of Education*, 2d ed., Harper and Row, New York, 1968, Chap. 18.

educator can be certain that all members of a group are alike in kind as well as degree of mental development, he or she still will need to realize that they may be distinctly unlike one another in physical, emotional, and social development. Much has been written about homogeneous grouping. Strictly speaking, there is no such thing as homogeneous grouping of complete individuals. Attainment of homogeneity in a group may be approached only when based on one particular characteristic of the individual, for example, age, vocational interest, reading skill, or IQ. Members of any class—studied as complete individuals—are found to be unlike one another in more than one respect. Moreover, it is well known that the intelligence of a person functions in relation to all other aspects of his being.

All the physiological, psychological, and sociological differences among students produce differences among them in scholastic achievement. It has been found that youngsters completing work in the elementary school have a range of performance of about six years in such subjects as reading and arithmetic. Some freshmen in high school read no better than an average fifth-grade child, while others in the same class read at the level of many high-school seniors. That the same approximate range of differences exists in other subjects may be assumed. If a battery of achievement tests is given to freshmen and seniors in high school, it will be found that an impressive percentage of the freshmen will make scores as high as several of the seniors.[5]

The variety and the extent of individual differences have strong implications for teaching, particularly in the study period. A flexible procedure may make it possible to adapt to the many individual needs in any class. Even in a "homogeneous" group, the efficient teacher studies and teaches the individuals. Furthermore, considerable experimentation on the value of ability grouping has not provided conclusive evidence that it has served to improve learning as measured by standardized achievement tests. Likewise, research has not shown that such grouping contributes much to improvement of social traits.

In a recent report of experimentation on the value of ability grouping, the conclusion is that evidence bearing on the academic achievement of superior groups has been conflicting, usually inconclusive, and that the "slow" groups achieve better in a heterogeneous group. One reason for this poorer achievement by the latter groups seems to be lack of peer stimulation and help. Also their teachers may not show them much understanding and interest. Only 3 percent of the teachers expressed preference for a slow-learning class. With a feeling of discouragement and low self-esteem, these groups fulfilled their teachers worst expectations.[6]

[5] G. J. Mouly, *Psychology for Effective Teaching*, 3rd ed., Holt, Rinehart, and Winston, New York, 1973, Chap. 18.
[6] M. M. Hall and W. G. Findley, "Ability Grouping: Helpful or Harmful?" *Phi Delta Kappan* (May, 1971), 52, pp. 556-557.

Ability grouping recognizes differences in traditional academic ability to the neglect of other differences. It ignores the fact that two students may be dissimilar in academic ability but similar in social and vocational interests. A school that aims to develop the whole individual in a social environment of shared common interests may find that it defeats its purpose through the use of homogeneous grouping. However, if the classroom has flexible instruction, the teacher may effectively use temporary grouping of students around special abilities and common needs and interests. Yet it will still be necessary to use the many opportunities in study to direct students in individual undertakings. Indeed, through individualized instruction both the student's academic achievement and classroom behavior are improved.[7]

Individualized Procedure in Reading

Individualized study has been well demonstrated in the teaching of reading. There is, of course, a place for some real group instruction in reading. When the individual as an active member of the group is required to read to meet an obligation to the group, there is likely to be a strong incentive to read. Frequently, too, a student's motive for reading arises from group discussion of books that have been read by classmates. Nevertheless, because of the wide differences of students in abilities, interests, and needs in reading, each one can benefit by extensive individualized instruction in that skill. Although individualized procedure has been found to be helpful, especially to the retarded reader, it is of value to the efficient reader also. It raises the reading levels of all kinds of young people. Furthermore, if much of the instruction in reading is individualized for all the students, any stigma attached to that kind of instruction for poor readers is thereby lessened.

The teacher who uses the study period to individualize instruction in reading needs a classroom library of books and periodicals suitable for readers of different interests and levels. In this library or the central library, the student may well browse to discover materials of interest. The teacher may use some or all of the weekly periods devoted to reading in individualized directed study. Both within the classroom and the library, a series of individual conferences may be held while the other students are reading books or periodicals. In some conferences the teacher may draw on an interest inventory, a nonreading intelligence test, a reading test, and other means of diagnosis. Usually the student reports on what has been

---

[7] E. G. Dauw, "Individual Instruction for Potential Dropouts," *National Association of Secondary School Principals Bulletin* (September, 1970), 54, pp. 9-21; A. C. Ornstein, "Suggestions for Improving Discipline and Teaching the Disadvantaged," *Journal of Secondary Education* (March, 1969), 44, pp. 99-106; and V. N. Lunetta and O. E. Dyrli, "Individualized Instruction in the Science Curriculum," *School Science and Mathematics* (February, 1971), 71, pp. 121-128.

read, while the teacher expresses interest, observes, questions, and makes appropriate suggestions for improvement.

This kind of directed study in reading enables the teacher to deal with the particular interests, problems, and skills of each individual. It removes the pressures, tensions, and thwartings of ordinary procedure. Each student is allowed to choose what to read and on a level without comparison to others. This enables all to taste success and to develop self-respect. The student receives individual help from the teacher in an informal and friendly manner, and sees that someone is concerned about his or her particular needs. The relationship and attitude toward the teacher are thus improved. All such factors improve the young person's attitudes and habits in reading. The result is that the student reads much more. In doing so, many new words are learned in context and the habit of extensive reading is developed. There may also be a gain in inclination and ability to select suitable materials and in such traits as initiative, independence, and comprehension in reading. These are results that are not obtained as well through traditional group instruction in reading.

Individualized reading in any courses may meet the needs of the learners for improvement in mental health as well as in the reading process. Such reading may contribute to self-understanding, self-esteem, a sense of security, and the like. As young people read literature, biography, and history, they may perceive that other people have motives, difficulties, and anxieties similar to their own and that some of these people live happy and useful lives.[8]

Particularly in literature, the student needs to read materials from which to gain the most in the quest for self-development: an ability to think reflectively, an increasing number of personal and social interests, and a humanistic spirit of goodwill. Any selection of literature that functions effectively toward such ends must be connected with the reader's interests, be significant, and enlarge and refine present social concepts. In view of these facts, certain classics may be better than modern productions for some students. Conversely, a contemporary production may be more valuable for some than a classic. It is essential to recognize that some students can share better, both mentally and emotionally, with others by reading detective stories than by reading Shakespeare's plays. Adolescents are most likely to develop shared common interests in literature not through being required to do intensive work on the same selections but by reading different selections on problems of life that are vital to all.

Such personalization of instruction is especially helpful to slow learners. Mueller and Frerichs reported a study of programs for slow learners in

[8] See the section on materials for reading in Chap. 10. See also R. E. Botts, "The Climate for Individualized Instruction in the Classroom," *Journal of Secondary Education* (November, 1969), 44, pp. 309-314.

some junior and senior high schools in Illinois. They noted that the most effective programs were "need oriented." Moreover, most teachers agree that the best way to "hook" the learners is to involve them in suitable activities within and without the classroom. In each subject focus should be "on contemporary concerns and interests of these students. A multi-sensory, audio-visual approach is standard procedure, and student reaction is quite positive. . . . Whenever possible, class activities should be action-type and open ended, leading to suspenseful, 'Hitchcock' situations where the students fill in the endings."[9] By this kind of instruction, slow learners, like fast learners, develop attitudes, concepts, and generalizations which are of value in their academic, personal-social, and vocational development. This is essentially the program of instruction demonstrated and supported for all types of students throughout this book.

To the teacher who does not have time to direct the individual in study, we suggest that time be secured by dispensing with some of the routine, mass instruction that frequently is practiced. Moreover, such a teacher is likely to find that often the youngster gains more from a few minutes of special help than from an hour of random or impersonal instruction. Teachers must guard against spending so much time teaching a poor way that they do not have time to teach an effective way.

IMPROVEMENT OF STUDY

The period of study is particularly suitable for development of students in effective study. That the teacher should make use of the many opportunities to improve students in study has been emphasized by the fact that many of them have not developed well in attitudes and habits of study while in elementary school.

In the use of the study period to promote efficiency in study, the teacher must aim beyond the immediate goal of helping the student to do a particular task or to "master" certain subject matter. Students must have direction in their work so that they develop abilities, attitudes, and habits of general and lasting application. In any learning situation the teacher ought to help each student to develop the inclination and the ability for self-help. Moreover, the teacher should realize that students who make average or above average grades may be forming bad habits of study. Through trial and error in inadequate and defective learning situations, they may mainly memorize subject matter. To assist them in developing procedures in study that are broadly functional, the teacher must help them to adopt worthwhile goals and to work toward those goals through comprehending, discovering, generalizing, and applying.

9 R. J. Mueller and A. H. Frerichs, "A Look at Programs for Slow Learners," *Illinois Education* (February, 1968), 56, p. 244. See also A. C. Ornstein, "On High School Violence: The Teacher-Student Role," *Journal of Secondary Education* (March, 1970), 45, pp. 99-105.

Specific Habits or Practices

In undertaking to teach the individual to study, educators have not agreed at every point on what constitutes effective habits of study. We may see this when we investigate manuals on how to study. There has been, however, a degree of consensus on some of the habits of study attributed to the good student. Examples of them are having an intrinsic objective, planning a reasonable time budget, making use of the table of contents and the index, improving vocabulary, reading critically, and using the dictionary. Some of them, stated in the form of simple rules, are (1) try to find a quiet place, (2) read to find answers to thought questions, (3) make a preliminary survey of any material before reading it, (4) take notes in your own words, and (5) have a notebook and keep it with you.

Lists of useful practices in study have some value for students. However, too often the lists consist of suggestions or rules without reference to the kind of education desired. Effective study procedures in a course that emphasizes investigation and reflective thinking must be different from those in a course that emphasizes telling and memorizing. Furthermore, a student with ineffective study habits is more likely to develop good ones under the direction of a helpful teacher in the study period than by trying to follow a list of printed directions. In fact, such a student is most likely to improve study habits while acquiring worthwhile motives, attitudes, traits, and abilities. Following specified practices in study avails little unless the student has the ability and desire to learn and the personal characteristics necessary for efficient study. This view was indicated in our analysis of underachievers in Chapter 1.

For effective study the student needs the following abilities: (1) to read with normal comprehension and speed, (2) to discover truth through simple research, (3) to report on reading and research (including some skill in logical organization of thoughts in oral and written form), and (4) to think somewhat critically or reflectively. For acquisition and application of those abilities, the student needs strong motivation and sound mental health as shown by such personal characteristics as emotional stability, willingness to work cooperatively, a sense of belonging and of responsibility, and respect for the views and the rights of others.

Probably the most essential ability for efficient study is reading. Often the teacher does not need to look beyond poor reading to discover the chief, if not the sole, cause of unsatisfactory study. Boys and girls themselves often designate inability to read well as one of the principal reasons for their ineffective habits of study. Research has shown that even gifted children may be deficient in reading and that they have improved in both speed and comprehension after spending a few weeks in a remedial reading class. Some high schools have been systematically establishing remedial reading classes in which capable teachers provide students with suitable reading materials in individual and small group instruction. The result has been that nearly all of them showed marked progress in reading, which was followed by noticeable improvement in studying.

Some high schools have reading centers to which students are assigned one or more periods a week throughout a semester or year. Others have a course that is considered as half the work in English for the semester. Still others have instruction scheduled in periods the students would normally spend in the study hall, thereby taking no time from an English class. In all these plans English teachers who are specialists in teaching reading provide the instruction. However, there are high schools in which instruction in "developmental" reading is provided for specific purposes within different content areas. Research reveals that guidance in reading in such subjects as the social studies and science results in improvement of mastery in both subject matter and reading skills. In those two and other subjects, there is a growing supply of paperbacks and periodicals which are read by students of different abilities, interests, and needs. Moreover, some teachers are spending time toward development of purposes for reading. The result is reading with intrinsic motivation and meaning.[10]

Another necessary ability for the student's effectiveness in study is that of discovering truth through simple research. By research is meant the use of investigation or experimentation to discover truth which is new to the discoverer, even though it may be well known by many others. Study through research in school involves the learners in looking for answers to questions rather than merely in memorizing answers already given by the teacher or the textbook. This suggests that during study in any subject the classroom may well become a workshop or laboratory in which students work as individuals and small groups to search for ways to reach their goals. It indicates further that the knowledge sought may be found not only in the textbook or the teacher's lecture but also in the library, the laboratory, and the community.

The development of students in research skills during study depends partly on how well they were helped in the assignment period to acquire some understanding and acceptance of the objectives of the investigation and to possess some interest and ability toward finding ways to reach the objectives. In the study period the teacher must continue to provide an environment conducive to research. The teacher must be known to the class as an experimenter and investigator having strong aversion to prejudice and propaganda but a desire to use the scientific method to discover truth. In assisting students in their investigations, the teacher usually

---

[10] National Society for the Study of Education, *Innovation and Change in Reading Instruction*, Sixty-seventh Yearbook, Part II, University of Chicago, Chicago, 1968, Chaps. 4, 11; R. A. Bennett, "Building a Total Reading Program," *Journal of Secondary Education* (November, 1967), 42, pp. 321-327.

refrains from telling them but attempts to place them in situations that lead them to discovery. Furthermore, since, in most of their school experiences students have learned too often merely by memorizing the thoughts of others, the teacher must use strong means consistently to develop in students the desire as well as the skills to learn through research.

The first two requirements for effective study suggest the third one, the ability to report on reading and research. Extensive reading and simple research contribute to study even more when done in conjunction with the reports on the results of the inquiry. A report may include evaluations, generalizations, and applications of what is learned. Throughout the written work, the teacher provides individual guidance in clear expression, helping students to organize their new knowledge logically on paper—a skill which the teacher knows will serve students well in future experiences. Unfortunately, those experiences are withheld from students who are taught just from the textbook, who are given assignments only in terms of the next few pages, who are required only to memorize during study, and who encounter only short answer questions in subsequent "discussion" and examination. Those students, on the other hand, who read extensively and investigate and discover usually acquire worthwhile knowledge which they can be helped to report with considerable interest and skill.

The three abilities needed for efficiency in study contribute to and rest on the fourth ability, thinking critically or reflectively. We saw in Chapter 3 that this ability consists of both attitudes and habits. Like other attitudes and habits, thinking is best developed in early childhood. Unfortunately, many children in elementary school often do work satisfactory to the teacher without having to think. The same is frequently true of many in high school. These facts indicate that the teacher in high school who seeks earnestly to improve thinking has to change many student attitudes and habits set against thinking. In the use of study to promote thinking, the teacher must devise strong means to stimulate and assist students to plan and carry out plans. It is necessary to place them in situations requiring and challenging them to think. If they have many vital experiences in thinking, they develop significantly in the desire and ability to think.

As the teacher endeavors to promote thinking during study, all the steps in a complete act of thought may be dealt with while focusing on one or two. If the assignment provided well for recognition and definition of the problem and for setting up suggestions or hypotheses for its solution, directed study may concentrate on gathering data in the process of testing the hypotheses. The teacher assists the students to discover facts bearing on the acceptance or the rejection of the suggested ways of solving the problem. This may include a well-planned and executed field trip and diligent investigation in the library and the laboratory. By precept and example, the teacher may help students to suspend judgment and search for pertinent and reliable information before they reach conclusions. Thus they may be directed toward formation of scientific habits of thinking.

Basic Importance of Motivation and Mental Health

The development and use of all four of the abilities necessary for efficiency in study depend largely on the student's motivation. Unless the learner has an intrinsic desire to read, investigate, report findings, and think through problems, it is unlikely that effective functioning and development will take root. The individual with only ordinary mental abilities but with a compelling interest in learning will make satisfactory progress in study. It is well known that the correlation between the scores of students on an intelligence test and their marks in school subjects is not high. That motivation may be considered as the key to effective habits of study has been shown by experiments on what produces these habits. The conclusion from investigations is that if the teacher wishes to improve the student's work, coaching in the techniques of study is less important than assistance in acquiring strong motives for diligent study. Research confirms further what many teachers have observed, that there is a close relationship between the subjects students like best and those in which they make the highest grades. Past and present success of students is also significantly related to their goal seeking.

A related basic factor affecting the student's abilities in study is mental health. It has been found that the anxious, disturbed, and unhappy individual spends much time in introspection and in looking at objects in the classroom. Such a person is also inclined to take a negative attitude toward the ideas and suggestions of classmates and the teacher and to be rigid and noncreative in thought processes, being too inattentive, set, or antagonistic to study well. These traits have been found frequently in retarded readers. Leading writers on teaching the retarded reader have emphasized that improvement of mental health improves ability to read. They have found that neurotic aspects of personality tend to be negatively correlated with reading performance.[11]

In turn, progress in reading contributes favorably to mental health. There was an investigation of the effect of learning to read on delinquent boys who were retarded in reading by two years. They were provided with individualized instruction, attainable goals, and suitable materials. They improved perceptibly in reading, and their attitudes toward schoolwork and those in authority were significantly elevated.[12]

[11] C. M. Neal, "The Relationship of Personality Variables to Reading Ability," *California Journal of Educational Research* (May, 1967), 18, pp. 133-144.
[12] W. P. Dorney, "The Effectiveness of Reading Instruction in the Modification of Attitudes of Adolescent Delinquent Boys," *Journal of Educational Research* (July-August, 1967), 60, pp. 438-443.

Further analysis of the reasons poor mental health hinders some in study reveals that the neurotic, maladjusted person is typically unhappy, rigid in behavior, and fearful of undertaking something new. The individual with such characteristics is likely to have an emotional block which inhibits diligent, concentrated application in study. Nearly all boys or girls who are unable to do adequate schoolwork have emotional difficulties caused by frustrations and conflicts. They are so bombarded by personal problems that they are unable to concentrate on schoolwork. In turn, continuous failure in school has a deteriorating effect on their self-esteem and sense of security. It makes them feel even more inferior than they otherwise would and adds to the complexity of their problems. This suggests that the teacher should carefully investigate the mental health of the unsuccessful student to discover how it may be affecting attitudes and study habits.[13]

Effect of the Entire Educational Program on Study

Teaching an individual to study should not be a separate or isolated activity but an integral part of the educational program. Reaction to the whole educational environment determines whether or not a student studies well. A teacher who usually dictates assignments and asks questions about isolated facts in subsequent "discussion" and examination may contribute more to bad habits of study than to good ones. Students in such a learning situation are unlikely to profit much from rules on how to study—for example, read critically, organize material, read under headings and topics, and seek and acquire a motive. Unless they have adequate varied experiences in cooperative activity and problem solving in classroom procedure, they do not receive all necessary help toward forming good habits of study. Every teacher, consciously or not, directs students in study while directing them in learning during the assignment, the study period, the culminating period, the examination, the personal conference, and so on. This conclusion is based on experimentation. With reference to the examination in particular, research shows that students tend to study either through memorization of specific details or through organization of thoughts, according to whether the examination requires the former or the latter type of study.[14]

The subject matter and teaching procedure must be such that learners develop satisfactorily in the acquisition of worthwhile objectives and effective means of reaching the objectives. The learning situations thus provided direct the students to read purposefully and understandingly, to investigate and discover, to report in oral and written form on the findings, and to engage in reflective or critical thinking. Obviously, such experiences in

---

[13] M. F. Shore and J. L. Massimo, "The Alienated Adolescent: A Challenge to the Mental Health Professional," *Adolescence* (Spring, 1969), 4, pp. 19-34.
[14] See Chap. 15.

study may exist to a small extent or not at all in study involving filling out blanks in workbooks or in memorizing facts in page to page assignments in one textbook.

The point of importance here is that improvement of habits of study depends on improvement of the whole learner in the total environment. This means that a student's academic achievement is a result not only of intellectual development in school, but of intellectual, emotional, and social development in school, home, and community. Realizing how the out-of-school environments of some boys and girls hinder more than help them in school, an understanding, sympathetic teacher works toward having a compensating classroom environment. Specifically, the teacher endeavors to be an example of the democratic person in instruction and management of the class and to make the class a democratic group. The teacher also brings into the classroom a variety of learning materials, including those many youngsters have lacked in the home and community. A classroom of suitable vital experiences for youngsters develops in them wholesome interests and attitudes and basic understandings, and thereby directs them toward effective study. The results are their advancement in both desirable traits and academic attainments.

The conclusion we reach is that effective study may be promoted by extending and improving study. Much of the time of the traditional recitation, used largely in "hearing" lessons and telling learners, could well be diverted to directed study to assist the learners to find out how to reach their objectives. Extensive use of the laboratory or shop in such subjects as the new chemistry, home economics, and industrial arts has clear implications for teaching in other curriculum areas, for example, English composition.

There seems to be increasing use of part or all of the class hour to assist each individual to study. Unfortunately, some teachers in the study period may be observed merely supervising study as they grade papers or engage in other work. Rarely should the teacher be seated at the desk alone during the period of study. Occasionally a student is in need of an immediate conference. Often, the teacher can walk about the room, talking with one individual after another or holding a conference with a small group in the rear of the room. In any case, the teacher would not be teaching the same thing the same way to the class but would be directing the learning of different kinds of individuals as members of a group.

Such a teacher-student relationship is an essential phase of efficient teaching. Through it each individual receives help where and when it is needed. Those who do not need assistance at a certain point are not required to waste time listening to the teacher. Often, too, a brief conference with the individual is more valuable than a long lecture addressed to the whole class. The conferences can be expected to produce understanding, goodwill, and a spirit of sharing between the teacher and the several individuals in the class. The important point for the teacher to watch during study, therefore, is never just to sit and supervise but to be continuously alert in discovering and supplying the individual's real needs. In this period every teacher is obligated to seize all possible opportunities to engage in personal work and guidance. The expert special counselor is necessary in a large school, but even there, a counselor can never take the place of the classroom teacher. Through personal conferences and group instruction in worthwhile activities, the teacher may assist the learner to understand the work and to develop the necessary motivation, mental health, and abilities, for independent, reflective study.[15]

QUESTIONS AND ACTIVITIES

1. In small groups discuss how the study period is dependent on a good assignment.
2. Interview some high-school students for suggestions for making the traditionally supervised study hall a time for more meaningful learning. How would their ideas be implemented? Would they affect how a teacher teaches?
3. Why is improving student study habits one of the primary functions of the school? In answering this question, refer to your objectives of education.
4. In an actual teaching situation, show how guidance and counseling may be made an essential part of directed study.
5. Explain the possible use of the study period to deal with one or more of Dewey's steps in an act of thought.
6. Divide the class into small groups of similar subject matter areas. Now discuss the following as it applies to your teaching field: consider how the teacher of English, or another subject (yours) may provide time for directed study by reducing time spent in useless or inefficient instruction.
7. In modern education there is an emphasis on learning through individual and group activities in which there is discovering, performing, and constructing. Point out how the directed study period is especially suitable for the promotion of such learning.

[15] See the section on independent study in Chap. 12. See also J. P. Casey, "Independent Study—A Plan for All Pupils," Clearing House (November, 1971), 46, pp. 173-177.

8. Either in a short written paper or in a small discussion group, recount
your personal experiences with learning in high school. Specifically,
what conditions were present that assisted you in accomplishing more
meaningful learning as opposed to just learning?

SELECTED REFERENCES

Blount, N. S., and H. J. Klausmeier, *Teaching in the Secondary School,* 3rd
ed., Harper and Row, New York, 1968, Chap. 8.

Brembeck, C. S., *Social Foundations of Education: Environmental Influences
in Teaching and Learning,* 2nd ed., John Wiley, New York, 1971, Chap.
4.

Carter, H. L., and D. J. McGinnis, *Diagnosis and Treatment of the Disabled
Reader,* Macmillan, New York, 1970.

Dawson, H., *On the Outskirts of Hope, Educating Youth from Poverty
Areas,* McGraw-Hill, New York, 1968.

Duker, S., *Individualized Reading,* Charles C Thomas, Springfield, Illinois,
1971, Chaps. 5, 11, 13.

Hallahan, Daniel P., and W. M. Cruickshank, *Psychoeducational Foundations of Learning Disabilities,* Prentice-Hall, Englewood Cliffs, N.J., 1973.

Hardy, L. L., *How to Study in High School,* 3rd ed., paper, Pacific, Palo
Alto, California, 1970.

Harris, L. A., and C. B. Smith, *Reading Instruction Through Diagnostic
Teaching,* Holt, Rinehart and Winston, New York, 1972, Part V.

Henderson, G., and R. F. Bibens, *Teachers Should Care: Social Perspectives
of Teaching,* Harper and Row, New York, 1970.

Herber, H. L., ed., *Developing Study Skills in Secondary Schools,* International Reading Association, Newark, Delaware, 1965.

Massialas, B. G., and J. Zevin, *Creative Encounters in the Classroom:
Teaching and Learning through Discovery,* John Wiley, New York, 1967,
Chap. 3.

Mouly, George J., *Psychology for Effective Teaching,* 3rd ed., Holt, Rinehart and Winston, New York, 1973, Chap. 18.

National Society for the Study of Education, *The Educationally Retarded
and Disadvantaged,* Sixty-sixth Yearbook, Part I, University of Chicago
Press, Chicago, 1967, Chaps. 2-6.

Newman, H. E., *Reading Disabilities: Selections on Identification and
Treatment,* Odyssey, New York, 1969.

Strom, R. D., *Psychology for the Classroom,* Prentice-Hall, Englewood Cliffs,
New Jersey, 1969, Chap. 1.

Sund, R. B., and L. W. Trowbridge, *Teaching Science by Inquiry in the Secondary School,* Charles E. Merrill, Columbus, Ohio, 1967, Chaps. 6-7.

Thomas, E. L., and H. A. Robinson, *Improving Reading in Every Class: A Sourcebook for Teachers,* Allyn and Bacon, Boston, 1972.

Wilson, J. A. R., and others, *Psychological Foundations of Learning and Teaching,* McGraw-Hill, New York, 1969, Chaps. 18-20.

CHAPTER 6

Work on a learning activity—begun in the teacher-student assignment and advanced in the study period—culminates in the third major step of the teaching cycle. The traditional recitation, which is still common in practice, provides for students to recite only what the textbook and the teacher cited. It emphasizes testing and drilling on parts of subject matter that were assigned with little or no active participation by the students. In contrast, the third step or period in the teaching process concentrates on continuation of a learning process of inquiring, discovering, organizing, and thinking. It focuses on the pooling of findings from library and laboratory, leading to conclusions, generalizations, and evaluations.

ESSENTIAL CHARACTERISTICS

In the concluding activities of an effective teaching cycle, students continue to engage in a variety of learning activities. They may make reports based on extended, purposeful reading; have panel discussions; consider their learnings from pictures, field trips, and experiments; generalize from a wide range of facts; and evaluate their experiences in all the various activities. They experience much more than responding to numerous factual questions and listening to the repetition and supplementation of the answers by the teacher. This is because the teacher continues to direct their learning toward the needs of each student and our democratic objectives of education. Of course the teacher can incidentally check on how well they are progressing in worthwhile learning. Yet the chief goal is not hearing lessons to discover how well the learners memorized the elements of the assignment.

THE CULMINATING PERIOD

Concentration on Thinking and Facts

In the third step or period the teacher's primary aim is to continue to improve thinking in young people. Of course, this requires giving attention to teaching facts, but only relevant, useful facts. Moreover, the teacher endeavors to teach the facts through and for thinking. This is because students, even those who ordinarily earn A's, may memorize facts but be unable or unwilling to do much thinking. On the other hand, as a person's thinking develops the acquisition of useful information follows. Hence improving the art of thinking is more inclusive and fundamental than the acquisition of facts. This suggests that the teacher should include informal and formal reports on activities and readings, free exchange of ideas between teacher and student and between student and student, thought-provoking questions raised by students as well as by the teacher, expressions of generalizations made under the guidance of the teacher, and students' and teacher's evaluation of the work. In this kind of learning situation the student is called to task by classmates as well as teacher if the necessary facts are lacking to support the given position. Thus in activities involving thinking the class is led to acquire significant information. Far from neglecting to teach facts, the democratic, humanistic teacher does well in teaching them. Students who receive guidance in thinking in turn acquire the information necessary for thinking.

Adequate provision for development of thinking during the third teaching period often involves helping students to reconsider the first steps in the solution of a problem that was begun in the assignment and continued through the study period. After study has furnished the class with pertinent information, its members may be prepared to draw valid conclusions and to support generalizations. Thus the final period is the time when there may be retracing of all the steps in the work on a problem. However, the emphasis is usually on consideration of conclusions, generalizations, and evaluations, with only incidental reference to preceding steps in the complete act of thought.

It may be necessary to stress that students should form their conclusions, generalizations, and evaluations on the basis of an adequate variety of investigative, reflective experiences. They profit little from merely memorizing those items from the textbook or the teacher's lectures.

Concern for both thinking and facts may be shown in teaching social studies. The teacher who concentrates on thinking in the social studies has been accused of neglecting to teach facts. The truth is that the old type of teacher is the one who teaches facts poorly—almost entirely from the textbook and usually apart from problem solving and thinking. The scientifically minded teacher insists that students suspend judgment and search for all the facts before they draw conclusions. This teacher challenges students to support their conclusion or generalization with facts and thus encourages them to challenge one another. In doing this the teacher requires them to discover facts on all sides of an issue, not just on the side that may be given by the ordinary textbook. The facts are learned thoughtfully as they reveal to the learner the validity of a hypothesis or generalization. Thus a teacher may improve the teaching of facts by focusing on improvement of teaching generalizations. Facts thus learned are understandable and functional and are likely to be retained and used by the learner in the future as he faces propaganda in business and politics.

How facts can be learned with understanding in the process of constructing and supporting generalizations can be observed easily in the teaching of United States history through problem solving and thinking. For example, a question may be asked about what caused the Revolutionary War. One or more students may state only one cause, expressing it with the jingle, "taxation without representation," which they read in the textbook. Some teachers would accept this statement as an adequate expression of what caused the war. Others, however, would use a series of probing questions, leading students to examine and discuss the meaning of the expressed cause and to suggest other possible causes. The teacher could well ask the class to consider the opposition of the colonists to the increase of taxes in relation to a similar reaction of many people today to the raising of taxes. Or questions could be posed about possible hidden causes of the war, which are similar to hidden causes of actions by current leaders in our government. The teacher patiently and respectfully listens to the students' expressions and refrains from answering questions. Then the teacher directs them toward finding facts in the library for use in construction of sound generalizations about causes of the war.

Another example is in study of the current controversial problem of school busing of the majority or minority group. A class engaged in work on personal and societal problems would have a strong interest in defining the problem and in stating hypotheses or possible solutions of it. Expressions for and against that type of busing are freely given by students. The teacher and some of the students question the soundness of some of the statements, but the teacher refrains from making positive statements of personal views. Then the class may be ready to go to the library and elsewhere in search of data for support of their generalizations. When the students return to the classroom to continue consideration of the problem, some of them will be prepared either to defend or to restate their former generalizations about school busing. Some may have concluded that there must be no busing of either the minority or the majority group; others, that busing is necessary to improve the social condition of the minority group and thereby its educational achievement. In the accompanying discussion there is no direct pressure on any student to take a particular position and no ridicule of anyone's position. The procedure is democratic, providing each individual with the opportunity to express thoughts with freedom and responsibility.[1]

Obviously, this kind of instruction requires a library containing an adequate supply of reading materials, suitable for different students in each subject of the curriculum. Some high schools have this kind of library. An example is the Fairview High School, Boulder, Colorado, where the library was planned first and then the rest of the building was added. There is a large variety of media in the library, and students, as individuals and in small groups, go there to engage in research and learn by discovery.[2]

Students need to learn through such a procedure in every step or period of teaching. It is true that they may be unable to state generalizations in the polished form of the textbook or the teacher, but the important point is that the generalizations are their own. Only as students participate in the construction of generalizations will the ability and willingness to apply them intelligently be available in facing future problematic situations. This teaching procedure is necessary in any subject.

As students express and support generalizations, they may well evaluate what they have been doing during all their work on an activity, unit, or problem. The nature of their evaluation will depend largely on how well they shared with the teacher during the assignment in setting up goals and devising ways of reaching the goals and during study in working consciously and earnestly toward their objectives. Consider the reaction of a class to the teacher's request that they evaluate their success in studying a dictated chapter or page-to-page assignment. In all likelihood, their comments would be few and discouraging. In contrast, if they have participated actively in planning and carrying out plans in an undertaking, they are apt to have some desire and ability to evaluate the results reflectively. As learners engage in purposeful and useful activities, they acquire the necessary inclination and basis for evaluating those activities. A person does not evaluate anything well without an interest and a standard for the evaluation.

The process of evaluation may advance students in comprehension and interest. They may be helped by considering how intelligently they acted at each point in the undertaking being completed. They also may be assisted in choosing both ends and means involved in future similar

---

[1] M. P. Hunt and L. E. Metcalf, *Teaching High School Social Studies*, 2nd ed., Harper and Row, New York, 1968, Chap. 5.

[2] E. Fenton, "Inquiry Techniques in the New Social Studies," *High School Journal* (October, 1971), 55, pp. 28-40; O. McBride, "The Library Media Center of Today," *Educational Leadership* (November, 1970), 28, pp. 151-154. See also the section on the instructional materials center in Chap. 12.

work. Thus they may develop in working with purpose and meaning and gain in the attitudes and habits necessary for them as efficient and democratic people.

In assisting students in evaluating their work, the teacher must provide direction in each step of the teaching cycle. Evaluation is essential at various points in any activity thoughtfully performed. The plans and procedures of the teacher and the class during the assignment and the study period must be subjected to frequent evaluation before the end of a learning experience, resulting sometimes in changes being made. Evaluation at the end is merely a major, climactic act in the whole learning activity.[3]

Social Function

Another major function of the concluding period is development of students in shared interests, a sense of belonging, and a "we" spirit. The purpose of this social development is promotion of attitudes, values, and habits conducive to improvement of both democratic living and academic achievement. We saw in reports of studies in Chapters 1 and 5 that academic achievement in particular is affected by the learner's social situation and condition, showing that underachievers and overachievers are markedly different in social environment, status, and growth.

In view of research, educational sociologists and psychologists emphasize the importance of the social environment of the classroom. The teacher, some say, largely determines the condition of the classroom climate. What is needed is a warm heart and a cool head and a real, demonstrable interest in every student, which means talking with each one at appropriate times to provide personalized instruction. One of the teacher's major responsibilities, however, is the promotion of class unity directed toward worthwhile educational goals. Group support must be gained from the students for the educational objectives of the course. Unless the teacher is a strong leader of the class, one or more students will assume his or her role. However, we must recognize that in a class marked by common interests and cooperative activities, every student can and should at times be a leader, for example, when the best student in drawing leads in a class activity requiring that special skill.[4]

The chief action of the teacher toward developing group cohesiveness is helping students to acquire and pursue common objectives. Teachers do this by questioning students about personal and societal problems, by directing discussion of individual and group reports of projects, and by help-

---

[3] For further discussion of the importance and the means of instruction toward understanding and reflection levels of learning, see M. L. Bigge and M. P. Hunt, *Psychological Foundations of Education*, 2nd ed., Harper and Row, New York, 1968, Chaps. 21-22.

[4] M. B. Miles and W. W. Charters, Jr., *Learning in Social Settings: New Readings in the Social Psychology of Education*, Allyn and Bacon, Boston, 1970, pp. 122-133, 706-709.

ing students to evaluate learning activities and use these evaluations to perceive the next activities they need to confront. Furthermore, every student must be helped to participate as successfully as possible and then receive due recognition for achievements. Investigations indicate that students change in self-esteem and in interests, attitudes, and actions according to whether they feel accepted and liked by teacher and peers. Also the student tends to make those changes when perceiving that most of those in the group favor the changes.[5]

The conclusion is that group spirit and behavior are produced more by challenging, common goals than novel techniques. Hence the subject matter as well as the classroom procedure should be social, drawn frequently from life in the modern world. When young people confront subject matter which leads them to see vital goals and rational ways of reaching the goals, they tend to participate freely, actively, and reflectively. They have reason to exchange ideas and to think together in the give-and-take of asking and answering questions. This is especially true if they are required to learn through the process of discovering.

Goal-directed influence in the classroom should include concerns for both academic learning and the development of autonomous, self-starting students. Furthermore, we believe that focus on the task and social-emotional functions that were presented previously would be helpful for realizing goal-directed influence. If the teacher's leadership is shared so that many class members are performing both task and social-emotional functions, then goal-directed leadership, as we are thinking of it, will more likely be realized. It seems especially important that leadership in the classroom be dispersed so as to achieve a positive social climate. Our research has shown that classroom groups with diffuse power structures—in which most students have some degree of power over some other student—have more students with high self-esteem who are utilizing their intelligence. Classrooms in which only a few wield influence have more students who evaluate themselves negatively and who are not working up to their potential.[6]

As a class develops in social awareness, it may develop in scientific mindedness. Each of these two types of development may affect the other, each being unlikely to be developed well apart from the other. By word and action of the teacher or a classmate, a student may be challenged to support a statement, to avoid prejudice and propaganda, to draw valid and tentative conclusions, and the like. Hence as teachers use group activity to improve social attitudes and habits, they may also use it to improve reflective attitudes and habits.[7]

[5] Ibid., pp. 151-167; B. C. Mathis and others, *Psychological Foundations of Education: Learning and Teaching,* Academic Press, New York, 1970, pp. 658-684; W. J. Campbell, ed., *Scholars in Context: The Effects of Environments on Learning,* John Wiley, New York, 1970, Chaps. 7-8.
[6] R. A. Schmuck and P. A. Schmuck, *Group Processes in the Classroom,* paper, William C. Brown, Dubuque, Iowa, 1971, p. 38.
[7] See the section on social studies in Chap. 7 and on science in Chap. 8.

Improvement of Interests

The preceding paragraphs indicate that when teachers succeed in advancing students' thinking and social attitudes and habits, they also succeed in advancing worthwhile student interests. Through engaging reflectively in group activities in attacks on both group and individual problems, students may enlarge and refine their interests. In turn, their growth in interests improves their application to group undertakings and to reflective thinking. As has been repeatedly emphasized, motivation, which includes various interests, is one of the keys to effective learning.

The culminating period functions well in the promotion of interests when it conforms to the modern psychology of learning. We have seen that the ideal learning situation involves a provision for recognizing worthwhile goals and gaining insights into ways of reaching the goals. As the learner is placed into such learning situations, quantity and quality of objectives, meanings, and interests are developed. The point needing emphasis again is that interests are not developed well in isolation or through a few tricks of the teacher but as students gain in purposing, planning, and carrying out plans. The concluding period, no less than the assignment and the study period, should include subject matter and teaching procedure characterized by usefulness and meaning.

Continuous development of interests is necessary not only for promotion of learning but also for transfer of learning. As Bayles emphasized, an essential factor in a sound theory of the transfer of learning is the desire of the person to use the learning.[8] Interest as well as ability is necessary in functional learning. The failure of many teachers to grasp this fact may be seen in their teaching of the elements of English composition apart from the individual's self-expression. That this practice is still common is evident from visiting a few classes in English and from investigation. In one investigation it was found that a distinct majority of teachers approve and teach diagraming. It is well known that the workbook is used extensively in many classes of English. Yet one study revealed that the correlation between the ability to fill in blanks in that book and the ability to express ideas in written composition is very low. Studies have also shown correlation as low as .23 between scores on knowledge of grammar and those on written composition. On the other hand, it has been found that when students are taught oral and written expression through engaging purposefully in those activities, they develop the desire and ability to express themselves in speaking and writing.[9]

---

8 E. E. Bayles, *Democratic Educational Theory*, Harper and Row, New York, 1960, pp. 56-61.
9 See the section on teaching English composition in Chap. 7.

SOME USEFUL PROCEDURES

How can a teacher use the culminating period to develop students in reflective thinking, in social attitudes and habits, and in worthwhile interests? A general answer is by providing a favorable social environment in which there is social cohesion and a democratic, scientific climate used to meet the real needs of different members of the class. Some specific procedures a teacher may effectively employ are:

1. Take various steps to have every student actively involved in the process of learning; this includes participation in the choice of specific objectives and of ways to reach the objectives.
2. Through both competition and cooperation among students, lead the student to impose upon himself or herself valuable learning goals.
3. Use reports and discussions of individual projects to benefit the student engaged in the project and to lead other students to desire work on similar projects.
4. By the use of questions, class discussions, audio-visual aids, and reading materials, help the student to perceive ideas in conflict in a belief or value.
5. Use thought questions freely to place students in puzzling situations, and refrain from answering the questions even at the end of the period.
6. As often as possible, provide for every student to experience some success and make it a point to give due recognition for work.
7. Help students to relate their learning in the classroom to their learning in other classrooms and in the home and community.
8. Direct each student in the development of new interests, for example, introduce reading materials in new areas of reading.
9. Make the evaluations, generalizations, and conclusions points of departure toward new learning activities.
10. If a student does not have sufficient reading skills for satisfactory learning in the course, take all the necessary steps to develop the skills.[10]

Reporting Experiences

A procedure especially suitable in the kind of culminating period described in the preceding sections is having the students report their experiences. This procedure is often student initiated. At the beginning of the period, one or more students may voluntarily give information about what they discovered during the study period in the library, laboratory, or community, or they may ask questions about what others found. Similarly, at

---

[10] See Bigge and Hunt, *Psychological Foundations,* Chap. 19; and M. R. Loree, *Psychology of Education,* 2nd ed., Ronald, New York, 1970, Chap. 7.

times when the teacher enters the classroom after the class has assembled, it is found that the students are exchanging information they obtained during the study period. On these occasions the teacher may at once join the group in their conversation, becoming another active participant. Of course, often the teacher is required to plan and call for individual and small group reports. Such reports stem from simple research or from work on a project. The information therein is significant to the reporter and the listeners, and enjoyment is felt on both sides.

This rather ideal learning situation has been well demonstrated in the weekly meetings of groups of student teachers. Members of such groups want to share their experiences because they possess a strong common interest in learning how to become good teachers. This is the primary purpose of each student in voluntarily reporting experiences and questioning others about theirs. Moreover, aside from these reasons for their reports, students enjoy the exchange of information about experiences that are new to them, as their instructors can easily observe.

Similarly, the value of student reports is easily observed in high school classes in the practical arts, for example, in industrial arts and home economics.[11] In these classes there is extensive provision for individual and small group projects. These projects are part of the everyday lives of all members of the class and accordingly are of vital interest to them. After completing the project, the student usually wants to show it to other members of the class, telling them about both its difficult and easy steps. The classmates listen attentively because they are engaged in similar projects and want tips on how best to proceed. Also, they usually ask questions and offer comments freely.

The usefulness of student reports has been demonstrated also in academic classes. In a social studies class, for example, the class may be studying the problem of environmental pollution or of drug abuse. In a preceding period the class analyzed the problem and set up hypotheses toward its solution. Then some went to the library and others to the laboratory or to the community to gather data bearing on establishment of the hypotheses. Each student was then ready, intellectually and emotionally, to report findings to the whole class and also to listen to the reports of others. In this learning situation, like others of its kind, all members of the class were interested in the information from the reports because it was useful in meeting their common needs. The result was vital, dynamic class discussion, initiated by the students as well as by the teacher.

Dynamic Class Discussions

After students have involved themselves in reporting their experiences, they and their classmates are inclined to participate freely in class discus-

11 See Chap. 9.

sion. Thus the discussion is often initiated by the students, as some of them ask questions or give comments about the reports while the teacher does little except provide guidance. At times the teacher, of course, is required to use thought-provoking questions about the reports to stimulate discussion. Whoever may start the discussion, it tends to be self-propelling.

This discussion is quite unlike that of the traditional recitation in which teachers often seem satisfied when only a few students answer. Typically, the teacher abruptly announces the topic for discussion and then begins to ask questions. The loquacious students raise their hands and respond, while most of the class remains silent, some appearing inattentive. Furthermore, if those who did not volunteer are questioned there may not be real class discussion but a series of brief one-sided dialogues between the teacher and one student after another. One student responds to a question that requires a short answer. In case the answer is satisfactory, the teacher usually repeats it to be certain it was heard by everyone and to teach through repetition. Only if the answer is unsatisfactory does the teacher sometimes pass on the question or the answer to another student for comment. Consequently, what occurs is little more than expressions of memorized statements from the textbook and of personal feelings, prejudices, and unquestioned beliefs.

In ideal class discussion students have intrinsic objectives toward which they work through reflection, inquiry, discovery, and creativity in the study period. These objectives tend to stimulate and direct the discussion. Yet alert, continuous direction from the teacher is necessary. In problem solving, students need help in recognizing, comprehending, and sticking to the problem; in suggesting and testing possible solutions; and in supporting valid conclusions and generalizations. They also need assistance in learning to suspend judgment, to be objective, to regard the rights of others, to rely on facts rather than prejudice and passion, and to contribute to group thinking. They may be helped to improve in all such respects through the teacher's thoughtful and skillful use of questions and suggestions and especially through "practicing what he preaches."[12]

In guiding discussion, the teacher has to guard against providing either too little or too much direction. Someone may raise a question or offer comments on a particular issue or event but soon wander from it. As the discussion rambles the participants may merely rearrange and express their prejudices without ever engaging in reflective thinking. (This is a laissez-faire type of class discussion, similar to an out of class bull session.) At the other extreme is teacher dominated discussion. In it the teacher may either have an unwarranted fear of free and extensive discussion or a strong desire to demonstrate superiority in knowledge or to gain acceptance of a particular point of view. Accordingly, the teacher may express positive

[12] R. K. Bent and A. Unruh, *Secondary School Curriculum*, D. C. Heath, Boston, 1969, Chaps. 16-17.

answers to students' questions soon after the discussion begins and may take an immediate stand against any one who dares to challenge one of those answers. Such autocratic restriction of class discussion reduces its effectiveness. That this type of discussion still exists in high school may be observed by visiting a few classes.

Guidance in discussion also requires special attention to different members of a class. The reticent individual may be in special need of encouragement and tactful treatment. In extreme cases an individual conference is likely to help. Often a suitable stimulating question asked of a reticent student at the beginning of the discussion will contribute to his or her becoming involved. Otherwise the student may become so far behind or lost after several minutes have elapsed that it is futile to question. On the other hand, some of the loquacious, ever eager participants may at times need to be challenged by either the teacher or a classmate to draw on a reliable source for support of some of their assertions. Those who express themselves on the basis of investigation and study of course are encouraged and helped to participate on that basis. In fact, they may be used effectively sometimes to supplement, clarify, support, or refute what others have stated.

This suggests that the teacher must be alert to improve each student in kind as well as extent of participation. As discussion is in progress the teacher considerately recognizes the efforts of each one and may use questions to assist the one who is trying but faltering. Yet the teacher is alert to sense lack of preparation in some, in the talkative as well as the noncommunicative, occasionally requesting such students to find and view in print an expression bearing on an idea under discussion. This may serve both to impress the idea on the learner and to show how it could have been learned during the study period by efficient study.

An especially useful form of discussion is panel discussion. In preparation, each member of the panel searches for reliable information, not only to satisfy a personal desire to obtain the truth but also to meet the obligation to inform classmates adequately and to support the positions taken if someone challenges. In directing the panel discussion, teachers have many opportunities to help students recognize discussion that is above the level of merely airing and strengthening prejudices. This is done by questioning students about how the discussion follows the principles of scientific procedure and how they may apply these principles in other forms of discussion both in and outside of the classroom.

Efficient use of all such procedures in class discussion depends much on the teacher's relationship with the class. The required relationship is democratic, consisting of regard for the uniqueness, worth, and welfare of each individual and shared interests and free play of intelligence in the give and take of exchanging ideas. There must be mutual respect. The teacher who has never had a class with him or has lost it does not have reason to expect success in the direction of class discussion. It should go without saying that establishing and maintaining a good relationship with the class is accomplished not through force and fear but through desirable personal qualities and intelligent, democratic procedures such as we have outlined. Research indicates that learning in this type of class is very satisfactory.[13]

Construction and Use of Standards

The promotion of free and reflective class discussion requires that the class share with the teacher the formulation of standards of procedure for such discussion. In doing this the students may need more than one class period—plenty of time to raise questions, offer suggestions, and reach conclusions about how to have a good discussion. An evaluation of proper procedure in discussion may be made a valuable educational experience in itself. Furthermore, unless students participate in the selection and adoption of guides to class discussion, some of them may not be able or willing to follow the guides.

The standards or rules of procedure should be viewed as being flexible and alterable. In following the shifting requirements of classroom procedure, the teacher and the class may make exceptions in administering the rules and even change some of them. Among the rules that they may adopt are the following:

1. Members of the class must speak one at a time. Even when the interest is very high or an individual's position is attacked, all must wait their turn.
2. Before the student speaks, recognition from the teacher should be sought by raising a hand.
3. As soon as a student thus gains recognition, the hands of all others should go down and not be raised again until the first student has had ample opportunity for self-expression, or until the teacher indicates a desire for an expression from another person. An individual addressing a group deserves the undivided attention of all the other members, not their discourteous arm waving.
4. When several students indicate a desire to speak, the teacher usually recognizes the one who has not yet spoken or has participated the least. An exception may be made in case a student desires to answer a challenge.
5. The teacher is expected to distribute questions as much as possible, being certain to question the reticent students as well as those who volunteer to speak. In fact a discussion should often begin by suitably questioning one or more who are disinclined to express their views.

[13] Miles and Charters, *Learning in Social Settings*, p. 708.

6. To restrain a few students from monopolizing discussion, the group may set a time limit on the length of comments and on the number of times an individual is permitted to speak.
7. The teacher and each student must refrain from discrediting or disparaging remarks toward other members of the group. Specifically, there must be no reference to another person as being ignorant, stupid, or incapable.
8. Each member of the group should always consider whether thinking is reflective or is merely an expression and strengthening of personal prejudices.
9. In evaluating the discussion, each student should consider personal development in scientific and democratic attitudes and habits. In particular, each individual may fittingly ask whether he or she made a worthwhile contribution to the group, respected the views of others, and endeavored to present only reliable facts and to draw only valid conclusions.[14]

The teacher may improve the conduct of class discussion further by considering such questions as the following:

1. Did I talk too much by hastening to answer students' questions and to comment on their answers?
2. Did I succeed in getting such extensive student participation that my tendency to monopolize class discussion was checked?
3. Did I promote a democratic climate, dealing sympathetically and understandingly with the interests and needs of different individuals?
4. Did I so initiate and direct discussion that the class developed in desire and ability to search for truth?

The Teacher's Use of Questions

To have vital and deliberative discussion, the teacher must make adequate use of suitable questions. It is well known that the prevailing type of question in the high-school classroom is the factual, short answer type whose chief purpose is to drill or test for facts. What should also be recognized here is that many teachers rely too much on themselves for answering questions, stating facts, and expressing opinions, thereby neglecting the questioning of students. The teacher's positive, declarative statements often stifle discussion, but his questions may stimulate and direct it. Through patient, skillful questioning, the teacher may direct students in productive discussion, leading them to recognize, define, and attack problems.

14 See M. P. Hunt and L. E. Metcalf, *Teaching High School Social Studies,* 2d ed., Harper and Row, New York, 1968, pp. 210-211.

For the discussion period, a list of rules for asking questions is of little help. We need to recognize the obvious fact that even a four-year-old child can ask the mother more challenging, thoughtful questions than she can answer. If students share with the teacher in thinking during discussion, they as well as the teacher are busy asking and answering stimulating questions. After all, the particular form of the question or the way it is asked should be determined by the progress of the discussion and by the kind of learning it promotes. A skillful teacher, earnestly engaged in directing learning through thinking, will find appropriate ways of using questions.

To provide such learning a question and a request that the teacher should use freely are "How do you know?" and "Give an illustration." In asking students to explain why they make certain statements and to illustrate what they state, the teacher may be surprised at how frequently their learning consists of no more than just the memorization of words. When a student expresses reasons for holding a particular position and gives an example of what he or she has in mind, ideas are clarified and activated and it is evident how well learning through comprehension and application is taking place.

The "How do you know?" question may be used freely in any curriculum area. In mathematics, for example, a student might well be asked: "How do you know that a minus sign before a fraction should govern all the terms in the numerator of a fraction?" The answer might involve first explaining how the minus sign before a parenthesis affects all the terms within the parenthesis and then applying this answer to the numerator of a fraction. Similarly, in the social studies a teacher may ask the factual question, "Who was President of the United States during World War I?" Then the answer "Woodrow Wilson," may be followed with the question, "How do you know he was?" This would require the student to reach into his fund of information and to make such statements as, "Wilson was elected in 1912 and the war was started in 1914. He was criticized by Theodore Roosevelt for not declaring war on Germany after the sinking of the Lusitania, and Wilson headed the peace delegation at the end of the war."

This suggests that a student's answer may be used as a basis for questioning one or more additional students. Often, if the answer is correct teachers approve it, repeating it and sometimes adding a few statements. Only when the answer is unsatisfactory does the teacher sometimes question the student further or pass the answer to a classmate for acceptance or rejection and supplementary remarks. Thus what is called "class discussion" often consists of a series of brief exchanges between the teacher and one student after another. Instead, some teachers frequently withhold their remarks about the student's answer until they have secured expressions about it from one or more of the other students. They may do this often even when the original answer is acceptable. This procedure is beneficial for keeping all alert, for giving several of them opportunities for expression, and for encouraging and directing real class discussion and thinking.[15]

The quality of the questions may further encourage free discussion and thinking. Some teachers still concentrate on questions that require just memorization of bits of information from the textbook, neglecting investigation, discovery, and evaluation. A class receiving such questions is unlikely to be very attentive and thoughtful in discussion. Other teachers emphasize thought questions organized as often as possible around the student's experiences and the problematic situations confronting them in modern society. These questions usually lead from the concrete to the abstract. Further, they call for answers expressing relationship, criticisms, generalizations, and applications. As teachers ask such questions they may expect to have extensive and continuing attention and reflective thinking in discussion.

Some examples of those questions are:

1. Why have we had some demonstrations by youths in recent years?
2. What may be done to decrease the number of marriages of young people in high school?
3. How can we read literature to receive help in solving our personal problems?
4. How does *Uncle Tom's Cabin* throw light on race relations before the war between the States and at the present in our country?
5. Compare the Supreme Court's decision in favor of desegregation of public schools with its former decision of "separate but equal" public schools.
6. Point out any similarities or dissimilarities you see between the Vietnam War and the Korean War.
7. How does the function of wings of an airplane demonstrate the working of a law in science?
8. Explain how multiplication of a fraction by a fraction gives a product smaller than either of the two fractions.
9. Explain why a common denominator but not a common numerator is required in addition or subtraction of fractions.
10. Give and support your generalization or generalizations from your study of the research on possible causal relationship between cigarette smoking and lung cancer.

This kind of question requires reliance on facts bearing on the topic or problem of discussion. Often what the teacher as well as the student seems to consider worthwhile discussion consists of little more than expressions of preconceived notions with little or no support. Some teachers emphasize

---

[15] J. S. Cross and J. M. Nagle, "Teachers Talk Too Much," *English Journal* (December, 1969), 58, pp. 1362-1365.

learning facts apart from thinking, dealing only with those of the textbook and on one side of the issue. In contrast, others stress learning facts through thinking in the search for all possible information pertinent to a particular discussion. They are alert to challenge students to support their assertions, conclusions, or generalizations. They also thus lead them to challenge one another.

As an aid in using good questions, the teacher may construct them in advance of the discussion period. We suggested in Chapter 4 that a few pivotal thought questions may be given in the assignment for direction of students' learning then and subsequently in the study period. Those or similar questions may be raised for the culmination period. As assistance to the students, the questions may be written on the chalkboard. The teacher may begin the discussion by helping the students analyze the questions so that they may perceive the nature of the problems as stated. This procedure may be of assistance to the teacher later if one or more members of the class digress too far or too long from the problem.[16]

BARRIERS IN SHIFTING TO REFLECTIVE ACTIVITIES

A teacher confronts special difficulties or obstacles while beginning the sorts of activities described in this and preceding chapters. The course of action will not run smoothly, because it will be somewhat new both to teacher and students. The teacher may find, therefore, that the hindrances to its producing satisfactory results are primarily in himself or herself and the students.

This teacher may need to concentrate first on a self-reexamination. Perhaps accustomed solely to the routine of conventional teaching, this individual should not be surprised to find it difficult to change abruptly to a procedure characterized by flexibility and student involvement in investigation, exchange of ideas, and thinking. To make this change with some degree of success, the teacher needs educational objectives that provide strong interest in and diligent application to the undertaking. Teachers with little concern for democratic, reflective teaching are unlikely to employ the thought and effort necessary for increased success in such teaching.

In looking at the degree of success, the teacher may be helped by recognizing that both teacher and students learn through experience. Unfortunately, many teachers (when students themselves) experienced little in the way of challenging, deliberative procedure in the learning process. Some of them have been teaching as they were taught. It may require one

---

[16] N. M. Sanders, "A Second Look at Classroom Questions," *High School Journal* (March, 1972), 55, pp. 265-277. For further suggestions about how to have reflective learning in the classroom see E. E. Bayles, *Pragmatism in Education,* Harper and Row, New York, 1966, Chap. 6. Also see H. G. Hullfish and P. G. Smith, *Reflective Thinking: The Method of Education,* Dodd, Mead, New York, 1961, Chaps. 12-13, and Bigge and Hunt, *Psychological Foundations,* Chaps. 18-20.

or more years of following different theory and practice in teaching for them to become reasonably successful. This was found by Bayles to be true of teachers who engaged successfully in reflective teaching. Their second year of such teaching was significantly more successful than the first, as judged by the achievement of the students.[17]

In instructional procedures, a teacher may find that a barrier to success lies in continuing to do a poor job in involving students in the selection and pursuit of learning activities during the assignment and study periods as well as the culminating period. The teacher may need to increase the use of learning materials outside the textbook and assist students in relating some ideas of the course to other ideas within and outside of the course. Further, construction and use of thought questions may need improvement. In addition, the teacher may discover that the present way of managing the class requires change. Probably a further shift is needed toward democratic procedure. This, of course, does not mean moving toward laissez-faire or anarchy. Just as truly, it does not involve standing an inattentive student in the corner. In democratic class management, there is reliance on individual guidance or counseling. The teacher also may use a group conference in which students participate in discussing and constructing standards or rules for orderly and efficient discussion.[18]

Turning to the students, the teacher who initiates use of reflective group activities may see that some of the students react against the innovation and thus interfere with satisfactory results. Nearly all of these students may have spent eight or more years of school listening to many brief dialogues and short lectures. It has been found that among those who have been conditioned to learn by being spoon-fed by a few classmates or the teacher, some prefer continuation of such a learning process. Their set attitudes and habits are against the changes being made. Therefore, a teacher earnestly desiring to involve all members of a class in reflective learning will need to use more than a few tricks of the trade. It will require some basic changes such as suggested in this and the preceding chapters, especially in the direction of student sharing in choosing and planning schoolwork.

The conclusion seems to be that before individual teachers assert that it is impossible to provide this kind of teaching, they and their students must be considered as possible hindrances to immediate success. A teacher should not be too quick to cite the course of study or administrators and parents as the only or chief obstacles to success. A teacher who knows both

17 Bayles, *Democratic Educational Theory*, p. 31.
18 See Chaps. 10, 13-14. For additional discussion of how to meet barriers to reflective teaching, see L. E. Cole and W. F. Bruce, *Educational Psychology*, rev. ed., Harcourt, Brace, and World, New York, 1958, Chap. 16; E. J. Nussel and M. Johnson, "Who Obstructs Innovation? A Study of Teacher Perception of Possible Obstacles to Innovation," *Journal of Secondary Education* (January, 1969), 44, pp. 3-11; and J. R. Marshall, Jr., "The Roles of the School Teacher," *High School Journal* (April, 1972), 55, pp. 320-329.

the students and the subject matter thoroughly and feels a strong desire to develop students in social and scientific awareness will find ways to reach this goal. Furthermore, if the students reveal that the quality as well as the quantity of their learning has improved, the teacher is unlikely to receive opposition from administrators or parents.[19]

The teaching procedure suggested throughout this and the two preceding chapters stems from the concerns and needs of different students and is directed toward democratic objectives of education. That this kind of teaching actually accomplishes anticipated results has been an assumption underlying these chapters. The individual learns through interacting purposefully and understandingly with the environment. What is learned is always determined by the process of learning as well as by the subject matter studied. Hence the teacher who provides many classroom situations in which students experience sharing, cooperating, purposing, investigating, discovering, reflecting, and creating, thereby helps them to develop well in those respects as well as in academic achievement. Incidentally, he or she contributes to reduction of student unrest and the number of dropouts. These conclusions are supported by experimentation cited in other chapters.

QUESTIONS AND ACTIVITIES

1. Individually and then in a small group, list some essential steps the teacher must take to encourage more open and extensive class discussion and student thinking. Check the validity of your listing with experienced teachers.
2. Explain how the concluding work on a learning activity provides well for the acquisition of facts as it concentrates on the development of thinking.
3. Ask for some student volunteers to demonstrate the differences in the following two types of classroom discussion: conventional, teacher-dominated discussions; discussions encouraging respect, cooperation, and reflective thinking. What are the advantages and disadvantages of each? Which supports democratic principles of teaching and learning?
4. Through a total class brainstorming session, identify a list of criteria for democratic and scientific procedures in class discussions.
5. Present and illustrate the kind of concluding activities necessary for learning directed toward the major objectives of education.

[19] For further consideration of the role of the teacher in implementing a modern program of education, see the chapters that follow.

6. How may those activities be used by the teacher and the students to form, evaluate, support, and apply generalizations?
7. Referring to the nature and use of the question, explain how it may be made to contribute to effective learning. Demonstrate numerous ways of asking a question which encourage student involvement and thinking.
8. Hold a panel discussion to evaluate this third step of teaching—culminating activities—from the standpoint of both academic achievement and the development of desirable personal traits.

SELECTED REFERENCES

Bigge, M. L., and M. P. Hunt, *Psychological Foundation of Education,* 2nd ed., Harper and Row, New York, 1968, Chaps. 18-20.
Brembeck, C. S., *Social Foundations of Education: Environmental Influences in Teaching and Learning,* John Wiley, New York, 1971, Chap. 3.
Brown, G. I., *Human Teaching for Human Learning,* Viking, New York, 1971.
Eson, M. E., *Psychological Foundations of Education,* 2nd ed., Holt, Rinehart and Winston, New York, 1972, Chap. 8.
Hass, G., and others, *Readings in Secondary Teaching,* Allyn and Bacon, Boston, 1970.
Henderson, G., and R. F. Bibens, *Teachers Should Care: Social Perspectives of Teaching,* Harper and Row, New York, 1970.
Hoover, K. H., *Learning and Teaching in the Secondary School,* 2nd ed., Allyn and Bacon, Boston, 1968, Chaps. 6, 11, 15.
Hullfish, H. G., and P. G. Smith, *Reflective Thinking: The Method of Education,* Dodd, Mead, New York, 1961, Chaps. 12-13.
Loree, M. R., *Psychology of Education,* 2nd ed., Ronald, New York, 1970, Chaps. 12-13.
Massialas, B. G., and J. Zevin, *Creative Encounters in the Classroom: Teaching and Learning Through Discovery,* John Wiley, New York, 1967, Chaps. 4-5.
Schmuck, R. A., and P. A. Schmuck, *Group Processes in the Classroom,* William C. Brown, Dubuque, Iowa, 1971.
Sund, R. B., and L. W. Trowbridge, *Teaching Science by Inquiry in the Secondary School,* Charles E. Merrill, Columbus, Ohio, 1967, Chap. 8.
Tanner, D., *Secondary Curriculum: Theory and Development,* Macmillan, New York, 1971.
Wilson, J. A. R., and others, *Psychological Foundations of Learning and Teaching,* McGraw-Hill, New York, 1969, Chap. 17.

PART III

TEACHING SPECIFIC SUBJECTS

CHAPTER 7

Thus far there have been only incidental references to teaching particular subjects of the high-school curriculum. In this chapter and the next two the aim is to show how sound basic theory and practice may be applied to instruction in different areas of the curriculum. Our goal is to realize that the needs of youth in today's world, the democratic objectives of education, and an experimentally supported theory of learning can be used effectively to direct the teaching-learning process in any subject. As teachers perceive that the essentials of good teaching are the same in all subject matter fields, they thereby gain understanding and acceptance of those essentials in a particular field. Moreover, recognition of common purposes and procedures in teaching all subjects in secondary education can help teachers of different subjects to work cooperatively.

TEACHING LANGUAGE ARTS

It is generally recognized that language arts, being arts of communication, are fundamental in education. The efficiency of students in reading and in oral and written expression largely determines how well they will succeed in the study of any subject. In an increasing number of schools the current objectives on teaching the language arts course, commonly known as English, are (1) to develop students' interests, understandings, and skills in reading, (2) to assist them in reading literature to meet their personal and social needs, and (3) to help them improve in speaking and writing thoughtfully, clearly, and correctly.

The method of implementing those objectives, at least in theory, has been to guide students as groups and individuals, in planning, sharing interests, and thinking. Leading writers have given impressive attention to having students read as an aid toward solving their personal and social

LANGUAGE ARTS
AND SOCIAL STUDIES

problems. Further, writers have proposed that students be led to discover concepts or generalizations in oral and written expression through providing them with a variety of vital, meaningful experiences. Thus the teaching procedure proposed for English is similar to that for the new social studies and other new subjects of the high-school curriculum.[1]

Improvement of Ability to Read

Observation and research have revealed the serious problem of retarded readers in high school. It is well known that many high-school students read below the ninth-grade level, some as low as the fourth-grade level. Reports of investigations indicate that between one-fourth and one-third of high-school students do not read well enough to engage in the reading expected of them in high school.[2] Although elementary schools are doing a better job of teaching reading than they were a few decades ago, as shown by experimental evidence, the retention of an increasing number of poor readers in high school has enlarged the problem. It is encouraging to note, however, that some high schools are making a special, concentrated effort to raise the levels of students in ability to read.

To understand the problem of improvement of reading efficiency in junior and senior high school, we must realize that the reading of students is differentiated into abilities to do specific jobs within particular curricular areas. For one kind of reading a student may have strong interest and sufficient background but not for another. This suggests that teachers in each subject of the curriculum have the opportunity and the obligation to provide some guidance in reading. In fact, observation and research show that guidance of reading in any subject improves students' ability to grasp subject matter and skills in reading. Preceding a reading activity, teachers in science or the social studies, for example, may help students set up realistic and challenging goals. These goals provide the force and direction needed for successful reading and study.[3] Yet leadership in an adequate program of improvement of reading depends largely on teachers of English and specialists in the teaching of reading. A teacher of another subject often is inclined to concentrate on immediate results in acquisition of subject matter to the neglect of development of interest and skill in reading.

The special programs of reading instruction are in English classes or in classes to which English teachers are assigned part of the time. Some schools schedule reading during periods the students would normally spend in the study hall. In other schools the students may be assigned to a

---

1 See, for example, W. Loban and others, Teaching Language and Literature, Grades Seven-Twelve, 2nd ed., Harcourt, Brace and World, New York, 1969, Chap. 4.
2 M. A. Gunn, What We Know About High School Reading. What Does Research in Reading Reveal? National Council of Teachers of English, Champaign, Illinois, 1969, pp. 10-11.
3 Ibid., pp. 19-25; W. J. Moore, "What Does Research in Reading Reveal About Reading in the Content Fields?" English Journal (May, 1969), 58, pp. 707-718.

reading center two days a week during a semester or one day throughout the year. Another practice consists of having a semester course in reading in lieu of an English course or as a part of it. Some schools require all students to have some special instruction; but others, only the poor readers. Thus the programs vary, some directed toward remedial reading for poor readers and some toward developmental reading for all students.[4]

A unique program was reported from a school district in Los Angeles. Each of four high schools of the district has two complete reading laboratories, each laboratory having appropriate materials and equipment and a special reading teacher. All freshmen are required to do eight weeks of work in the reading laboratory. During the remainder of the year they spend indefinite time in supervised classroom reading. The regular freshman English teachers work with the reading specialist in advising and guiding students. The results have been impressive, the average gains being significantly above normal.[5]

Whatever may be the form or the administrative features of the reading program, its essential requirement is provision for the special needs of different youths. As we saw in Chapter 2, two requirements of effective learning are intrinsic objectives and meanings. The student develops interest in the reading activity as it assists him or her in reaching goals—personal, social, vocational, and educational. Suitable reading helps in the resolution of problems. Moreover, suitable reading materials not only apply to problems but are also at the proper level. When students have appropriate experiences in reading, they may be expected to read with purpose and understanding.

Of course, diagnosis of each student's reading needs is basically important. Students' satisfactory or unsatisfactory development in reading is the result of their physical, mental, emotional, and social conditions, as well as how well teachers have provided for developmental experiences in reading. Thus diagnosis of reading disability requires recognition of multiple causation. The whole student must be studied in the total environment. Furthermore, diagnosis should be continuous. Diagnosis helps the teacher perceive appropriate teaching methods and during instruction there arise additional opportunities to diagnose. Hence there is a reciprocal relationship between diagnosis and teaching. As a result of thorough diagnosis of each student, the teacher often finds that improving the student's personal qualities is a necessary basis for improving the techniques of teaching reading.[6]

Understanding the needs of different students in reading indicates the need for extensive provision of individualized instruction. Through tests,

4 Gunn, What We Know About High School Reading, pp. 40-82.
5 S. Berkey, "Reading and Study Skills Program in a High School District," Reading Teacher (November, 1962), 16, pp. 102-103. See also J. N. Hook, The Teaching of High School English, 4th ed., Ronald, New York, 1972, Chap. 4.
6 R. Strang, Diagnostic Teaching of Reading, 2nd ed., McGraw-Hill, New York, 1969, Chap. 2.

interest and personality inventories, cumulative records, and especially individual conferences, the needs of each student may be found. In the individual conference, the sympathetic, observant teacher not only can discover important points about the nature of the student but also can assist in improving the student's attitudes toward himself, others, and readings.[7]

In individualized instruction, especially for a low ability student and an underachiever, there is need for self-selection of materials and self-direction of procedure. Both teacher and student keep records of interests, needs, and accomplishments. There are scheduled conferences in which the student may read briefly and join in discussion of past and future reading. The teacher may draw on such aids as the Science Research Associates Reading Laboratory for suggestions about procedure and on Western novels, Landmark Books, Big Little Books, and the like for suitable reading materials.[8]

An example of reading instruction adapted to the particular needs of individuals was reported by two teachers. In a Chicago high school a group of students who were retarded in reading were chosen for special instruction. As a first step the teacher and the librarian selected some books of strong appeal to adolescent boys and girls, as shown by surveys of the interests of youths. Other books were added as individuals of the retarded group revealed their special interests. In the teaching procedure there was provision for necessary freedom of movement for the students so that they could browse in the classroom or school library and select their reading materials. Also, the teachers reserved much time for individual conferences in which they questioned and advised students and listened to their progress reports. There was, however, some group instruction stemming from, and directed toward, group objectives. The report indicated very satisfactory results.[9]

There has been extensive research showing that the individualized method is superior to conventional procedure. In one experiment with junior-high-school students, some students received individualized instruction in which there was a one-to-one relationship between teacher and student, each student in conference with the teacher choosing what would be best to read. Students of the control group had a basal textbook and received conventional group instruction. The experimenters found evidence indicating that the individualized method is definitely superior to

---

[7] Ibid., Chap. 12.

[8] For Reading Laboratory and for books on personal and social problems of adolescents, write Science Research Associates, 259 East Erie Street, Chicago, Illinois. See also S. A. Cohen, *Teach Them All to Read: Theory, Methods, and Materials for Teaching the Disadvantaged,* Random House, New York, 1969.

[9] B. J. Ehrenwerth and M. M. McAuliffe, "Developmental Reading Program for High School Students," *Chicago Schools Journal* (April, 1963), 44, pp. 315-319. See also H. L. Whalen, "English Teaching: Past, Present and Future," *English Journal* (November, 1971), 60, pp. 1072-1079.

the conventional method.[10] More convincing is the survey of 39 investigations of the effectiveness of the individualized method. Nearly all of the results showed distinct superiority of the individualized procedure over conventional group procedure.[11]

Individualized instruction can be improved by effective group instruction. In fact, group procedure, efficiently conducted, functions as a base for individualized procedure. At times instruction of the whole class may provide situations that lead every student to read with intrinsic motivation and meaning. The teacher can use the physical and the social environment of the classroom so that students of different skills and interests in reading can set up and read toward suitable objectives. Among the means the teacher employs are various audio-visual aids, thought questions, and class discussions. The chalkboard, the bulletin board, and of course the classroom library, which contains books written particularly for adolescents, are freely used resources. A focal point of discussion is often on the reactions of different members of the class to books they have seen, heard about, or read. The exchange of ideas by young people about their reading has a strong effect on each individual's attitudes and habits in reading.[12]

Development in Appreciation of Literature in and Through Reading

As in improvement of reading skill, leaders in English are advocating adjustment of instruction in literature to the needs of the individual. Ability to read is basic for engagement in, and enjoyment of, reading. Yet it is known that many people who can read well seldom or never read any literature of the past or present. They did not develop sufficient interest in reading literature for it to compete with many other interests in modern society.

The traditional course in literature has consisted largely of units of subject matter presented uniformly to the whole class. This may involve teaching a list of classics or a collection of choice passages contained in a textbook. Routine, inflexible teaching of literature to a group, through use of set content, is a difficult and unsatisfactory undertaking. Reading is a personal activity. Recognizing this, some teachers, particularly in junior high school, are supplementing or even supplanting a list of classics or a textbook of selected readings with extensive, well-directed individualized reading. In doing this they have received assistance from the growing popularity of the paperback.

Some support for emphasis on individualized reading of literature may

10 F. W. Davis and J. S. Lucas, "An Experiment in Individualized Reading," *Reading Teacher* (May, 1971), 24, pp. 737-743.
11 P. Groff, "Comparisons of Individualized (IR) and Ability-Grouping (AG) Approaches as to Reading Achievement," *Elementary English* (March, 1963), 40, pp. 258-264; see also R. Karlin, "What Does Research in Reading Reveal About Reading and the High School Student?" *English Journal* (March, 1969), 58, pp. 386-395.
12 For sources of a variety of books and magazines, see Chap. 10.

be found in research. For example, Burton and Simmons reported Lou LaBrant's follow-up study of students taught by that procedure. The students had received only individualized reading instruction during their six secondary years, having some required readings but plenty of guidance through conferences. Twenty years later they were reading more and better books than members of any other group with whom they were paired. In a similar study, reported by Gunderson, B. C. Appleby experimented with individualized instruction given to high-school seniors. This group was superior to a control group in appreciation of the techniques of fiction and in reading fiction voluntarily to gain information about themselves and sociocivic affairs.[13]

Group instruction is needed of course with individual instruction. The way group-individual procedure is used is important. In this dual method of teaching, student involvement in "active" learning is essential. Unfortunately, too many teachers depend largely on a lecture or telling method, neglecting real class discussion of group and individual purposes for reading. This was found to be true in the National Study of High School English Programs, sponsored by the University of Illinois and the National Council of Teachers of English. More than 50 percent of the teachers stated on the questionnaire that they used the discussion method most frequently. But the observers of the National Study recognized discussion in only 18 percent of the class periods, more of the class time being given to question-and-short-answer reciting and to lecturing. The explanation of the difference between the report of the teachers and that of the observers hinges on the conception of discussion. In the opinion of the observers, discussion involves distinct interaction between teacher and student and between student and student. Also it is directed toward a common objective and the process is dynamic and meaningful. Happily, this type of discussion was observed in some classrooms.[14]

In another report of the National Study, similar findings and recommendations were given. Too often lessons in literature were found to be ends in themselves rather than means toward freeing students to read widely and well. There was too much lecturing about literature in large and small groups. In place of such instruction, the investigators recommended increased reading of individual texts, with much guided reading built upon intelligent use of classroom book collections. In addition, the report suggested class discussion of personal and social problems as a basis for the selection and study of readings.[15]

Such group instruction can provide extensively for direct and indirect

13 D. L. Burton and J. S. Simmons, *Teaching English in Today's High Schools—Selected Readings,* Holt, Rinehart, and Winston, New York, 1965, p. 14; D. V. Gunderson, "Research in the Teaching of English," *English Journal* (September, 1971), 60, pp. 794-795.
14 R. K. Applebee, "National Study of High School English Programs: A Record of English Teaching Today," *English Journal* (March, 1966), 55, pp. 273-281.
15 J. R. Squire, "National Study of High School Programs: A School for All Seasons," *English Journal* (March, 1966), 55, pp. 282-290.

guidance of the individual. During directed study or the free reading period, the teacher has scheduled and unscheduled conferences with individuals and small groups. In the conference the student may consider some personal and educational concerns. Typically, youths are concerned about physical fitness and prowess, ability to get along with others, acceptance by others, choice of a vocation, and their involvement in economic, social, and political justice. Research indicates that these concerns provide suggestions for guidance in reading.[16] An important instructional procedure is that the teacher and the librarian, working together, collect and display suitable reading materials. They may place colorful books on open shelves in the library and classroom and may attach the covers of some of those books to the bulletin board.[17]

In effective group procedure all members of the class are encouraged to express themselves in a free, orderly manner. Different individuals may state choices of books for the classroom library and exchange ideas about a book, read and reported on by an individual or a group. The views of a book expressed by a student's peers may affect that student's attitudes and habits of reading more than the views of the teacher. Thus group instruction in reading may contribute to improvement of the quantity and quality of a student's free, independent reading.

This purposeful, functional approach to teaching literature has been demonstrated by the way some teachers direct their students in reading to find help in dealing with personal and social problems. On the first or second day with a class, the teacher may raise questions about anxieties and concerns troubling old as well as young people. Examples of such questions are:

---

1. What especially interesting program on television have you viewed within the last few days?
2. From reports of news on television or radio and in the press, what seem to you to be the most serious current problems facing us in our home, community, and nation?
3. What seem to you to be some possible solutions to these problems?
4. How may the reading of literature help us gain understanding about the inter-relationships and the complexities of these problems and increase our concern about their solution?
5. Do you know of any pieces of literature that seem to have effected changes in the course of history?

Since such questions may be asked by students as well as the teacher, there is an exchange of ideas between teacher and student and between

16 Gunn, *What We Know About High School Reading,* pp. 29-36. See also W. Loban, "Literature and the Examined Life," *English Journal* (November, 1970), 59, pp. 1086-1090. For reading materials and other aids for teaching literature, see current and past copies of *English Journal* and write National Council of Teachers of English, Champaign, Illinois. See also Chap. 10.
17 Loban and others, *Teaching Language,* pp. 50-58.

student and student. The discussion is so directed that almost all in the class make a contribution. In the process the teacher begins to discover the needs and interests of each member of the class, and students begin to analyze their own problems and classmates' problems and to perceive possible contributions of literature toward solutions of those problems.

At points in the discussion both teacher and class may refer to examples of literature, particularly novels and biographies that seem to have influenced major issues and movements of the past. Examples of these are *Les Miserables, A Tale of Two Cities, Oliver Twist,* and *Uncle Tom's Cabin.*

After the class has agreed on a problem of special concern for study, the teacher and some students may recommend suitable reading materials for group and individual reading. The materials should be available in the school or the classroom library or in the community library. Some questions for the direction of reading and reporting on a book are:

---

1. What is the purpose and meaning of the book as a whole?
2. What are the most impressive and significant scenes and events?
3. What are the author's interpretations of the actions of the main characters?
4. What is the soundness of the basic assumptions and facts presented by the author?
5. How may this book affect the understandings and sensitivities of people concerning the nature and solution of the problem of immediate concern to our class?
6. How has the book affected your insights and attitudes relative to the problem being studied by our class?

In this kind of procedure students tend to study literature purposefully and reflectively. Often literature is presented to a class merely as aspects of a body of subject matter having value solely within itself apart from the perplexities of the time. If literature is assigned primarily on the basis that a book is a classic or represents a type of literature being studied, it stirs few students. The effect of literature on the ideals and actions of the reader is enhanced significantly while reading for assistance in confrontation with vital, pressing problems.

Literature thus taught may be expected to develop in students social understanding and reflective thinking. Their goal seeking, meaningful readings provide them with experiences that help them form valuable ideals of conduct. Such teaching of literature is effective in a social studies course as well as one in literature. In either course a skillful teacher can use realistic characters of literature to effect beneficial changes in the social attitudes and intellectual habits of the student.[18]

---

[18] N. L. Arnez, "Racial Understanding Through Literature," *English Journal* (January, 1969), 58, pp. 56–61.

The foregoing suggestions for teaching literature have as an end the improvement of self-directed reading. Students are assisted in choosing and reading the best books according to their abilities, interests, and needs. Literature is good not only in itself or in the abstract but for particular boys and girls. *Gone with the Wind* may be best for one student while *Ivanhoe* is best for another. To stimulate and enlarge the student's choice of worthwhile reading, it is helpful to provide for browsing in libraries. The teacher also needs to be an independent, self-directing student of literature—not a slave to tradition or the textbook but an innovator and improviser. Drawing on his or her own knowledge of literature and of each student, the teacher thoughtfully helps everyone in the class choose suitable materials and activities.

Although a personalized procedure is appropriate for superior students, it is imperative for the disadvantaged or slow learner. Tinchner, a member of the staff of the Detroit Public Schools, noted from a study of poor learners that many of them have few friends and that they retreat or act belligerently when confronted with perplexing problems. Hence literature for them in particular must deal with their home and community problems. They also require unconventional or unorthodox methods of instruction. This is not to say that they will not be directed at all toward enjoying reading what educators consider to be good literature. This is best done, however, through their finding enjoyment in reading for individual and group objectives. The literature program for underprivileged students, and all others, should include books that deal with personal and social issues directly and searchingly. Literature thus taught may be expected to develop in students appreciation of its function and meaning as well as its form and style.[19]

An example of the group-individual way of teaching literature was reported from a high school in Bedford, New York. The teacher had the class participate in planning the course. Teacher and students brought various reading materials to class, including paperbacks and magazines. Some literature was read and discussed by the group toward a common goal. On many of the days, however, there was individual reading in class. Thus the class period was used chiefly to expose students to attractive reading materials and to guide them in reading according to their interests and needs. A similar report was given by an English teacher in a high school of Los Alamos, New Mexico. Through extensive discussion, the class adopted group and individual goals and a variety of reading and writing projects, sharing with one another through work on all the projects. In both schools the

---

[19] E. Tincher, "Helping Slow Learners Achieve Success," *English Journal* (April, 1965), 54, pp. 289-294; M. Smiley, "Gateway English: Teaching English to Disadvantaged Students," *English Journal* (April, 1965), 54, p. 273.

enthusiasm of the students was very gratifying, because they experienced decision making and were learning how to learn.[20]

It should go without saying that learning in literature directed toward genuine appreciation should be evaluated according to that end. Yet, as is well known, many teachers rely chiefly on the objective test as a means of evaluation. It will be seen in Chapter 15 that this kind of test has low validity for determining appreciation in any area of human activity. Some leaders in teaching English advocate a good essay examination for measurement of understanding and enjoyment of literature. If thought questions have been used freely in class discussion, similar ones are appropriate in an examination. However, the most dependable means for evaluating appreciation of literature is observation of the students' reading habits and their expressions of understanding and enjoyment in individual conferences and class discussion.[21]

Written Composition

Teaching reading and literature is closely related to teaching written composition. As a student improves in reading understandingly and critically, he or she may be expected to improve similarly in writing. There is transference of learning from reading to writing. In an investigation of poor and good writers, one significant finding was that "good writers did more voluntary reading and had a better self-image." Evidently, ideas gained from reading may produce helpful ideas in both content and form of writing.[22]

Thought is fundamental in written composition. This is because writing a composition is an artistic experience, a creative activity. Clearness of a student's thoughts promotes clearness of expression. In turn, clarification of expression contributes to clarification of thoughts. To write clearly and correctly, the students need to be in learning situations that help them gain meaningful objectives for writing and perceive the content and form of expression required to reach their objectives.

This point of emphasis has been expressed repeatedly by writers on teaching composition and has support from experimentation. For example, Baird investigated the errors of two classes in composition in high school during a school year. Her two related conclusions were (1) that increasing the number of compositions written has little or no affect on improvement of the compositions and (2) that the basis for effective writing is effective

---

20 G. Ehrenhaft, "Combatting Apathy: Literature and the 'General' Class," *English Journal* (September, 1969), 58, pp. 840-846; P. Shipp, "Step to the Back of the Class: An Approach to Individualizing Learning," *English Journal* (January, 1972), 61, pp. 87-91.
21 R. J. Morsey, *Improving English Instruction*, Allyn and Bacon, Boston, 1965, pp. 148-151.
22 N. S. Blount, "Summary of Investigations Relating to the English Language Arts in Secondary Education," *English Journal* (May, 1970), 59, p. 679.

thinking.[23] In a similar investigation, in which the writing errors of high-school graduates were studied, it was found that most of the errors were the result of illogical thinking.[24]

Development of skills or techniques in writing is best accomplished, as in all other activities, through purposeful and thoughtful involvement of the learner in the activity. Since a composition is a creation or production, the writer must be an active participant in determining both content and form of expression. It does not suffice to write a paragraph merely to apply one or more rules of grammar or to receive drill on the mechanics of ex-pression. Rather, what is wanted is writing that stems from the personal, social, and academic needs of young people and is produced in a class-room atmosphere of understanding, cooperation, and sharing.

One way to start a class toward writing with purpose and meaning is to provide for exchange of compositions between the class and another class. Each class would read and evaluate the compositions of the other class. A student secretary would be chosen by each class, whose duties would in-clude assigning each student a number and handling all the exchanged compositions of the classes. The students of each class might decide on a topic of interest to themselves and of probable interest to the other class. Each student would write a composition in class, and the teacher would offer suggestions and render necessary assistance. Then the students would meet in small groups to read and evaluate the compositions of the group. All the compositions might be sent to the other class or only a few con-sidered to be the best.

Another way to promote understanding, thinking, and interest in writ-ing is through encouraging each student to write, within the English class-room, a report on a project in another class, for example, in science, industrial arts, or the social studies. Of course the teacher would also relate literature and composition by having students write reports on indi-vidual and group readings.

This way of teaching written composition requires a kind of workshop situation in which students, as individuals or small groups, plan and carry out writing projects with the assistance of other students and the teacher. Such a shop or laboratory situation often exists in teaching science, home economics or industrial arts. As we will see in Chapter 9, it rarely occurs to the teacher of industrial arts or home economics to announce to the

---

[23] R. C. Baird, "A Survey of Errors in English Compositions," *Journal of Educational Research* (January, 1963), 56, p. 235. See also J. S. Shermin, *Your Problems in Teaching English: A Criti-que of Research*, International Textbook, Scranton, Pennsylvania, 1969, pp. 157-161; and R. L. Trezie, "The Hilda Taba Teaching Strategies in English and Reading Classes," *English Journal* (April, 1972), 61, pp. 577-580.

[24] W. M. Thomas, "Technical Errors in the Compositions of the Average High-School Senior," *School Review* (Summer, 1963), 71, p. 194. See also Bertha Berman, "The Composition Mystique," *Clearing House* (October, 1972), 47, pp. 99-102.

class that each student is requested to make an article and bring it to class ready to be handed in on a certain date. Instead, the teacher typically provides that the work be done in class with some supervision. There is group discussion of what individuals and small groups may do and how it may be done well. As the class members work individually or in small groups, the teacher walks about the room questioning and suggesting, anxious to render help when it is needed and to observe the process of producing the finished article. Encouragingly, reports indicate that an increasing number of teachers of written composition are following this workshop procedure.

In writing class, a teacher works with a student, as need be, in each step in the production of a composition, assisting the student in setting up large and small objectives and in discovering means of moving toward goals. Occasionally, the teacher may organize the students into small groups so they can read one another's papers and offer suggestions for improvement of content, organization, and sentence structure. If a student knows that a classmate, as well as the teacher, may read someone's composition before or after the final draft, there is an additional incentive for diligent, thoughtful application to writing. Thus the student may advance in written expression through purposeful and meaningful use of skills during the writing. Furthermore, the students who read and criticize a peer's composition receive valuable suggestions toward improving their own compositions. Finally, in this workshop-laboratory method of teaching composition, the teacher may learn so much about a composition while it is written in class that the time required to read it out of class in its final form may be markedly reduced.[25]

Teachers who say they do not have time for effective teaching of written composition are reminded that some teachers with more than 100 students are finding extra time through student involvement in workshop procedure. In this method of teaching, each student assumes increasing responsibility for thoughtful writing and revising, which reduces significantly the time the teacher usually needs to spend in correcting papers in the classroom and at home. Furthermore, by dispensing with practices that work unsatisfactorily, the teacher can find time to use practices that have been found to work satisfactorily. Of course it is preferable that a teacher of composition have not more than 100 students for provision of adequate individual instruction.

Such a way of teaching written composition has some support from experimentation. For instance, Lynch studied the individual conference method in comparison with the conventional procedure of writing and reading papers without conference. He found that having the individual

25 R. Botts, "What Means This End? Some Unexamined Classroom Practices," *English Journal* (January, 1971), 60, pp. 88-92.

theme conference with each member of the experimental group resulted in significant improvement over the control group. Moreover, additional improvement may be expected if the conference is accompanied by revision of the paper in class. From this and other investigations there is evidence that the teacher of English needs to consider carefully whether the long hours spent out of class reading and commenting on compositions are paying dividends in student improvement.[26]

That students respond favorably to the foregoing kind of instruction was indicated in a study by the Kanawha County English Association in West Virginia. Three significant findings were that the students wanted objectives and procedures in advance of writing, a choice in the selection of a topic, and access to other themes or to a model production as a guide. They also preferred short themes, which they wrote in class with the help of other students and the teacher. They wanted adequate time for an exchange of themes in order to read some of those written by classmates. In view of these student preferences, the reporter of the investigation advised scheduling conferences in which the student and the teacher and the student and one or more classmates could discuss the improvement of themes. Another recommendation was that students be encouraged to discover and correct their errors, using grammar handbooks and the dictionary.[27]

Provision for Independent Creative Writing

The group-individual procedure of teaching composition can be used to promote independent, creative writing. This is because it is possible to make it a flexible method of teaching in which the teacher is alert to the many opportunities to care for individual differences. Although the teacher must spend time guiding the learning of the whole class working together, much time should also be spent in direct guidance of individuals working in small groups or alone. This is suggested in preceding paragraphs in the recommendation for extensive use of individual conferences. Group instruction, especially small group instruction, in composition is for the stimulation and assistance of students toward becoming independent, creative writers.

This method of teaching requires free use of the classroom as a workshop, especially during the study or work period. Several of the students may be writing reports on individualized reading while others are engaged in that kind of reading. The teacher is busy observing and conferring with one individual after another. In small groups, students read the writings

[26] J. J. Lynch, "The Conference as a Method in the Teaching of English Composition in the Junior-Senior High School," *National Association of Secondary School Principals Bulletin* (February, 1962), 46, pp. 119-120. See also Loban and others, *Teaching Language*, pp. 342-343.
[27] L. A. Anderson, "Ways and Means in the Teaching of Writing," *English Journal* (December, 1962), 51, pp. 621-624. See also V. P. Redd, "Teaching Writing in the Junior High School," *English Journal* (April, 1970), 59, pp. 540-547.

produced by other students of the group. They exchange ideas about the content and form of each production and give and receive suggestions for its improvement. Often these suggestions affect the students as much as the teacher does.

Creative writing is promoted especially well through individualized reading. After reading a book of his or her choice that answers some puzzling questions and assists in dealing with personal-social and vocational problems, a student is inclined to communicate with others about the results of the reading. In writing the report, there is inherent motivation and meaning in the selection of both the content and the form of expression. The student constructs an outline or pattern for use in deciding what contents of the book to include in the report and how to organize effectively what is included. While a helpful suggestion from the teacher or a classmate may prove useful, the sole responsibility for the report rests with the student, as he or she is fully aware. The student alone knows his or her thoughts and how to express them. Hence every word, every sentence, and every paragraph is viewed in the light of how well it expresses particular thoughts. Thus the student is involved in an independent, creative activity.

The English teacher can duplicate those valuable experiences for the student by arranging for written reports of projects in other subjects. Obviously, this can be done easily when the English teacher and the social studies teacher, for example, are engaged in team teaching. However, with little effort it can be done in other teaching situations.

Of course, the best way to develop students in creative writing is by encouraging them to do what is commonly called "creative writing," which would include writing a story or a poem. In this type of writing the student uses imagination freely. No student should be *required* to engage in this kind of writing, but every student should receive help toward trying it. This can be done by providing each student with suitable, enjoyable experiences in reading and listening in the areas of prose fiction and of poetry. Also, a student who voluntarily writes a poem or a short story could stimulate other students by reading the production in class. The point of importance here is that participation in this kind of writing absorbs the students in an effort to improve writing so that they as well as others will enjoy reading it. Thereby skills are developed toward becoming an independent, creative writer. The most successful of the students in creative writing probably will continue it as a hobby or even become professional writers.

Speech

As in learning to write through writing, one learns to speak through speaking. This is evident from the well-known fact that, on an average, children at six years of age have a vocabulary of at least 2500 words. These words are not acquired by formal instruction but through extensive and varied experiences in oral expression. Similarly, the student improves in speaking when engaged in speaking—to inform, convince, or entertain. Ideas have to be put over, and words are organized accordingly. This may not occur on "speech day," when a dozen or more are called on to give talks primarily to practice rules of speaking. On that day students often find something just to meet the requirements of the assignment. In contrast, they are likely to talk with intrinsic motivation and meaning if reporting on an experiment in science, an article constructed in industrial arts, or an enjoyable experience outside of school. The student speaks when he or she has something to say and may be the only one giving a talk on a particular day.

When one of the writers was visiting a fifth-grade class, the teacher said to one of the girls, "Would you like to tell our visitor how your committee proceeded to construct your part of our new classroom mural?" The girl stood at the mural and used a pointer as she explained step by step the procedure her committee followed. She would look at the mural and then at the visitor as she spoke with the ease of an effective public speaker. (In fact, once when a certain public speaker was asked by a speech teacher whether he had ever studied speech, he replied simply that he had had a message to deliver and became absorbed in the process of delivering it.) When students have something to say and the desire to communicate, they too are likely to apply themselves to the acquisition and application of useful techniques.

There is a place, of course, for the class to make a special study of the content, the form, and the technique of good speaking. As in other areas of English, the inductive approach is preferable. An appropriate beginning may be a study of models: radio and television programs, including newscasts and political speeches; tape recordings; assembly programs; and talks by the teacher and students. As the students observe different types of oral expression and engage in giving talks themselves, they may gain from reading about good speaking. From the directed experiences of the students in observance of and engagement in oral expression, they may be assisted in constructing a code for evaluation of speeches. This code may include choice of a subject, content, organization, language, and physical presence. Such a code may be used by the student in preparation of talks and in evaluation of the talks or speeches of others.[28]

A basis for the provision of vital experiences in the study of speechmaking may be encouraging the thoughtful participation of some students in real class discussion. A reticent student may need first to develop

---

[28] Morsey, *Improving English*, pp. 86-89.

ability for expression in oral discussion before being ready to give a talk of educational value. As we have seen, genuine class discussion does not consist only of a series of questions and short answers between the teacher and one student after another. Rather it requires a common, challenging objective that requires in turn clarification and advancement of ideas, often in preparation for subsequent action. This awareness of group purpose underlying all discussion is fundamental. As indicated in Chapter 6, such discussion is promoted and students are helped when they are encouraged to note with the teacher (1) how well the point at issue is understood, (2) the degree of advancement toward the objective, (3) their intellectual, social, and emotional growth, and (4) their progress in clear, accurate, and forceful expression.

Oral and Written Expression and Grammar

In oral and written expression, as in other areas of human activity, the techniques of action are best acquired in the process of self-directed activity. Hence grammar, which includes techniques of expression, is best learned while being used in real self-expression. There has been a long and major controversy over the nature and usefulness of teaching grammar for the promotion of correctness in oral and written communication. It will be seen from research that there has been little transference of knowledge from grammar to composition. Grammar must be taught so that the learners are both able and willing to transfer the knowledge to oral and written expression.

Much of the criticism of grammar results from the disproportionate or wasteful amount of time given to it. From the upper grades of nearly all elementary schools through senior high school, students are presented with the same grammatical ideas in a formal, repetitious manner. The results do not justify the time and effort put forth in this endless repetition. Surely there is a more efficient, economical way to teach grammar for correct usage. Having received about five years of instruction in formal grammar, many students in the twelfth grade do not have a functional knowledge of the subject. Many are unable or unwilling to apply their knowledge of grammar, as shown on tests, to improvement of their written expression.

The common belief that the formal study of grammar is fundamental for skill in composition has lacked support from experimentation. Several years ago investigations failed to show the extensive effectiveness of grammar in eliminating usage errors. There was no scientific evidence of the value of grammar that warranted its existence as a prominent feature of the course of study. Research indicated that the coefficient of correlation between *knowledge* of grammar and *performance* in composition was about .25. It revealed further that a student with a given grade in grammar was as likely to have approximately the same grade in history, for example, as in composition.[29]

According to later writers on teaching English, experimentation has continued to condemn emphasis on the study of formal grammar. A typical statement is "The research findings show clearly and overwhelmingly that direct methods of instruction, focusing on writing activities and the structuring of ideas are more efficient in teaching sentence structure, usage, punctuation, and other related factors than are such methods as nomenclature drill, diagraming, and rote memorization of grammatical rules."[30] The conclusion from all the investigations on the functioning of grammar in composition as given by two writers is "The lack of relationship between information about grammar and the use of this information points up the need to seek opportunities for teaching grammar and usage that grow naturally out of reading, writing and speaking units."[31]

This suggests that to teach grammar as a functioning tool in speaking and writing it must be taught as it is needed and used in those activities. To discover the grammatical needs of the class in oral and written expression, it is helpful to study those needs in each of those forms of expression at the beginning of the course. A diagrammatic chart on which the strengths and weaknesses of each student are listed may help determine the points of emphasis in the course.

The teaching process should be centered on the development of concepts rather than on acquisition of terms. Toward this end the inductive approach is generally considered by leaders to be superior to the deductive or rule approach. Two examples of this method of teaching grammar may be seen in the illustrations of the discovery type of assignment in Chapter 4.

Linguistic Grammar

In recent years much has been written about linguistics, particularly its grammar. The linguists have condemned what they call "traditional grammar," stating that it is inaccurate and inconsistent and does not deal adequately with changes in correctness of speech derived from usage. One can admit that there is a degree of truth in those criticisms and yet reasonably ask: "How is linguistic, or structural, grammar an improvement over

[29] W. Asker, "Does Knowledge of Formal Grammar Function?" *School and Society* (January 27, 1923), 17, pp. 109-111; W. Loban, "Studies of Language Which Assist the Teacher," *English Journal* (December, 1947), 36, pp. 518-523; D. V. Smith, *Instruction in English*, U.S. Bulletin 17, No. 20, U. S. Government Printing Office, Washington, D.C., 1932, pp. 35-42; and Shermin, *Problems in Teaching English*, p. 132.
[30] R. R. Braddock and others, *Research in Written Composition*, National Council of Teachers of English, Champaign, Illinois, 1963, pp. 37-38.
[31] J. S. Lewis and J. C. Sisk, *Teaching English, 7-12*, American Book, New York, 1963, p. 439.

traditional grammar and how well may this new grammar be taught to students in the secondary school?"

There are leaders in the teaching of English, including some linguists, who believe that linguistic or structural grammar is unsuitable for the secondary school. There is lack of agreement among the "pure" linguists on the constituent elements of their grammar, including the relationship of grammar and usage. One may find at least four currently respectable points of view. Hence there is not one complete new grammar for adoption in high school. In addition, the new ideas can be understood by professors of English and by some secondary school teachers but by few high-school students. The terminology of linguistic grammar is so varied and extensive and so difficult to define that even those teachers eager to understand it have been unable to interpret it to students with assurance. Structural grammar is far too complex to be readily adapted to the needs of secondary students. Some teachers find it requires more time than traditional grammar. We may recall here that research has shown that the extensive time spent on traditional grammar cannot be justified by the results. So far there has not been enough research to indicate that linguistic grammar is superior to traditional grammar for high-school students.[32]

It seems evident that the key to improvement of grammar as a tool of oral and written expression is not in the substitution of the new grammar for traditional grammar but in the adoption of an efficient method of teaching grammar. The terminology and even the ideas contained in the content of grammar are of no value to students unless these students learn with intrinsic interest and meaning. In fact, some teachers have found no significant difference between the old and the new grammar in the improvement of writing. Neither type seems to contribute much. A valid conclusion seems to be that, in high school, the teacher does well to concentrate on the teaching of grammar that is understood, as it is involved in the student's speaking, reading, and writing.[33]

Evaluation of Progress in Oral and Written Expression

Instruction in oral and written expression directed toward the development of young people's desire and ability to express themselves thoughtfully and correctly requires a means of evaluation in agreement with that goal. According to Morsey, "Research does not support the assumption

[32] Burton and Simmons, *Teaching English*, pp. 247-257; J. Verbillion, "Is Linguistics the Key to Language Instruction?" *Chicago Schools Journal* (February, 1963), 44, pp. 217-223; P. Roberts, "Linguistics and the Teaching of Composition," *English Journal* (May, 1963), 52, pp. 331-335; J. J. DeBoer, "The 'New' English," *Educational Forum* (May, 1968), 32, pp. 393-402; S. McGrady, "What You Need to Know about the New Englishes," *School Management* (October, 1968), 12, pp. 57-62; and R. C. O'Donnell, "Does Research in Linguistics Have Practical Applications?" *English Journal* (March, 1970), 59, pp. 410 ff.

[33] E. R. Fagan, "Unified English: Salvaging the Disaffected," *Clearing House* (January, 1971), 45, pp. 259-264. Textbooks in linguistic grammar, grades 7-9, are published by Harcourt, Brace, and World, New York.

that objective test scores will match students' speaking and writing abilities." He added that a study revealed that scores of more than 500 high-school seniors on the New Purdue Placement Test in English had a low correlation with scores on an essay they wrote. He stated that some principals announce to the PTA proudly that their students are above the national norms in English, even though their writing may contain sentence fragments, run-on sentences, and misspelled one- and two-syllable words. Similarly, some teachers boast at the end of the school year that their students gained two years in English, but the reason for the gain is often concentration on workbook exercises containing items resembling those in the test. As has been indicated, the most dependable way to determine the progress of students in speaking and writing is to observe the process as well as the product of their engagement in those activities. Their attitudes and habits are revealed by words and actions in individual conferences, group discussions, and work periods.[34]

Implications for Teaching Modern Foreign Languages

The foregoing presentation of ways to teach English suggests similar procedures in teaching modern foreign languages. A parallel exists between learning a first and a second language, but it is not a complete one. This is particularly true if the learner is at or above the high-school level. Secondary school students are capable and often desirous of drawing on our native language when studying a foreign language. Hence they do not acquire a second language entirely as the first. The student starts out with the second language already possessing some concepts for interpreting it.[35] Yet each language is best acquired in a setting involving actual use of the language in a variety of experiences.

The present trend in the teaching of modern foreign languages is toward use of the audio-lingual method. The procedure emphasizes learning a second language as the first was learned: through direct oral response to one's environment without the intervention of translation from another language. Particularly in the beginning course, the instruction depends largely on a series of organized dialogues for the promotion of learning through mimicry and memorization. The strict audio-lingual teacher excludes reading during the first two to five months of instruction, and grammar during a longer period. Obviously, this method is in contrast to traditional procedure, which incorporates reading and grammar, along with oral expression, in every course and relies on translation in the process of learning.

This new method has merit, especially in its emphasis on the oral expression approach. Unfortunately some of its adherents are extremists who tend to reject any procedure associated with the old method. An example

---

[34] Morsey, *Improving English,* Chap. 10.
[35] C. S. Kersten and V. E. Ott, "How Relevant Is Your Foreign Language Program?" *Modern Language Journal* (January, 1970), 54, pp. 9-13.

is in their attitude toward any use of the source language in the classroom. Of course concentration on translation must be repudiated. Yet investigations do not support the belief that any use of the native tongue is ineffective. The experiences of the students in acquiring their native language can be duplicated only to a limited extent in the classroom.

A factor of special importance is the position of the new method on the role of grammar. After observing that the audio-lingual movement is sound in some respects, one specialist pointed out that it needs modifications, one being a provision for explanations about how structures of the language work. The best students in particular request this. This indicates that the teacher may occasionally promote interest and meaning by assisting learners to gain insight into peculiar and troublesome expressions of the language. One way to do this is by directing the students to consider a parallel expression in English. As has been shown in teaching other subjects, an incidental, comparative process has been found to be effective. What is important in teaching a foreign language, therefore, is not to choose between formal grammar and no grammar at all but to adopt the proper way of teaching functional elements of grammar. Thus viewed, grammar may be used to add understanding to the study of both oral and written expression.[36]

A modification of the audio-lingual position on the inclusion of reading in the program also seems necessary. Some adherents believe that reading should be postponed two or more months after the beginning of instruction. Others, for instance in New York, provide in the syllabus the introduction of reading in the second month. In fact, New York City has planned a program of instruction in foreign languages that combines what is best in the new with what is best in the old. In addition to its early inclusion of some reading, the program involves from the beginning grammatical points which formerly did not come until much later. It was found that some students were loath merely to repeat structures. They also wanted an explanation.[37]

An experiment at the University of Colorado is significant. There was a study of results from the audio-lingual habit theory in comparison with results from the grammar-translation-cognitive theory. The findings were not decidedly in favor of either theory. There was no difference between the two in listening and reading, but the new theory seemed to be superior in speaking and the old theory in writing. Similar findings were reported from a study at Purdue University. Both investigations indicated that what is needed is selection of the best elements of the two theories and the

36 T. Huebener, "The New Key Is Now Off Key," Modern Language Journal (December, 1963), 47, pp. 375-377; L. Livingstone, " 'Organic' vs. 'Functional' Grammar in the Audio-Lingual Approach," Modern Language Journal (November, 1962), 46, pp. 304-307.
37 T. Huebener, "New York City's Foreign Language Program," Modern Language Journal (February, 1963), 47, pp. 62-65.

teaching of the elements according to sound principles of learning.[38] Two such principles suggested by both Carroll and Chastain are (1) that a variety of experiences in different settings facilitates retention and use of learning and (2) that the learning of a skill occurs not through repetition alone but also through development of insights or understandings.

TEACHING SOCIAL STUDIES

We have indicated the relationship between language arts and social studies. As an individual speaks, reads, or writes, interaction with one or more persons occurs. A language is best acquired and used in real social situations. In turn, people are developed in social mindedness and become a community through communication. Students in social studies who actually communicate in give and take discussions on common problems and engage in reading and writing on those problems improve significantly in social understandings and attitudes. Seeming to recognize those inter-relationships between communication and social values, some teachers in English and in social studies have taught the two subjects cooperatively. Each of those two curriculum areas may be made to draw on and contribute to the other area.

Overview and Objectives

There has been an extensive demand by educators in social studies for vitalization and modernization of the subject in secondary education. One writer states there is general agreement on the need for changes but little agreement on the what and how of changing. Others point out that the content and method of the courses are essentially the same as they were decades ago. There is inadequate study of current problems, and learning consists largely of memorization of facts and generalizations from the textbook. Some add that too often zealous persons accept innovations without thorough, thoughtful consideration. They insist that intelligent and realistic judgments as to the reorganization of social studies require a view of the proposed patterns in relation to objectives based on a sound psychology and philosophy.[39]

The inclusive aim of social studies is to educate youth for democratic living in present-day society. This broad aim consists of two objectives: (1) improvement in adoption of democratic values and (2) development in

---

[38] J. B. Carroll, "The Contributions of Psychological Theory and Educational Research to the Teaching of Foreign Languages," *Modern Language Journal* (May, 1965), 44, pp. 279-281; and K. D. Chastain, "A Methodological Study Comparing the Audio-lingual Habit Theory with the Cognitive Code-Learning Theory—A Continuation," *Modern Language Journal* (April, 1970), 54, pp. 257-266.

[39] J. M. Becker, "Prospect for Change in the Social Studies," *Social Education* (January, 1965), 29, pp. 20 ff.

free use of reflective, or scientific, thinking. These two democratically oriented objectives may be used to assist young people to grow in interests,
attitudes, ideals, and beliefs that provide them with a spirit of "live and
help live." They furnish direction in providing situations for boys and
girls to employ reflection instead of prejudice and propaganda in their
confrontation with problems of a changing and complex social order. They
may be helpful to the teacher also in evaluating the old and the new in
social studies.

The Courses

For implementation of these or other such objectives, the teacher will
find that the courses usually required of students in junior high school are
geography, in seventh grade; United States history, in eighth grade; and
civics, in ninth grade. In the senior high school, the pattern of required
courses is more set than in the junior high school. The predominant requirement in the tenth grade is world history; in the eleventh grade, United
States history; and in the twelfth grade, a problems course. In some
schools, particularly the large ones, economics, sociology, and psychology
are among the electives. All these courses are about the same as they
were in the 1920's.

Some schools are engaged in the revision of offerings in social studies.
Some report revision of units on "isms," particularly communism. Apparently, provisions are being made also for increased study of non-Western geography, history, and culture. Another significant trend indicated
by some schools is toward emphasis on challenges of the present, in history as well as other courses. Significantly, the pattern of curriculum revision in social studies usually has been restricted to changing subject
matter within existing courses.[40]

Examples of Proposed Changes

An example of proposals of change within conventional courses is in
world history. Some social science educators realize that world history
can no longer consist of a complete story of humankind. Hence they are
suggesting some departure from chronological organization for one
around themes or movements, especially as these bear on problems of
the modern world. Examples are (1) governments and the development
of democracy, (2) the contributions of science and technology to civilizations, (3) people's struggle to make a living through industry and commerce, and (4) religions of the world in relation to governments,
institutions, and cultures. The student studies such lines of thought through

---

40 B. G. Massialas and F. R. Smith, *New Challenges in the Social Studies, Implications of Research
for Teaching*, Wadsworth, Belmont, California, 1965, pp. 22-30.

viewing the evolution of the present from the past. Thus a perspective may be gained through a sense of continuity in cause-and-effect relationships.

A similar recommendation of change in world history is a shift to a cultural area approach. This consists of concentration on the ways peoples have lived, including their values, aspirations, and problems. By a comparative study of various cultures of the world, students may improve their understanding of how those cultures evolved and may take an intelligent attitude toward each of them.[41]

Likewise, geographers have proposed the reorganization of world geography according to cultural areas. Since geography is a part of social studies, it is inappropriate to organize it around physical regions. Among the cultural areas of the world are Western Europe, the Soviet Union, and Southeast Asia. Each area is an inclusive, cohesive basis for the study of crops, industries, religions, governments, languages, customs, and other such aspects of cultures. The primary objective of this organization is the development of cultural empathy, a sympathetic understanding of other cultures, particularly those unlike our own.[42]

How United States history also may be made vital and functional may be seen in a course organized around major historical problems, designed by the Secondary School History Committee. This Committee consisted of representatives from the faculties of Amherst College and the University of Massachusetts and of five high schools adjacent to Amherst. As the Committee began meetings in the academic year 1959-1960 it noted that classes in United States history in the eleventh grade typically repeated study of the topics of the eighth grade. Furthermore, students read only from the textbook for answers to the questions in recitation and examination, with the teacher supplementing the short oral answers. As a result the Committee constructed several units devised to organize history around problems common to the past and the present. Examples are (1) race relations in the United States since the Civil War and (2) the adoption and role of the federal Constitution. Ideally, the students may begin to study the first unit through analysis of one or more civil rights problems and, the second, through conflicting interpretations of provisions of the Constitution made by contemporary politicians.[43] This procedure requires critical discussion in class and research in the library to provide for student involvement in discovering and creating. Materials and questions are used

41 Ibid., pp. 46-47.

42 W. B. Conroy, "The Cultural Region—Framework for Teaching World Geography," *Social Studies* (February, 1966), 57, pp. 71+; N. M. Sanders and M. L. Tanck, "A Critical Appraisal of Twenty-six National Social Studies Projects (16. High School Geography Project, University of Colorado, pp. 425-428)," *Social Education* (April, 1970), 24, pp. 383-449.

43 V. R. Halsey, Jr., "American History: A New High School Course," *Social Education* (May, 1963), 27, pp. 249-252+. See also L. D. Miklos and M. O. Miklos, "Historical Inquiry as a Method of Teaching American History on the Secondary Level," *Social Studies* (March, 1971), 62, pp. 113-117; and H. G. Miller, "American History—Innovating or Enervating?" *Clearing House* (April, 1971), 45, pp. 483-487. To purchase the Committee's materials, write to D. C. Heath, Boston.

to provide the inductive approach; and on the basis of both direct and vicarious experiences, students are requested to construct their own generalizations. Thus the units do not present the generalization and then give examples, but they attempt the reverse process. This method is expected to develop students for interpretation of current events.

The Inclusion of Current Problems

Whatever the course in social studies may be, it must come to grips with current problems confronting the young and the old. A social science educator, after he had visited many classrooms and talked to many teachers, reached the conclusion that only a few teachers have an adequate comprehension of why they are teaching social studies. Some of them seemingly teach just to cover ground consisting of the "safe" topics, particularly those of the past. The result has been a neglect of such vital current problems as air and water pollution, public transportation in metropolitan areas, civil rights for all Americans, and overpopulation in many countries. While directing students how to face such issues, the teacher may help them to draw on one or more of the other courses for pertinent information. All the disciplines of the social sciences are interdependent and should be taught as such.[44] Examples of questions on current problems suitable in each social study are:

1. How can our city solve some of its problems through urban planning?
2. How have welfare programs affected people?
3. What attitudes do we have in my family and neighborhood toward all minority groups?
4. How can we learn to live with automation?
5. Why can we not control our behavior on the highways so as to reduce death and injuries?
6. What effect have farm subsidies had on the farm problems?
7. How may we reduce crime in our country?
8. What steps need to be taken to improve the physical and mental health of our people?
9. How may international goodwill and peace be promoted?

The Contribution to Reorganization by Project Social Studies

Recognizing the need in the classroom for vitalization and modernization of the subject matter and for adoption of a problem-solving method, several social science educators formed committees to engage in more than 40 development projects. These projects have been financed by the

44 R. E. Banister, "A Social Studies Program for the Space Age," *Social Studies* (October, 1965), 56, pp. 166-172. See also R. W. Johns, "Identity and Inquiry," *Social Studies* (October, 1970), 61, pp. 203-213.

Department of Health, Education, and Welfare; the National Science Foundation; and some private agencies. The projects conducted are at centers, usually in universities with one or more faculty members in charge; the others are in public school systems or private agencies. Members of some groups consist of scholars from social science departments, experts on learning from departments of education, and specialists in educational measurement.

Drawing on tested educational theory and the demands of modern society, these projects have aimed at improvement of content and teaching procedure in the social studies classroom. Nearly all projects have undertaken both to revise courses and to provide suitable instructional materials, but some, merely to improve the quantity and quality of materials for use in existing courses. Almost without exception, the projects are directed toward teaching generalizations or concepts through investigation in more than one discipline of the social sciences. For instance, the new history course incorporates much more material from economics, sociology, and anthropology than does the traditional course. In fact, emphasis on these three areas is a distinguishing feature of the new social studies.

In method of teaching, nearly all the projects have shifted from almost exclusive emphasis on expository and deductive procedure toward emphasis on investigative, inductive-deductive procedure. Students have access to a variety of research data and are encouraged to set up and test hypotheses, draw valid conclusions, develop generalizations, and relate and apply ideas. Moreover, in the study of any course in social studies, students are to be led to transfer learnings from the other courses. Thus, there is a recommendation of a multimedial process of learning for the promotion of inquiry and reflective thinking.[45]

For assistance to classroom teachers in their adoption of the new social studies, the projects have been designing suitable instructional materials. Almost without exception, directors of the projects have indicated that they will not write textbooks but will provide a large variety of source materials and units. Some of these have been devised to supplement work in traditional textbooks, but others, to cover an entire year's work in place of a text. The materials have been tested in classrooms.[46]

The University of Minnesota Project

The center at the University of Minnesota demonstrates what has been done by some of the projects. The aim of the project was to provide social studies instruction directed toward helping young people to deal with

---

[45] E. Fenton and J. M. Good, "Project Social Studies: A Progress Report," *Social Education* (April, 1965), 29, pp. 206-208. See also J. Eulie, "Structure and Strategies in the New Social Studies—an Evaluation," *Journal of Secondary Education* (January, 1969), 44, pp. 16-17.
[46] For information about instructional materials, write U. S. Office of Education, Washington, D.C.

today's perplexing problems. Toward this end, the emphasis was on a teaching process devoted to use of up-to-date subject matter to provide conceptual and reflective learning. As stated by a reporter on this project:

Needless to say they were intent upon bringing the social studies curriculum up to date in terms of interpretations and emphases. This meant, to give but one example, a change in emphasis in political science from a structural to a behavioral approach. The staff believed the prime purpose of the social studies curriculum should be to develop citizens capable of coping with problems of the modern age. They found no dichotomy between this goal and that of teaching pupils sound social science. The goal did, however, seem to demand an increased emphasis upon the behavioral sciences and upon the non-Western World.

. . . Greatest emphasis is given to concepts of the widest scope and application, to analytical concepts, and to other key concepts from the individual disciplines. Above all, the staff has tried to provide the development of thinking process among students, including the ability to conceptualize for themselves, to apply generalizations, and to think critically.[47]

Each course in the junior high school consists of content from more than one discipline of the social sciences. The staff of the project emphasized materials which provide concrete cases from which students may develop concepts, generalizations, and values. In senior high school, the courses show little resemblance to those in the typical high school. During one year there is a study of cultural areas based on anthropology as well as other social sciences. There is also a study of a series of problems facing the United States at home and abroad and one which assists students to compare economic, social, and political life in the United States with that in other parts of the world.

Further understanding of the social studies program produced by the Minnesota Project may be obtained from a later report. The program advocates more than one teaching strategy but emphasizes the method of inquiry, a method that includes helping students to recognize personal and societal problems and to set up and test hypotheses, accompanied by teacher-led discussions. As aids to this type of teaching-learning process, guides have been produced for the teacher and background papers for the students. The tenth-grade course emphasizes interrelationships among the social, economic, and political systems of each period of United States history. The eleventh-grade course uses ideas from all the social science disciplines to study the cultures and problems of Europe, China, and India. And the twelfth-grade course examines the values, conflicts, and policies of underdeveloped nations in the areas of civil liberties.[48]

47 E. West, "An Articulated Curriculum for Grades K-14," *Social Education* (April, 1965), 29, pp. 209, 211. For information about materials, write to Project Social Studies, University of Minnesota, Minneapolis.
48 N. M. Sanders and M. L. Tanck, "A Critical Appraisal of Twenty-Six National Social Studies Projects (Project Social Studies, University of Minnesota, pp. 402-404)," *Social Education* (April, 1970), 34, pp. 383-449. Versions of teacher guides, resource units, and student background papers are available from Green Printing Company, 631 Eighth Avenue North, Minneapolis, Minnesota.

The University of Illinois Project

Another example of a project is in the center at the University of Illinois. This center had as its objective development and dissemination of the first three courses of a five-year sequence, beginning in the seventh grade. These courses focus on study of social orders and cultures in relation to the individual. They draw on all the social sciences, including sociology, economics, and anthropology.

The first course of the three-year sequence begins with study of the family. The students examine the American family of today and then the New England family of the past, noting the reasons for the differences. This may be followed by a related study of families in one or more other countries. The same pattern appears in the units on economic and political institutions. Starting with the present in our society and shifting to an earlier period and then to selected models in other societies, those units may help students to enlarge and deepen their understanding of similarities and differences among cultures. They may also recognize some forces tending to solidify or to change institutions and customs in cultures.

Building on the concepts introduced in Course 1, the emphasis in the second course is on those historical developments that affected all mankind rather than on the individual experiences of one people or another. Selected simple cultures as well as advanced regional cultures in Eurasia and Indo-America will be needed to determine the way of life that man developed to cope with recurring problems that gave rise to social, economic, and political institutions. Concepts in geography, cultural anthropology, economic history, and art are used to assist students to develop a global view.

The third course as presently planned will focus on major non-Western cultures and Latin America. The approach will be to examine, first the existing conditions largely in terms of economic, political, and social institutions in each of the regions studied, and then the using of selected events to explain the historical origin and development of present-day culture and institutions. Emphasis on the institutional organization of the culture of each region studied will require students to examine the values and goals of other people and our own in comparison with one another.[49]

The foregoing accounts of new programs in the social studies reveal a provision for learning directed toward social values and critical or reflective thinking. The emphasis of the programs is on promotion of social and scientific awareness for life in a world of interdependence, change, and confusion. This requires a democratic, reflective teaching procedure such as we considered in Chapters 4-6. This places special demands on the teacher, who must have a logical mind, understand students, and be very

---

[49] E. C. Leppert, "A Sequential Junior-Senior High School Curriculum," *Social Education* (April, 1965), 29, p. 214. For materials of instruction, write to Project Social Studies, University of Illinois, Urbana.

patient while asking thought questions and waiting for discerning answers. The role is chiefly that of a moderator and questioner.[50]

Reflective Thinking and Democratic Values

In line with Project Social Studies, some leading writers on teaching the social studies in high school have explained how classroom procedures may provide for democratic values and scientific or reflective thinking. Hunt and Metcalf, for example, base their teaching procedure on the goal-insight view of learning directed toward the democratic ideal.[51] Of importance here is their explanation of how a teacher may follow, in a flexible manner, Dewey's steps in a complete act of thought, which we described briefly in Chapter 4.

The beginning of an act of thought in the classroom, as elsewhere, is recognition of a real problem. Accordingly, the teacher encourages students to suggest study problems by having them discuss their findings from various reading materials and from newscasts. The teacher also uses this procedure to discover the present understandings, interests, and needs of the students, asking probing questions about their common beliefs. As they see their cherished beliefs challenged, they may be led to recognize conflicts and inconsistencies among their values. As a result, they may be helped to perceive several problems they need to study for reorganization of their system of values. Among the problems the students are very likely to suggest for study are (1) the improvement of public welfare and (2) the promotion of world peace. Let us assume that the leader approves immediate work on the first problem.

After recognition of the welfare problem, the second step to be taken is defining or limiting the problem. Students may begin by suggesting that it be structured to read: "How may the public welfare system be improved so that recipients will have an adequate living standard?" Later they may decide that a preferable form would be: "How may the public welfare system be improved so that both the welfare recipients and the taxpayers will be benefited?" In the process of formulating the problem, the teacher uses probing questions and discussion to assist the students to discover the most reasonable way to state the problem. It usually is helpful to have a student stand at the chalkboard to write some of the students' suggestions. The final statement of the problem may be left on the chalkboard for reference as work on the problem continues.

After the students formulate the problem, the next logical step is to de-

---

50 See J. R. Steinkamp, "The Demands on the History Teacher Using the Inquiry Method," *Social Studies* (March, 1970), 61, pp. 99-102; and June R. Chapin and R. E. Cross, "Making Sense out of the Terminology of the New Social Studies," *Social Studies* (April, 1972), 63, pp. 147-155.

51 M. P. Hunt and L. E. Metcalf, *Teaching High School Social Studies*, 2nd ed., Harper and Row, New York, 1968.

termine possible solutions or hypotheses. Questions are asked and propositions are made and evaluated. The discussion is directed so that students are led to express alternative beliefs. At least one student is likely to propose that the sole means of welfare reform is increased benefits. Other students, using information from reliable sources, will present other basic ways of improving welfare—for example, improvement of the staff and the professional services of welfare agencies.

The fourth step is the study and testing of the hypotheses developed by the class. The aim is to find whether the hypotheses have adequacy as predictive tools. The students engage in sufficient reliable reading to obtain the necessary facts. In the process the class may find tentative adequacy of some suggested solutions and final inadequacy of others. Thus through research and reasoning the hypotheses are evaluated, some being rejected forthwith and others retained for testing through further investigation.

The final step in direction of a complete act of thought is drawing conclusions. Students are urged to express conclusions only after there has been adequate study of reliable data. Moreover, they have been provided with a give and take situation in which they as well as the teacher are led to criticize the proposed conclusions of others. Each conclusion is examined on its merits on the basis of support from adequate, dependable evidence. Students thus may be led to recognize that in confrontation with problems of values in human relationships, they must reject prejudice (prejudgments) in the process of scientific or reflective thinking.[52] One conclusion that the class working on the welfare problem may logically draw is that since there are many causes of an unsatisfactory welfare system, many remedies are required for it to become a reasonably satisfactory system.

In the process of thinking reflectively on human values, students need assistance toward weighing all factors in a problematic situation of the home, community, nation, or world. Prejudices thrive on concentration on one point while other pertinent points are disregarded. Likewise, provincialism prevails in dealing with problems of common interest between groups when, through deficient communication, there is lack of intelligent application of all important facts bearing on the problem. Often a person's argument is based on standing up for a specific principle. What he or she does not seem to realize is that a moral problematic situation requires due recognition of more than one principle. For example, one may be obligated to choose between cooperation and competition, as in a choice between free enterprise and a degree of governmental support and control of capital and labor. This realization is especially necessary in a

52 Ibid., pp. 170-175.

world of interdependence. Problems of today have extensive ramifications and must be considered in a broad setting.

In addition, reflective procedure requires helping students to engage in *thoughtful discussion* of problems. Active involvement of a class in discussion occurs when they have a common, challenging goal or objective. Thus involved, the students as well as teachers pose thought questions bearing on the point at issue. Rather than always answering questions promptly, the teacher often replies by asking a question. Likewise the teacher frequently refrains from approving, disapproving, or commenting on a student's answer, instead, using the answer to draw a response from another student. For intelligent cooperation of students in such discussion, it is helpful to have them participate in setting up guideposts, such as may be seen in Chapters 4 and 6.

Further, reflective thinking on human relationships is best developed in a democratic group. The class needs to be a miniature democratic society in which individuals share ideas and skills, engage in speech and action reflectively, and give due consideration to the rights of others. Teacher and students endeavor to view democratic ends and means as they attack current perplexing problems. Too often expressions of belief and conduct, in and outside of the classroom, are based on prejudice, passion, and propaganda and are directed solely toward individual interests. The democratic ideal provides a rational and social point of reference as a guide to teacher and student as they work cooperatively in pursuit of classroom activities.[53] For assistance in implementing that ideal, each student may well ask the following questions:

1. Am I actively sharing in setting up and working toward the group goals?
2. Am I giving due consideration to the interests and needs of other members of our group?
3. How well am I trying to follow scientific procedure as I deal with individual and group problems?

With reference particularly to the teacher's procedure in a democratic classroom, Hunt and Metcalf specifically state:

One rule is that a teacher should treat student opinions with respect. This does not necessarily mean that a teacher expresses approval; but he avoids ridicule or sarcasm, or any expressions which might be so interpreted by students. He does not cast aspersions on the intelligence or motives of students who render serious opinions. . . . When a teacher wishes to challenge an opinion expressed by a student, he should do it in such a way that conflict is internalized. That is, the student is made to feel the conflict within his own personality. He may not feel a

53 Ibid., Chap. 9.

problem, or at least not the problem which the learning situation demands, if he sees the conflict merely as a contest between himself and someone else. For this reason a teacher should not argue with a student. . . . The learning enterprise should focus on raising questions about what will come of acting in accordance with a given proposition or hypothesis. An opinion may be converted into a proposition by saying, "Here is an opinion which is before the class. Let us take it as a proposition to be tested."[54]

Verification of how reflective instruction in a democratic climate has been used with good results is in the Indiana experiments.[55] In reports of four investigations at Indiana University, the investigators expressed as a primary objective of social studies the development of reflective thinking for democratic living in the modern world. The procedure of each experiment employed a reflectively oriented method of teaching based on the field theory of learning. The problems for class study arose from springboards, which consisted of either generalizations or contradictory statements found by students and teacher in readings in the textbook. Dewey's steps in a complete act of thought, as applied by Hunt and Metcalf to the teaching of the social studies, were used as a frame of reference by the experimenters in both the process of teaching and the evaluation of results. Models of the reflective process based on those steps were constructed and used. In three of the four experiments, a control group termed Group B was taught conventionally, with instruction directed primarily toward factual learning.

An illustration of such teaching procedure reported by one of the experimenters is in a study of the conflict between the United States and Mexico which led to war. For stimulation and direction of insightful reading and similar discussion preceding and following the reading, some thought questions were posed. Examples are:

---

1. What does "the eyes of the United States turned toward the Southwest" mean?
2. Was the attitude of those who would take Mexican territory consistent with the idea that we should be honest and with the idea that man has a right to his own property?
3. Since Mexico had a law against slavery, how would you justify the bringing of slaves into that country by settlers from the United States?
4. Why would the Mexican government expect settlers to obey laws that the setters did not help to establish?[56]

These questions are distinctly different in function from questions such as the following: "Who was the leader of the first United States settlers in

[54] Ibid., pp. 197-198. See also R. D. Van Scotter, "A Prescription for Teaching Social Studies in the Seventies," Social Studies (April, 1972), 63, pp. 170-176.
[55] B. G. Massialas, The Indiana Experiments in Inquiry: Social Studies, Bureau of Educational Studies and Testing, Indiana University, Bloomington, 1963.
[56] Ibid., pp. 43-44.

Texas?" and "When did the United States acquire Texas?" Efficient use of thought questions to stimulate and direct critical reading and discussion of cultures in conflict may help students to evolve two significant generalizations: (1) that cultural contacts result in varying degrees of conflict and (2) that when two cultures come into conflict, one will gain control over the other or the two will merely exchange ideas and customs and a composite culture will gradually emerge. These generalizations may provide students with insights into causes and resolutions of hostility and strife among some nations of today.[57]

One significant conclusion from the Indiana experiments is that students instructed in classes in the social studies using the problem-solving approach acquire as much information as those taught with emphasis on acquisition of facts. Moreover, the information is meaningful and useful for attacks on personal and social problems in present-day society. Not less important is the conclusion that students, receiving instruction directed purposefully toward development in the skills of critical thinking, showed significant improvement in those skills. Massialas listed the skills or processes to which the experimental group was much more sensitive than the control group:

In terms of the model of critical thinking as defined by the writers, students in Group A demonstrated a relatively high sensitivity to skills, abilities and processes relating to (a) hypothesizing, (b) defining and clarifying, (c) enlarging the perspective, (d) identifying and probing assumptions, (e) drawing logical implications, (f) producing relevant information, (g) generalizing and distinguishing among different kinds of generalizations, (h) recognizing material fallacies in propositions, and (i) relating propositions to one another in terms of consistence and extent of explanatory power. . . . Very few of the above skills were identifiable in student demonstrable behavior within Group B.[58]

A Final Suggestion to the Doubting Teacher

The teacher who still fears that problem-solving procedure prevents satisfactory preparation for a standardized test at the conclusion of the course may still teach by that procedure until the test is near. The interest and meaning generated by problem solving will improve the reaction of students to any concluding teaching concentrated on acquisition of facts for the test. The closeness of the test is also a motivating factor. There is little reason for drilling on facts three or four months in advance of an examination.

The results of reflective, democratically oriented teaching depend largely on the teacher. Educational philosophy is a determining factor: if the

---

57 Ibid., p. 45.
58 Ibid., p. 33.

teacher believes strongly in the desirability and possibility of that kind of instruction, ways of overcoming difficulties will come to light. Along with the students, the teacher will improve in understanding and accepting the method because of the variety of interesting and meaningful experiences it brings with it. Among the discoveries the teacher will make is the necessity for increased alertness to the different needs of youths, to the climate of the classroom, and to the ways the course relates to problems of home, community, and nation. Also, the teacher will discover how to direct challenging and critical discussion devoted not to airing prejudices but to probing basic assumptions and supporting assertions or conclusions. The democratically, scientifically minded teacher learns how to achieve results comparable to those revealed by the experiments on problem-solving teaching.

QUESTIONS AND ACTIVITIES

1. How does the Gestalt or field view of learning support a shift from the rule-drill procedure to the inductive-experience procedure in teaching the language arts?

2. Interview teachers of English or social studies to find out how they individualize instruction and how they evaluate student learning using that approach.

3. Compile a list of the essential characteristics of an effective approach to teaching oral and written expression and reading and literature. How well are these characteristics supported by learning theory? Discuss your listing with other English majors, experienced English teachers, the class, and/or high-school English students.

4. In view of the findings of research on the usefulness of formal grammar for improvement of English composition, state and support your position on teaching grammar in English courses. Debate your position in class or create a survey containing the points in your position, and submit it to experienced English teachers for sampling and analysis.

5. Have a panel of language majors, language teachers, and/or foreign language students from a high school evaluate the audio-lingual emphasis in comparison with the grammar-reading emphasis in the teaching of a modern foreign language.

6. Point out differences between how a student in high school may learn a modern foreign language and the way a young child may learn the language.

7. In a small group composed of English and social studies teacher candidates, discuss ways these two groups might work cooperatively to improve instruction in both subjects.

8. Apply the general objectives of education, as given in Chapter 3, to teaching social studies. Discuss this in class.

9. It is well known that courses in social studies often have little effect on improvement of values and thought processes of the students. What do you think are the causes and the remedies? You might want to interview both experienced social studies teachers and/or social studies students in a high school to discover their ideas.

10. Give an illustration of how you would direct students in taking the steps of scientific or reflective thinking in the study of a particular problem in a social study. Then make a video tape of this illustration or a mini-portion of it and invite feedback from class members and/or the instructor.

11. Demonstrate the differences between the conventional use of a topic from a textbook and its use to provide springboards in democratic reflective teaching.

12. Have a few students volunteer to demonstrate how a lecture presentation can be used for problem raising—creating questions and dichotomies in students' minds as a means of encouraging reflective inquiry —rather than simply to present facts and content.

13. Have a small group of students select a topic, interest, event, or curiosity from English or social studies and prepare a bulletin board display that will motivate students to seek additional information related to the motivational event.

SELECTED REFERENCES

Language Arts

Association for Supervision and Curriculum Development, *Changing Curriculum: Modern Foreign Language,* National Education Association, Washington, D.C., 1968.

Burton, D. L., and J. S. Simmons, *Teaching English in Today's High Schools —Selected Reading,* 2nd ed., Holt, Rinehart, and Winston, New York, 1970.

Cohen, S. A., *Teach Them All to Read: Theory, Methods, and Materials for Teaching the Disadvantaged,* Random House, New York, 1969.

Conlin, D. A., *A Modern Approach to Teaching English,* paper, American Book, New York, 1968.

Daigon, A., and R. T. Laconte, eds., *Challenge and Change in the Teaching of English*, paper, Allyn and Bacon, Boston, 1971.

Daly, M. E., *Teaching English in the Secondary School*, Macmillan, New York, 1969.

Dechant, E. V., *Improving the Teaching of Reading*, 2nd ed., Prentice-Hall, Englewood Cliffs, New Jersey, 1970.

Dechant, E. V., *Reading Improvement in the Secondary School*, Prentice-Hall, Englewood Cliffs, New Jersey, 1973.

Duker, S., *Individualized Reading: Readings*, Scarecrow, Metuchen, New Jersey, 1970.

Grittner, F. M., *Teaching Foreign Languages*, Harper and Row, New York, 1969.

Hipple, T. W., *Teaching English in Secondary Schools*, Macmillan, New York, 1973.

Hook, J. N., *The Teaching of High School English*, 4th ed., Ronald, New York, 1972.

Jenkinson, E. B., and P. B. Daghlian, eds., *Teaching Literature in Grades Ten through Twelve*, paper, Indiana University, Bloomington, 1968.

Jenkinson, E. B., and J. S. Hawley, eds., *Teaching Literature in Grades Seven through Nine*, paper, Indiana University, Bloomington, 1967.

Jenkinson, E. B., and D. A. Seybold, *Writing as a Process of Discovery: Some Instructive Theme Assignments for Grades Five through Twelve*, Indiana University, Bloomington, 1970.

Loban, W., and others, *Teaching Language and Literature, Grades Seven through Twelve*, 2nd ed., Harcourt, Brace and World, New York, 1969.

Malmstrom, J., and J. Lee, *Teaching English Linguistically: Principles and Practices for High School*, Appleton-Century-Crofts, New York, 1970.

Marchwardt, A. H., *Linguistics and the Teaching of English*, Indiana University, Bloomington, 1968.

Morsey, R. J., *Improving English Instruction*, 2nd ed., Allyn and Bacon, Boston, 1969.

National Education Association, *Language Laboratory and Language Learning*, rev. ed., National Education Association, Washington, D. C., 1967.

National Society for the Study of Education, *Innovation and Change in Reading Instruction*, Sixty-seventh Yearbook, Part II, University of Chicago, Chicago, 1968, Chaps. 4-5.

Shepherd, D. L., *Comprehensive High School Reading Methods*, Charles E. Merrill, Columbus, Ohio, 1973.

Strang, R. M., *Diagnostic Teaching of Reading*, McGraw-Hill, New York, 1969.

White, M. E., *High Interest–Easy Reading for Junior and Senior High School Students*, 2nd ed., Citation, New York, 1972.

Witty, P. A., and others, *The Teaching of Reading: A Developmental Process*, D. C. Heath, Boston, 1966.

Wolfe, D. M., *Creative Ways to Teach English: Grades 7-12*, 2nd ed., Odyssey, New York, 1966.

Social Studies

Banks, J. A., and A. A. Clegg, Jr., *Teaching Strategies for the Social Studies: Inquiry, Valuing, and Decision Making*, Addison-Wesley, Reading, Massachusetts, 1973.

Brubaker, D. L., *Innovations in the Social Studies: Teachers Speak for Themselves*, paper, Thomas Y. Crowell, New York, 1968.

Brubaker, D. L., *Secondary Social Studies for the Seventies: Planning for Instruction*, paper, Thomas Y. Crowell, New York, 1973.

Clark, L. H., *Teaching Social Studies in Secondary Schools*, Macmillan, New York, 1973.

Estvan, F. J., *Social Studies in a Changing World: Curriculum and Instruction*, Harcourt, Brace and World, New York, 1968.

Fenton, E., *New Social Studies for the Slow Learner*, Holt, Rinehart and Winston, New York, 1970.

Fenton, E., *Teaching the New Social Studies in Secondary Schools: An Inductive Approach*, Holt, Rinehart and Winston, New York, 1966.

Gardner, W. E., and F. A. Johnson, eds., *Social Studies in Secondary Schools: A Book of Readings*, Allyn and Bacon, Boston, 1970.

Hunt, M. P., and L. E. Metcalf, *Teaching High School Social Studies*, 2nd ed., Harper and Row, New York, 1968.

Keller, C. W., *Involving Students in the New Social Studies*, Little, Brown, Boston, 1974.

Kenworthy, L. S., *Guide to Social Studies Teaching in Secondary Schools*, 2nd ed., Wadsworth, Belmont, California, 1966.

Krug, M. M., and others, eds., *The New Social Studies: Analysis of Theory and Materials*, F. E. Peacock, Itasca, Illinois, 1970.

Massialas, B. G., and C. B. Cox, *Inquiry in Social Studies*, McGraw-Hill, New York, 1966.

Massialas, B. G., and F. R. Smith, *New Challenges in the Social Studies*, Wadsworth, Belmont, California, 1965.

Morgan, J. C., and J. E. Schreiber, *How to Ask Questions*, National Education Association, Washington, D. C., 1969.

National Council for the Social Studies, *Effective Thinking in the Social Studies*, paper, National Education Association, Washington, D. C., 1967.

Oliver, D. W., and J. P. Shaver, *Teaching Public Issues in the High School*, Houghton Mifflin, Boston, 1966.

Sistrunk, W. E., and R. C. Maxson, *A Practical Approach to Secondary Social Studies*, William C. Brown, Dubuque, Iowa, 1972.

Smith, F. R., and C. B. Cox, *New Strategies and Curriculum in Social Studies*, paper, Rand McNally, Chicago, 1969.

CHAPTER 8

Educators recognize, at least in theory, a significant relationship between science and mathematics. Mathematics is an essential tool in science, and science in turn provides a method and some content for mathematics. This mutual relationship becomes obvious when instruction is made quantitative in science and concrete and investigative in mathematics. It is especially evident when each subject is taught inductively. Hence teaching in these two distinct disciplines may appropriately be considered in the same chapter.

TEACHING SCIENCE

Roots of the Current Trend

Science in secondary education is in a period of accelerated transition. It is moving away from regarding science courses mainly as bodies of ready-made subject matter didactically taught and toward thinking of these courses as knowledge to be acquired through the student's own use of the scientific method. There is both growing concern about the process, as well as the product, of learning and increasing recognition that the basic objective is to develop in all students the attitudes and habits of the scientist.

This trend in teaching science has its roots in the first quarter of this century. A few leading writers showed how instruction definitely could be improved by gearing it to the needs of different students and the demands of modern society and of the democratic ideal. They believed the student should become actively involved in observing, investigating, and experimenting and, thereby, learn to organize acquired knowledge. Such an approach could develop in the student the scientific spirit and procedure.

SCIENCE AND MATHEMATICS

These former writers recognized that the distinguishing feature of science is its method of inquiry and discovery. Science, of course, is not the only field with organization or system. Yet scientific knowledge is uniquely organized with reference to successful scientific inquiry. "The more one emphasizes organization as a mark of science, then, the more one is committed to the recognition of the primacy of method in the definition of science. For method defines the kind of organization in virtue of which science is science."[1] In applying the method of science to the method of education, Dewey added:

There is a strong temptation to assume that presenting subject matter in its perfected form provides a royal road to learning. What is more natural than to suppose that the immature may be saved time and energy and be protected from needless error, by commencing where competent inquirers left off. . . . Pupils begin their study of science with texts in which the subject is organized into topics according to the order of the specialist. Technical concepts, with their definitions, are introduced at the outset. Laws are introduced at a very early stage, with at best a few indications of the way in which they were arrived at. The pupils learn a "science" instead of learning the scientific way of treating the familiar material of ordinary experience.[2]

The chronological method which begins with the experience of the learner and develops from that the proper modes of scientific treatment is often called the "psychological" method in distinction from the logical method of the expert or specialist. The apparent loss of time involved is more than made up for by the superior understanding and vital interest secured. What the pupil learns he at least understands. Moreover, by following, in connection with problems selected from the material of ordinary acquaintance, the methods by which scientific men have reached their perfected knowledge, he gains independent power to deal with material within his range, and avoids the mental confusion and intellectual distaste attendant on studying matter whose meaning is only symbolic.[3]

This idea of having the student follow the learning process of the scientist was applied by Twiss to the laboratory. He pointed out that in an ideally arranged course in science, students do not go to the laboratory to do stunts, to "perform experiments," to verify laws, or to fix principles in the mind. Rather they go there as scientists to engage in methodical investigation of a scientific problem; they observe, experiment, and discover. "A project for the laboratory should provide the means of answering some question or questions that constitute essential steps in the solution of some problem that is significant to the students."[4]

Such ideas on how to improve science teaching, as expressed by some educators in the first quarter of this century, had little effect on practice in secondary schools. Undoubtedly, some teachers did not become ac-

1 J. Dewey, Democracy and Education, Macmillan, New York, 1916, p. 224.
2 Ibid., p. 257.
3 Ibid., p. 257-258.
4 G. R. Twiss, A Textbook in the Principles of Science Teaching, Macmillan, New York, 1917, p. 131.

quainted with the ideas and many others were content with conventional practice and were unwilling or unable to overcome obstacles to improvement. There were reports of how individuals had experimented on teaching science scientifically, with encouraging results. Before the dreams of those pioneer educators could come true, however, a combination of favorable forces was necessary.

One of the chief forces toward the improvement of science instruction in recent decades has been increased international competition, economic and political. The competition was heightened by the launching of *Sputnik*. For domestic as well as international reasons, we have become increasingly apprehensive about the quality of scientists and engineers for industry and of science teachers for schools. There has been growing concern about the preparation of youths for citizenship and vocation in a complex, technological society. Gradually, too, a purposive-cognitive conception of learning seems to have permeated the minds of many educators. All these forces combined to produce marked improvement in science instruction through a new school science.

The New Sciences

In the early 1960s, groups of scientists and educators, supported by the National Science Foundation, produced new school sciences in the four areas of physics, chemistry, biology, and earth science. One or more curriculum study groups covered each of these four sciences. The groups designed textbooks, laboratory manuals, teachers' guides, films, and other material aids. The evolving courses were tried in thousands of high schools and were revised on the basis of the resulting suggestions.

Although each of the curriculum study groups worked independently, an impressive similarity of educational ideas and practices prevailed. Their common purpose was to produce courses to promote learning current scientific knowledge and the scientific method. The new sciences are different from the conventional ones in content and method. Only part of the subject matter of a new course is new; but it is organized to develop themes or lines of thought, to provide for relationships, unity, and meaning in learning. The method of teaching and learning is that of the scientist. The laboratory activities are designed to be less descriptive and illustrative but more quantitative and investigative than formerly. A way of teaching consistent with the aims and content of the new courses is required. The new movement provides not only for up-to-date subject matter but also the method of problem solving, open-ended experimentation, and reflective thinking.[5]

[5] P. D. Hurd and M. B. Rowe, "Science in the Secondary School," *Review of Educational Research* (June, 1964), 34, pp. 286-297; J. W. Renner, "Why Change Science Teaching?" *School Science and Mathematics* (May, 1964), 64, pp. 413-420; and B. Glass, *The Timely and the Timeless: The Interrelationships of Science, Education, and Society*, Basic Books, New York, 1970, pp. 13-38.

It is important to note here that results from the new sciences depend largely on the attitudes, understandings, and skills of the teacher. The teacher must demonstrate the spirit and behavior of the scientist in the laboratory. It is well known that many science teachers are unaccustomed to directing students in genuine problem solving and research. These teachers are inclined to teach the new sciences almost entirely through the conventional process of explanation, demonstration, and memorization. In some instances, therefore, unimpressive results have stemmed not from the new courses but from the deficiencies of the teachers.[6]

Nearly all teachers of science in secondary schools need special preparation for implementation of the new science curriculums. This preparation includes gaining a functional understanding of what is new to them in the teaching procedure as well as in the subject matter. Every teacher may find specific, helpful information among the curriculum materials produced by the National Science Foundation study group.[7] When, as often happens, however, these materials alone do not suffice, some teachers must additionally attend a kind of workshop. In large schools a teacher well prepared to use the new course may instruct others in the science department. In fact, it is possibe for some to teach themselves —those well acquainted with current scientific knowledge and experienced in teaching conventional courses scientifically.

In adopting the new sciences, modifications usually are necessary. This is because of conditions peculiar to a school. Skillful teachers working toward a common, worthwhile goal may be using different but equally effective approaches or techniques, as some of the NSF curriculum study groups have recognized. As we will see, the biology group designed three approaches, and the chemistry group, two. Indeed, some teachers may choose to retain conventional courses but, in the process of teaching, to employ some of the suggestions of content and method from the new courses. Whatever may be the nature or extent of adoption of the new sciences, thorough knowledge and critical implementation are essential.

The Aims

For the school sciences, designated as either new or conventional, the basic aims as specified or implied by current writers are (1) acquisition of meaningful and useful knowledge of natural phenomena and (2) development in acceptance, understanding, and application of the scientific method. These two aims recognize science as a particular body of subject

---

6 R. Janu, "The New Science Curriculums: How to Get Your District Ready," *School Management* (June, 1963), 7, pp. 58-69; and D. E. Newton, "Educating Teachers for the New Science Curriculum: a Dilemma," *School Science and Mathematics* (January, 1971), 71, pp. 17-23.

7 For information about availability of materials, write J. R. Major and A. H. Livermore, AAAS, 1515 Massachusetts Avenue, Northwest, Washington, D. C.

matter (the product) and as a method of inquiry (the process).

An understanding of the significance of the first aim requires seeing the relationship of scientific knowlege and technological knowledge. The two are not the same but are closely related, each contributing to the advancement of the other—as we saw in the discovery of additional information about the atom in science research laboratories preceding invention of the atomic bomb. This does not imply that technology may not provide valuable content in a science course. On the contrary, one of the best ways to help students enjoy and understand science is to encourage them in analyzing technological products of science. Yet, in a science course the primary purpose is to teach science.

It is important to recognize further that scientific knowledge consists of related ideas organized around laws and major concepts resulting from scientific inquiry. It is not an aggregation of bits of information to be learned mainly through memorization and verification. It is a system of findings, discovered facts, generalizations, and concepts, which are best learned using the scientific method of inquiry.

The second basic aim, development in the scientific method, includes developing in students the characteristics of the scientist or the scientifically minded person. Expressed as attitudes or habits, these are:

1. *Curiosity*. This characteristic consists of desire to come to grips with problems and to discover cause-and-effect relationships and what is true. It is the driving force, interest, or motivation necessary for persistent engagement in scientific investigation.
2. *Suspended judgment*. Without this quality persons "jump at conclusions." Possessing it, they are willing to withhold decisions or postpone acceptance or rejection of a conclusion until all necessary data have been acquired and adequate testing has been done.
3. *Open-mindedness*. This characteristic does not mean that the individuals must be without opinions or must refrain from drawing tentative conclusions. Instead, they hold beliefs on the basis of all the best evidence. However, there is a willingness to reconsider and change ideas in the light of new evidence.
4. *Objectivity or single-mindedness*. Unity of purpose constitutes this quality. In research there is avoidance of trying to serve two masters: objective pursuit of scientific truth and the prejudicial desires of oneself or others. Instead the investigator possesses intellectual integrity, honesty, and sincerity. Specifically, there is discount of data furnished by those having vested interests, economic or social.[8]

---

[8] See R. E. Haney, "The Development of Scientific Attitudes," *Science Teacher* (December, 1964), 31, pp. 33-35; J. Dewey, *Democracy*, pp. 203-211.

Further analysis of the second objective suggests that students develop the competencies of the scientific investigator. Some of these competencies are:

1. *Ability to locate and define problems in complicated situations.* The neat, ready-made problems of the typical textbook do not suffice. Young people need experiences of sensing and expressing problems in a context of irrelevances and false issues.
2. *Competency in analyzing and outlining logical steps in the solution of problems.* This may be developed as individuals and groups work on problems, particularly through the questions, criticisms, and challenges of class discussion. It may involve assisting the students to examine their basic assumptions and to detect the logical or illogical conclusions stemming therefrom. They may thereby recognize the difference between rational and "wishful" thinking.
3. *Ability to recognize and obtain relevant and sound information.* This involves distinguishing between valid and invalid data—determining which sources of information are authoritative and dependable and which are directed by ulterior motives.
4. *Comprehension of extensive usefulness of science.* This involves an increasing understanding of science as an efficient, reliable method of inquiry, with recognition of its potential usefulness in all areas and also its limitations in problems of human relationships.[9]

General Science

The two major objectives just considered are as imperative for general science as for the other courses in science. More students enroll in general science than in any other science course in high school. For many of them it is the last formal study of science. Furthermore, their attitudes and habits may be changed more easily at this time than at a later age. The course is one in which the potential dropout, along with other students, may begin a lasting interest in science. For these reasons general science should be offered in each grade of the junior high school.

Leaders differ on how to improve general science. Some believe that the teacher should organize instruction around central themes, concepts, or generalizations—like instruction in the new science courses of the senior high school. Others would organize around current ecological problems, believing that the method of teaching must involve students in the use of the concept or generalization while they are in the process of discovering

9 See R. W. Burnett, *Teaching Science in the Secondary School,* Holt, Rinehart and Winston, New York, 1957, pp. 34-35; W. A. Thurber and A. T. Collette, *Teaching Science in Today's Secondary Schools,* 3rd ed., Allyn and Bacon, Boston, 1968, Chap. 1; N. S. Washton, *Teaching Science Creatively in Secondary Schools,* W. B. Saunders, Philadelphia, 1967, pp. 42-43; and D. Vitrogan, "Characteristics of a Generalized Attitude Toward Science," *School Science and Mathematics* (February, 1969), 69, pp. 150-158.

it. Studying a central theme or principle of ecology usually requires experience in observing adverse environmental conditions. This ecological approach is especially helpful to immature students in the junior high school. It is a valuable approach also in the senior high school, whether the course is traditional or new. The enterprising teacher, dedicated to meeting the needs of students in a perplexing, technological society, will find ways to help students raise questions as they study the environment and then turn to science for the answers.[10]

There is a need for a sequence of science courses in junior high school in which the teacher and the students may concentrate on a limited number of topics, units, or problems as they draw on biological and physical science. Yager reported an example of such a course constructed in a three-year sequence in the junior high school of the University of Iowa. The seventh-grade course was organized around the concept of matter, the content consisting largely of chemistry and geology. The offering in the eighth grade concentrated on life matter, requiring study chiefly of biological science. In the ninth grade the sequence was completed with a study of specific factors affecting matter; the course was entitled "energy and space" and consisted mainly of physics and astronomy.[11] These courses provided for relational, insightful learning.

A one-year course for the eighth or ninth grade was constructed by the Secondary School Science Project, commonly called the "Princeton Project." It was designed by some who worked on the Physical Science Study Committee for physics. This new general science course is based on the assumption that the student must be an investigator. It is organized around the theme of study of the physical world and it consists of many sequential investigations. For example, the study of matter does not begin by reading about the three states of matter. Instead, various visual experiences with matter challenge the student to discover its nature. In the process three states of matter emerge. "He then investigates properties of various materials and develops a notion of the difference between a 'pure' substance and an impure substance (mixture)."[12]

A general science course organized chiefly around earth sciences has been adopted for the ninth grade in several states, particularly New York, Pennsylvania, and New Jersey. It was designed to provide "solid" subject matter in science between the general science of the preceding years and the offerings in science of the senior high school. Schools adopting the

10 M. Harmin and others, "Teaching Science with a Focus on Values," Science Teacher (January, 1970), 37, pp. 16-21; A. D. Roberts and O. E. Dyrli, "Environmental Education," Clearing House (April, 1971), 45, pp. 451-455.
11 R. E. Yager, "A Junior High School Sequence in Science," School Science and Mathematics (December, 1963), 63, pp. 719-725. See also N. S. Washton, Teaching Science Creatively in Secondary Schools, W. B. Saunders, Philadelphia, 1967, pp. 74-76.
12 B. M. Berlin, "New General Science Curriculum Features Direct Experimentation," Chicago Schools Journal (November, 1964), 46, p. 65. For teaching materials, write to Secondary School Science Project, Princeton University, Princeton, New Jersey.

course may draw on the textbook, teacher's guide, or laboratory manual and use visual materials recommended by the Earth Science Curriculum Project (ESCP) under the general theme of investigating the earth.

The ESCP approach stresses the concept of science as inquiry. The written materials for the earth science course are not merely collections of current scientific facts to be acquired in the conventional way. Rather, they are designed to produce learning through active investigation. For example, the student is not told the number of miles in the sun's diameter but is assisted in the use of simple visual experiences to discover its length. Examples of thought questions that may be raised at certain points in the course are "How do we know that the earth is spherical?" "What does this experiment show?" and "What further investigation does it suggest?"[13]

Unfortunately, teaching in general science has not been well directed toward the objectives of science. Frequently the attempt has been to cover too much ground without adequate provision for depth and understanding. Often the emphasis has been on recalling bits of information in either oral recitation or on written exams, to the neglect of scientific attitudes and competencies. Most of the classes have been too large for the necessary quantity and quality of laboratory experiences, the average size being above 30. Especially disturbing is that only about 30 percent of the classes are taught by full-time science teachers.[14]

Some valuable suggestions about how to create real scientific investigation in the laboratory of the junior high school were given by some science teachers in Michigan:

1. In the use of all teaching materials, the teacher must be resourceful. He must be able to draw on sources outside as well as within the school and be skillful in use of thought questions to secure the reactions of students to their experiences.
2. The laboratory experiences should be open-ended; the students ought not to receive answers to the questions in advance of the laboratory activity.
3. Direct the experiences toward solution of a problem and development of an idea. The problem should be clear to the students and be accepted as their own, so that they may relate all applicable procedures to it.
4. Provide a minimum of directions. As far as possible, let the student acquire the needed information as he engages in the research.[15]

13 J. H. Shea, "The Earth Science Curriculum Project: A Progress Report," *Science Teacher* (February, 1965), 32, pp. 43-45. See also R. B. Sund and L. W. Trowbridge, *Teaching Science by Inquiry in the Secondary School*, Charles E. Merrill, Columbus, Ohio, 1967, pp. 56-61. For teaching materials, write to R. L. Heller, Earth Science Curriculum Project, Post Office Box 1559, Boulder, Colorado.
14 C. H. Heimler, "General Science in a State of Flux," *School Science and Mathematics* (December, 1964), 64, pp. 755-764.
15 W. C. Van Deventer, "Michigan Prepares Project on Junior High School Science," *Science Teacher* (November, 1964), 31, pp. 29-30.

To these four suggestions a fifth one may be added: provision of voluntary, individualized laboratory activities. This is required by the differences in interests, needs, and abilities of a class. It is one of the best ways to make science meaningful and interesting to the slow learner, the potential dropout, and the capable student. It can be used well, of course, only in classes of moderate size.

Biology

Usually general science in the ninth grade is followed by biology in the tenth grade. If the general science course draws mainly from the physical sciences, the students are thereby provided a basis for the study of biology. It is recognized by scientists that until developments in the physical sciences evolved adequate, useful generalizations about matter and energy, biology could be little except a description of plants and animals. Teachers of biology are challenged to incorporate new knowledge from both the physical and the biological sciences, into the laboratory sessions, to make their teaching truly scientific and effective.

Conventional biology in high school reflects few of the recent advances of biology in research laboratories. There is a gap between the biology of the scientist and that of many textbooks and teachers. This led a group of scientists and educators in the early 1960s to produce a program and appropriate materials for teaching contemporary biology through scientific inquiry in the secondary school. The American Institute of Biological Sciences, supported by the National Science Foundation, established the Biological Sciences Curriculum Study (BSCS),[16] whose aim was to place biological knowledge in its fullest modern perspective. The study group was concerned not only with the subject matter presented under the title of biology but also with the method of presentation. It advocated focus on the continuous search for meaning rather than on acquisition of ready-made ideas. It condemned the cookbook type of exercise, mere naming of structure, and answering questions only by use of the textbook. The key to good instruction was seen in meaningful laboratory and field study involving sincere attacks on real problems.[17]

The curriculum materials and teaching aids produced by the BSCS are very valuable. Materials incorporating the advance in biology through research laboratories had been quite limited in secondary schools. Furthermore, the typical teacher had been educated in biology about 1940 and was not using the laboratory approach in teaching the subject. Accordingly,

16 National Research Council, *Guidelines for Development of Programs in Science Instruction,* National Academy of Sciences, Washington, D. C., 1963, pp. 23-24. See also P. W. Richard, "Experimental Individualized BSCS Biology," *Science Teacher* (February, 1969), 36, pp. 53-54 ff.
17 National Research Council, *Guidelines,* pp. 24-27. See also A. B. Grobman, *The Changing Classroom: The Role of the Biological Science Curriculum Study,* Doubleday, Garden City, New York, 1969.

the study group produced up-to-date textbooks, laboratory manuals, and teachers' guides. The materials provided for three approaches to teaching biology, designated as the Blue, Green, and Yellow versions. Books were bound in these three colors according to the version. Although the approaches and emphases of the three versions differ, there is considerable overlapping of content and method.[18]

The Green Version lays special emphasis on ecology. The central concern in this version is the interaction of populations, communities, and the world biome. The Yellow Version focuses on the cellular approach to plants, animals, and microorganisms. The Blue Version emphasizes the molecular and cellular concepts. It treats most of the topics appearing in the Yellow and the Green versions, but the level of presentation is somewhat more advanced and there is concentration on teaching biology to illustrate the methods of scientific inquiry.[19]

The chapter headings of the three textbook versions, in comparison with those of conventional textbooks, indicate the differences between the two types. The emphasis in the BSCS books is on unity, relationships, and broad understanding; for example, the interdependence of structure and function and the relationship of organism to environment. Furthermore, the manual of each version differs from the ordinary manual in that it does not include blanks to be filled in and the laboratory work is not mainly illustrative but is focused on inquiry.

The use of the new biology in a secondary school may be seen in an example of the Green Version approach reported by a teacher of the Barringer High School, Newark, New Jersey.

The first unit is ecology. We lead into it by observing how some familiar animals respond to changes in their environment. Because insects are easily collected in September, we present them on the first or second day of school as our first laboratory animal. . . .

Each group of students is given two jars that contain several ants and told to write CONTROL on one jar. The importance of this jar is emphasized throughout the lesson and in the discussion that follows. The laboratory sheet guides the class into testing the insects for reactions to environmental changes in temperature, light intensity, the presence of food, the presence of an unusual substance (alcohol). . . . Each student observes and records results and is encouraged to express himself in clear, simple language. When the results are reported to the class, a great deal of discussion evolves, even if occasionally no response is observed in a given situation. We have found that some ants prefer potato chips to bread crumbs or sugar. . . . On one occasion we had collected larva along with the ants from a particular colony and observed the adults' preoccupation with their offspring took precedence over other responses. Each of these lessons took

[18] For material of the Blue Version, write to Houghton Mifflin, Boston; of the Green Version, Rand McNally, Chicago; and of the Yellow Version, Harcourt, Brace Jovanovich, New York. For materials designed particularly for low ability learners, write to Holt, Rinehart and Winston, New York.

[19] National Research Council, *Guidelines*, p. 25; Janu, "The New Science Curriculums," p. 60.

an unexpected turn, but they made good learning situations. They were open-ended investigations that could, if the interest was there, provide work for more than a few days.[20]

All the textbooks and other materials for the three versions of the new biology provide valuable suggestions for any teacher of biology in a secondary school. In a school where necessary steps for a shift to the new course are being taken, the materials may assist the teacher in the choice and use of one version or a combination of the three. If a school is retaining the conventional course and textbook, the materials provide current content in biology and help in teaching it scientifically. In any situation, teachers need access and acquaintance with the program and teaching aids of the BSCS group. How they use these materials depends on their different attitudes and abilities and the situations in the schools and communities.

Results from use of the new biology courses have been pleasing. According to Grobman, investigations demonstrate that BSCS students gained more in inquiry-oriented behavior than did control students. He added that for evaluation of outcomes from those courses, factual tests alone are inadequate, tending to direct both teacher and students away from a teaching-learning process centered on problem solving and discovery.[21] Accordingly, the teacher must rely chiefly on observations of the student's performances in laboratory and library research and in class discussions, supplemented by well-constructed, problem-solving essay examinations. We point this out in Chapter 15.

Physical Sciences—Chemistry and Physics

In a majority of secondary schools, general science and biology are followed by chemistry in the eleventh grade and physics in the twelfth. The first two courses are frequently required, but the last two are elected. This fact along with the increase in dropouts near the end of the tenth year, causes relatively few students to take chemistry and physics. Those electing either course are likely to have interest and ability above the average.

In some high schools chemistry and physics have been fused together into a new course called "physical sciences," which is offered in one or both of the last two years. Some students have schedules that permit their electing only one year of science in either the junior or the senior year. It may be better for most of them to take a course which includes both chemistry and physics rather than only one of the two. Furthermore, some science teachers believe that fusion of these traditionally separate courses contributes to learning through sensing relationships and the development of understanding.

---

[20] E. Liberson and E. Fabiano, "Teaching Biology to Non-Academic Students," *Science Teacher* (November. 1965). 32, p. 30.
[21] Grobman, *The Changing Classroom*, p. 136.

The integrated course may consist of broad topics, themes, units, or problems involving some study of content from earth science as well as chemistry and physics. Since all the ground of the conventional courses cannot be covered in the fused course, some teachers effectively use the "block and gap" method of choosing the content. They select from the available subject matter the essential areas and deal with them in some depth, recognizing and leaving out inconsequential gaps in the process. Some of these teachers also organize the course around ecological problems.

In some high schools the physical sciences course has been a poor substitute for separate chemistry and physics courses but, in others, satisfactory results have been reported. An example of a report is from Barringer High School, previously cited. The students in physical sciences showed on tests that in knowledge of content they compared favorably with students in chemistry and physics. Moreover, in classroom and laboratory activities they showed unusual interest, resulting in their development in the spirit and method of the scientist.[22]

Unfortunately, many high schools do not have a teacher sufficiently educated in both chemistry and physics to do a good job of teaching both courses together or separately. Ideally, every teacher of science in a secondary school should have enough preparation in both of these physical sciences to draw freely on each to put meaning into the other and to teach science scientifically. In some schools, team teaching by the physics teacher and the chemistry teacher may be required. Whether the course is taught by one or more teachers, the focus must be on providing students with sufficient laboratory experiences and thought questions to help them form functional concepts and generalizations.

The New Chemistry

Chemistry in school has lagged behind chemistry in research laboratories. In the 1950s leaders among science educators noted that chemistry as taught in the typical classroom lacked adequate provision for contemporary knowledge and for the scientific method of acquiring and organizing the knowledge. There was too much emphasis on memorization of facts, formulas, processes, and compounds without development of unifying concepts and a feeling for science as an open-ended search for truth. Most of the entries in notebooks required only perusal of the textbook, without reference to real research in the laboratory.[23]

In an effort to modernize both the content and the method of the chemistry course, some chemists and educators met during the summer

---

22 M. R. Lerner, "Integrated Science: Physics and Chemistry," *Science Teacher* (February, 1964), 31, pp. 37-38; Washton, *Teaching Science*, pp. 194-196.
23 National Research Council, *Guidelines*, pp. 20-21.

of 1957 and produced a textbook and other materials for a new course known as the "Chemical Bond Approach." Two years later a similar group, known as the "Chemical Education Material Study" (CHEM Study), designed another new course. Both groups received support from the National Science Foundation. In addition to providing new content for the course, both groups advocated a method of teaching centered on student involvement in observing, experimenting, and discovering.[24] The emphasis of CHEM Study on the experimental approach to learning is indicated in the title *Chemistry—An Experimental Science* on the cover of the textbook, the teachers' guide, and the laboratory manual. It may be seen further in the preface or the foreword of each book and in the material throughout the book. An example of this emphasis, taken from the foreword of the textbook, is as follows:

The title, *Chemistry—An Experimental Science,* states the theme of this one year course. A clear and valid picture of the steps by which scientists proceed is carefully presented and repeatedly used. Observations and measurements lead to the development of unifying principles and then these principles are used to interrelate diverse phenomena. Heavy reliance is placed upon laboratory work so that chemical principles can be drawn directly from student experiences. Not only does this give a correct and nonauthoritarian view of the origin of chemical principles, but it gives maximum opportunity for discovery, the most exciting part of scientific activity. This experimental theme is supported by a number of films to provide experimental evidence that is needed but not readily available in the classroom because of inherent danger, rarity, or expense.

The initial set of experiments and the first few textbook chapters lay down a foundation for the course. The elements of scientific activity are immediately displayed, including the role of uncertainty. The atomic theory, the nature of matter in its various phases, and the mole concept are developed. Then an extended section of the course is devoted to the extraction of important chemical principles from relevant laboratory experience. The principles considered include energy, rate and equilibrium characteristics of chemical reactions, chemical periodicity, and chemical bonding in gases, liquids, and solids. The course concludes with several chapters of descriptive chemistry in which the applicability and worth of the chemical principles developed earlier are seen again and again.

There are a number of differences from more traditional courses. The most obvious are, of course, the shift of emphasis from descriptive chemistry toward chemical principles to represent properly the change of chemistry over the last two decades. Naturally, this reconstruction of the entire course gives a unique opportunity to delete obsolete terminology and out-moded materials. Less obvious but perhaps more important is the systematic development of the relationship between experiment and theory. Chemistry is gradually and logically unfolded, not presented as a collection of facts, dicta, and dogma. We hope to convey an awareness of the significance and capabilities of scientific activities that will help the future citizen assess calmly and wisely the growing impact of techno-

---

[24] National Research Council, *Guidelines,* pp. 21-23; Sund and Trowbridge, *Teaching Science,* pp. 52-53. A textbook using the CBA approach may be purchased from Webster Division, McGraw-Hill, St. Louis. For materials of CHEM Study, order from W. H. Freeman, San Francisco; Prentice-Hall, Englewood Cliffs, New Jersey; Houghton Mifflin, Boston; and D. C. Heath, Lexington, Massachusetts.

logical advances on his social environment. Finally, we have striven for closer continuity of subject matter and pedagogy between high school and modern freshman chemistry courses for those students who will continue their science training.[25]

The same point of emphasis in the teaching-learning process in chemistry is addressed to the student in the preface of the laboratory manual.

The CHEM Study course approaches the study of chemistry as an experimental science. It is a *laboratory-centered* course which:

1. features experiments which will permit you to make your own discoveries of the regularities and principles which unify chemistry and make it easier to understand,
2. emphasizes the making of careful observations and quantitative measurements under controlled experimental conditions,
3. stresses the preparation of well organized tables for recording data and the results of calculations so that you can more readily make deductions and recognize the regularities which exist,
4. uses challenging discussion questions which will help you to apply the principles observed in the experiments to new situations.[26]

In the teaching-learning process of the CHEM Study, experimentation, which often precedes reading and discussion, is used to produce as well as to answer questions. The student begins work in the laboratory and may not be introduced to the textbook until near the end of the first week. The first experiments initiate some of the fundamental ideas of concern to chemists. Briefly, the emphasis is on building concepts and principles, discovered, developed, and applied in an experimental setting.[27]

The New Physics

Like chemistry in high school, physics during the 1950s needed to be modernized in content and method. According to one group of leading scientists:

For years physicists in the United States have been uneasy about the state of secondary school physics teaching, about the caliber of teachers and their training, and about the materials contained in texts and laboratory manuals. Careful analysis of many texts, films and classes in physics provided the conclusion that little twentieth century physics was portrayed satisfactorily in the secondary school course. As mentioned earlier in the report, science has moved far beyond the stage of a search for absolute laws: leading to the contemporary view . . . that the process of science is an open-ended search best taught by allowing the student to participate in the search.[28]

25 G. C. Pimentel, *Chemistry—An Experimental Science*, W. H. Freeman, San Francisco, 1963, pp. vii-viii.
26 L. E. Malm, *Chemistry—An Experimental Science: Laboratory Manual*, W. H. Freeman, San Francisco, 1963, p. v.
27 Pimentel, *Chemistry*, Chap. 1-2.
28 National Research Council, *Guidelines*, p. 17.

This condition of instruction in physics led some physicists, with the support of the National Science Foundation, to meet in the summer of 1956 to plan a new course. The group, known as the Physical Science Study Committee, began work toward production of a new textbook, laboratory manual, equipment, films, and supplementary reading materials. They endeavored to present the old and the new of physics in an integrated manner, through the organization of all the subject matter around meaningful, major concepts. One such concept is that time, space, and matter cannot be separated.

As in the other new sciences, the laboratory is of primary importance. Experiments have been designated for more than fifty topical areas. The experiments are used to explore a field and to lead the student toward formation of concepts or generalizations. The Committee holds that experiments should be real, not mere accumulations of data to support a conclusion already known; they should be guided by previously developed ideas; they should encourage further work along suggested lines, leading to development of theoretical ideas; and, if possible, they should be performed by simple equipment which the student can use. Finally, in the descriptive material accompanying each experiment, the Committee "attempts to open doors for students, without leading them step by step to an inevitable conclusion or generalization. Prescriptions are avoided. The old pattern of experiment by filling in blank spaces or numbers in an equation is gone."[29]

Some Reports of Adoptions

Colby, director of junior and senior high-school science, Marblehead, Massachusetts, reported that they first tried PSSC physics, which is the most difficult new program. The enrollment increased markedly, so they discarded the conventional course and adopted the new one. They found, however, that it is not a course for a student of low ability, but they recognized that this also was true of traditional physics. Significantly, the students adapted more easily to the new subject matter and method than the teachers. The teachers had difficulty in casting out old notions and in grasping new objectives and procedures. This required reeducation and experience. After a time they learned that experimentation is of prime importance. They realized further that the students were learning what it is like to be a scientist, to make discoveries, to interpret data, and to act on their own.[30]

Another example of successful adoption of the experimental approach

[29] Ibid., p. 19. For materials, write to Jerrold Zacharias, Educational Services, Watertown, Massachusetts; and D. C. Heath, Lexington, Massachusetts.

[30] E. G. Colby, "The New Science Curriculums," *School Management* (November, 1964), 8, pp. 83-88.

to science teaching is in Portland, Oregon. In preparation for the transition, the teachers attended institutes and workshops to study how to use the revised science curriculum, how to make free use of the laboratory and library, and how to assist students to engage in investigation and discovery. They spent much time in developing a local science program, in producing appropriate activities, and in providing suitable materials for the activities. Through the use of well-equipped laboratories and libraries and audio-visual materials, the schools are employing the method of inquiry to assist students to acquire and apply scientific principles. The courses are adjusted to the differences of the students. Through experiences in the laboratory and exposure to colorful books and magazines in the library, students of various interests and abilities can begin to engage voluntarily in individual experimentation and reading.[31]

Whether a school professes to use new or conventional courses in science, it is important that both content and method meet the needs of youths in the modern world. In a society in which all young people are consumers of the technological products of science and many will be participants in the production process, it is fitting that teachers draw freely on those products to teach different students the concepts of science purposefully and meaningfully. The approach to learning activities, through observation and examination of technological products, is recommended for the gifted student as well as the potential dropout or the slow learner. To provide for a degree of differentiated instruction, some educators have proposed special classes, but they have not been found to be the only or the best solution. "There is considerable evidence indicating that a wide variety of students can follow the same general course, especially when they can make some choices of their own as to how deep or how fast they can go."[32]

As aids to such instruction, leaders in the teaching of science are recommending that laboratory facilities be improved and that simple equipment be used when possible. They also have advocated what some schools have accomplished, the lengthening of the laboratory period. In addition, some of them have proposed, and some teachers have practiced, having suitable books and magazines for individual research in the central or the classroom library.

Using all these facilities in study or work periods, the alert, dedicated teacher assists different students to recognize, define, and attack problems. In fact, one of the best indications of effective teaching in a science course, conventional or new, is the extent to which students voluntarily work

[31] D. W. Stotler, "Secondary School Science in Portland, Oregon," Science Teacher (May, 1963), 30, pp. 29-35. For sources of teaching materials, some of which are inexpensive or free, see issues of Science Teacher.

[32] National Science Teachers Association, Planning for Excellence in High School Science, National Education Association, Washington, D. C., 1961, p. 43. For further discussion of this method of teaching science, see Sund and Trowbridge, Teaching Science, Chaps. 4-5.

on individual projects in and outside of school hours. This indicates learning through intrinsic motivation and meaning.

Impressive results from this problem-solving, laboratory method of teaching have been revealed by research. Some significant conclusions from a review of several investigations are as follows:

1. Students in newer course improvement projects achieve at least as much traditional content as do students in conventional courses and achieve more in the content area defined by the new course.
2. The background and philosophy of the teacher are important if a new course is being taught. Any given student will achieve more in a traditional course with a traditionally oriented teacher than he would have if the traditional teacher had taught a new course. Thus, new courses can be successful only if the teacher is adequately prepared and philosophically oriented to teach the course.
3. Inductive, problem-solving, and laboratory-centered methods seem preferable to deductive-demonstration methods if outcomes other than knowledge are sought and if retention of knowledge over time is felt to be important.
4. Instructional procedures can be designed to teach students to think critically and to deepen their understanding of the scientific enterprise.
5. A desirable attitude change can be taught by carefully designed instructional procedures; this applies to all ability groups.[33]

It seems that students of the new courses surpass those of the traditional courses in acquisition of course content and in development of scientific attitudes and habits—including students with low levels of ability. However, the teacher of either type of course seems to be a strong determiner of the students' achievements in the course. Yet, disturbingly, an investigation reveals that many science teachers had few experiences with the discovery method of learning science when they were students in high school and in college.[34] Accordingly, steps taken to improve courses in science must be accompanied by steps taken to improve teachers. There are reasons to believe that this generalization also applies to mathematics and the other high-school subjects.

TEACHING MATHEMATICS

As is true of science in secondary schools, mathematics consists of the conventional and the new. The number of schools adopting modern mathematics is impressive, but many schools still retain the traditional mathematics. Some teachers are teaching conventional courses, however, so that they incorporate some essential features of modern mathematics.

33 G. A. Ramsey and R. W. Howe, "An Analysis of Research on Instructional Procedures in Secondary School Science. Part I—Outcomes of Instruction," *Science Teacher* (March, 1969), 36, p. 68.
34 Newton, "Educating Teachers," pp. 17-23.

Others who are using the textbooks and other teaching materials of the new courses are continuing use of a teaching procedure characteristic of conventional mathematics. Encouragingly, some are incorporating the new mathematics into their teaching, in both content and method.

Former Efforts in the Improvement of Teaching Algebra

We saw in Chapter 4 that some leading educators in the mathematics of preceding decades were advocating significant changes in the subject matter and the teaching procedure of the traditional courses. Algebra received particular criticism. For example, the Commission on Post War Plans wrote: "Let no one assume that all is well with first-year algebra. There is a wide gap between first-year algebra as it is commonly taught and what good teachers everywhere have long demonstrated."[35] Quoting from a committee representing the Mathematical Association of America, the Commission added that elementary algebra had changed little in theory and symbolism since the seventeenth century. Excessive time was often spent on abstract, useless work in such areas as fractions, factoring, simultaneous equations, and radicals. This condition was deplored in view of the principle that mathematics is valuable not as a "disciplinary" subject but only as it is meaningful and functional in vocation and leisure in a technological society.[36]

Further condemnation of the status of algebra in the ninth grade was furnished by Reeve, a former editor of *The Mathematics Teacher*. He urged removal of the "deadwood" from the course, saying: "No one who makes a careful study of the situation can any longer justify the teaching of any other types of factoring in the ninth grade beyond taking out a common monomial factor, the factors of a perfect square, and possibly the difference of two squares. . . . Many more or less complicated operations on polynomials and equations are no longer of any real importance and should be relegated to the algebra museum."[37] Reeve disapproved of the typical course in algebra further as he pointed out the undesirable results from teaching it as a pure course, devoid of elements from other courses in mathematics. Referring to all the ordinary courses of high-school mathematics, he stated that our traditional watertight compartment method of teaching algebra, then plane geometry, then intermediate algebra, and so on caused unnecessary repetition of subject matter, resulting in the loss of much time and energy.[38] Reeve specified that this loss was evident as stu-

---

[35] Commission on Post War Plans, "The Improvement of Mathematics in Grades 1 to 14," *Mathematics Teacher* (May, 1945), 38, p. 207.

[36] F. N. Freeman, "Teaching Mathematics for the Million," *California Journal of Secondary Education* (May, 1944), 19, p. 249.

[37] W. D. Reeve, "Editorial: Elimination of Obsolete Material in Mathematics," *Mathematics Teacher* (February, 1947), 40, p. 89.

[38] W. D. Reeve, "Coordinating High School and College Mathematics," *Mathematics Teacher* (December, 1946), 39, p. 354.

dents took eleventh-grade algebra, when a large part of the time was spent, if not wasted, in reteaching ninth-grade algebra, which they did not use in the intervening course in geometry. He could have added appropriately that many students found algebra and other traditional mathematics courses in high school so meaningless that they were unable to remember or use much of what was taught.

Various suggestions for teaching algebra meaningfully and usefully were offered. For example, Kinsella proposed improving students' understanding in algebra by directing their attention to the relationships of numbers in arithmetic as bases for understanding the same relationships of symbols in algebra.[39] Obviously, this procedure first required acquisition of a basic stock of meanings in arithmetic. Trump agreed: "In order that algebra instruction be rich, it must be built upon a rich foundation in arithmetic instruction. This is not to say that the algebra teacher is warranted in excusing himself merely because the child's arithmetic teachers may have fallen short of the mark. . . . One major purpose in the teaching of algebra must be added enrichment of the arithmetic background."[40]

Expressing a similar line of thought, Hendershot suggested drawing extensively on the real problems of science for the problems in algebra. Being a teacher of the same group of students in algebra and physics, he found that they "knew" algebra when they were studying it but not when studying physics. Their knowledge of algebra simply did not carry over into physics and into other allied fields.[41] The reason for this prevailing situation, he believed, was that emphasis in algebra had been on the blind manipulation of symbols and on solving useless and meaningless problems in the textbook. Students were introduced to algebra through drill on the various operations of signed numbers, apart from any problems, verbal or real. Later, when they were asked to work verbal problems, a frequent statement was: "Show me how to work one, and then I can do the others." Many of them, in the words of Hendershot, "go on a sit-down strike. Here are problems that require thinking and the pupils are not prepared to think. In fact when it comes to thinking they are conscientious objectors. They do not believe in it. But the question is: Who made them that way?"[42]

Some teachers, however, were approaching the study of equations and formulas in the process of solving simple, realistic problems in science. In like manner, some were teaching graphing not as an isolated topic, but as it may be used in the whole course of algebra and in other areas in and outside of the school. They were providing for the inclusion of mathe-

---

[39] J. J. Kinsella, "A 'Meaning' Theory for Algebra?" *School Science and Mathematics* (December, 1947), 47, pp. 775-780.

[40] P. L. Trump, "Enrichment of Mathematics Instruction," *Mathematics Teacher* (December, 1947), 40, p. 365.

[41] W. G. Hendershot, "A Suggested Program for Teaching the Function Concepts in High School Algebra," *Mathematics Teacher* (March, 1946), 39, p. 121.

[42] Ibid., pp. 122-123.

matical problems from the school laboratory and shop and from industrial technology.

An essential feature of the improved ways of teaching algebra, suggested by some of the preceding statements, is direction of students toward finding out meanings for themselves. Definitions and rules are evolved from many mathematical experiences, involving concrete laboratory investigations. This is the inductive-deductive, discovery, or experience way of teaching algebra. This method of teaching the course is also a distinguishing feature of the new mathematics. It is the meaningful approach in contrast to the manipulation-of-symbols one. Specifically, the youngsters do not have to "learn" the rule for the signs of terms removed from parentheses and then apply this rule. Instead, the teacher provides them with experiences with genuine problems, requiring the addition and subtraction of several terms, separately and collectively, in arithmetic and algebra. For example, a student may be asked to point out the two ways of showing the change from $5 after a person has made purchases of $1.50 and $1; namely, through subtracting from $5 the cost of each item alone and then subtracting the sum of the two. In such experiences objects and visual aids also may be used to clarify meanings.

That this method of teaching algebra is effective is indicated by both psychology and experimentation. The method obviously includes proper provision for two factors in effective learning: (1) the student's goal and (2) insight toward reaching the goal. Experimentation cited in preceding chapters reveals that interest and meaning in learning contribute to retention and transfer. There also has been significant research on teaching through inquiry in arithmetic, showing that the method results in improvement of quality and use of the learning.[43] The similarity between the subject matter of arithmetic and algebra indicates that an effective procedure followed in the former may well be followed in the latter.

In an experiment on teaching algebra through discovery, the experimenter had a control group of students taught through the conventional expository approach, in which the teacher stated the principle, or rule, and then explained and applied it. In contrast, the experimental group first was given learning materials and thought questions designed to raise a problem in the learners' minds. This was followed by a request that they attack the problem any way they could, without being required to verbalize their process at once. In the results it was found that the two groups were about the same in acquisition of subject matter, but the experimental group excelled in thinking. An additional finding of significance is that some students had difficulty changing from habits of passive receptivity

---

[43] See, for example, D. C. Tredway and G. E. Hollister, "An Experimental Study of Two Approaches to Teaching Percentage," *Arithmetic Teacher* (December, 1963), 10, pp. 491-495.

to active pursuit. Yet nearly all of them developed marked interest in the process of learning through problem solving and discovering.[44]

Former Efforts in the Improvement of Teaching Geometry

In like manner, some writers of preceding decades presented revolutionary recommendations for improvement of content and method in geometry. The principal objectives of this course, commonly expressed by teachers as well as writers, had been the development of the ability to think. The importance of this goal had been placed into relief by many new and perplexing problems in the modern world. Yet leaders in the field of mathematics seriously questioned that this goal was actually achieved through the usual course in geometry.[45]

This doubt about the effectiveness of the course in the promotion of thinking resulted partly from observations of "learning" geometry through memorizing rather than through thinking. Very often students themselves expressed with delight how they beat the game by memorizing the theorems. Unsatisfactory learning was evident also in reports from examinations given to a large number of students. This was shown, for example, by New York Regents Examinations.[46] Likewise, a thorough analysis of the results of the Every Pupil Plane Geometry Test, taken by students in Ohio, revealed that often the reasons they gave for statements seemed to be devoid of a thought process and were equivalent to guesses or nonsense syllables. These facts indicate that "demonstrative geometry has not greatly improved the ability of the students to reason accurately even within the narrow confines of the subject."[47] In view of this, one does not have reason to expect it to improve thinking in nongeometric situations.

Reasons why the old type of course in geometry is unsuitable for high-school students were expressed by leaders in the field of mathematics teaching. One writer mentioned that traditional demonstrative geometry, having undergone no essential changes since it was transferred from the college to the high school about 100 years ago, was above the mental maturity of ordinary high-school students.[48] He also pointed out that the course as it was usually taught caused students to concentrate on studying ready-made proofs rather than on the development of their own proofs. Furthermore, the course confined any kind of study of proof to geometry, neglecting any parallel study of it in economic, social, or political areas.

---

44 H. Ballew, "Discovery Learning and Critical Thinking in Algebra," *High School Journal* (February, 1967), 50, pp. 261-270.
45 National Council of Teachers of Mathematics, Thirteenth Yearbook, *The Nature of Proof*, Bureau of Publications, Teachers College, Columbia University, New York, 1938, pp. 6-10.
46 S. Welkowitz, "Tenth-Year Geometry for All American Youth," *Mathematics Teacher* (March, 1946), 39, p. 99.
47 National Council of Teachers of Mathematics, *The Nature of Proof*, p. 8.
48 Ibid., pp. 2-3.

The result was poor transfer of the learning to everyday problems.[49] Another writer expressed a similar criticism, stating that the effort to teach geometry for "power" has resulted in its being studied through sheer memory and without application.[50] Others, referring particularly to the importance of teaching geometry so that there is transfer of learning outside the subject, emphasized that we must no longer assume inherent transfer value in geometry but we must teach for transfer.[51] Thus several leaders in mathematics no longer held that geometry had inherent disciplinary value and declared, rather, that it must be taught from the standpoint of both content and method so that it functions in both mathematical and nonmathematical situations.

To teach geometry in harmony with the general objectives of education, especially the objective of thinking, the teacher must aim to promote understanding and use of proof both in and outside the subject. To meet this challenge, at least a few teachers distinctly changed their teaching procedure. For instance, eight teachers in Lincoln High School, Lincoln, Nebraska, reorganized their classroom procedure along lines expressed in the following suggestions:

1. Introduce, through the use of everyday situations, the reasoning patterns necessary for understanding and mastery of geometry content.
2. As the geometry situations become more complex, parallel them, so far as possible, with like situations from nongeometric material, interweaving the two so that each is an aid in understanding the other.
3. Make the transfer of training a conscious and continuous procedure—from geometry to nongeometric problems and vice versa.
4. Through the use of many and varied types of materials, help pupils to recognize the reasoning patterns of geometry in everyday life situations and make them a part of their everyday thinking.[52]

In undertaking these changes in teaching geometry, four teachers from this group worked together during a semester, collecting data for the experiment and studying the progress of other teachers who had made similar changes. While the experiment was in progress, they met in conference once a week to discuss their problems and make plans for continuation of the work. About one-fourth of the class work was devoted to nongeometric subject matter. Later the four teachers were joined by four others. Three teachers who continued to use the ordinary teaching procedure constituted a kind of control group. To determine the results of the two methods of teaching geometry, a series of different tests on reasoning

49 Ibid., pp. 7-17.
50 Welkowitz, "Tenth-Year Geometry," pp. 100-101.
51 The National Council of Teachers of Mathematics, *Emerging Practices in Mathematics Education*, pp. 269-284; E. Murray, "Conflicting Assumptions," *Mathematics Teacher* (February, 1944), 37, pp. 57-63.
52 I. Cook, "Developing Reflective Thinking Through Geometry," *Mathematics Teacher* (February, 1943), 36, p. 79.

and on achievement were given. The experimental group gained about 30 percent more in ability to reason in nongeometric situations than the control group. Although the experimental group spent only about three-fourths as much time on ordinary geometry as the control group, the former slightly surpassed the latter in achievement in the subject.[53]

Similarly, Fawcett advocated and used this method of teaching geometry. He believed: "What particular theorems are covered is not a matter of great concern, since the emphasis is to be placed on the nature of the process by which these theorems are proved and not on the theorems themselves."[54] He also concentrated on teaching the nature and the use of proof in both geometric and nongeometric situations. He assumed that students understand the nature of proof when they understand:

1. The place and significance of the undefined concepts in proving any conclusion.
2. The necessity for clearly defined terms and their effect on the conclusion.
3. The necessity for assumptions or unproved propositions.
4. That no demonstration proves anything that is not implied by the assumptions.[55]

In actual teaching, Fawcett emphasized that the student must not only understand proof but must use it in various kinds of problematic situations. That is, it must help the student to behave intelligently. The behavior of the student who understands proof is marked by the following characteristics:

1. He will select the significant words and phrases in any statement that is important to him and ask that they be carefully defined.
2. He will require evidence in support of any conclusion he is pressed to accept.
3. He will analyze the evidence and distinguish fact from assumption.
4. He will recognize stated and unstated assumptions essential to the conclusion.
5. He will evaluate these assumptions, accepting some and rejecting others.
6. He will evaluate the argument, accepting or rejecting the conclusion.
7. He will constantly re-examine the assumptions which are behind his beliefs and which guide his actions.[56]

As the first step for learners toward understanding the nature of proof, Fawcett undertook assisting them to see the importance of the definition of terms in all precise thinking. At the first meeting he surprised the class by presenting the proposition that awards should be granted for outstanding achievement in school. In the argumentation that followed, strong disagreement developed. In summarization of the discussion, he

[53] Ibid., pp. 79-82.
[54] National Council of Teachers of Mathematics, *The Nature of Proof*, p. 24.
[55] Ibid., p. 10.
[56] Ibid., pp. 11-12.

assisted them to see that their different statements resulted partly from their failure to define *award* and *outstanding achievement*. In the next few class periods they had other experiences in clarifying definitions. Their growing interest led them to propose terms that needed to be defined. Some of their questions were as follows: "What is an aristocrat?" "What is 100 percent Americanism?" and "What is the labor class?" Finally, they concluded that definitions are necessary for precise thinking, that conclusions depend on assumptions, some of which are unrecognized, and that it is difficult to agree on definitions and assumptions in the discussion of controversial issues. Thus that teacher used materials in the social, economic, and political areas to lead learners in geometry to comprehend the function of terms and basic assumptions in proof.[57]

At this point the class began the construction of definitions and assumptions in geometry. They considered the meaning of space, side, triangle, square, cube, and the like, expressing their own definitions. They also made their own assumptions. Examples are as follows: (1) A line can be drawn through any two points. (2) Vertical angles are equal. (3) Two straight lines can intersect at one and only one point. In such work they had experiences in inductive as well as deductive proof. For example, some of them, noticing the use of *interior* in the theorem on the sum of the angles of a triangle, asked whether a triangle has exterior angles. Various illustrations of the exterior angle enabled them to develop concepts of it.[58]

Parallel with work on the creation of proof in geometry was work on the creation of it outside the subject. Examples of propositions that they considered thoroughly are as follows: (1) Once an amendment to the Constitution has been submitted to the people, the time required for ratification is slightly over a year. (2) Would the history of the United States have been changed if it had been made clear that the assumption was that all *white men* are created equal?[59]

The results from this type of course in geometry may be expected to be satisfactory. That the young people taking the subject were not low in achievement is evident from their scores on the Ohio Every Pupil Test in plane geometry. That they did transfer their thinking in geometry to their attack on personal and social problems is revealed from the reports of, and the observations by, teachers and parents.[60]

Thus during the preceding decades there were beginnings in theory and practice toward reformation of the conventional courses of algebra and geometry. The recommendations for improvement included modernization of the subject matter and provision for a method of discovery and conceptualization. There was some use of laboratory procedures and some

57 Ibid., pp. 30-34.
58 Ibid., pp. 34-75.
59 Ibid., pp. 75-100.
60 Ibid., pp. 101-116.

development of mathematical concepts through drawing on natural and social science. As was expected, the result was significant improvement of students in attitudes toward mathematics and in ability to think in the mathematical and the nonmathematical field.

Modern Mathematics

The isolated, individual efforts to reform mathematics in secondary education produced meager results. Traditional courses continued, seemingly from inadequate knowledge of up-to-date subject matter and the inductive-deductive method, from the tendency to follow custom, and from satisfaction with the status quo. After World War II, however, there was acceleration of technological innovations, such as computing machines. Industry and international competition were demanding an increasing number of capable mathematicians to function as scientists and engineers. Moreover, during the first half of this century, changes made in mathematics from research had been almost as extensive as those in chemistry, physics, and biology. An example is in the area of probability and statistics, which has numerous applications in both the physical and the social sciences.[61]

Those conditions stimulated at least eight groups of educators and mathematicians to engage in the reformation of mathematics in high school. The two making the greatest impact have been the School Mathematics Study Group and the University of Illinois Committee on School Mathematics. The former, supported by the National Science Foundation, and the latter, by the Carnegie Corporation of New York, were largely responsible for the production of modern mathematics.

Modern mathematics consists of both new and old subject matter. The reorganization is around units or lines of thought, involving study of the constituent elements of mathematics in relation to one another. Leaders of the National Council of Teachers of Mathematics emphasized that all the programs they discussed attempted to avoid presentation of new material as a series of unrelated topics. They stressed unifying ideas in mathematics through construction of valid generalizations in the study of such major topics as the following: structure of mathematics, operations and their inverses, measurement, graphical representation, systems of numeration, properties of numbers, statistical inference, probability, and sets.[62]

A distinctive characteristic of modern mathematics is the concentration on developing in students the concept of sets. People commonly use the word set in reference to things that belong, or are used, together; for example, a set of furniture, dishes, or tools. Similarly, mathematicians use the term to show a relation between mathematical elements with re-

---

[61] National Council of Teachers of Mathematics, *The Revolution in School Mathematics,* National Council of Teachers of Mathematics, Washington, D. C., 1961, p. 22.
[62] Ibid.

spect to their properties or functions. Two examples are sets of positive real numbers and sets of even real numbers. Classification of elements into sets may begin, for instance, when students can recognize relationships between equations and inequations and between terms in numerators of fractions and terms within parentheses.

It is important to perceive here that mathematics in high school may be taught so that students relate ideas and learn with high purpose and insight without any use of the word set. As has been seen, some teachers of mathematics were doing a good job of assisting students to organize their thoughts and to develop rich concepts before the new mathematics arrived on the scene. In fact, they were surpassing some teachers of today who are endeavoring to teach sets and other concepts through a telling-demonstrating procedure. However, since concentration on sets can result in a large measure of reflective, meaningful learning, it behooves teachers of mathematics in high school to study the textbooks and manuals of the new mathematics for help toward teaching sets through the method of concrete experience and inquiry.

The newness of modern mathematics is, for many teachers, not just in the subject matter but also in the teaching procedure. It has been found that the new approach to teaching either traditional or new content is the most difficult aspect of the new programs. Commenting on this, Beberman, former director of UICSM, stated that appraisals of the new programs should not center on the newness of the content but on whether the method of instruction uses both new and old content to assist students to acquire skills through insightful investigation and discovery.[63]

In method of teaching, the new programs provide for the discovery approach, but it is the central theme of the UICSM program. In this method the procedure is from concrete examples and experiences to abstract ideas, or thoughts. Effective use of the method requires a teacher to have special preparation, including understanding and skill in both mathematics and the teaching-learning process. "The teacher must be an expert interrogator, secure in his knowledge of mathematics, patient when pupils are slow to discover the obvious, capable of following some unexpected pupil suggestions, and considerate in rejecting others."[64]

Referring particularly to how the UICSM program provides for student discovery, the National Council of Teachers of Mathematics added:

Exploration exercises appear frequently, and these are very useful in encouraging and guiding the student in the discovery of generalizations. One of the first places where important generalizations are discovered is in the unit on the

63 M. Beberman, "The Old Mathematics in the New Curriculum," *Educational Leadership* (March, 1962), 19, pp. 373-375.
64 National Council of Teachers of Mathematics, *The Revolution in School Mathematics*, p. 79. See also H. P. Fawcett and K. B. Cummins, *The Teaching of Mathematics from Counting to Calculus*, Charles E. Merrill, Columbus, Ohio, 1970, pp. 87-88.

operations with signed numbers. The rules are not stated as such, but are discovered by the students after finding several interpretations of the symbols of signed numbers. Simple equations and inequations (inequalities) offer another topic in which discovery is of extreme importance. The students are led to discover their own methods for solving many kinds of equations. The pervading discovery techniques are intended to help the students when they are confronted with new problem situations and in the understanding of the mathematics developed. UICSM holds to the belief that the learning process is deepened by presenting a sequence of activities from which students may independently recognize some desired knowledge.[65]

Thus the focus of the teaching method recommended by UICSM was on assisting the teacher in directing the student to find out the why and the how of mathematics. The Committee realized that a high-school student may remain silent and ask no *why* questions and yet do the required homework correctly by just imitating the teacher and following the rules in the book. Its textbooks, therefore, do not place a concept or generalization immediately after the exercises from which it is supposed to evolve. Instead, they provide for engagements in observations, operations, and discussions, leading toward perceptions of an idea. The student is not just told and shown but is involved in investigation.

A point of special importance in the promotion of learning through inquiry in mathematics is provision for adequate concrete experiences in advance of a request for verbalization of the concept or generalization. The writers have observed teachers violate this principle in conventional courses. These teachers will be inclined to continue this practice if they undertake teaching modern mathematics. Students must engage in various problem-solving activities leading them to check on the why and the how of the mathematical operation. They should not be pressed for precise verbal expressions until their performance in solving problems indicates understanding of the generalization or concept toward which the instruction has been directed. Premature verbalization encourages students to substitute words for thoughts, which often occurs in traditional procedure. Of course precise expression of ideas is essential at appropriate points in the teaching-learning process.

A teacher endeavoring to improve instruction according to new programs needs help from the instructional aids produced by SMSG and UICSM. This is true whether or not the school has adopted the new mathematics. In case the teacher must use conventional textbooks adopted by the school, some progress toward modernization of content and development of concepts is possible through the use of materials of the two new programs. Of course, in schools having a new program, most of the

---

[65] National Council of Teachers of Mathematics, *An Analysis of New Mathematics Programs*, National Council of Teachers of Mathematics, Washington, D. C., 1963, p. 60. See also Herman Boeckmann, "The Discovery Approach Strategy for Mathematics Teachers," *School Science and Mathematics* (January, 1971), 71, pp. 3-6.

teachers also will need special preparation in content and method. They may acquire this in or outside the school.

SMSG has provided textbooks, teachers' guides, and supplementary pamphlets for courses or major topics in mathematics in elementary as well as high school. These include a textbook in trigonometry and a book, *Mathematics Through Science,* in which several science units containing simple science experiments are presented for use in developing some basic mathematical concepts.[66]

Similar instructional materials, including some films, have been produced by UICSM for grades 9-12. The materials provide eleven major units, which may be used in teaching courses or aspects of courses. Examples are The Arithmetic of Real Numbers; Generalizations and Algebraic Manipulations; Equations and Inequalities; Geometry; and Circular Functions and Trigonometry. The titles of chapters of the textbook for the first course indicate that they contain subject matter from arithmetic, algebra, and other conventional courses. Examples are Properties of Real Numbers; Operations and Inverses; Deductive Organization; Order and Sets; Equations; Inequations; and Problems.[67]

Qualified and dedicated teachers in modern mathematics have been obtaining encouraging results. The teacher also gains new interest and understanding in mathematics, which is transferred to the students. Before long, parents detect a marked improvement in the attitudes and habits of their children and they want to know why. "Students are beginning to experience the thrill of discovering mathematics principles. . . . One of the chief problems in teaching mathematics is motivation of the student. These new programs have a built-in motivation factor and it is exciting to watch it operate under the guidance of a well qualified teacher."[68]

Particularly revealing is the reaction of "good" students in comparison with "poor" ones. Teachers have found that some of the students rewarded with A's and B's have difficulty when they are required to find out for themselves and learn through thinking. On the other hand, they have observed that there are underachievers who respond enthusiastically as they study and experience a teaching procedure that challenges them to seek goals, catch on, and reason.[69] As the National Council of Teachers of Mathematics adds:

Students who had gone unnoticed before were thrilled because for once they were allowed to ask "off beat" questions or to disagree with accepted reasons

[66] Order materials from A. C. Vroman, SMSG, Cedar Hall, Stanford University, Stanford, California.
[67] Order materials from D. C. Heath, Lexington, Massachusetts.
[68] W. E. Ferguson, "Current Reforms in the Mathematics Curricula—A Passing Phase or Progress?" *Mathematics Teacher* (March, 1964), 57, p. 143.
[69] Ibid., p. 145.

for doing things. They were allowed to find answers for themselves . . . You must interest adolescents in mathematical ideas themselves. It is of little value to try to obtain student interest by promises of utility in adult life. . . . Students become interested in mathematics because it gives them quick access to a kind of intellectual adventure that is enticing and satisfying.[70]

In use of this inductive-deductive method of teaching mathematics, the following specific practices have been found to be helpful.

1. Provide laboratory-type materials within the classroom.
2. Patiently use many questions to lead students to discover, create, and reflect.
3. Assist students to recognize, define, and attack problems drawn from experiences outside the mathematics classroom.
4. Provide learning situations that help students understand mathematics by perceiving the interrelationships of its functional parts.
5. Use simple problems, material aids, and questions to lead students to develop a concept or formulate a rule.
6. At appropriate times, call on students to state how or why an operation works in solution of a problem.
7. Challenge students to demonstrate different ways of working a problem.
8. Encourage students to ask questions and to participate in setting up new goals of investigation.
9. Through purposeful, meaningful activities, cause students to enjoy working mathematical problems for the reason that some people enjoy working puzzles.

In helping students to learn equations in algebra, for example, the approach may be to offer them a fresh look at the meaning of reducing a fraction to its lowest terms and of the ratio of one number to another. Then the teacher may write one or two easy equations on the chalkboard and request every student to solve them by any process whatsoever and using any helpful material aids. After considering the results, the teacher may ask some leading questions, without any class discussion, and then assign additional equation problems, to be followed by class discussion. The teacher should question individuals patiently to help them solve equations using their knowledge and skills in other mathematical operations. In the beginning students are not expected or pressed to explain their solutions precisely, and the teacher carefully refrains from answering any of the questions posed.

The teacher follows a similar procedure in teaching word problems. Once students understand the process of solving equations, it may be necessary to concentrate on helping them acquire the nonmathematical

[70] National Council of Teachers of Mathematics, *The Revolution in School Mathematics*, p. 32.

concepts of the word problems. In all the procedure there is provision for both group and individual instruction.[71]

Investigations of the student-discovery method of teaching mathematics reveal pleasing results. Students learning mathematics by this method were found to be at least normal in acquisition of mathematical content but to be significantly above normal in development of interest and understanding. As stated by Fawcett and Cummins: "Studies indicate that discovery approaches are exceedingly effective in increasing understanding of, and improving attitudes toward, mathematics. Skill and grasp of content are not impaired; if anything, these are improved too."[72]

Mathematics for the Slow Learner

Modern mathematics is geared to challenge and direct the superior and the "average" student. It has been seen that in the new courses some underachievers come alive as they are placed in situations leading them to engage actively in pursuing objectives and gaining insights. There are, however, some learners so low in ability and interest that they require special and persistent help to progress in either new or conventional mathematics. For many of them a well-taught course in general mathematics may provide the best and last formal instruction in mathematics.

Encouragingly, the National Council of Teachers of Mathematics took steps toward provision of modern mathematics for low achievers. It appointed the Committee on Mathematics for the Non-College Bound to study and help that group of students. This committee prepared a book, *Experiences in Mathematical Discovery, 1971.* In fact, much of the Council's recent drive toward improvement of mathematics has been directed specifically toward meeting the needs of the underprivileged or backward learner. Some mathematics teachers have been rediscovering what some educational psychologists and mathematics teachers discovered decades ago, that the slow learner is in special need of motivation and understanding in the teaching-learning process. A teacher experimented with motivation stemming from intellectual curiosity and from social and vocational utility. He found these types of motivation to be effective. He also gained further evidence for the belief that when instruction is determined by each student's particular interests and needs, achievement is significantly improved. This involved dealing with the cultural backgrounds of slow learners.[73]

---

71 See Fawcett and Cummins, *The Teaching of Mathematics,* Chap. 5; and J. A. McIntosh, Editor, *Perspectives on Secondary Mathematics Education,* paper, Prentice-Hall, Englewood Cliffs, New Jersey, 1971, Chap. 2. See also National Council of Teachers of Mathematics, *The Continuing Revolution in Mathematics,* National Council of Teachers of Mathematics, Washington, D. C., 1968.

72 Fawcett and Cummins, *The Teaching of Mathematics,* p. 42.

73 B. Holtan, "Motivation and General Mathematics Students," *Mathematics Teacher* (January, 1964), 57, pp. 20-25; and K. R. Johnson, "The Culturally Disadvantaged—Slow Learner or Different Learner?" *Journal of Secondary Education* (January, 1970), 45, pp. 43-47.

Another teacher experimented with slow learners in general mathematics in grades seven and eight. The median of the IQ's of the seventh grade was about 100; of the eighth grade, about 95. The experimenter used modern and traditional materials. The classes were organized so that the causes of low achievement could be treated as much as possible. Concepts were introduced through concrete materials and purposeful experiences. Motivation occurred largely from the student's taste of success for the first time. When the instructor was working with one group at the study corner, the rest of the youngsters were working at their desks toward suitable individual goals. From the experiment three significant conclusions were drawn:

1. Modern mathematics can be blended with traditional material into a successful program.
2. Such a program may be effective in adding three years to a low achiever's grade level in mathematics.
3. Small group instruction with independent study is possible in a secondary classroom of thirty students.[74]

That low achievers in ninth-grade classes in particular are in need of improved instruction may be seen in a report by another investigator. In a school district in California, twelve teachers were requested to teach classes in general mathematics as they chose. The classes were distributed in the seventh, eighth, and ninth grades. Achievement in grades seven and eight was satisfactory, but several students in the ninth grade made no measurable progress, the course being ineffective for about 25 percent of the students. Apparently, by the time young people reach the ninth grade their attitudes and habits are so firmly set that it is very difficult to change them. They are in special need of gaining interest and understanding in mathematics through laboratory types of experiences accompanied by patient questioning, resulting in tastes of success.[75]

We see that mathematics, like science, is undergoing revolutionary changes in secondary education. In both there have been extensive recommendations and steps toward reformation in content and method. Teachers of each are challenged to acquaint themselves with new ideas and implement them to provide inquisitive, investigative learning experiences for different students in preparation for reflective, democratic living in a complex, technological world.

[74] Adapted from K. E. Easterday, "An Experiment with Low Achievers in Arithmetic," *Mathematics Teacher* (November, 1964), 57, p. 468.
[75] G. W. Brown, "Improving Instruction in Problem Solving in Ninth Grade General Mathematics," *School Science and Mathematics* (May, 1964), 64, pp. 341-346. See also J. W. Ogle, "Unfinished Revolution: Mathematics for Low Achievers," *High School Journal* (February, 1970), 53, pp. 298-309; K. P. Kidd and others, *The Laboratory Approach to Mathematics,* Science Research Associates, Chicago, 1970, Chap. 6.

QUESTIONS AND ACTIVITIES

1. Individually, explain to a small group the accelerated efforts in recent years toward changing the teaching of science and mathematics.
2. Identify, then discuss, the elements of modern educational theory, as presented in Chapters 1-3, as support for the new sciences and the new mathematics.
3. Drawing on suggestions in Chapters 4-6 about the major steps in teaching any subject, formulate a set of guidelines describing how best to teach science and mathematics. Compare these guidelines with other class members and/or obtain the remarks of experienced teachers in these subjects.
4. Analyze what the teacher of either mathematics or science needs to possess in knowledge, attitudes, and skills to use effectively the subject matter and method proposed in the new program of the subject.
5. As a class, brainstorm ideas that might help a teacher of science or mathematics, in a school that has not adopted the new program, to improve teaching of conventionally organized courses.
6. Either in an actual mini-lesson demonstration or by playback of a video tape you make, demonstrate how you would employ the steps of scientific reflective procedures in teaching a concept or generalization in science or mathematics.
7. Research the most recent studies comparing the teaching of science and/or mathematics conventionally with the discovery method. Share your findings with the class.
8. Select some experienced science and mathematics teachers and have them appear on a panel to discuss their experiences in teaching their subjects traditionally and/or following the inquiry method. To what degree do their preferences for a method rest on learning theory, unfounded research, good luck, or personal bias?

SELECTED REFERENCES

Science

Andersen, H. O., *Readings in Science Education for the Secondary School*, paper, Macmillan, New York, 1969.

Andersen, H. O., and P. G. Koutnik, *Toward More Effective Science Instruction in Secondary Education*, Macmillan, New York, 1972.

Carin, A. A., and R. B. Sund, *Teaching Science Through Discovery*, 2nd ed., Charles E. Merrill, Columbus, Ohio, 1970.

Esler, W. K., *Modern Physics Experiments for the High School,* Parker, West Nyack, New York, 1970.

Glass, B., *The Timely and the Timeless: The Interrelationships of Science, Education and Society,* Basic Books, New York, 1970.

Grobman, A. B., *Changing Classroom: The Role of the Biological Sciences Curriculum Study,* Doubleday, Garden City, New York, 1969.

Heimler, C. H., *New School Programs in Science,* David McKay, New York, 1967.

Hittle, David R., and others, *Sourcebook for Chemistry and Physics,* Macmillan, New York, 1973.

Hurd, P. D., *New Directions in Teaching Secondary School Science,* paper, Rand McNally, New York, 1969.

National Science Teachers Association, *Conditions for Good Science Teaching in Secondary Schools,* National Education Association, Washington, D. C., 1970.

National Society for the Study of Education, *The Changing American School,* Sixty-fifth Yearbook, Part II, University of Chicago, Chicago, 1966, Chap. 2.

Romey, W. D., *Inquiry Techniques for Teaching Science,* Prentice-Hall, Englewood Cliffs, New Jersey, 1968.

Sund, R. B., and L. W. Trowbridge, *Teaching Science by Inquiry in the Secondary School,* Charles E. Merrill, Columbus, 1967.

Thurber, W. A., and A. T. Collette, *Teaching Science in Today's Secondary Schools,* 3rd ed., Allyn and Bacon, Boston, 1968.

Voss, B. E., and S. B. Brown, *Biology as Inquiry: A Book of Teaching Methods,* C. V. Mosby, St. Louis, 1968.

Washton, N. S., *Teaching Science Creatively in the Secondary Schools,* W. B. Saunders, Philadelphia, 1967.

Mathematics

Butler, C. H., and F. L. Wren, *The Teaching of Secondary Mathematics,* 5th ed., McGraw-Hill, New York, 1969.

Davis, R. B., *The Changing Curriculum: Mathematics,* National Education Association, Washington, D. C., 1967.

Fawcett, H., and K. Cummins, *The Teaching of Mathematics: From Counting to Calculus,* Charles E. Merrill, Columbus, Ohio, 1970.

Fremont, H., *How to Teach Mathematics in Secondary Schools,* W. B. Saunders, Philadelphia, 1969.

Kidd, K. P., and others, *The Laboratory Approach to Mathematics,* Science Research Associates, Chicago, 1970.

Kinsella, J. J., *Secondary School Mathematics,* Center for Applied Research in Education, New York, 1965.

Krulik, S., *Handbook of Aids for Teaching Junior and Senior High School Mathematics*, W. B. Saunders, Philadelphia, 1971.

McIntosh, J. A., ed., *Perspectives on Secondary Mathematics Education*, Prentice-Hall, Englewood Cliffs, New Jersey, 1971, Chap. 2.

National Council of Teachers of Mathematics, *The Continuing Revolution in Mathematics*, paper, National Education Association, Washington, D. C., 1968.

National Council of Teachers of Mathematics, *Mathematical Challenges*, National Education Association, Washington, D. C., 1965.

National Society for the Study of Education, *Mathematics Education*, Sixty-ninth Yearbook, Part I, University of Chicago Press, Chicago, 1970, Chap. 6.

Paige, D., and others, *Mathematics Methods for Junior High School Teachers*, paper, Prindle, Weber and Schmidt, Boston, 1968.

Willoughby, S. S., *Contemporary Teaching of Secondary School Mathematics*, John Wiley, New York, 1967.

Wooton, W., *SMSG: The Making of a Curriculum*, Yale University Press, New Haven, Connecticut, 1965.

CHAPTER 9

The purpose of this chapter is to assist teachers to provide instruction in the practical and fine arts (music in particular), toward meeting vocational and avocational needs of high-school students. The focus is on helping them to see that the potential value of these subjects extends beyond training students in skills that are peculiar to performance in particular areas of human activity. Far from being narrow, specialized subjects, they can be taught so that they enrich and broaden the student's education for life in both work and leisure. Thus like other subjects of the curriculum, practical and fine arts require specific objectives and teaching procedures directed toward meeting the student's various needs and reaching our general democratic objectives, as discussed in Chapter 3.

TEACHING BUSINESS

Functions and Offerings

For provision of suitable education for all students, a business curriculum typically consists of (1) an introductory, general, or basic course and (2) specific courses in fields of concentration. The general course may provide students with background, understanding, and guidance for the specialized courses. It may also introduce them to our economic system and develop in them underlying business concepts. The four areas of specialization are secretarial, bookkeeping and recording, general clerical, and retail selling. Distinct courses in all four areas are likely to be offered in only large high schools.

THE ARTS—BUSINESS, INDUSTRIAL ARTS, HOME ECONOMICS, AND MUSIC

General Business

General business is commonly offered in the ninth or tenth grade of high school. Among the courses in business it ranks fourth in terms of enrollment. It is commonly viewed as an introductory or basic course for specialized business offered in subsequent years—typewriting, stenography, bookkeeping, and others. As such, its function is often chiefly vocational. It may be taught, however, so that it contributes much to the student's general or cultural education. Some leaders in business education deplore the prevailing practice of teaching the course almost entirely according to the vocational objective. They insist that the course must educate for consumption as well as production, providing instruction to promote economic competencies and a clear understanding about how our business systems operate. In the words of one writer: "Leaders in business education, in dealing with the objectives and major purposes of business education, uniformly stress the importance of basic, general, or social business education. They indicate that, without an understanding of the fundamental principles of business, techniques are valueless."[1]

General business does . . . provide a logical vehicle for orienting the student's thinking, not only in terms of himself as an economic entity, but also in terms of the functioning of the total society of which he is a part. The consumer approach which is used in most general business textbooks provides an excellent springboard for leading students to the point where they can see the importance and significance of some of the areas they study—money and banking, use of credit, saving and investing—not only to themselves, but also to business firms and our total economic society.[2]

The teacher should organize the course around current issues, interests, and problems confronting the individual as a worker and citizen. Some of the areas of organization may be vocational opportunities, hiring minorities, family budgeting for the year, owning or renting a home, banking services, transportation services, consumer record keeping, investments and savings, types of insurance, forms of taxation, principles of buying and selling, the welfare situation, and the capitalistic economic system in comparison with the socialistic.[3]

In introducing and assigning units or problems, such thought questions as the following may be used:

1. Why is it necessary for a boy or girl to evaluate vocational opportunities in choosing a vocation?

[1] H. A. Tonne and others, Methods of Teaching Business Subjects, 3rd ed., McGraw-Hill, New York, 1965, p. 333.
[2] L. L. Garrison, "Economic Concepts Can Be Taught in the General Business Course," Business Education Forum (March, 1964), 18, p. 10. See also R. Fussel, "Economic Concepts Enrich Course," Business Education Forum (December, 1970), 25, pp. 7-9.
[3] G. W. Maxwell, "Contemporary Issues Create Excitement in General Business," Business Education Forum (April, 1971), 25, pp. 64-65; D. R. Malsbary, "Including New Subject Matter in Basic Business," Business Education Forum (February, 1971), 25, pp. 52-53.

2. How may budgeting for the year assist a family to operate on a sound financial basis?
3. Under what conditions may it be advantageous for some people to own a home and for some to rent one? Explain.
4. How may a bank provide services to a family in buying a home?
5. The family is planning a vacation. What are the advantages and disadvantages of different modes of travel? How may they deal with problems confronting them as they plan their vacation?
6. For what reasons would you invest savings in stocks or bonds or in a savings and loan association?
7. Why do so many people have some form of insurance? What are the advantages and the disadvantages of different forms of insurance?
8. What are the essential differences between our economic system and that of the Soviet Union?

Such questions may be used effectively in the teacher-student assignment to promote recognition and defintion of, and an initial attack on, a problem; in the study period to assist in gathering data to test hypotheses; and in discussion of results to aid in the drawing of valid conclusions. Skillful use of such questions along with a variety of concrete experiences develops important concepts or generalizations. The aim of teaching insurance, for example, is not a complete study of the field for acquisition of a body of information. Rather it is to assist students to evolve fundamental ideas and principles toward sound practices in insurance. With specific reference to teaching term insurance, Tonne states:

Term insurance is the simplest form of insurance and the one most easily taught. . . . If the facts are made simple enough and if round numbers are used, junior high school students, including students with below-average ability, can be given a simple understanding of the basic concepts of term insurance in one period. In succeeding days this basic learning can be developed more fully. On the second day, for example, students can be taught the manner in which five-year term insurance operates; on the third day, straight life insurance. In succeeding periods, limited life, endowment life, and other forms might be presented. In each case, the basic concept presented on the first day is used over again and is further developed.
   Students may not remember everything they learn about insurance, but they will have mastered the fundamental concept of term insurance because it will have been used and reused many times. . . . Only as each unit of learning is expanded around a simple idea to be mastered will learning really take place.[4]

Leaders in business education, as is true of those in other subjects of the curriculum, are increasingly recognizing that in general business learning must involve active student participation. It should promote learning through intrinsic objectives and meanings. There is the need and possi-

[4] Tonne and others, *Methods of Teaching Business Subjects*, pp. 357-358.

bility of mentally challenging each individual toward maximum self-development in choosing, evaluating, and thinking. This interdependent, changing world requires producers and consumers who can make and execute intelligent decisions.[5]

What needs to be recognized here is that concepts of teaching expressed in preceding chapters are applicable to teaching general business. Leading writers in business education are specifying the need for development of students' goals and understandings in the teaching-learning process. They advocate use of concrete experiences, such as participation in making out an income tax form and in studying advertisements and labels. They express the importance of problem solving, discovering, and thinking. As aids, they use audio-visual materials, the library, and community resources.[6] All these procedures in teaching general, or basic, business also have been recommended for teaching bookkeeping[7] and, to some extent, the other specialized courses in business, including typewriting.

Typewriting

Of all the courses in business, typewriting is first in the number of students enrolled. Typewriting is viewed not only as essential in the vocation of business, but also as having high value for personal use. In fact, more students take the course for personal than for vocational reasons. Specifically, many nonbusines students plan to use typing to write papers and letters while in high school and college and for such reasons after completion of their formal education.

Promotion of effective learning in typewriting requires recognition of what was pointed out in Chapter 2, that acquisition of any skill is more than a mechanical process; it is also mental. (In sports, for example, the ball player gains a skill by a series of insights acquired in practice.) This conception of modern psychologists has been applied to teaching typewriting by current writers in business education. In the teaching-learning process, they advocate provision for continuous extension of student objectives and understandings. As stated by some writers:

Without some understanding of the whole process and the relations of its parts to one another, the learner is confused, can have no clear goal toward which to work, finds himself constantly rebelling inwardly and is likely to give up. . . . Today all master teachers make use of the principle of teaching parts in proper

[5] V. A. Musselman, "Motivating Student Interest in Basic Business Classes," *Business Education Forum* (January, 1971), 25, pp. 27-28. See also a series of articles on involvement of students in creativity and thinking in "Basic Business," *Business Education Forum* (March, 1969), 23, pp. 3-14.

[6] See L. V. Douglas and others, *Teaching Business Subjects*, 2nd ed., Prentice-Hall, Englewood Cliffs, New Jersey, 1965, Chap. 8.

[7] Ibid., Chap. 9. For an example of such teaching in the Sheldon Community High School, Sheldon, Iowa, see N. B. Dover, "Individualized Instruction Offers Challenge," *Business Education Forum* (December, 1970), 25, pp. 17-18.

relation to the whole to which they belong. . . . That is why many typewriting teachers now have students writing complete sentences during the first day in class.[8]

This statement emphasizes the function of wholes, patterns, or relationships for the promotion of understanding in the process of learning. There is also reference to the contribution of understanding to the production of student goals. In fact, provision for students to acquire goals and insights is of basic importance in the teaching procedure. Accordingly, on the first day the teacher may effectively demonstrate use of the whole keyboard and direct instruction toward writing one or more words and even short sentences. The whole keyboard approach seems to be the most effective. Nearly all authorities agree that the student should carefully observe the pattern of the keys and watch his or her fingers move in accordance with the pattern. This provides a mental picture of the keyboard and a feel for the reach of each key.[9]

Of course there is a place for practice or drill in the teaching-learning process. However, the reason for the practice, including the specific objective, must always be clear to the student. Each period or part of a period should have a definite objective which the student recognizes. The most important objective of the first few days of work is developing the correct concept of the pattern of the expert typist. The execution of this concept is then achieved through practice.[10]

Group drills may be helpful toward development of required patterns, but individual drills are likely to be especially effective in advancing students in accordance with their particular needs. The goal for each student must be attainable. In analyzing present achievement and the determination of future needs, teacher and student must work together.[11] The student thus may be helped to assume some responsibility in the selection of objectives and procedures in practice. Ideally, the student develops desire and ability to typewrite with little direct supervision, to find and correct errors, and to use reference books as aids for improvement of punctuation and in other respects.

A summarization of the steps in building the skill of typewriting is (1) a demonstration-imitation of the whole process, (2) a recognition of particular techniques needing improvement, (3) goal-directed practice, and (4) conducting timing procedures for immediate determination of results. Unfortunately, the fourth step is repeated by some teachers to the neglect of the first three. The teacher must be on guard against this practice.

There is evidence that using varied materials and activities in teach-

[8] Douglas and others, *Teaching Business Subjects,* p. 60.
[9] Ibid., pp. 132-133.
[10] Tonne and others, *Methods of Teaching Business Subjects,* pp. 131-138.
[11] Ibid., Chap. 4.

ing is more effective than just repeating one kind of learning experience. This is quite likely to be true if some of the different activities and materials provide use of the typewriter as a writing as well as a copying machine. As students use the typewriter to write personal letters, report on reading and laboratory experiences, and the like, they tend to gain in purpose and meaning. They have a reason for typing beyond that of correctly writing a specified number of words a minute. It has been found further that they are likely to develop incidental skills in the art of writing, in the construction of sentences and paragraphs, and in punctuation and spelling. This is true especially if the teacher often asks questions requiring written answers of various lengths.[12]

Such procedures in teaching typewriting and the other courses in business are based on the needs of the student, the democratic objectives of education, and a sound conception of learning. These ways of teaching, as shown by experimentation reported in preceding chapters, have been quite effective.

TEACHING INDUSTRIAL ARTS

Courses in industrial arts in high school have potential value for both the college-bound and the terminal student. Such courses provide both general and vocational education and contribute to education for a profession as well as for a trade. This becomes evident as one recognizes that technology and industry dominate the economic, social, and political life of today.[13] Also, the courses can broaden and enrich the education of both girls and boys.

Objectives and Programs

In the 1960s some states and cities began reconstructing their industrial arts programs to increase their relevancy to students for life in an industrial, technological society. Among the states constructing a program definitely geared to the study of industry and technology was Maine. In the process of reconstruction, it adopted the following objectives:

1. To develop in each student an insight and understanding of industry and its place in society.
2. To discover and develop student talents in industrial-technical fields.

---

12 C. H. Duncan, "Motivation in Typewriting," *Business Education Forum* (March, 1971), 25, pp. 23-24; M. R. Guthrie, "More to Typewriting Than Speed and Accuracy," *Business Education Forum* (April, 1971), 25, pp. 60-61; A. L. Kaisershot, "Composition at the Typewriter," *Business Education Forum* (December, 1969), 24, pp. 24-25. For further discussion of purposeful, insightful procedure in teaching typewriting, see the series of articles in *Business Education Forum* (November, 1968), 23.

13 D. F. Hackett, "Study of American Industry is Essential to Liberalizing General Education," *Industrial Arts and Vocational Education* (April, 1964), 53, pp. 25-28+.

3. To develop problem-solving abilities related to the materials, processes, and products of industry.
4. To develop in each student skill in the safe use of tools and machines.[14]

Using this list of objectives, the State Department of Education in Maine produced a six-year industrial arts program beginning in grade 7. It provides for study of broad categories of American industry, including the technological phases of the industries. The work for each year is divided into units, which are organized around aspects of industry but include study of woods, metals, electricity and electronics, drafting and design, and other offerings of traditional industrial arts to be taught as they are required in study of the units. The outline of that program is:

Grade 7—*Manufacturing Industries* (technology and civilization, household accessories, and personal accessories)
Grade 8—*Manufacturing Industries* (camping equipment, hunting and fishing equipment, and communication equipment)
Grade 9—*Manufacturing Industries* (tools and home workshop equipment, small furniture for the home, production industries, and model power industries)
Grade 10—*Manufacturing and Construction Industries* (tool and machine industries, residential construction, and transportation construction)
Grade 11—*Power and Transportation Industries and Electrical-Electronics Industries* (thermal power, residential wiring, and wire and wireless communication)
Grade 12—*Service Industries* (small service business management, appliance servicing, automotive servicing, repair and refinishing industries, and specialization in one of the major areas).[15]

The Maine program and similar new programs make at least two significant contributions to the improvement of industrial arts instruction: (1) gaining knowledge and skills of industrial arts in the broad setting of industry and technology and (2) providing suggested units of instruction and aids to the teacher for the teaching of the units. Of course a school is not advised to adopt that program or any other such program without modifying it according to conditions in the school. For example, a school may decide to change the program to provide for a course in introduction to vocations in grade 7. Likewise, the teacher should have freedom to adjust instruction to the class.

For successful implementation of the new program in industrial arts most of the teachers will need some in-service education, especially in the area of contemporary industries. This was found to be true in Maine.[16] In addition, it is necessary for them to be provided with a comprehensive laboratory. For acquisition of this type of laboratory, some schools have

14 L. H. Cochran, *Innovative Programs in Industrial Education,* McKnight and McKnight, Bloomington, Illinois, 1970, p. 84.
15 Ibid., pp. 85-86.
16 Ibid., pp. 83-84.

secured financial aid from the Ford Foundation or the U. S. Office of Education.

The Teaching Procedure

Whether a school has a new or a traditional program, the well-educated, dedicated teacher will go as far as possible toward the promotion of learning for a changing technological and industrialized society. For this purpose the fundamental objective is development of students in problem-solving abilities related to the materials, processes, and products of industry. Emphasizing this, two writers in industrial arts state: "In fact . . . the development of ability to think has been identified as the central purpose of American education."[17]

Some schools having the traditional program include individual and group projects; research in laboratory, library, and community; problem solving and creative activities; and reflective discussion, resulting in discovery learning similar to that in the new industrial arts and academic subjects. This way of teaching is clearly in contrast to the cookbook procedure still found in some classes in industrial arts and science.

Instruction in drafting, for example, may require a high intellectual operation of students as teachers discard practices of the old manual arts era in which students engaged in predetermined exercises of copying to develop a list of mechanical skills. There can be some work on problems drawn from industry and from projects designed by teacher and students. Work on the problems develops the students' interest and understanding, which assist them to grasp the fundamentals of drafting. The likelihood of good results is enhanced if there is adequate provision for use of the library as well as the laboratory. For learning through experimentation, discovery, and creativity, the student in industrial arts, as in other subjects, may draw on reading along with observation and experimentation.[18]

Teaching procedure in another course, power mechanics, also may be directed toward promotion of motivation, understanding, and thinking. For attainment of these outcomes of instruction, the learners need to use all their senses in finding out for themselves. Often they may best accomplish this by tearing down and studying a real engine. Old engines may be purchased at no more cost than models, and they are superior to models in the provision of trial-and-error learning, involving, analyzing, synthesizing, perceiving, and discovering. Of course there are models and other such instructional aids that can be purchased and used with good results.[19]

As indicated, there is considerable reliance on the project in courses

17 G. O. Wilber and N. C. Pendered, *Industrial Arts in General Education*, 3rd ed., International Textbook, Scranton, Pennsylvania, 1967, p. 263.
18 H. J. Auer, "Let's Do Away with the Copy Method in Drafting and Use Creative Thinking," *Industrial Arts and Vocational Education* (April, 1964), 53, pp. 33-35.
19 See Wilber and Pendered, *Industrial Arts in General Education*, Chaps. 12-13.

in industrial arts. Some writers, however, urge improvement of project teaching by teacher-student planning. Any planning procedure will be effective to the extent that it enables the student to visualize the project. Student research, experimentation, and creativity must be included in planning and executing plans. Otherwise students will not be assisted toward development of skills in problem solving and in understanding our complex industrial society. As a specific means of such planning, thoughtful and critical class discussion is necessary. Further, there is a need for visual representation of some kind—at least by a drawing or sketch, simple or complex. The quality and level depend on the situation.

It must be remembered that the project is not an end in itself but merely a means to an end; it is a vehicle by which certain behavior changes can be effected. A project is not educationally acceptable unless the teacher is thoroughly convinced that by making it the student will acquire certain behavior patterns considered to be desirable. Thus the choice among many possible projects becomes critical in terms of whether it meets the needs of the particular student and will help attain the objectives of the course.

A true industrial arts project is a high form of problem solving. The steps involved in critical thinking and in the project method of teaching are similar. A true project arises in the mind of a student based upon felt need or real interest. Upon recognizing the problem, the student then proceeds to formulate a tentative solution or hypothesis based upon facts, observations, and previous experiences. This corresponds to the planning stage in the project method. The student now proceeds to test his hypothesis by collecting data, learning how to perform processes, experimenting, and constructing. Upon completion of the constructive or data-gathering stage, the student evaluates his solution (the finished project) in terms of his original goal.[20]

Adequate use of teacher-student planning leads to proper use of the teacher-student assignment. There are teachers in industrial arts, as in other subjects, who have developed the habit of making routine or perfunctory assignments. They need to reflect on whether they are developing minds equal to development of manipulative skills. The assignment is the period in which there may be initiatory stimulation and direction of students toward willing assumption of work on a project or problem. The process of making a good assignment requires student participation. The teacher uses laboratory experiences and thought questions to lead students to set up goals and to gain insights toward reaching those goals. Together, teacher and students draw on the home, the community, the news media, and other sources for points of departure for reflective class discussion and planning.

Such a group assignment leads to individual assignments. The latter may evolve partly in individual conferences during the work or study period.

[20] Ibid., pp. 116-117. See also D. L. Jelden, "Learner-Controlled Education," Journal of Industrial Arts Education (November-December, 1968), 28, pp. 39-41.

As pointed out previously, a good conference is one of the best ways of meeting the needs of different students.

Instruction Toward Careers

The teaching procedure presented previously is directed toward helping students acquire attitudes and skills required to deal with various problems in a complex and changing industrial society. An absorbing problem of the student is choice and preparation for a suitable occupation. The direction of courses in industrial arts toward assisting students in the solution of that problem makes the courses relevant to the students, often causing them to improve their schoolwork not only in these courses but also in other courses. Furthermore, teachers of every subject, especially those in industrial arts, are obligated both to the students and society to provide instruction toward reduction of the large number of young people who end their formal education at or before graduation from high school without adequate preparation for satisfactory entrance into the world of work.[21]

In provision of such instruction for some high-achieving students, it helps to recognize a demand for the craftsman and the technician. These two workers become members of a team with the professional engineer and the scientist. Specifically, industry needs electronic technicians, engineering technicians, and electrical technicians. Manufacturing companies have shown special interest in electronics, for example, through their preparation of teaching materials in that vocation, and some schools have made it one of the main offerings in industrial arts.[22] This course, which requires at least average understanding of science and mathematics, may provide education toward a career for some students or it may contribute to their education for leisure.[23]

Another industry that is very promising to the high-achieving student is plastics. The growth of this industry can be observed in the increasing number of plastic articles in and outside the home. "Only the plastic industry has been growing at a rate of between 12 and 14 percent (as compared to a rate of about 4.5 percent for all U. S. manufacturing)."[24] Because of the large demand for workers who have engaged in extended study of plastics, some schools provide for students to begin the study in high school, expecting them to continue it in college.

21 For an appraisal of the career-education project recently initiated by the U. S. Office of Education, see the section on vocational education in Chap. 1.
22 B. R. Showmaker, "Some Thoughts on Technical Education," *Industrial Arts and Vocational Education* (October, 1964), 53, pp. 29-30+.
23 J. L. Feirer and J. R. Lindbeck, *Industrial Arts Education*, Center for Applied Research in Education, New York, 1966, pp. 84-85. See also R. Miller, "Careers for the 1970's in Electronics," *Industrial Education* (March, 1973), 62, pp. 89-92.
24 J. P. Toner, "Careers for the 1970's in Plastics," *Industrial Education* (May-June, 1973), 62, p. 14. For information about the leading current careers, see *Dictionary of Occupational Titles*, Vols. I and II, U. S. Government Printing Office, Washington, D. C.

Similarly, writers express concern about careers for low-achieving students. Their plea is for a suitable industrial arts education for many students who lack the educational background to become engineers or even engineering technicians but can be equipped for occupations requiring less education and skill. These students have opportunities for work in construction, operation, and service jobs. A necessary feature of their education may be cooperative work-study experiences; that is, on-the-job education for those whose shop performance has shown their readiness for employment. Moreover, since the occupational and geographical mobility in this group of workers is rather high, they need to receive some breadth of experiences, at least to the extent of having education for a cluster of careers.[25]

Education of the student for a cluster of careers is a practice that was studied and recommended by a group of leading educators in industrial arts education. An example of a cluster of careers is in the occupational area of service worker. The cluster could be business machines, air conditioning and refrigeration, radio and television, and home appliances. Adoption of this concept would not only improve the student's chance of securing employment but also add to his understanding in each career of the cluster.[26]

For further provision of understanding and usefulness in the study of industrial arts, the subject should be taught in relation to other courses of the curriculm, especially science, mathematics, social studies, and English. Some schools offer a fused course of industrial arts and science or mathematics. Others leave the structure of the courses as it is but use a form of team teaching, not only in science and mathematics but also in social studies and English, as related to industrial arts. Even if the school does not make any special provision for integration of industrial arts with at least one other subject of the curriculum, the broadly educated, enterprising industrial arts teacher can find many opportunities to improve learning in this subject by teaching it in relation to parts of other subjects.[27]

The foregoing suggestions for improvement of instruction depend largely on the desire and the ability of the teacher for implementation. Lacking either an adequate general education or a specialized and professional education, the teacher will be unable to perceive and use many opportunities to promote goal seeking and insight in the learning process. The teacher needs to adopt a sound view of learning and to meet the demands of present-day society and of the democratic ideal to be able to

[25] H. Siegel, "The Imperatives of the High School Industrial Arts Program," Industrial Arts and Vocational Education (May, 1964), 53, pp. 34-36.
[26] See D. W. Kratochvil and L. J. Thompson, The Cluster Concept Program, American Institutes for Research in the Behavioral Sciences, Palo Alto, California, 1972, particularly p. 5.
[27] See R. S. Seckendorf, "Where Should We Be Going in Industrial Arts?" National Association of Secondary School Principals Bulletin (November, 1969) 53, pp. 98-107; D. W. Olson, "Industrial Arts Recast," Journal of Industrial Arts Education (May-June, 1969), 28, pp. 5-7.

actualize the potentialities of industrial arts. This type of teacher promotes industrial arts education not only for careers but also for democratic citizenship.

TEACHING HOME ECONOMICS

Home economics provides education for improvement of family living. As is well known, the home is a social, economic, and educational unit of the community, the state, and the nation. It affects, and is affected by, life in each of these areas. Life in the home is interwoven with life outside. This has become increasingly true in our interdependent society. Hence, as home economics centers on education for family living, it contributes to and receives contributions from education for complete living. Thus viewed, home economics can make a valuable contribution to the education of both boys and girls.

Role in the Curriculum

Contemporary writers on the teaching of home economics view the function of the subject broadly. At least in theory, this area of secondary education is not directed solely toward teaching skills in cooking and sewing. Instead, it is made to include additional points of emphasis: development of attitudes, interests, concepts, and generalizations in social and economic aspects of life. Examples are parent-child relationships and consumer competence. In these aspects of family living lie perplexing problems, especially for young parents. One investigation found that nine out of ten young mothers were frustrated in their ability to deal with children, to organize a home, to handle money, and to grapple efficiently with demands from inside themselves and from other members of the home and community.[28]

This broad subject is extended to include relationships of the home with other social and economic groups. An understanding of the interdependence of home and society should underlie instruction in all courses in home economics.

Young people need help . . . in interpreting the potent influences on their lives; both the constructive and the destructive contributions of families to society, and the influences and pressures exerted on the family by forces outside the home. They can become aware then of the different values and goals held by other individuals and families and the influence their values and goals have on the way others live. These interrelationships between the family and the community can be made clear whenever various community services (such as family welfare, child welfare, education, recreation, housing, and shopping services) are

---

28 B. I. Coon, *Home Economics Instruction in the Secondary Schools,* The Center for Applied Research in Education, New York, 1966, pp. 4-5.

evaluated. Of equal importance is the concrete help pupils can gain in understanding themselves and their relations with their peers, their family, and their friends.[29]

Such a comprehensive view of home economics suggests a contribution to education that is not only practical or vocational but also cultural or liberal, to assist in meeting the personal, social, and economic needs of different students in a society of increasing complexity and change. The objectives and teaching procedures for this type of school subject are appropriately based on democratic ideals, such as those presented in Chapter 3. As stated by one leading writer in home economics: "Our philosophy will be founded on the democratic ideals that our country has always valued so highly—respect for the worth and dignity of the individual, cooperation for common purposes, and the application of intelligence to the improvement of man's lot."[30]

In line with the purposes and practices of teaching home economics, expressed by leading writers in the subject, is the following list of objectives:

1. Recognition and adoption of democratic values toward meeting socially desirable and personally satisfying needs in the home, community, nation, and world.
2. Development of inclination and ability to engage in problem solving in dealing with personal, social, and economic concerns.
3. Appreciation of the importance of intelligent, harmonious living within and outside the home, and development of the required traits for such living.
4. Comprehension and acquisition of appropriate homemaking skills such as the following: planning, preparing, and serving wholesome meals; making, purchasing, and caring for suitable clothing; recognizing and placing appropriate furnishings; and managing family finances.[31]

Implementing the Objectives

This representative list of current purposes of home economics indicates the need for the selection of subject matter of extensive and recent derivation. One home economist wrote that in our rapidly changing society it is as important "to focus new insights from psychology, natural science, economics, and sociology on homemaking as it is to focus them on other occupations."[32] The significance of these statements is heightened in view

---

[29] Ibid., p. 7. See also R. M. Leverton, "The Future of Home Economics Research," *Journal of Home Economics* (March, 1965), 57, pp. 169–172.
[30] H. C. Fleck, *Toward Better Teaching of Home Economics*, Macmillan, New York, 1968, p. 103.
[31] Adapted from O. A. Hall and B. Paolucci, *Teaching Home Economics*, 2nd ed., John Wiley, New York, 1970, p. 162.
[32] Coon, *Home Economics Instruction in the Secondary Schools*, p. 5.

of how technological, social, and economic changes have so affected the family that there is an accelerated need in home economics for the study of family relationships, child development, consumer education, family economics, home management, and the like. The many new and shifting situations facing families today have made the home economics of a few decades ago about as outdated as the science of that time.

Families, frequently mobile, whether living in cities, suburbs, or rural areas, demand a background for decision making not required in the relative isolation of the rural economy of the early 1900's. This becomes more necessary with many wives and mothers working outside the home, with new types of contacts for all family members, with mass media of communication reaching every individual, with new products to be evaluated, new research to be mastered, and with new problems arising every day. A program incorporating new types of consumption, human relationships, and management problems within the community, as well as the national and international implications, is essential in the second half of the twentieth century.[33]

The purposes of home economics also must be directed toward providing for the needs of different students. Certainly, those of high academic ability and from privileged homes may improve their adjustment and efficiency in the contemporary home through taking appropriate courses in the subject. However, those of average or below-average academic achievement, who come from economically and culturally deprived homes and are potential dropouts and teen-age parents, are in special need of suitable courses. Most of them lack the knowledge, interests, attitudes, and traits required for successful and happy homemaking. This is indicated in a recent study, which revealed that most of the teen-age mothers in the investigation did not provide their families with adequate amounts of milk, vegetables, and fruits for a balanced diet.[34] The teacher is challenged to go as far as possible toward adjustment of instruction to those who most need help.

Adjustment of the course to the student requires the teacher to study the student in the home, community, and school. For directions in doing this, the following questions may be asked:

1. How much time does the family spend together as a group?
2. What are significant characteristics of the relationships among members of the family?
3. What members of the group are responsible for the preparation of food?
4. What kind of household appliances does the family possess?
5. What is the economic and cultural condition of the community?

33 Ibid., p. 33.
34 M. S. Van DeMark and V. R. S. Underwood, "Dietary Habits and Food Consumption Patterns of Teenage Families," *Journal of Home Economics* (October, 1971), 63, pp. 540-544.

6. In what ways do members of the family interact with the community?
7. What are the personal and academic needs of each student for improvement of living in home and community?

For finding answers to such questions, home visitation, individual conferences, an interest and a personality inventory, a sociogram, and student writings are quite helpful. Visitation to the home is of prime importance. Of course, this is often difficult, but it is necessary for the rational provision of suitable instruction for the individual.[35]

Knowledge of the home is especially necessary for the teacher in junior high school. It is well known that many teen-agers do not remain in school beyond the ninth grade. Most of those leaving school have lived in underprivileged homes. The members of these families generally lack the motivation, knowledge, and skills needed for satisfactory family living. They are in special need of improvement not only in human relationships but also in such areas as health, nutrition, clothing, communication, acquisition and retention of a job, and the use of money. All these facts apply particularly to the girls who are likely to marry at sixteen. Between six and ten times more of them experience divorce than those who marry at twenty.[36]

Family Relationships

The role of home economics in the education of adolescents suggests an imperative need for a course in family relationships. Ways of teaching this and other courses in home economics are basically the same as those for other subjects, as presented in this and preceding chapters. Writers on teaching in home economics seem to agree that this area of the high-school curriculum should promote learning characterized by relationships, common interests, problem solving, and thinking.[37]

Using knowledge of students in home and community, teachers in family living may formulate suitable, tentative goals before making an assignment. In the classroom they help students to perceive challenging objectives, using their experiences within and outside the classroom. Teachers and students draw on their personal interests and needs in the home and community for help toward choosing valuable and attainable objectives. All such steps in cooperative planning should not be too difficult to follow in home economics, particularly in family living, because the subject matter deals with difficulties and responsibilities frequently

[35] Hall and Paolucci, Teaching Home Economics, Chaps. 3-5.
[36] R. K. Bezant, "Marriage and Family Living in the Homemaking Curriculum," Journal of Home Economics (January, 1965), 57, p. 13; R. O. Herrmann, "Economic Problems Confronting Teen-Age Newlyweds," Journal of Home Economics (February, 1965), 57, pp. 93-98.
[37] See Chaps. 2-3.

confronted in homes. An example of such planning toward class goals is given below:

One teacher of an eighth-grade class heard her pupils discussing their baby-sitting experiences. Entering the conversation, she learned that 80 percent of them were taking care of children two to eight years old and that they were having some problems they did not know how to meet. Inquiry revealed that they would like help with these problems. The teacher's suggestion of some books and magazine articles to read and a visit to a kindergarten to see how a teacher deals with some of the problems presented by this age group were readily accepted. Their further study helped them to make out an observation sheet to use during the visit to the kindergarten. They planned with the teacher for their part as visitors. An analysis of the observation sheets after the visit helped pupils to draw a few conclusions about the interests of children and the kind of relationships that might be established with them. This led to further study of stories, toys, and games suitable for children of different ages. With the help of some parents, they developed an instruction sheet with information needed for babysitting and suggestions of things to do if an emergency arose. Later a children's party at school was planned and carried out, and this helped in a further analysis of children's interests, reactions, and abilities and in their own relations to children.[38]

This example of teacher-student planning is also an example of teacher-student problem solving. It illustrates how a teacher who is committed to the general objective of the development of students in reflective thinking is alert to opportunities to provide them with experiences in the solution of real problems. In fact, some teachers begin each semester and each unit by having students state their problems for class consideration. In some homes, students must care for the younger children, purchase and prepare food, keep the house clean and in order, manage time and money, and the like. All the learners may have problems in the areas of physical and mental health, boy-girl relationships, grooming, and manners. By having as objectives the solutions of vital problems, the students learn through purpose, meaning, and thinking.

Classroom procedures focused on problem solving have been given by leaders in home economics.[39] They have explained how students may be led through concrete experiences and discussion to recognize, understand, and accept problems for study. One problem that may be studied is "How can I improve my relationship with my parents?" As the discussion progresses, some may suggest possible solutions. Others may question particular assertions of classmates or the teacher. The teacher or some students may suggest various causes of the unsatisfactory relationship: inadequate physical facilities of the home, poor physical condition of the parents, both parents working away from home, the inability of the teen-agers to understand themselves and their parents, and poor com-

---

[38] Coon, *Home Economics Instruction in the Secondary Schools,* pp. 70-71.
[39] Ibid., Chap. 5; Fleck, *Toward Better Teaching of Home Economics,* Chaps. 9, 15.

munication and mutual distrust. These suggestions, especially the last one, may stimulate and direct students in an effort to find causes of poor relationships between themselves and their parents. At this point the class may be directed to the library and the community to find facts bearing on their questions and suggestions toward solution of their problems.

Foods

Such a purposeful, significant procedure in family living also may be practiced in the course on foods. The instruction may be made so broadly functional that it contributes to the student's practical and cultural education, including physical and mental health. Teacher and students may appropriately choose such topics as nutrition, menu planning, marketing, food preparation, serving, table manners, food preservation and storage, feeding the sick, and food for large groups on special occasions. To this list may be added food as an item in budgeting, food and the growth of children, and habits of eating in relation to emotional development. When such a broadly conceived course is evolved through directing young people in attacks on their personal, social, and economic problems, it can be made to function extensively in their lives.

The particular topics selected and the order in which they are studied depend on the nature and the needs of the class. A class may begin with a study of the foods commonly used by people of that locality or with the lunches brought to school or selected in the cafeteria. As another approach, all members of the class may keep records of their diets during a week. Each day they would list the foods eaten, and at the end of the week each member of the class would evaluate all the diets, using a score card constructed in terms of the basic foods. An investigation of special importance would involve research on how to improve the nutrition of children, especially infants.

Whatever the approach may be, the work should be patterned to some extent according to common situations and activities in the home and the community. For example, in the preparation of food, the work usually could be planned around an entire meal or a series of meals rather than a single dish. Likewise, in marketing for food, the students need to learn how to make up complete market lists, judge the quality of foods, consider seasonal variations in foods, and weigh factors which contribute to the cost of foods. Thus the teacher may provide a course characterized by flexibility, integration, broad comprehension, and functional learning.

In general, the method used to teach about foods effectively is one in which students share mentally and emotionally with the teacher in planning and carrying out projects. This is the democratic, reflective method through which young people discover and apply truth for themselves. It places them in learning situations that enable them to comprehend and feel the necessity of cooking and eating for health. It deals with the reaction of the whole learner to the whole environment.

This is saying that the emphasis should be on discovering and on understanding rather than on just following the cookbook. As far as possible, the teacher of home economics should endeavor to aid students in the development of skills in cooking as they have occasion to use them in actually preparing and serving meals. The aim is to place the students in goal seeking situations so that they may be led to assume responsibilities and to practice thinking. When they inquire about a particular step in cooking, the teacher assists them in the kitchen or library to discover the needed information themselves. Thus students may experience problem solving and thinking in the study of foods so that they are able to adjust themselves to new and problematic situations in this area.

Clothing

As in teaching about foods, instruction in clothing needs to be quite inclusive. It includes sewing but much more than this skill. It also must consist not of mere training in skills but of experiences in investigating, finding out, constructing, and generalizing. It could involve study of such problems as the following: planning a wardrobe for a period of time, considering quality and style in aiming to purchase clothes economically, deciding between purchasing a ready-made garment and the materials for making one, considering the cost of one's clothes in relation to the family budget, judging styles and colors becoming to oneself, and studying how best to care for different garments. Each of these problems may well be attacked in relation to the other problems. Far from requiring merely mechanical skills, the good course in clothing requires comprehension, insight, and thinking.

Students may develop interest, understanding, and skill in sewing as they make simple things from materials that are easy to handle. The teacher and the class may discuss making various articles of clothing—scarfs, ties, aprons, slips, shorts, dresses, or pants—out of cotton goods, letting each student choose what is made. In the process of constructing these items, students are assisted in discovering for themselves how to lay out, cut, and sew the materials. As they proceed to construct various articles of clothing, they study the characteristics of different fabrics. While the work progresses, they make clothes that require them to attack new and increasingly difficult problems. Furthermore, all may be done toward the goal of providing each student with a suitable wardrobe. Each student is directed in making or altering garments that supplement present wearing apparel, fit the budget, and enhance appearance.

In these and other experiences in sewing, the emphasis is not on teacher demonstration but on student discovery. Some teachers of sewing refrain from just showing or telling how to do the work. The students are directed not only in finding out for themselves, but also in sharing their findings with other members of the class. Such direction requires use of the home economics library and the laboratory for investigation. It also may demand free class discussion of the clothing problems of each student as they pertain to having a suitable wardrobe.[40]

Evidently, methods of effective teaching in home economics are basically the same as those in other subjects. For example, one writer devotes a chapter to the development of students in attitudes and habits of thinking. Commenting specifically on research in the classroom, this writer states:

There are limitless opportunities to make research a part of daily class activities. Research can prove to be an interesting and intellectually stimulating challenge to students, and will interest parents, too. Research can be done as group or individual assignments. Following are a few suggestions for research projects.

1. Test the wearability of paper clothes.
2. Set up taste panels of a food marketed in various forms, such as fresh, canned, and freeze-dried white potatoes.
3. Compare the cost and adequacy of dry cleaning a certain type of garment at home, in a service dry cleaning machine, and by professional cleaners.
4. Analyze the snack habits of peers, according to types of foods eaten, nutritional values, amounts of money expended, social customs, and so on.
5. Survey the spending habits of a sample group of students.
6. Explore the breakfast habits of a sample group of students.
7. Determine the sources of the favorite recipes of a sample group of homemakers in the community.[41]

The same writer emphasizes the values and ways of improving students in common interests and social understandings. In her words:

When students share among themselves they are contributing to joint purposes and thus develop a concern for the welfare of the group. Responsibility tends to promote a "we" rather than an "I" feeling. The group should work to get all its members involved, including the timid, the sad, the sullen, and the rejected. Every member sooner or later should be given an opportunity to serve in the office of chairman, recorder, or observer. The observer is an especially responsible office, for its function is to determine how well a group is doing. Groups must evaluate their growth and make plans for improved development. Much of this can be done by its members, especially the observer, while the group is in action, by determining the extent to which goals are being realized and what forces are at work reducing group efficiency. When group work is continually evaluated, students become expert in using this important method. . . .

In a home management unit, students might be divided into groups, each to try out certain management procedures. One group might experiment with a

40 F. M. Horn, "Using Independent Study in Home Economics," *Illinois Teacher for Contemporary Roles* (June 9, 1969), 12, pp. 293-301.
41 Fleck, *Toward Better Teaching of Home Economics*, p. 283.

time-and-motion study on the easiest and quickest way to make a bed or to prepare a simple salad. Another group could compare different ways to clean silver-
ware. A third group might devise novel ways to use vacuum cleaner attachments
or test various methods of shampooing upholstered furniture. . . .

Group work is very desirable in carrying out community studies. One class, for
instance, was interested in the age and type of houses in different sections of the
community. A map of the community was studied and divisions made for each of
several groups, which brought back reports to the class. Naturally there was
thorough preliminary discussion of how to make the needed observations and
to secure the necessary information.[42]

In all courses in home economics, group procedure should be accompanied by individualized procedure. Teachers in no other field have better
opportunities to engage in instruction and counseling of the individual.
This is because they must work with the students in many laboratory situations. The alert and committed teacher employs all possible means to learn
about each student, including the use of individual conferences. The
teacher advises students on personal and academic problems and assists
them in choosing and working on projects. Thus the teacher meets the
obligation to provide for the all-round needs of different students.[43]

TEACHING MUSIC

Like the practical arts in the secondary school the fine art of music is
taught to a limited number of students. There is some requirement of
music in junior high schools, but the subject usually is an elective in the
senior high school. Although it may not be considered an essential of the
curriculum, it may contribute to the complete education of many teen-
agers. For vocation or avocation, it is vital to the education of many students. Much depends on the kind of experiences each course is made to
provide.

Courses in music offered in secondary schools may be classified as follows: (1) general music, (2) vocal music, (3) instrumental music, and (4)
musical theory and history, which is offered only in large senior high
schools. In addition, there are the performance groups, vocal and instrumental, which are common in both junior and senior high schools and are
on an elective and selective basis.

In methods of teaching, the principal objectives expressed or implied
by music educators are (1) promotion of enjoyment, (2) development of
concepts or understandings, and (3) production and improvement of performance skills. Overemphasis on any one of these aspects of music education, to the neglect of the other two aspects, results in an unbalanced

42 Ibid., pp. 171-172.
43 A. E. Summerfelt, "Individualized Learning in Home Economics," Journal of Secondary Education (April, 1970), 45, pp. 185-187.

and ineffective program. Focus on all three in relation to one another is necessary for a clear and adequate view of the ends and means of music education. In each learning situation it is important to recognize that learnings are multiple. In fact, music education may be made to develop students not only in music but also in social cohesiveness.

General Music

Promotion of these interrelated outcomes of the student's music education may be seen in teaching general music, a course that may be required in the first year of the junior high school. As is true of all required courses, distinct differences among the students may be found. Some have had a good musical background in the home and elementary school. For them this course may be a stepping stone toward further study and growth in music through high school and college. They are promising performers; they have a consuming desire to progress in fundamental understandings and skills. Others in the course are low in interest and deficient in background and talent. Some of them can learn to perform at least in vocal groups in the home and community, and all of them can be improved in their appreciation and enjoyment. They especially need suitable, rich experiences in music. General music can provide such experiences.

Writers have expressed emphatically the necessity and means of using general music to advance students toward the essential objectives of music education. In this course it is basic to improve the students' interests in music. Focus on the development of their interests contributes to improvement of their understandings and skills, which in turn improve their interests. To obtain these related outcomes, the teacher provides students with a variety of suitable experiences in performing, observing, and listening. Audio-visual aids, thought questions, discussions, and demonstrations likewise involve students in choosing, planning, and evaluating.

This suggests that on the first day of school a teacher may question students about their likes and dislikes in music and then spend time in letting the students listen to different kinds, including rock music. Thus the teacher would begin with the present interests of students as a basis for development of their interests. This procedure probably would help toward improvement of the attitude of some students who entered the class with a negative attitude toward music.

Teaching of knowledge and skills in general music is accomplished through enjoyable experiences in listening and performing and requires careful adjustment to the different abilities and needs of the students. Instruction in notation or reading, for example, can be significant and functional to some, especially if it stems from enjoyable performance and listening. Continuous emphasis on reading music, however, resulting in neglect of other points of concentration, may hinder rather than promote enjoyment and appreciation. Some students of general music do not have the ability or the need to go very far in learning to read music. With reference to need in particular, some writers in music have recognized that not many unselected students will be required to read music. Only a few of them will become members of singing groups in the community, and there are places in those groups for those who learn to sing the songs by imitation and repetition.[44]

Thus general music and similar music courses may be used to help students develop musical concepts and appreciations and, in addition, group spirit. Of special importance in the teaching-learning process is student involvement in the method of discovery in the development of musical concepts. The class may beneficially share with the teacher in planning and in carrying out plans. Instead of relying on telling and dictating in the approach to and pursuit of an activity, a teacher may effectively use listening, audio-visual aids, class demonstrations, thought questions, and class discussion to assist students in discovering.

Performance Groups

As in general music, instruction in instrumental and choral groups should be directed toward developing the students in all the essential aspects of music education. It is true that pressures on the teacher may cause judging success with those groups almost entirely in accordance with nearness to perfection in performance. Teachers may be led to make skills in performance such a dominant aim that they neglect opportunities to promote understanding.

An investigator studied the development of musical concepts in performance experiences. The findings showed that some students with considerable performance experience were decidedly lacking in understanding of musical concepts. There was a low correlation between the amount of that experience and the degree of concept formation. The investigator recognized that a shortage of time prohibits extensive attention to concept formation in rehearsals but that timely questions and comments on the nature of the music involved could improve understanding.[45]

In rehearsals, the teacher has the problem of providing proper attention to all the objectives of music education. In the full rehearsal, brief periods can be spent effectively in questioning and informing students about improvement of their musical understanding. The extent and nature of this procedure should be weighed in relation to the musical program and the various needs of the group. The small performance classes, however, pro-

44 I. C. Singleton and S. V. Anderson, *Music in Secondary Schools*, 2nd ed., Allyn and Bacon, Boston, 1969, pp. 35-36. See also B. Reimer, *A Philosophy of Music Education*, Prentice-Hall, Englewood Cliffs, New Jersey, 1970, Chap. 3.
45 N. C. Deihl, "Developing Musical Concepts Through Performance," *Music Educators Journal*, (November-December, 1964), 51, pp. 61-62.

vide extended time and opportunities for the teacher to study individuals and give them instruction toward understanding. In all promotion of performance, the ideal is to make teaching purposeful and thoughtful to all students.

Our concern here for development of understandings and concepts in relation to performance has been expressed by music educators.[46] Writers emphasize that a provision for enjoyable, perceptual experiences with music, particularly in performing but also in listening and composing, constitutes the foundation for learning music. Each realistic musical experience may provide a laboratory experience in which the student may acquire knowledge and skill and develop understanding and appreciation. For example, notation should be introduced by purposeful, enjoyable experiences with music, both vocal and instrumental. Only through providing such experiences may the study of syllables or numbers clarify tonality or tonal relationships for most of the students. How to provide such learning opportunities for youngsters is expressed below:

The teacher raises questions about music experienced, encourages the pupil to raise questions, and assists him in answering questions and in applying his learning to the musical task at hand, whether it be more artistic performance, more perceptive learning, or mastering some musical technique. . . . The teacher, as a guide to the pupil in his exploration and discovery of musical meanings, assists him in developing a method of attacking musical problems.[47]

Learning takes place only as the learner has meaningful experiences; mere exposure and passive reception are not sufficient. The teacher must structure a situation in which the learner, having identified and accepted a problem, is able to release energy in the solution of the problem. For example, in developing fine tone quality, in playing or singing, the teacher first brings about awareness of differences in tone quality by presenting examples of good and poor tone quality and demonstrates the superior expressive effect attained by fine tonal quality. The pupil develops a concept of good tone quality and evaluates his own playing or singing in relation to his concept.[48]

Suggestions from the Revised Hawaii Music Curriculum

The method of discovering, creating, and forming concepts is recommended in the revised music curriculum for the schools of Hawaii. This curriculum was produced by a staff of experts, advised by the Hawaii State Department of Education and the Music Department of the University of Hawaii. The music curriculum differs from the traditional one in both content and form.

A prominent feature of the new curriculum is the focus on development

[46] See, for example, W. E. Kuhn, *Instrumental Music: Principles and Methods of Instruction*, 2nd ed., Allyn and Bacon, Boston, 1970, pp. 89-94.
[47] C. Leonhard and R. W. House, *Foundations and Principles of Music Education*, McGraw-Hill, New York, 1959, p. 246.
[48] Ibid., pp. 251-252.

of musical understanding, which includes musical appreciation and provides a basis for musical performance. Through various purposeful, significant experiences in listening and performing the students develop useful concepts. The concepts include tone, rhythm, melody, texture, tonality,
form, and harmony, which are not to be considered as a once-for-all-times
model list of musical concepts.[49]

In specific reference to performance of music, the Hawaii curriculum
rejects the traditional practice of focusing on public performance with inadequate promotion of the student's musical understanding and growth.
A fundamental principle of this curriculum is that musical understanding is the paramount goal and that progress toward that goal must be
interwoven with perfection of skills in performance. "The members of this
Project hold that music education cannot allow the role of performance in
the curriculum to overshadow listening, composing and discussing, nor
[can] these pursuits be allowed to supplant performance."[50]

The kinds of listening activities advocated in this curriculum also require
special consideration. Every formal listening period must provide students
with a purposive experience. They should have realistic, relevant goals.
These goals can be sharpened and strengthened by involving the students
in class discussion that stems from their past relevant experiences in
music. This kind of class discussion should both precede and follow the
listening experiences. When listening activities are thus conducted, students engage in creative activities as they listen.[51]

Another difference between this curriculum and the traditional curriculum can be seen in the instruction provided within special classes, particularly instrumental and ensemble classes. In an effort to improve
musical understanding through performance, a class in beginning strings,
for example, spends about two-fifths of the class time in listening, composition, and notation and in development and discussion of concepts,
which are made relevant to instrumental work. Similarly, in ensemble
groups, the student's musical growth is not neglected because of a narrow
view of technical efficiency. An impressive part of the rehearsal time is
spent in discussing the music sung and in listening to the performances of
other ensembles.[52]

The implementation of this new curriculum necessitates improvement of
the music classroom by making it soundproof and equipping it adequately
with musical instruments, records, tapes and other teaching-learning aids.
Another necessity is an instructional media center to which the teacher may
go for audio-visual and reading materials and for help in using these

49 W. Thompson, The Hawaii Music Curriculum Project: The Project Design, Hawaii State Department of Education, Honolulu, 1969.
50 Ibid., p. 6.
51 Ibid., p. 20.
52 Ibid., pp. 25-26.

materials. Of primary importance is the teacher, who must possess sufficient understanding and approval of the curriculum to direct the teaching toward its implementation. This requires that some teachers experience reorientation in their professional education.[53]

Some Conclusions and Suggestions

Such purposeful, useful instruction involves the selection of musical compositions suitable for a particular class. The teacher avoids choosing a composition merely because it is in a textbook or because it may be considered as a classic to which every student should be exposed. Instead, there is the continuous recognition that in music, as in other areas of the curriculum, the value of subject matter is relative to the interests, abilities, and needs of the students.

These facts suggest the need for a flexible and thoughtful procedure in the choice of music for different students in high school. Frequently the students may be actively involved in the process. The teacher, of course, should refrain from spending too much time on the use of selections characterized by discordant sounds and a monotonous rhythm, except in an effort to provide comparisons with music of harmony and of variety in rhythm.

Students well directed in performing and listening to different types of music may improve their choices from among the various types. Their choices require recognition of differences not only among types of music but also among compositions within each type. Since many students appreciate scarcely any music except the type commonly called "popular music," the class may need a variety of vital experiences with this kind of music for help toward discovering that some of the compositions are superior to others in harmony, melody, and richness of expression.

There should be experiences leading to recognition of differences in performance. Too much of the playing and singing on radio and television sounds like impromptu performance. Some of the singing in particular is painful to some listeners, who feel that it is little more than moaning, groaning, screaming, and noise. Listening to the recordings of familiar songs as sung by one or more ordinary singers and then as sung by Joan Sutherland or Franco Corelli, for example, could be quite revealing to the students. They may gain further insight into the nature and need of skillful performance through listening to a tape recording of their singing soon after they begin practice on a song and later when they are ready to sing it on a program. By providing young people with a variety of such experiences, the teacher may direct them toward improving their enjoyment, understanding, and skill in music.

[53] Ibid., p. 31.

It is seen that in music and the other arts, educators express close agreement on basic educational procedures. That this also is true of all other areas of the high-school curriculum is shown in preceding chapters. By explicit or implicit expressions, current writers on instruction in all school subjects approve a teaching-learning process stemming from the following fundamentals: (1) the nature and needs of adolescents in modern society, (2) a goal seeking, conceptualizing view of learning, and (3) the democratic objectives of education. The methods of teaching they advocate are directed toward the development of young people in socially desirable interests, understandings, and skills. There is repeated stress on provision of learning situations in which students find out for themselves. They become actively involved in purposing, reflecting, investigating, and discovering. Thus learning in all areas of secondary education may be improved in quality as well as quantity.

QUESTIONS AND ACTIVITIES

1. Prepare a set of interview questions covering the philosophy of the arts, courses in a school's curriculum, the content and means of instruction in this area, and the financing or budgetary policies regarding the arts. Possible interviewees are school board members, citizens, students, and teachers of the arts and other related subject areas. Summarize and evalaute your findings.

2. Explain and illustrate similarities between practices recommended by educators in the arts and those recommended by educators in other subjects of the curriculum.

3. How may students in the arts be taught so that they develop not only in skills of performance but also in attitudes and habits of the democratic-minded individual?

4. How does a purposeful-insightful view of learning support practices proposed by some writers in each of the arts?

5. Unless you are a student majoring in practical arts you may not be aware of what really occurs in this dynamic field. Plan a field trip to visit a large high school or technical center and spend the day observing, talking, and participating in the practical arts. Following this visit, either in writing or orally, evaluate your impressions in light of democratic educational objectives.

6. Review recent articles and research describing the career education movement. Debate the pros and cons of this trend in light of the present "needs" of society.

7. Appraise how the reflective method of teaching might be employed by practical arts teachers.

8. How may a teacher of English composition, for example, adapt the laboratory procedure of instruction in industrial arts and home economics to teaching written English?

SELECTED REFERENCES

Business

Anderson, R. I., and others, *Teaching Business Subjects,* 3rd ed., Prentice-Hall, Englewood Cliffs, New Jersey, 1973.

Daughtrey, A. S., *Methods of Basic Business and Economic Education,* Southwestern Publishing Company, Cincinnati, 1965.

Douglas, L. V., and others, *Teaching Business Subjects,* 2nd ed., Prentice-Hall, Englewood Cliffs, New Jersey, 1965.

Musselman, V. A., *Methods in Teaching Basic Business Subjects,* Interstate Printers and Publishers, Danville, Illinois, 1971.

National Business Education Association, *Business Education Meets the Challenge of Change,* National Education Association, Washington, D. C., 1966.

National Business Education Association, *Emerging Content and Structure of Business Education,* paper, National Education Association, Washington, D. C., 1970.

National Business Education Association, *New Media in Teaching the Business Subject,* National Education Association, Washington, D. C., 1965.

Nolan, C. A., and others, *Principles and Problems of Business Education,* 3rd ed., Southwestern Publishing, Cincinnati, 1967.

Roman, J. C., *The Business Curriculum,* rev. ed., Southwestern Publishing, Cincinnati, 1966.

Rowe, J. L., and J. Smith, *Methods of Teaching Typewriting,* New York University Campus Stores, New York, 1965.

Tonne, H. A., *Principles of Business Education,* 4th ed., McGraw-Hill, New York, 1970.

Industrial Arts

American Industrial Arts Association, *Developing Human Potential through Industrial Arts,* paper, National Education Association, Washington, D. C. 1965.

American Industrial Arts Association, *Guide for Equipping Industrial Arts Facilities*, paper, National Education Association, Washington, D. C., 1967.

American Industrial Arts Association, *Guidance in Industrial Arts Education for the 1970's*, paper, National Education Association, Washington, D. C., 1971.

American Industrial Arts Association, *Industrial Arts Education: Purposes, Program, Facilities, Instruction, Supervision*, National Education Association, Washington, D. C., 1970.

Bakamis, W. A., *Improving Instruction in Industrial Arts*, Bruce Publishing, Milwaukee, 1966.

Barber, J. W., ed., *Industrial Training Handbook*, A. S. Barnes, Cranbury, New Jersey, 1969.

Brown, R. D., *Industrial Arts Laboratory Planning and Administration*, Bruce Publishing, Milwaukee, 1969.

Cochran, L. H., *Innovative Programs in Industrial Education*, McKnight and McKnight, Bloomington, Illinois, 1970.

Littrell, J. J., *Guide to Industrial Arts Teaching*, Charles A. Bennett, Peoria, Illinois, 1970.

National Society for the Study of Education, *Vocational Education*, Sixty-fourth Yearbook, Part I, University of Chicago, Chicago, 1965, Chaps. 1-6.

Thompson, John F., *Foundations of Vocational Education: Social and Philosophical Concepts*, Prentice-Hall, Englewood Cliffs, New Jersey, 1973.

Wilber, G. O., and N. C. Pendered, *Industrial Arts in General Education*, 3rd ed., International Textbook, Scranton, Pennsylvania, 1967.

Home Economics

Coon, B. I., *Home Economics Instruction in the Secondary Schools*, The Center for Applied Research in Education, New York, 1966.

Fleck, H. C., *Introduction to Nutrition*, Macmillan, New York, 1971.

Fleck, H. C., *Toward Better Teaching of Home Economics*, Macmillan, New York, 1968.

Hall, O., and B. Paolucci, *Teaching Home Economics*, 2nd ed., John Wiley, New York, 1970.

Hatcher, H. M., and L. C. Halchin, *The Teaching of Home Economics*, 3rd ed., Houghton Mifflin, Boston, 1973.

Home Economics Association, *Choosing Techniques for Teaching and Learning*, paper, National Education Association, Washington, D. C., 1970.

Home Economics Association, *Reaching Out to Those We Teach*, paper, National Education Association, Washington, D. C., 1969.

National Education Association, *Contemporary Issues in Home Economics*, National Education Association, Washington, D. C., 1965.

National Education Association, *Innovation in Home Economics,* National Education Association, Washington, D. C., 1967.

National Education Association, *Techniques for Effective Teaching,* rev. ed., National Education Association, Washington, D. C., 1966.

Music

Andrews, J. A., and J. F. Wardian, *Introduction to Music Fundamentals,* 3rd ed., Appleton-Century-Crofts, New York, 1972.

Edelson, E., *Secondary School Music Program from Classroom to Concert Hall,* Prentice-Hall, Englewood Cliffs, New Jersey, 1972.

Glenn, N. E., and others, *Secondary School Music: Philosophy, Theory and Practice,* Prentice-Hall, Englewood Cliffs, New Jersey, 1970.

Gordon, E., *Psychology of Music Teaching,* paper, Prentice-Hall, Englewood Cliffs, New Jersey, 1971.

Green, E. A., *Teaching Stringed Instruments in Classes,* Prentice-Hall, Englewood Cliffs, New Jersey, 1966.

Hoffer, C. R., *Teaching Music in the Secondary Schools,* 2nd ed., Wadsworth, Belmont, California, 1972.

Jipson, W., *High School Vocal Music Program,* Prentice-Hall, Englewood Cliffs, New Jersey, 1972.

Kaplan, M., *Foundations and Frontiers of Music Education,* Holt, Rinehart and Winston, New York, 1966.

Kuhn, W. E., *Instrumental Music: Principles and Methods of Instruction,* 2nd ed., Allyn and Bacon, Boston, 1970.

Labuta, J. A., *Teaching Musicianship in the High School Band,* Prentice-Hall, Englewood Cliffs, New Jersey, 1972.

Leonhard, C., and R. W. House, *Foundations and Principles of Music Education,* 2nd ed., McGraw-Hill, New York, 1972.

Marsh, M. V., *Explore and Discover Music: Creative Approaches to Music Education in Elementary, Middle, and Junior High Schools,* Macmillan, New York, 1970.

Monsour, S., and M. Perry, *Junior High School Music Handbook,* 2nd ed., Prentice-Hall, Englewood Cliffs, New Jersey, 1970.

Moses, H. E., *Developing and Administering a Comprehensive High School Music Program,* Parker, West Nyack, New York, 1970.

Nielsen, F., and R. J. Folstrom, *Music Fundamentals: A Creative Activities Approach,* paper, Addison-Wesley, Reading, Massachusetts, 1969.

Singleton, I. C., and S. V. Anderson, *Music in Secondary Schools,* 2nd ed., Allyn and Bacon, Boston, 1969.

Sur, W. R., and C. F. Schuller, *Music Education for Teenagers,* 2nd ed., Harper and Row, New York, 1966.

Winold, A., *Elements of Musical Understanding,* Prentice-Hall, Englewood Cliffs, New Jersey, 1966.

PART IV

SPECIAL MEANS
AND PROCESSES

CHAPTER 10

Thus far there have been incidental references to the role of instructional materials in the teaching-learning process. At this point there is need of special attention to how material aids may be used efficiently to improve the quality as well as the quantity of learning. Specifically, our immediate concern is not with materials to provide variety and spice for repetitious, meaningless instruction. Rather it is with how best to incorporate suitable materials into instruction in accord with objectives and methods of teaching expressed in the preceding chapters.

USING AUDIO-VISUAL MATERIALS

Basic Views of Audio-Visual Instruction

As is well known, the medium of instruction most extensively used by the school is language. Words, spoken and written, are of course essential and of necessity constitute the chief means of teaching. In fact, one of the major defects of instruction in high school is insufficient use of suitable reading materials. However, a parallel fault of teaching is the frequent dependence solely on reading and talking, the result being a kind of learning commonly called "verbalism." Verbalism exists in learning when the learner acquires little or nothing except words, which of course are only the symbols or vehicles of ideas and thoughts. Growth of ideas and concepts is basic in significant, useful learning. These are inadequately developed apart from sensory experiences. The learner may secure the sensory experiences necessary for accurate and rich concepts through having direct, immediate contacts with the realities of life or through various media such as models, pictures, and drawings. Of importance here is the realization that the student can experience meaning in learning

USING MATERIALS
OF INSTRUCTION

through written or spoken words only to the extent that a sensory background enables putting sufficient meanings into words to receive additional meanings in return.[1]

Any teacher can find out the extent of verbalization in the classroom, simply by requiring students to go beyond stating a few words from the textbook and by requesting them to explain, interpret, generalize, illustrate, or apply. The teacher who does this may find that much of what many teachers commonly accept as satisfactory learning is disturbingly inadequate and inaccurate.

There is increasing need for efficient use of audio-visual aids for promotion of goal seeking, insightful learning. A few decades ago only capable young people were likely to continue their formal education through high school. They were able to learn reasonably well from books. Even some of them, however, were too bookish and impractical when they completed high school. Today a large percentage of boys and girls in high school cannot be expected to learn satisfactorily from books alone. They need various audio-visual experiences as a basis for their reading. Furthermore, all young persons live in a world of increasing complexity and change. The secondary school may assist them to adjust to the physical and social environments of such a world through improving their understanding of these environments.

Proper use of audio-visual materials in teaching requires viewing them in relation to the whole teaching process. The teacher must guard against including these materials chiefly to break the boredom of poor teaching procedure or to reduce the dislike of unsuitable subject matter. As these aids function toward promoting intrinsic interest and meaning in learning, their use is justified. For advancement of such learning, however, appropriate reading materials also are essential. Moreover, in the process of using audio-visual materials, the learners need to share in planning and carrying out plans. The teacher must avoid too much talking or thinking for them. There is little place for the teacher-demonstration method commonly called the "lecture-demonstration method." Instead, there is need for a method of teaching that involves the students in observing, perceiving, experimenting, problem solving, discovering, generalizing, and conceptualizing. For this kind of learning, sensory experiences are basic. They enrich the student's background, which in turn, contributes to the enlargement and enrichment of his or her generalizations and concepts. They form links in the whole chain of the teaching-learning process.[2]

[1] W. A. Wittich and C. F. Schuller, *Audio Visual Materials: Their Nature and Use*, 4th ed., Harper and Row, New York, 1967, Chaps. 1-2.
[2] E. Dale, *Audiovisual Methods in Teaching*, 3rd ed., Holt, Rinehart and Winston, New York, 1969, Chaps. 1-4, 18.

Community Resources

Every community has some resources that may provide students with real, direct experiences of essential value in their education. Of course every young person has learned much through interaction with the community environment in everyday living, some of the experiences being educative and some miseducative. This suggests that assisting youths toward improved use of community resources to advance their education is a chief function of the high school.

To perform that function it is important to recognize how the community is a more realistic society than the typical school and that it is in varying degrees a replica of distant and large societies. Particularly in urban and suburban communities, there are nearly all kinds of individuals and groups. Human relationships in these communities are quite representative of those elsewhere—local, national, and international. Hence the community may well be considered a laboratory in which students are directed in investigating and discovering significant phenomena in physical and social environments. The materials of instruction are people as well as things.

In some localities the community is surveyed by a committee composed of school administrators, teachers, students, and some lay citizens. The committee may use a list of questions to gain information from places the students might visit and study. Examples of items of information thereby obtained are whether visitors are welcome, the name of the person in charge of arrangements, the observational experiences available, the best time of day for the visit, the number in the group preferred, the provision for a guide and for a talk to the students, and the procurement of any audio-visual or printed materials of value in the classroom. After the committee receives such information from the questions, a teacher may visit each place and evaluate the resources. At the conclusion of the study, the data are presented and a printed guide to the educational resources of the community may be produced.

An example of that type of survey was provided in Warren, Michigan. More than fifty teachers, with the cooperation of the Chamber of Commerce and local industries, made a thorough study of the community's educational resources. They produced a handbook that contained more than a thousand potential resources, including locations for field trips and of citizens having available interests and skills. Similarly, educators and community leaders of San Diego County, California, jointly produced a directory of regional libraries and of audio-visual aids, obtainable, for example, in a planetarium and in the local United States Navy hospital.[3]

[3] J. W. Brown and others, *A-V Instruction: Media and Methods*, 4th ed., McGraw-Hill, New York, 1973, pp. 389-394.

A committee of interested parents and teachers of Manhasset, New York, studied the community's resources with reference particularly to available contributions from some of its citizens.

The committee began by interviewing professional and business people to discover what skills and abilities they had that would enrich learning situations in the classroom. This information was then catalogued for reference by interested teachers. In this way the committee discovered, for example, that a very able lawyer could be available when the social studies class was investigating personal rights and the techniques and procedures of court action. The local nurseryman who had developed certain grafting techniques would explain them to general science students. A local ceramist was willing to explain and demonstrate glazing techniques to an art class. The local music-store proprietor, who happened to be a skilled cello player, was willing to help the members of the cello section of the school orchestra.[4]

Such studies of the resources of the community help the teacher to choose intelligently among various available aids of instruction. Using the directory of resources, the teacher may decide to invite a specialist to instruct the class, to secure educational materials from an organization, or to go on a field trip. The choice may include employment of all three aids.

Field Trips

The field trip, which is potentially a very effective aid to learning, requires special thought in selection and use. It is relatively time consuming, and it often takes students from other classes of the day. Hence the teacher needs to raise the question: "Is this field trip the best possible means at hand for improvement of learning in study of this unit, problem, concept, or skill?" Other items of consideration may include school board regulations and a state law pertaining to field trips. The fact remains, however, that in a field trip scenes, things, and people may be studied firsthand in their settings and schoolwork may thus be incorporated with everyday life.

After the teacher has chosen a field trip and has made at least preliminary arrangements with the principal, there are three steps to take with the class: preparation of the class, taking the trip, and follow-up. For the trip to serve well as an aid to learning, students need to view it as an integral part of the learning activity. Toward reaching this end, they and the teacher may participate in asking and answering questions about what should receive their special attention during the observation experience. Discussion and organization of orderly conduct on the trip also may be helpful. Thorough preparation for the trip results in reduced need for the teacher's direction of the class during the experience. In the follow-up

4 Wittich and Schuller, *Audio Visual Materials*, pp. 240-241.

period there is time for thoughtful considerations of what was done and learned. This may include discussion of impressions, evaluations, generalizations, and applications. The students may relate their learnings on the trip to those of their former readings and use the relationships to direct future study. They also may plan writing a report of both the proceedings and the findings of their trip for their use and that of other classes.

An important result from a field trip may be research studies of the community conducted by capable and interested students. In a quest for information bearing on contemporary local problems, these students may work as individuals or groups, visiting places that have resource materials, questioning specialists, and reading in the community library. Some of these research studies may extend beyond the locality to include state and national conditions.[5]

The Model and the Specimen

In case it is not feasible to take the class away from school to study phenomena in natural or social environments, the school may provide for study of some models and specimens within the classroom. Through these materials students may study aspects of remote as well as local environments. Although the aids are viewed out of their natural or social setting, they have the advantage of being three-dimensional. They can be effective toward promoting understanding and interest in inquiry learning.

The model is an imitation or representation of a real thing and, as such, provides for a contrived experience. Examples are the models of regional terrains, the ocean floor, a colonial village, and the bodily organs. Models are used in an effort to include the advantages of the direct experience without the disadvantages. Some features or aspects of the students' environments are not accessible or are too complex for direct study. (This can be seen in the examples just given.) In some instances, therefore, the study of models may be more useful for sensory learning than the direct study of certain phenomena in the complete environment. Thus, from the standpoint of both accessibility and learning, it is often better to bring the model to the classroom than to take the class to what the model represents.

A specimen is an object or substance that is one of several things or a part of something. Thus it may be called a "sample" or "segment." Examples are a boll of cotton, a piece of coal, a rock, an ear of corn, or a bottle of crude oil. Obviously the specimen is limited in its educational value in that it is separated from context or natural setting. Specifically, the boll of cotton is viewed apart from the cotton field and the piece of coal from the coal mine. Yet it is not a representation of something but a sample of the real thing. As such, it has high value for concrete, realistic learning.

Either the model or the specimen may be used in the classroom at the moment it may be needed to reduce vagueness and inaccuracy in learning and to encourage investigation and problem solving. To provide a background for the model or the specimen, still and motion pictures, readings, and other media may be added in the learning situation.

Since the model and the specimen have high potential value for concrete learning, the high school does well to acquire an adequate supply of these material aids. Students may assist through collection of specimens or through construction of models. Of course, it is important to catalog and file the materials in cabinets so the teacher may have ready access to real and contrived materials for sensory learning.[6]

Still Pictures

An effective supplement of, or substitute for, means of direct experiences is the still picture. This is particularly true when the object of study does not involve motion or when intensive study of a step in an event or a process is necessary. Furthermore, this type of picture has the advantage of being inexpensive and easily available. This is not to mention the ease and speed with which it may be shown in numerous and various learning situations.

The still picture is very valuable for the study of both immediate and remote environments. Seeing pictures of the past and the distant is frequently necessary for satisfactory learning. For example, in the study of history, students need to see pictures of peoples of the ancient world and, in the study of geography or science, pictures of natural phenomena in remote regions.

Pictures contribute to comprehension and interest in learning. Evidence of this may be seen in the seed and nursery catalogue. A written description of an improved or a new plant usually does not produce clear and adequate perception—a picture is also necessary. Besides, the picture, especially a colored one, may be needed to induce the observer to read about the plant and ultimately to become sufficiently interested to make a purchase. In like manner, students respond to pictures in books and other printed matter. Through pictures they experience representations of persons, animals, plants, and objects in real situations and against recognizable backgrounds. Pictures add to their understanding and motivation, often stimulating them toward reading or another learning activity.

Pictures are among the most common visual materials used in school.

6 Ibid., Chap. 8.

This is shown by studies of practices in some of our large cities and in rural areas. The modern textbook, particularly in science and the social studies, contains vivid and stimulating pictures, some of them being in color. In addition, some school systems purchase numerous pictures, which are mounted and placed in central distributing offices. In presentation of the picture to a class it can be placed on the bulletin board, held by the teacher, or projected onto a screen.

Because of the accessibility and usability of the still picture, it can be made very helpful to students, especially in their study of problems. The teacher can stimulate interest in a problem by presenting one or more pictures. He can present additional pictures as the students are in the process of taking the steps toward the solution of the problem. In social studies, for example, a picture or pictures could show conflicting interpretations of a controversial event in history. As the teacher presents each picture, students are invited to comment and are questioned in an effort to help them perceive important points they might miss.

Graphic Materials

Like pictures, graphical materials are visual symbols of reality which are relatively easy to obtain and use. Examples are maps, globes, charts, graphs, and diagrams. These visual aids lack the completeness of details produced by a picture. Rather, they provide a simplified and emphatic form of visualization of significant factors in situations. They can pointedly express relationships of quantities, sizes, conditions, positions, and the like, which pictures cannot express. These aids are especially valuable for adding reality to abstractions, generalizations, and broad concepts.

Maps and globes are common and potentially effective as visual aids. Every social studies classroom is expected to have a globe and some maps. Other classrooms—for example, in teaching English—could be improved by these aids in the equipment. They may assist students to understand the relative sizes and positions of various land and water areas as these may affect human relationships—economic, social, or political. Thus they provide answers to questions by students about phenomena of physical and social environments.

The occasion for using the globe or the map is its need by students for understanding what they are studying. When the classroom becomes a kind of workshop and the class is engaged in study, a student may be helped by a globe and maps to find answers to questions. Likewise, in class discussion these aids should be used freely and carefully at opportune times. In the process, the teacher usually refrains from telling and pointing out but encourages the students to discover and to express. The endeavor is always to lead young people to perceive significant relationships in their study of various locations and areas of the world. Thus the map or the globe is not just to be shown briefly by the teacher but also to be studied at some length by the learners.

A similar visual symbol is the chart. It is a graphic representation of a course, process, or system. It consists of lists, pictures, tables, or diagrams used to summarize, classify, compare, or contrast. Examples are a family tree, a bus or airplane schedule, and an organization of a school system or a government. The chief value of the chart is its brief and vivid expression of related facts. Pages of narration and description may not present adequately and clearly the information provided by a chart of not more than one page. Effective learning often requires that the learner view the relationships among the parts of a body of knowledge, which the chart supplies.

Teachers and students may spend some time valuably in the construction of charts. Some may be constructed temporarily on the chalkboard and others, for future as well as present use, on large sheets of paper. As in map use, charts in books or periodicals may be projected onto a screen, a large sheet of paper, or the chalkboard. If on the two latter surfaces, the chart may be easily drawn for future use. Thus there are many opportunities and ways for the enterprising teacher to use this visual aid to increase meaning in learning.

Another kind of visual symbol requiring special attention is the graph. This means of instruction presents quantitative data in an abbreviated, diagrammatical, picturesque, and vitalized form. The graph has become an important visual aid because of the increase of research in social science as well as natural science. The findings of scientific investigations are commonly presented through a graph. Some young people need help in comprehensive and accurate reading of results of experiments expressed in a graph. Furthermore, they need to learn to construct and use this visual aid in making reports of their own investigations as, for example, of some phase of the school or community. In thus employing the graph, they may gain not only in comprehending the results of the experiments but also in understanding and utilizing graphs.

A common graphical aid is the diagram. It consists of lines which present the "skeleton" of an object or process. As is true of other such materials, its primary function is to explain and emphasize characteristics of a phenomenon. Its relative simplicity of construction makes it a convenient as well as a valuable visual aid.

It is possible and desirable to make extensive use of the diagram. It is an available and effective means of clarifying and vitalizing the perception of an object and a process. Often the teacher can construct a diagram on the chalkboard while going through the process of leading pupils to understand. This visual material does not need to be drawn artistically but just accurately and clearly. Of course, if it expresses something complex and is not ready-made, the teacher may need to draw it in advance of the instruction. As is true of other graphical visual aids, some diagrams can be collected from books, magazines, and newspapers, and they can be shown by use of a projector. In addition to the teacher's own use of this aid are opportunities to assist students to include it in their reports of investigations and activities.[7]

The Chalkboard

For use of the diagram and any other graphical visual symbols, the most common device is the chalkboard. This visual aid is very valuable also in instruction through verbal symbols (which are considered in the next section of this chapter). In fact, many teachers confine their employment of the chalkboard almost entirely to verbal symbols, as in teaching words, sentences, paragraphs, and outlines; in giving a short examination; and in solving numerical problems. Some claim that they are unable to draw a picture or diagram. Aside from the fact that little of artistic skill in drawing is required, it is the teacher's obligation to cultivate this skill sufficiently for frequent use in teaching.

Among the advantages of the chalkboard is that it is inexpensive and is immediately and continuously available. Besides, like the motion picture machine, the film-strip lantern, and the projector, the chalkboard is a means of presenting visual material to the whole class at one time. It is a very valuable means of providing visual experiences toward group undertakings, as when the class is working together in investigating or creating. It affords teacher and students various opportunities to employ their ingenuity in demonstrating as well as in stating their ideas. In making reports, some of the most artistic students may utilize comics or cartoons as well as graphs or diagrams. The most inefficient teacher in drawing can construct a circle to indicate the limit of a concept, a line to show the division between two concepts, or an arrow to express a causal relationship between the two. With a little thought and practice, ways can be effectively devised to inject chalkboard aids into a variety of learning situations.[8]

Among the practical suggestions for use of the chalkboard is that lengthy or complex material be copied on the board in advance of the class period. Several minutes of the learners' time should not be taken by the teacher for what could have been done outside the class period. An additional suggestion is that the teacher refrain from sending several students to the board for practice or demonstration. They may like to go to the board, but this does not justify having a dozen or so there at one time to do exercises. Whether the assignments are the same or different, some will complete the work soon and be idle, while others will flounder and need

---

[7] Ibid., pp. 519-522.
[8] Wittich and Schuller, *Audio Visual Materials*, Chap. 3.

individual help. If the purpose of sending several to the board is to provide practice or to test, either purpose usually can be accomplished more efficiently at the seats than at the board. However, if the objective is to demonstrate or to teach something new, the teacher can produce learning through discovery by questioning the students and having one student at the board to do the necessary writing.

For example, a class that has seen a motion picture at school or has taken a field trip may be preparing to make a written report of the experience. The teacher may request a student who writes legibly to go to the board to act as recorder. Then, through questioning different individuals, the teacher may lead nearly all members of the class to express themselves with reference to the topic, the outline, the content, and at least the first paragraph of the report. The class evaluates each of those items before, and in some instances after, it is written on the board. To supplement, clarify, and vitalize the written material on the board, the teacher may add diagrammatical or graphical symbols. Through such experiences, students may be assisted in finding out how to write a good report.

Overhead Projection

In showing pictures and graphical materials, overhead projection has become an effective means. The projection may be either transparent or opaque. Transparent projection is provided by transparencies in the form of slides or films, many of which are made at school. Improvements in the technique of processing transparencies have reduced the time and skill formerly required.[9] In opaque projection, the materials are projected by reflected light. Thus there is no need for the processing of materials. Pictures, maps, and graphs taken from a book may be projected as they are. Even small three-dimensional materials, such as coins, shells, or insects, may be projected in silhouette. After purchase of the projector, there is scarcely any expenditure in time or money. Furthermore, materials of present occurrences can be projected immediately. For instance, a clipping from the morning newspaper may be shown on the screen in the first period of the morning. Likewise, parts of a composition can be projected in the period in which compositions are returned and discussed.

The prime reason, of course, for either type of projection is that all members of the class are to be able to view the item shown at the same time. Thereby there is avoidance of the distracting, inefficient practice of passing a picture or other visual material around the class for each one to view apart from the others while the teacher is endeavoring to lecture or direct discussion. As all look at the projected material together, some may

---

9 C. W. H. Erickson, *Fundamentals of Teaching with Audiovisual Technology*, 2nd ed., Macmillan, New York, 1965, pp. 140-145.

ask questions and make comments that may assist in the clarification and formation of concepts. Simultaneous reception of vital sensory experiences by everyone in the class promotes free and thoughtful discussion in which even reticent students may voluntarily participate.[10]

Related to the potential contributions to learning by overhead projection are those of projection by the film strip and the film strip lantern. There has been a significant change in some film strips such as those produced for teaching the new social studies and sciences. In contrast to many film strips, which consist only of facts about an area of subject matter, some new ones provide for the study in depth of a process, event, or problem in a subject. The aim is toward promotion of goal seeking, understanding, and thinking in the process of learning. The film strips are not loaded with facts, which easily can be obtained through reading a book. Instead, they include chiefly source materials—documents and pictures, maps, charts, and the like.[11]

Motion Pictures

Through motion pictures, events and processes can be effectively presented. Still pictures may show an event or process at certain stages, but they cannot completely show the course of action. The motion picture provides for continuity in the learning process. Furthermore, it can take a class over an area of the world or through a period of history in an hour. It also can record and present very slow movements, as in the growth of a plant, and very fast movements, as in activities of a ball game. All these real and vital features of the motion picture, along with the absence of distraction in the darkened room, make it effective in improvement of understandings and attitudes.

The maximum value of the motion picture in school depends on the way it is used. The teacher should utilize it strictly as a means of education, not to break the monotony or to put life into poor teaching. It always ought to be considered as an integral part of the whole teaching procedure and as only one means of promoting motivation and meaning in learning. In some instances a motion picture is the most feasible or suitable of the audio-visual aids but, in other instances, it may be less appropriate than the other aids or may best be used only to supplement them. There also are times when books in the school library could be made to contribute more to learning than one or more motion picture films.

In the process of teaching through the motion picture, special attention should be given (1) to preparation of the students for what they will be shown and (2) to discussion, evaluation, and application of what they have

[10] M. J. Schultz, The Teacher and Overhead Projection, Prentice-Hall, Englewood Cliffs, New Jersey, 1965, Chap. 2.

[11] To purchase these filmstrips and other audio-visual materials, write to companies listed in footnotes in the section on the new social studies in Chap. 7, and on the new sciences in Chap. 8.

seen. The teacher may assist the students to be ready for the film through making some statements about its purpose and content and through questioning them on what they are about to see. In thus leading them to recognize what they do and do not know on the subject of the picture, the teacher may help them to view it with maximum interest and insight. Obviously, this necessitates that the teacher preview the film. Students well prepared for a suitable picture are ready for the follow-up discussion. In this discussion they may be helped to review and reconstruct their experiences. Their analyzing, relating, and applying what they saw should indicate what they did or did not understand or like in the picture.

The step in the teaching procedure best suited for showing a film varies according to the nature of the unit or activity and of the particular class. However, a good case can be made for placing the picture in the initiatory step. That is the point where the learner is likely to need additional sensory experiences to increase reality, purpose, and meaning in the learning activity. A suitable, well-presented motion picture in that step may lead into such valuable educational activities as research in the laboratory or library, making reports, and constructing graphs and charts.

Disk Recordings and Tape Recordings

The disk recording and the tape recording provide useful audio aids for instruction. By no other means could many valuable learnings be produced in the classroom. To quite a degree the recording dispenses with the barrier of distance, time, and expense. Its availability is immediate and permanent. These features provide the teacher with considerable freedom in the determination of the point in the learning process where those learning aids may be employed effectively. The materials may be used at length with a particular class and with other classes over a period of years. Time in the teacher's preparation and planning also may be saved.

Among the subjects in high school on which disk recordings have made an impact are music, English literature, social studies, and foreign languages. In music there are many recordings of various types, instrumental and vocal. There are symphonies, operas, operettas, folk songs, cowboy songs, spirituals, and classical selections. In English literature, a number of Shakespearean plays, as well as dramatizations of novels and readings of poems, have been recorded. The recordings in social studies include those of great events and speeches involving rulers and other prominent persons. The events are from past and present periods, and the recent speeches are in the actual voice of the speaker. Likewise, the foreign languages in high school have records that enable students to learn through dependable and impressive auditory experiences. Since they rarely live with people who speak a foreign language, recordings can provide an effective substitute means of hearing a language spoken and of gaining correct pronunciation and diction.

The tape recorder is being used increasingly to record and reproduce instructional materials from various sources. Examples are class discussions, group playing or singing, talks by a visiting specialist, reports of individual research by students, and radio programs. Some of the recordings are of students' performances and some of other people's. As students listen to a taped reproduction of their own statements in class, they may be assisted to evaluate both the content and the form of their expression. Recordings of discussions of the same topic by two classes may be quite revealing to each class. Likewise, a class in a social study is likely to be affected in understandings and attitudes by listening to and discussing a recording of a newscast or a political speech given on radio or television the previous evening. Social studies teachers recognize that recordings break time-space barriers by enabling students to hear in any class period ideas on current issues expressed by leaders throughout the country.[12]

Although the tape recorder has a variety of uses in each area of the curriculum, it is obviously of special value in music and the language arts. A teacher or a student of music may record an opera singer heard on radio or television and bring it to class the next day for enjoyment and analysis. Students also may gain interest and insight in vocal music as they listen to a recording of their singing soon after they begin practice on a song and later as they approach singing it on a program. Likewise, in the language arts they may use tape recordings to listen to artists and specialists in speech in either the native or a foreign language. Then each may listen to his or her own voice and, by comparison, judge what is needed for improvement of expression. By hearing themselves as others hear them—their expression, tone, pronunciation, and speed—they may recognize their particular errors and inadequacies. A brief talk made by a student at the beginning of a semester and again a month later also may be quite helpful to both student and teacher in the direction of procedures in speech correction.

Students studying a foreign language in many high schools use tape recordings as they engage in directed laboratory experiences in speaking the language. The number of language laboratories has increased as a result of (1) the shift from the grammar translation method to the audiolingual method and (2) the provision of aid in the National Defense Education Act of 1958.

In the language laboratory, the teacher, by use of a device known as a "console," may talk to individual students or to a group. The students may listen alternately to the teacher's voice, their own voices, or the voice

12 J. S. Kinder, *Using Audiovisual Materials in Education*, paper, American Book, New York, 1965, pp. 85-101.

on tape. It thus is possible to note a similarity or difference between their own expressions and the correct one. In a sense each student has a private tutor while sitting apart from other students. For such learning experiences, many recordings, including those of native speakers, are available.[13]

Television and Radio

As aids to instruction, television and radio have some common features, problems, and functions. Both function through broadcasting, and this poses the problem of scheduling many classes for the broadcast. For full and efficient use of each, some schools are relying on audio and video recordings. Both have high educational potential for changing understandings and values. They present in a vital, realistic manner activities and events of the modern world, including athletic events, political activities, and musical programs. Since television is radio plus motion picture, procedures in the use of television in education imply similar procedures in the use of radio.

In some schools radio is still employed as a substitute for television, its chief function being transmission of music and news. From broadcasts, tape recordings may be made and stored, particularly for classes in social studies, music, and speech, and may be used as needed. Some cities and states have broadcasting facilities for presentation of carefully prepared educational programs. Television, however, overshadows radio in education.[14]

There are two categories of television, broadcast and closed circuit. Many education programs for both broadcast and closed-circuit television have been produced. Some of the programs are for whole courses in science or mathematics, for example. The program includes different materials of the audiovisual field—pictures, film strips, diagrams, specimens, tape recordings, and so on—along with reading materials, thought questions, and teaching procedures, such as those suggested in courses in the new mathematics and the new sciences. It constitutes an educational synthesis involving a variety of materials and methods for use toward purposeful and insightful learning. The specialist engaged in the production has ability, time, and facilities for assistance of the learner in complex learning situations that the ordinary teacher does not.

Whatever may be the access of some schools to broadcast television or to closed-circuit television, all schools can have recordings of televised programs. The video tape is rather expensive, but a kinescope or telefilm may be used at relatively little expense. This means of recording is in essence a motion picture film which is produced by making a continuous

13 For tapes in modern foreign languages, write to National Tape Library, 930 F Street, Washington, D. C.; National Tape Repository, University of Colorado, Boulder, Colorado; and Audio-Visual Center, Kent State University, Kent, Ohio.
14 Brown and others, A-V Instruction, pp. 335-340.

motion picture record of a television program as it is being telecast. It can be used later in the classroom as a standard 16 mm sound film.[15]

Television instruction requires extensive involvement of the classroom teacher, who, in schools having closed-circuit television, often consults with the teaching specialist working in the laboratory on production of programs. In any school using commercial telefilms, the teacher functions in the choice of suitable films for the library, and further, must decide in the process of teaching whether to use a telefilm, another audio-visual aid, or other instructional materials. Except in instances of using a live broadcast, he or she can and should preview the telecast.

To make television relevant to the needs of students, the three steps— preparation, presentation, and follow-up—should be used. In preparation the learners are assisted to draw on their past experiences, within and outside the classroom, for interpretation of the live or filmed telecast. The teacher raises and answers questions and encourages students to do the same. The chalkboard is another teaching aid for use at this time. Following presentation of the telecast, there is continuation of the discussion begun in preparation, using the same or similar means toward development of purpose and insight in learning. Such television instruction may be expected to be effective toward enrichment of concepts and improvement of values. Indeed, television efficiently used can be made to excel all the other audio-visual means of instruction for provision of a class with suitable sensory experiences.[16]

AUDIO-VISUAL MEDIA IN LEARNING THROUGH DISCOVERING AND CONCEPTUALIZING

Beginning in Chapter 2, the focus has been on stimulation and assistance of students toward finding solutions to their problems and, in the process, forming concepts for use in future confrontation with those problems. It also was pointed out in that chapter that the richness and value of students' concepts are determined largely by their perceptual backgrounds. This throws into relief the basic importance of the student's past and present sensory experiences for learning, especially learning that is directed by purpose, understanding, and reflection.

The usefulness of audio-visual materials to improve learning has been recognized increasingly by teachers in every subject of the curriculum. Unfortunately, many teachers, in using the materials, employ either the

---

15 Wittich and Schuller, *Audio Visual Materials*, p. 423. Kinescopes may be purchased from educational television stations and from television film companies. Write to Educational Television and Radio Center, Ann Arbor, Michigan; National Association of Educational Broadcasters, University of Illinois, Urbana, Illinois; and Audio-Visual Center, Indiana University, Bloomington, Indiana.
16 Brown and others, *A-V Instruction*, Chap. 11; Dale, *Audiovisual Methods in Teaching*, pp. 383-393.

lecture-demonstration method or what may be called the "textbook-demonstration method." In each procedure the students are presented with information in advance of audio-visual media, which are frequently required for most of them to acquire satisfactory meaning from the information. Then in a subsequent period of instruction the audio-visual experience or experiences are presented, seemingly as an afterthought of the teacher. In advance of listening to a teacher's lecture or to reading a textbook, students can profit from concrete, sensory experiences. Use of audio-visual media in the teacher-student assignment improves the students' understanding and purpose for the work at hand. They need to use the sensory experiences from the sensory media to throw light on their reading in both the textbook and the library while searching for answers to their questions.

Some of the best examples of the use of audio-visual materials in provision for discovery learning toward development of important concepts are in the new sciences. (This is indicated in the section on teaching science in Chapter 8.) The groups of educators who designed the courses of the new sciences emphasized the laboratory approach of the scientist, which enables the student to begin study of a scientific problem through use of the sensory organs. In the textbook and the teacher's manual of some courses, there is provision for the class to spend about the whole first week in the laboratory. The students observe and experiment to find answers to questions stemming from laboratory experiences and class discussion. Throughout the course the textbook provides the students with some information, but it raises more questions than it answers and sends the students to the laboratory to find the answers.

Along with provision for extensive experiences of students in the school's laboratory, the designers of the new courses produced films to provide students with important sensory experiences they could not obtain at school. Sources from which schools may purchase these films are given in footnotes in Chapter 8.[17]

Likewise, producers of the new social studies design instructional aids, including audio-visual materials, for basic use by students in learning through inquiry. In fact, some groups of producers did not revise the old courses but concentrated on the production of lists of suitable instructional aids.[18] Similarly, some leaders in the teaching of music are emphasizing discovery learning. Hence they stress listening and performance and understanding as related points of emphasis in instruction and recommend use of audio materials.[19]

[17] For further reference to the emphasis of the new sciences on the use of sensory materials for the discovery of scientific concepts see Dale, *Audiovisual Methods in Teaching*, pp. 424-425.
[18] See the section on social studies in Chap. 7 for descriptions of these courses and for sources of the materials.
[19] See the section on teaching music in Chap. 9.

In the selection of instructional aids, the teacher is obligated to the students to aim toward choosing the aid that best meets their special needs. Of course this objective can be closely approached only in a school that provides a large variety of materials for the teachers. An instructional media center within the school or the school district would be helpful. In the process of choosing media according to student needs, the teacher should consider the differences between the environmental backgrounds of students, past and present. For example, the needs of urban students for audio-visual experiences are usually distinctly different from those of suburban and rural students. Also, teachers must avoid choosing an aid chiefly because it is entertaining and must continually ask themselves the question: "Is this medium the best available aid for use as an integral part of this learning activity?"

All teachers, especially those in social studies and in music, need to appraise the value not only of the students' audio-visual experiences at school but also of those experiences out of school. On radio and television, for example, they have extensive opportunities to have realistic sensory experiences about conditions in the economic, social, and political areas of our society. From the same sources they have almost continuous opportunities to listen to music throughout each day. Also, through travel and attendance of group meetings, they have opportunities to have various experiences. Accordingly, the teacher would do well to question students about their out-of-school audio-visual experiences, to form a partial basis for the choice and use of their in-school audio-visual experiences. Also, discussion of the students' out-of-school experiences will improve their perceptual backgrounds for their learning activity.

PRODUCTION OF MATERIALS

The teacher in a high school well supplied with instructional media has little need to produce materials. Most of the commercially produced materials are superior to those the teacher can produce and are little, if any, more expensive. Yet there can be a time when a teacher-made transparency for overhead projection, for example, is more suitable for the special need of a particular class than a commercial transparency. The transparency is not difficult to make, and not much equipment is required. If a school has a copy machine, all the teacher needs is the proper film and a little training to be ready to produce.

A production that is easy for any teacher is the still picture. A good camera to take indoor and outdoor pictures at school can be very enjoyable and useful. Also, it is not difficult to make simple super 8 instructional motion pictures, but 35 mm slides can be made more quickly and at less cost. For production of these slides, the school or the teacher will need to own a 35 mm, single lens, reflex camera. The techniques of making the slides can be easily learned.

A resourceful teacher and some students can use a super 8 or a 16 mm camera to shoot a short film of an important demonstration, process, or activity, without much cost. By use of a magnetic recording motion picture projector and a synchronizing system for super 8 motion picture camera and cassette tape recorder, a sound track can be added to the picture. Some teacher-made pictures could be more useful as teaching aids than some commercial pictures. For the production of sound motion pictures and other technical instructional media, teachers frequently need help from the school's technician.[20]

With no special training or help, any prospective teacher can well begin a collection of pictures that will be quite useful in teaching a given subject. These pictures can be collected from magazines, newspapers, posters, and other sources and catalogued and stored systematically. These pictures should be in the possession of the teacher at the time they are needed in the classroom. By the use of an opaque projector, all members of a class can view each picture together. Such pictures can be used effectively in any class, especially social studies.[21]

OPERATING THE EQUIPMENT

Teachers may need to operate equipment so that they will be free to use a particular instructional aid at an appropriate time. Even though a school has assigned a well-trained operator for the equipment, the operator may not always be available during the period the teacher needs aid. Furthermore, some teachers may need to know how to operate the equipment so that they can teach their students how to use it individually in the learning carrels of the classroom or of the instructional media center.

Some teachers are afraid to try to operate some of the equipment. Any teacher can acquire the necessary skills by simple application to the task of learning. Fortunately for prospective teachers, many teacher-education institutions provide help for them toward mastery of the operations. These institutions require of education students some laboratory practice with audio-visual equipment before they engage in student teaching or receive a certificate. At times, however, the student may receive inadequate experiences for mastery of the equipment. Sometimes, also, the brand of the equipment is not the same as the brand used in the high school.

In some teacher-education programs there is provision for an instructor

---

20 See C. W. H. Erickson and D. H. Curl, *Fundamentals of Teaching with Audiovisual Technology*, 2nd ed., Macmillan, New York, 1972, Chap. 8. See also R. V. Wiman, *Instructional Materials*, paper, Charles A. Jones, Worthington, Ohio, 1972, Sec. 7.
21 For additional examples of what teachers may do toward production of useful audio-visual materials see books on the use of these materials.

to teach students how to operate the equipment. In others, carrels are provided for the student's self-instruction. In each carrel there is a program broken down into demonstration-practice segments. The student is free to choose the order for studying the equipment, but is advised to begin with the simplest pieces.[22]

A statewide program to give teachers in-service training in the use of audio-visual materials within their home districts was designed by the Texas State University. Similarly, the Department of Education and the State University of New York developed a course designated as "A Multimedia Course in Instructional Technology for Teachers" to be taught within the teacher's home district. These are examples of what some leading state educators are doing to advance the technical skills of in-service teachers toward effective utilization of multimedia materials.

Where this type of training does not exist, a teacher can, as a last resort, take steps in self-training. Ordinarily, help is available from at least one member of the teaching staff or from the school technician.[23]

Every high school, small or large, should have an instructional media center. As a beginning, it may be necessary to place the center in a reserved corner of the school library with only a part-time teacher directing it. The center is important for both storing and distributing the materials. The ideal, of course, is a large center in which there is a full-time director and an adequate staff. It is well supplied with a variety of materials and equipment, and there are several carrels for the students to use the media individually. Also, some members of the center's staff can assist teachers to choose appropriate media and improve their skills in operating the equipment.[24]

In conclusion of our consideration of audio-visual materials in instruction, it is encouraging to note that research indicates the usefulness of these media toward improving learning.[25] This is what we should expect. The value of sensory experiences in the process of learning has been recognized by many leading educators from the time of John Amos Comenius, who produced what is widely accepted as the first illustrated text, *Orbis Pictus*, in the seventeenth century. Of course this does not suggest reduction in the use of reading by the teacher, who must use both means of instruction wisely, weighing the strength and the weaknesses of each in the learning situation. The question to ask repeatedly is "Will this particular medium be superior to others for improvement of the quality as well as the quantity of learning?"[26]

[22] Erickson and Curl, *Fundamentals of Teaching with Audiovisual Technology*, Chap. 9.
[23] J. Tanzman and K. J. Dunn, *Using Instructional Media Effectively*, Parker, West Nyack, New York, 1971, Chap. 4.
[24] For further appraisal of the need for this center see the section on instructional materials center in Chap. 12. See also Tanzman and Dunn, *Using Instructional Media Effectively*, Chap. 3.
[25] Ibid., p. 158.
[26] Ibid., Chap. 7.

USING MATERIALS FOR READING

The Necessity of Sufficient, Suitable Reading Materials

Along with adequate, appropriate audio-visual materials, sufficient, suitable reading materials are necessary for satisfactory learning. Sensory experiences do not reduce but increase the importance of reading in the learning process. Audio-visual aids contribute to goals and understandings in the reading experience. Each type of experience interacts with the other toward making learning intrinsically interesting and meaningful. This is true in all subjects, for example, in science, English, and the social studies. Significantly, programs of the new sciences include research in the library, in addition to the laboratory, as being essential for learning through the scientific method.

The need of ample provision for suitable reading materials in high school is obvious in view of the low level of reading shown by many of the students. It is seen in Chapter 7 that some of them read at about a fourth-grade level. One obvious cause of their poor reading is that they never had adequate opportunities for successful reading of appropriate materials. In fact, it may be assumed that many youths in high school are not reading according to their needs and abilities.

High schools are increasingly setting up programs for instruction in reading. Nearly all the programs, however, have been limited to remedial reading, in which only extremely retarded students and reading specialists and English teachers have been involved. Few schools have provided a developmental reading program which is for all the students and is conducted by all the teachers. Such a program is directed toward improvement of every student's desire and ability to read.

In some respects a teacher of science, social studies, or any other "content" subject is in a strong position to help students develop in reading. Here the focus is more in the direction of reading to learn than of "learning to read." Observing students in various learning situations and endeavoring to adjust instruction in the subject to the needs of the individual, this teacher can discover and provide for individual needs in reading and also can assist students to acquire attitudes and skills in reading conducive to finding answers to questions and solutions to problems. Concentrating on directing the learner to acquire subject matter from reading, results in development in the art of reading.[27]

Any teacher can improve students in learning through reading by careful preparation of the assignment. Preceding a reading activity, time is well

[27] R. G. Stauffer, *Directing Reading Maturity as a Cognitive Process*, Harper and Row, New York, 1969.

spent in promotion of purpose and meaning. In doing this audio-visual materials accompanied by thought questions and class discussions have been found to be effective. It is important to note further that presentation and discussion of the findings from readings also may contribute to preparation of students for future reading. Briefly, good teaching, as expressed in preceding chapters, includes leading students to set up and evaluate objectives of study and thus to have incentive and direction for reading.

Such promotion of learning through reading depends on direction of each student in selection and use of printed matter in accordance with his or her ability and need. As was seen in Chapter 5, that can be done in classes of about thirty students, as there is improvement and reduction in group instruction resulting in increased time for individualized instruction. Adequate provision for directed study affords the teacher many opportunities to observe and confer with students about how they may best read to learn.[28]

Obviously, provision for such teaching through reading requires a central library well supplied with a variety of books, pamphlets, and periodicals. A classroom library also is essential. In preceding chapters it was seen that leading educators in each curriculum area have emphasized the value of making the classroom a laboratory or workshop in which students learn by finding out for themselves. The classroom library provides for an immediate shift from lecture or discussion to investigative study. It contributes to a climate in the classroom conducive to the spirit of exploration and discovery instead of mere lesson learning.

The results from varied and extensive reading have been encouraging, according to research given in preceding chapters. This was also revealed in Michaels' investigation of the use of reading in teaching United States history. In his study it was incidentally found that only about 50 percent of the teachers involved supplemented the textbook with additional reading. His chief finding, however, was that classes experiencing reading beyond the textbook surpassed in analysis and comprehension the classes confined to the textbook.[29] Investigations reveal further that in a school that has a developmental reading program involving all teachers in an effort to provide suitable reading materials to meet the individual needs of students, there are significant increases in interests and skills in reading.[30]

[28] R. G. Stauffer, *The Language-Experience Approach to the Teaching of Reading,* Harper and Row, New York, 1970.

[29] M. L. Michaels, "Subject Reading Improvement, a Neglected Teaching Responsibility," *Journal of Reading* (October, 1965), 9, pp. 16-20.

[30] J. B. Tremonti, "Responsibilities of the Secondary-School Teacher in the Reading Program," *Journal of Developmental Reading* (Summer, 1964), 7, pp. 290-306.

AVAILABILITY OF INSTRUCTIONAL MATERIALS

Proper use of instructional materials depends to a large degree on the teacher's knowledge of the availability of materials. The beginning teacher in particular is likely to be deficient in such knowledge. Even though the school or district has an instructional materials center, the teacher needs to know about outside sources to turn to for additional learning aids suitable for the content and method of a subject.

An especially helpful source of materials is the United States government. Among the federal agencies on which the teacher may draw are the departments of the Cabinet. The Department of Agriculture, for example, provides printed materials that are useful in agriculture, science, social studies, home economics, industrial arts, and other subjects. Pamphlets are free or inexpensive. The publications are based on extensive research and written by specialists. Also, this department distributes such materials as maps, posters, still pictures, film strips, and motion pictures. Examples of its publications are *Background on Our Nation's Agriculture* and *Food for Fitness: A Daily Food Guide*. The Department of the Interior distributes materials on such topics as Indian affairs, national parks, wild life, and mines. The Department of Health, Education, and Welfare contains as a division, the United States Office of Education, which offers instructional aids and information about the aids. Two examples of its publications are *Science Books for Boys and Girls* and *Teaching Aids for Developing International Understanding*.

The central source for most of the federal publications is the U. S. Government Printing Office. Relatively few of its large number of publications are produced specifically for schools, but several can be adapted to classroom use and be made to furnish information unavailable elsewhere. Continuous information on valuable materials distributed by the Office may be obtained in the bulletin, *Selected United States Government Publications*, sent free on request.

The state governments also provide low-cost or free learning aids. Among the agencies on which a teacher may draw are Fish and Game, Highways, Motor Vehicles, Mental Health, Insurance, and Natural Resources. A copy of the state's governmental organizations may be obtained from the state's Secretary of State. Some state agencies have local branches that may help. These are located in the telephone directory under "Government." The state's colleges and universities are also important sources. These usually have bureaus of audio-visual aids at which motion picture films and other aids may be rented.

The National Education Association, 1201 Sixteenth Street, Northwest, Washington, D. C., is an extensive distributor of instructional materials. It publishes *Today's Education*, each issue of which has a section on materials. The Association has commissions, committees, and departments, the latter being of special help to teachers. The Department of Audiovisual Instruction, for example, publishes two magazines, *Audiovisual Instruction* and *Audiovisual Communication Review*, each of which has a section on sources of audio-visual materials. This Department also issues guides on the availability and uses of materials. Nearly all the other departments are organized around curriculum areas, each one distributing teaching materials for its area. Each also publishes one or more magazines in which sources of materials—some free or inexpensive—may be found. The departments and the magazines are:

1. American Association for Health, Physical Education, and Recreation—
   Journal of Health, Physical Education, and Recreation.
2. American Business Education Association—*Business Education Forum* and the *National Business Education Quarterly.*
3. American Industrial Arts Association—*The Industrial Arts Teacher.*
4. Department of Home Economcis—*Journal of Home Economics.*
5. Music Educators National Conference—*Music Educators Journal* and *Journal of Research in Music Education.*
6. National Art Education Association—*Art Education.*
7. National Council of Teachers of Mathematics—*The Arithmetic Teacher* and *The Mathematics Teacher.*
8. National Council for the Social Studies—*Social Education.*
9. National Science Teachers Association—*The Science Teacher.*

For the teacher of English, the National Council of Teachers of English, 508 South Sixth Street, Champaign, Illinois, publishes various audio-visual and printed materials, including the *English Journal*, which has a section on the nature and availability of materials.

Other national organizations, professional and nonprofessional, distribute a variety of free or inexpensive learning aids to schools. Some of those sources of aids are listed below:

AFL-CIO, Department of Education, 815 Sixteenth Street, Northwest, Washington, D. C.

American Automobile Association, Department of Public Education, 1712 G Street, Northwest, Washington, D. C.

American Bankers Association, 90 Park Avenue, New York, New York

American Bar Association, 1155 East Sixtieth Street, Chicago, Illinois

American Civil Liberties Union, 156 Fifth Avenue, New York, New York

American Dental Association, 211 East Chicago Avenue, Chicago, Illinois

American Institute of Family Relations, 5287 Sunset Boulevard, Los Angeles, California

American Medical Association, Bureau of Health Education, 535 North Dearborn Street, Chicago, Illinois

American Petroleum Institute, Department of Information, 1271 Avenue of the Americas, New York, New York

Anti-Defamation League of B'nai B'rith, 315 Lexington Avenue, New York, New York

Association of American Railroads, Schools and Colleges Services, 815 Seventeenth Street, Northwest, Washington, D. C.

Automobile Manufacturers' Association, 320 New Center Building, Detroit, Michigan

Chamber of Commerce of the United States, Audiovisual Services Department, 1615 H Street, Northwest, Washington, D. C.

Institute of Life Insurance, Education Division, 277 Park Avenue, New York, New York

National Association for Advancement of Colored People, 20 West Fortieth Street, New York, New York

National Association of Manufacturers, 277 Park Avenue, New York, New York

National Association for Mental Health, 10 Columbus Circle, New York, New York

National Audubon Society, 1130 Fifth Avenue, New York, New York

National Conference of Christians and Jews, 43 West 57th Street, New York, New York

National Safety Council of America, Film Service Bureau, 425 North Michigan Avenue, Chicago, Illinois

National Tuberculosis Association, 1790 Broadway, New York, New York

National Urban League, 14 East 48 Street, New York, New York

Public Affairs Committee, 381 Park Avenue South, New York, New York

Other sources of teaching materials are corporations, for example, the major automobile manufacturers. Partly as advertisement and partly as public service, a corporation conducts a public relations department, which distributes a variety of teaching aids— pictures, charts, pamphlets, film strips, motion pictures, and the like—all centered on the particular industry of the company and free or at nominal cost. Addresses of the corporations may be acquired from advertisements or from a local dealer or agent of the company.

For further assistance toward the discovery of the vast supply of learning aids, the teacher may turn to published guides. The cost of most guides is in the range of $5 to $15. Each of those presented below may be helpful in more than one curriculum area, particularly toward the acquisition of free or inexpensive materials.

A-V Instructional Materials, Department of Audiovisual Instruction, 1201 Sixteenth Street, Washington, D. C. Published monthly except July, August, and September. Provides continuous extensive information on the nature and availability of different materials.

Basic Book Collection for High Schools, American Library Association, 50 East Huron Street, Chicago, Illinois. Approximately 1500 annotated titles of appropriate books and magazines for students in senior high schools.

Basic Book Collection for Junior High Schools, American Library Association, 50 East Huron Street, Chicago, Illinois. Many annotated titles in fiction, science, social studies and other categories. The association also distributes motion pictures.

Books for You, National Council of Teachers of English, Champaign, Illinois.

Catalogue of Free Teaching Aids, Gordon Salisbury, Riverside, California. Annotated lists of pamphlets, models, film strips, etc.

Educators Guide to Free Films, Educators Progress Service, Randolph, Wisconsin. Briefly describes approximately 4,000 motion pictures available from large companies on a free-loan basis.

Educators Guide to Free Tapes, Scripts, and Transcriptions, Educators Progress Service, Randolph, Wisconsin. A guide similar to the preceding one on free films.

Educators Index to Free Materials, Educators Progress Service, Randolph, Wisconsin. Pamphlets, books, maps, charts, etc. are listed by curriculum areas.

Free and Inexpensive Learning Materials, Division of Surveys and Field Services, George Peabody College for Teachers, Nashville, Tennessee. Approximately 4,000 items presented under about 300 subject headings.

Free and Inexpensive Materials of World Affairs, Public Affairs Institute, 2912 P Street, Southeast, Washington, D. C. A variety of materials suitable particularly for social studies classes.

Gateways to Readable Books, H. W. Wilson Company, 950 University Avenue, Bronx, New York. An annotated list of more than 1,000 books in various fields for adolescents who find reading difficult.

Guides to Newer Educational Media, American Library Association, 50 East Huron Street, Chicago.

How and Where to Look It Up, McGraw-Hill Book Company, New York. A guide to the vast resources of the federal government for instructional materials and to a wide range of nongovernment sources.

National Tape Recording Catalogue, National Education Association, 1201 Sixteenth Street, Northwest, Washington, D. C. Lists of tapes available in different school subjects.

Paperbound Books in Print, published monthly by R. R. Bowker Company, 1180 Avenue of the Americas, New York, New York. Gives distributors of inexpensive books in fiction and non-fiction, including books of art, biography, business, cooking, crafts, games, literature, music, science, and social science.

Teaching Aids in the English Language Arts, National Council of Teachers of English, Champaign, Illinois. Lists books, magazines, and free helps.

Your Reading, National Council of Teachers of English, Champaign, Illinois. A catalogue of books in several areas of subject matter for students in junior high school, including some paperbacks and those easy to read.[31]

This chapter has attempted to assist the teacher in efficient use of different teaching materials. It has been pointed out that provision for either a sensory or a reading experience is no assurance of good teaching. Attention must be focused on the suitability of the particular aid and on the way it is used. Audio-visual and printed materials are used well only as they add purpose, meaning, and function to learning directed toward the all-round education of different young people for democratic living.

QUESTIONS AND ACTIVITIES

1. Why are audio-visual materials considered to be of special importance in modern education?
2. Illustrate how a teacher may use audio-visual aids and still be a poor teacher.
3. In a small group discussion, consider this question: "Why is it necessary to have both concrete and abstract learning experiences for effective learning?
4. In small discussion groups of similar subject majors, list and evaluate criteria for the selection of appropriate audio-visual materials for a specific learning situation in your subject.

---

[31] For additional lists of sources of audio-visual aids, see textbooks on the use of these aids, for example, Wittich and Schuller, *Audio Visual Materials,* Appendix; and Brown and others, *A-V Instruction,* Glossary, Part IV.

5. During class discussion time, consider several ways in which the teacher with a limited fund for audio-visual materials may obtain materials at little or no cost.

6. Demonstrate the proper use of some audio-visual aids in teaching a topic in your field of specialization. It may be beneficial to visit the audio-visual department of your college or a nearby high school for additional insights into the varied uses of these aids.

7. Invite an experienced audio-visual specialist and/or a classroom teacher who uses audio-visual aids a great deal into your class to demonstrate and discuss audio-visual materials about your subject area.

8. As a class, consider this statement: "Situations exist in teaching where additional reading may improve learning more than audio-visual experiences might."

9. During an observation in a high-school course, count the number of times the teacher uses an audio-visual aid in teaching. Can you suggest ways of improving that lesson by either eliminating or increasing the number and/or quality of those devices?

10. Modern learning theory suggests that a teacher may want to create psychological conflict in content by presenting information in a dynamic yet perplexing fashion. Demonstrate how this might be done in your subject area so as to encourage tentative mental perplexity, motivation, and inquiry.

SELECTED REFERENCES

Brown, J. W., and others, *A-V Instructions: Media and Methods*, 3rd ed., McGraw-Hill, New York, 1969.

Brown, J. W., and others, *A-V Instruction: Technology Media and Methods*, 4th ed., McGraw-Hill, New York, 1973.

Cohen, S. A., *Teach Them All to Read: Theory, Methods, and Materials for Teaching the Disadvantaged*, Random House, New York, 1969.

Dale, E., *Audio-Visual Methods in Teaching*, 3rd ed., Holt, Rinehart and Winston, New York, 1969.

Erickson, C. W. H., and D. H. Curl, *Fundamentals of Teaching with Audio-visual Technology*, 2nd ed., Macmillan, New York, 1972.

Gordon, G. N., *Classroom Television: New Frontiers in ITV*, Hastings House, New York, 1970.

Haney, J., and E. J. Ullmer, *Educational Media and the Teacher*, paper, William C. Brown, Dubuque, Iowa, 1970.

Kemp, J. E., *Planning and Producing Audiovisual Materials,* 2nd ed., Chandler, San Francisco, 1968.

Kinder, J. S., *Using Audio-Visual Materials in Education,* paper, American Book Company, New York, 1965.

Kinder, J. S., *Using Instructional Media,* Van Nostrand, Princeton, New Jersey, 1973.

National Education Association, *Teachers in Television and Other Media,* paper, National Education Association, Washington, D. C., 1969.

Pula, F. J., *Application and Operation of Audiovisual Equipment in Education,* John Wiley, New York, 1968.

Schultz, M. J., *The Teacher and Overhead Projection: A Treasury of Ideas, Uses, and Techniques,* Prentice-Hall, Englewood Cliffs, New Jersey, 1965.

Stauffer, R. G., *Directing Reading Maturity as a Cognitive Process,* Harper and Row, New York, 1969.

Stauffer, R. G., *The Language-Experience Approach to the Teaching of Reading,* Harper and Row, New York, 1970.

Tanzman, J., and K. J. Dunn, *Using Instructional Media Effectively,* Parker, West Nyack, New York, 1971.

Wittich, W. A., and C. F. Schuller, *Audio Visual Materials: Their Nature and Use,* 4th ed., Harper and Row, New York, 1967.

CHAPTER 11

During the past two decades, special innovational forms of instruction have been publicized and adopted in some high schools. Each of these procedures has had proponents who seemed to consider it almost as a panacea for curing educational ills. This chapter and the next analyze and appraise these special means of instruction, beginning with the two seeming to rank highest in extent of publicity and adoption. The purpose throughout the two chapters is to provide some answers to the question: "For humanistic teaching, are these innovational forms of instruction superior to the forms that they are designed to supplement or supplant?"

PROGRAMED INSTRUCTION

Characteristics of the Program

An analysis of the program in programed instruction reveals that it typically consists of a portion of subject matter presented to the learner in small steps or frames, precisely organized into a logical sequence. In the steps, the student is given information, cues, questions, and reinforcements and ordinarily is required to respond overtly by filling out blanks in the program. Reinforcement, a key essential, is provided through a comment on the nature and consequence of the response. Since the learner is moved by small, strictly controlled steps through the program, few errors are likely, the ideal being less than 10 percent. Responses are rigidly determined by the explicit, external stimuli and the effects or reinforcements.[1]

The preceding characterization of the program is of the linear type,

[1] W. L. Garner, *Programed Instruction*, The Center for Applied Research in Education, New York, 1966, Chap. 2.

PROGRAMED INSTRUCTION AND TEAM TEACHING

designed and promoted by B. F. Skinner, a psychologist of Harvard University. In this type every learner moves over the same prescribed path without provision for detours, including the low-ability student. The frames are supposed to be constructed so small and easy that any student capable of learning in conventional instruction can progress through the program satisfactorily if permitted to set the pace.

A slightly different program designed by N. A. Crowder and commonly known as a "branching" or "intrinsic" program, deserves passing attention. Its pattern provides for branches or by-paths from the main course. In its construction the programmer includes additional information and direction to assist the poor student to clarify ideas and correct erroneous responses. Incorrect responses require learning detours, but correct responses require an allowance of long steps along the regular path. In contrast to the linear program, which contains the same sequence of stimuli for every learner and rigidly controls the responses, the intrinsic program contains a variety of stimuli and uses some responses to discriminate among learners and lead them into separate paths.[2]

Presently, branch programing for care of individual differences faces an almost insurmountable task. The cost of an adequate supply of branching programs to provide for the educational needs of different young people is virtually prohibitive. Moreover, for that educational goal, a good teacher can be quite resourceful and adjustable. At any rate, nearly all the programs now developed for commercial use are of the Skinnerian linear type.[3] They obviously can be more easily constructed than those of the branching classification. It is Skinner's linear program that has usually been designed for the teaching machine and the programed textbook and has become a center of controversy in educational theory and practice.

Using the Program

In comparison with much conventional teaching, the program has proved itself to be a desirable special means of instruction. Among the areas where it has been used with satisfactory results are in the study of a foreign language and in training for a particular job in industry or military service. Furthermore, the program is designed for thoroughness of learning in any subject of the school curriculum, whatever may be claimed about the usefulness of the learning. The teacher, however, needs to understand the program's limitations, which some of its enthusiastic proponents recognize. In some situations and for some students, the program can be used to improve a student's interests and skills in a subject. A promoter of this form of instruction states that, for its best usefulness, it should

2 Ibid., pp. 16-20.
3 K. E. Myers, "What Do We Know About Programed Instruction?" *Clearing House* (May, 1965), 39, pp. 533-538.

not be provided as a steady diet in the classroom. In fact, he suggests that its use could well be mainly in homework.

. . . A classroom diet of straight programmed texts is possible, and remarkably effective, but it is unlikely to achieve the best possible results. The teacher may even decide to use the programmed text material partly or mainly for homework, allowing some time in class for raising questions prompted by it. The remaining class time—which may be virtually all of it—can be devoted to exploration of other approaches and material, with the whole class or with subgroups that are on the same section of the programmed text, such as presenting the programmed text material in a different way, introduction of novel examples not given in the text, use of audiovisual materials, field trips, group discussions, group or individual projects, student presentations to the class, laboratory work, individual consultations with students about their examination results or programmed text progress, discussions or debates on course topics, use of game or play materials keyed to subject matter, and visiting lecturers.[4]

Proponents of the program assert that its use relieves the teacher of being a dispenser of information by paced lectures. The question that may well be raised here is "Does relevant, useful instruction require either a teacher or a program to dispense bits of information to students?" In the teaching-learning process that has been described and illustrated repeatedly in preceding chapters, the teacher provides learning situations that involve students in use of the laboratory and library to search for information they need for solution of their problems and accomplishment of their projects. Information thus acquired by the student has been found to be understandable, retainable, and transferable.

The suggestion here to teachers is to have an open mind about programed instruction and the other innovational special means of instruction; each of these means of instruction should be appraised in the light of educational psychology, philosophy, research and, of course, the students' needs in contemporary society.

Psychological Basis

The psychology of learning on which Skinner's programed instruction partially rests is Thorndike's theory, which is presented along with the Gestalt or field theory in Chapter 2. However, Skinner says he has taken more seriously the Law of Effect than Thorndike did. He explains that whereas Thorndike applied this law by provision of a reward at the end of a learning activity, he has applied it by a series of rewards distributed throughout the activity. Skinner's psychology is in line with J. B. Watson's behaviorism of the 1920s, which emphasized learning as conditioning. In a psychological laboratory, Skinner conditioned pigeons by supplying

[4] M. Scriven, *Programmed Instruction: Bold New Adventure*, A. D. Calvin, ed., Indiana University Press, Bloomington, 1969, Chap. 1, p. 25.

reinforcement after each move within the act, as is done by the typical animal trainer. Referring to his achievements in the laboratory, he said that the techniques followed enable one "to shape the behavior of an organism almost at will."[5] He added that "through gradual advance to complex interrelations among responses, the same degree of rigor is being extended to behavior which would usually be assigned to such fields as perception, thinking, and personality dynamics."[6]

Thus, according to Skinner, learning is a process of what he calls "operant conditioning," whether it occurs in a person or a pigeon. Through precise stimuli, responses, and reinforcements, a program directs the student step by step to a terminal performance. Hilgard and Bower express recognition of this when they state that in Skinner's application of his psychological principles to programed instruction, "he arrived at his methods through an attempt to generalize to education what he had learned through the study of operant conditioning in rats and pigeons."[7]

Skinner's view of learning as solely a conditioning process is considered by many psychologists and educators to be inadequate for an explanation of human learning. Unlike the other leading conception of learning, the goal-insight theory, it does not deal sufficiently with purpose and meaning. Nearly all prominent psychologists have recognized the importance of cognitive and purposive factors in the learning situation. Thorndike recognized these essentials for effective learning in people, but he preferred to express them in what he considered scientific terminology. Skinner, however, seems to minimize or even reject such forces as purpose, incentive, and meaning in learning as he explains them as projection into the past without due recognition of their power in creative perception of future consequences.

Statements which use such words as "incentive" or purpose are usually reducible to statements about operant conditioning and only a slight change is required to bring them within the framework of natural science. Instead of saying that a man behaves because of the consequences which *are* to follow his behavior, we simply say that a man behaves because of the consequences which *have* followed similar behavior in the past. This is, of course, the Law of Effect or operant conditioning.[8]

We are left to decide about the simplicity and value of this explanation of purpose or incentive and the like in effective human learning. A person draws on past experiences for stimulation and guidance in self-direc-

5 B. F. Skinner, *Teaching Machines and Programed Learning*, A. A. Lumsdaine and R. Glaser, eds., National Education Association, Washington, D. C., 1960, Chap. 14, p. 99.
6 Ibid., p. 103. See also B. F. Skinner, "Reflections on a Decade of Teaching Machines," *Teachers College Record* (November, 1963), 65, pp. 168-177.
7 E. R. Hilgard and G. H. Bower, *Theories of Learning*, 3rd ed., Appleton-Century-Crofts, New York, 1966, p. 132.
8 B. F. Skinner, *Science and Human Behavior*, Macmillan, New York, 1953, p. 87.

tion in learning but, simultaneously, may view the future imaginatively and evaluate the probable consequences of some future acts. Thus may intrinsic goals and meanings enter into the process of learning. Each step has meaning as it moves the person toward an objective. This is the position of Gestalt psychologists and other psychologists who hold that learning is inadequately explained solely in terms of external stimuli and observable responses produced by an associative process. They believe that "a complete learning theory must have something to say about reasoning, creative imagination, and inventiveness." Skinner, however, has presented a behavioristic psychology for support of his programed instruction; his programs "depend on conditioning as a behavioral base."[9]

Philosophical Basis

In a further effort to support programed instruction, Skinner has presented a philosophy of determinism. It emphasizes control of the individual by the physical and social environment without sufficient recognition of how the individual may in turn control the environment. As already indicated, this point of view includes little of what occurs within a person who decides, thinks, acts, and learns; it centers on observable responses emitted as result of external stimuli. In addition, Skinner believes that his science of human behavior is opposed by the Western democratic philosophy, which advocates freedom, responsibility, and initiative of the individual. He states that the traditional view of human nature in Western culture is well known and that it pervades our beliefs and practices. Then he adds:

The use of such concepts as individual freedom, initiative, and responsibility, has, therefore, been well reinforced. When we turn to what science has to offer, however, we do not find very comforting support for the traditional Western point of view. The hypothesis that man is not free is essential to the application of scientific method to the study of human behavior. The free inner man who is held responsible for the behavior of the external biological organism is only a prescientific substitute for the kind of causes which are discovered in the course of scientific analysis. All these alternative causes lie *outside* the individual. . . . The environment determines the individual even when he alters the environment.[10]

Although Western democracy created the conditions responsible for the rise of modern science, it is now evident that it may never fully profit from that achievement. The so-called "democratic philosophy" of human behavior to

[9] Myers, "What Do We Know About Programed Instruction?" p. 535. For further presentation of Skinner's psychological view, see M. L. Bigge and M. P. Hunt, *Psychological Foundations of Education*, 2nd ed., Harper and Row, New York, 1968, Chap. 15; B. C. Mathis and others, *Psychological Foundations of Education: Learning and Teaching*, Academic Press, New York, 1970, pp. 51-71.

[10] Skinner, *Science and Human Behavior*, pp. 447-448. See also Bigge and Hunt, *Psychological Foundations of Education*, pp. 356-357.

which it also gave rise is increasingly in conflict with the application of the methods of science to human affairs. Unless this conflict is somehow resolved, the ultimate goals of democracy may be long deferred.[11]

We are unable to see that there is a conflict between Western democracy and the science of human behavior. History seems to show that in the last few centuries science and democracy have advanced perceptibly by the contributions of each to the other. Both have emphasized freedom and responsibility of the individual to discover and abide by the truth. Apparently, Skinner conceives of Western democracy as advocating absolute freedom of the individual and the science of human behavior as demanding complete control of the individual. As shown in Chapter 3, leading writers on democracy in education have viewed freedom, responsibility, and initiative not as absolute but as relative concepts, related both to one another and to the environment. In government, too, proponents of democracy consider the individual to be self-directing but always within the frame of the physical and social environment. Likewise, an adequate concept of a science of human behavior requires some emphasis on control by the individual along with some by the environment. As has been seen in preceding chapters, many experiments in psychology and education indicate that ideas, concepts, interests, and the like function with the environment in stimulation and direction of effective learning. When democracy and a science of human behavior are thus conceived, there is agreement and mutual support between the two.

Skinner has restated his educational psychology and philosophy in a recent book.[12] His psychology is still mechanistic and behavioristic and his philosophy, deterministic. In explanation of human behavior, he eliminates giving a role to feeling, purpose, or will. He continues to believe that human beings are controlled by their environment and, therefore, cannot possess autonomy and freedom, which is a point of view in conflict with not only our democratic philosophy but also an experimental psychology. What we must realize is that a person is not controlled completely and is not absolutely free. Freedom is limited by the environment; but of primary importance is that the environment can also enlarge a person's freedom through provision for various wants and needs.

It is important to note that because of having different environments, individuals vary in inclination and ability to engage in self-direction. The degree and kind of control a person has over the environment, social or physical, depends partly on opportunities for past experiences in such control. Specifically, an adolescent who has lived from babyhood in an environment of repression and dictation in home and school tends to be

11 B. F. Skinner, *Cumulative Record*, enlarged ed., Appleton-Century-Crofts, New York, 1961, p. 3.
12 B. F. Skinner, *Beyond Freedom and Dignity*, Alfred A. Knopf, New York, 1971, especially Chaps. 1, 9.

either submissive or rebellious. In contrast, one who has lived and learned through sharing objectives and procedures with others and has been allowed limited, socially oriented freedom and responsibility is likely to experience a fruitful, satisfying give-and-take with the environment. The degree and kind of guidance and control needed in school are shown in Chapters 13 and 14. The question requiring an answer here is "Does a philosophy of determinism and its product, programed instruction, contribute well to self-guidance or self-discipline of the individual?"

Implications of Modern Educational Theory and Practice

How well does programed instruction provide for the essentials of a suitable education for young people today? In preceding chapters we have seen repeatedly that writers in education, including those in each curriculum area, have advocated instruction aimed at meeting the real needs of different students. They have made specific recommendations in accord with suggestions from a purposeful, insightful view of learning, the democratic ideal, and an unpredictable, complicated social order. An emphasis in their proposals of classroom procedures is on placing the student in many learning situations similar to those of the scientist and the artist—to explore, investigate, and create. In the process various experiences in recognizing, defining, and setting up problems and in suggesting and testing hypotheses are gained. The process involves pursuit of group and individual interests through reflective discussion in the classroom and through investigative, creative work in the library and laboratory.

The method described above places emphasis on providing the student with various concrete experiences and with freedom to use the experiences to explore, inquire, find out, create, and generalize while moving toward objectives in learning activities. In contrast, a distinguishing feature of programed instruction is its precise, rigid control of the learner's every step toward the final objective of the program. It also may be characterized by its usual adherence to verbal stimuli and verbal responses. For example, a program may be used by even a fourth-grade student to express the terminology of scientists in an explanation of the condensation of vapor with scarcely any understanding of the phenomenon. A safe inference is that some of the learning from the program is little more than verbalization.[13]

Reports of Programed Instruction in High Schools

In reading about adoption of programed instruction in secondary schools, one gets the impression that it has not been very rapid. This was

---

[13] S. Shimabukuro, "Guidelines for the Classroom Use of Programed Courses," *Journal of Teacher Education* (December, 1965), 16, pp. 469-476.

indicated in a survey of high schools in northern Illinois. The reporter of the survey concluded that the chief reasons for the hesitance of many schools to use the method are that (1) almost without exception it is concerned exclusively with factual material and routine, recall skills and (2) it is chiefly verbal, lacking provision for a concrete, meaningful approach.[14] Another writer, in light of a review of its use, is convinced its effectiveness has fallen short of its expectations and that the principles on which programs have been based require considerable reexamination.[15]

A report about the use of programs in ninth-grade algebra in Lakewood High School, Lakewood, Ohio, is representative. In expressing the results, the reporter stated that nearly all the students were motivated through the definite assignments and the opportunity to proceed at different rates. Almost without exception, they revealed a favorable attitude toward the instruction, and their achievement on standardized tests was satisfactory. Also, the teacher was assisted toward provision of individualized instruction. However, it was found that programs do not provide for the student to discover and generalize and that they rely too much on the "rule-example" approach, which many mathematicians deplore.[16]

Findings from three years of experiences with the program at Medford High School, Medford, Massachusetts, also are revealing. This school placed specially selected students in programed classes. On achievement tests they did as well or better than those taught by the conventional method. Some members of the program group completed four years of mathematics in about two years. Several of the group, however, were not highly motivated. In reply to a question about how far the instruction may be boring, the reply was that the students did not find it any more so than conventional instruction and that inspiration is something caught from a good teacher. An additional observation reported is that if teachers allow the program to take over teaching of the class, they are simply not on the job, and that teachers using programs must spend an average of three hours more work per week than conventional teachers.[17]

From these two reports one significant conclusion indicated is that programed instruction is designed to help conventional teachers more than modern teachers, who spend nearly all of their time not on dispensing information directly but on encouraging the learner to discover it. As the reader recalls, one major change that programs produce in the classroom

14 S. H. Frey, "The Case Against Programed Instruction," *Clearing House* (September, 1965), 40, pp. 27-29.
15 R. T. Heimer, "Designs for Future Explorations in Programed Instruction," *Mathematics Teacher* (February, 1966), 59, pp. 110-114. See also C. Helwig, "Innovation: What's It All About?" *Clearing House* (October, 1971), 46, pp. 82-85.
16 P. McGarvey, "Programed Instruction in Ninth-Grade Algebra," *Mathematics Teacher* (November, 1962), 55, pp. 576-579.
17 J. Houston, "Programed Math Passes Three-Year Test," *Nation's Schools* (August, 1965), 76, pp. 40-43.

is that they free the teacher who continuously supplies factual information to the group to provide individualized instruction.[18]

Trial of the program in another high school led to raising some basic questions. The DeWitt Clinton High School in New York tried to use a programed textbook, *The American Constitution* (Doubleday, Garden City, New York). This program provides the student with small amounts of information, each followed by multiple-choice answers. The learner selects an answer and then turns to the page indicated to learn whether the answer is correct. Instruction for the next step is determined by the correctness or incorrectness of the answer chosen. Because of uncontrolled variable factors occurring in the use of this program, the reporters stated that positive conclusions about results could not be reached. This experience with a programed textbook in a social study, however, led them to ask whether programed instruction, which limits freedom of thought and encourages conformity, can properly be used in social studies, which aim to promote critical thinking, involving suspending judgment, and searching for and weighing evidence before reaching conclusions.[19]

Analysis of Research

A look at investigations of results from programed instruction reveals that comparisons are made almost invariably between this technique of teaching and conventional teaching. We agree with Skinner and other writers that conventional procedure often has been found to be quite ineffective. However, one needs to recognize that improvement of conventional teaching involves improvement of learning in quality as well as quantity. Educators are not restricted to a comparison between only conventional instruction and programed instruction. Unfortunately, research has neglected to compare programed instruction with the modern type of instruction, which provides for active student participation in the choice and pursuit of objectives, exploring, solving problems, experimenting, and discovering. An important question is "Does research show that programed instruction is superior to instruction that provides content and method for the student's use toward development in goal seeking, organization and expression of thoughts, reflection, creativity, and the like?"

That students may learn more from programed instruction than from ordinary instruction has been indicated by some investigations. A review of 36 reports of studies comparing the program method with the conventional method showed that in 18 the program is superior; in 17, no significant difference exists between the two; and in 1, superiority of the conventional was seen.[20] Other reviewers of research report similar findings,

[18] Calvin, *Programmed Instruction,* p. 38.

[19] D. Feins and G. Leinwand, "Programed Instruction in the Social Studies," *High Points* (October, 1965), 47, pp. 13-14.

[20] Hilgard and Bower, *Theories of Learning,* p. 558.

stating that only a small number of experiments indicated superiority of programed instruction over conventional procedure and that in the other experiments there is lack of demonstrable superiority of either method.[21] They also have found evidence that merely reading the content of a program may be as effective in production of learning as the reading plus the required responses of a program. According to Pressey, reviews of the most adequate research have reported that the program method is often no more efficient than the usual study-reading method and nearly always more clumsy and expensive.[22]

Of further significance are the specific findings from research on the constituent elements of a program, considered as essentials by Skinner and others. Some studies of sequence of frames or steps in the program do not indicate superiority of ordered sequence over random sequence. Likewise, investigations have not shown an appreciable advantage of small steps over large ones. Another significant finding is that there is insufficient evidence to show that in individual study of a program there is any advantage of self-pacing over controlled pacing. Finally, there is some evidence that frequent, external reinforcement is not essential for students to learn well.[23]

A finding of special importance is that the conventional textbook may be superior to the program for promoting understanding in learning. This seems to be true particularly for the least capable student. This student typically lacks the background and breadth of view necessary for insightful learning of a program's meager content. The experimenter concluded: "It is possible that learning is maximized by the studying of material which is organized into large meaningful wholes rather than material which is broken down into small response units."[24] In a similar investigation, the investigators concluded that the textbook seems to be superior to the program in providing understanding in learning and thereby permanence of retention and application of the materials learned.[25]

In another study two investigators studied how well programed instruction may provide for individual differences among learners. They drew the conclusion that "only higher ability students should be permitted to work on programs in out-of-class situations" and that the other students

21 L. J. Briggs and D. Angell, "Programed Instruction in Science and Mathematics," *Review of Educational Research* (June, 1964), 34, pp. 354-373.
22 S. L. Pressey, "A Puncture of the Huge 'Programing' Boom?" *Teachers College Record* (February, 1964), 65, pp. 413-418.
23 Garner, *Programed Instruction*, pp. 42-43; J. M. Furukawa, "A Chunking Method of Determining Size of Step in Programed Instruction," *Journal of Educational Psychology* (June, 1970), 61, pp. 247-254.
24 M. E. Feldman, "Learning by Programed and Text Format at Three Levels of Difficulty," *Journal of Educational Psychology* (June, 1965), 56, p. 138.
25 M. H. Goldberg and others, "Comparison of Programed and Conventional Instruction Methods," *Journal of Applied Psychology* (April, 1964), 48, pp. 110-114. See also Pressey, "A Puncture of the Huge 'Programing' Boom?" p. 416.

should be required to work in class under teacher supervision. This study, along with reports from schools using programed instruction, indicates that this type of instruction should not be expected to reduce the teacher's work in class as much as some writers have suggested or to provide well for the individual needs of low-ability students.[26]

Thus experimentation on programed instruction reveals a significant gap between the promise and the practice of this way of teaching. Some claims of leading exponents of the program have little support from research. As just seen, such constituent elements of the orthodox program as the small step and an immediate reinforcement have not been shown by experimentation to be essentials for effective learning in the classroom. There is some evidence that program procedure has been used to increase an observable, behavioral type of learning, but none that it also has increased a purposive-conceptual type. In fact, some findings indicate that the ordinary textbook may surpass the program in production of such important results as understanding in learning and thereby increase the retention and transfer of the learning. As Garner states, the program is effective in production of learning in the form of behavior, but its effectiveness may contribute to development of harmful or useless ideas and attitudes. In more detail he says:

Programming produces changes in behavior effectively; but dangers arising from this effectiveness exist and preventive steps must be taken, since it is possible that unproductive ideas and handicapping attitudes can be initiated in learners. . . . Students can get a notion that learning is always a process of tracking an easily followed sequence of fragmentary units and that information and concepts will always be ready-made for their consumption. If they are protected from complexity, they will be unadjusted to the fact that the life they will be leading will be anything but neatly arranged and simplistic.[27]

In conclusion, we recognize that the program has shown impressive results in areas of instruction requiring training in operational skills, as in preparation for some jobs in industry or for service in a branch of the armed forces. It has also proved its value as an aid in acquisition of specific skills in any school subject. This does not imply, however, that extensive employment of this form of instruction in the American high school is necessary for effective learning. Instead, the school may wisely concentrate on having well-educated, socially adjusted teachers, a modernized curriculum, and adequate and suitable materials of instruction with only some supplementary use of programed instruction.

[26] A. B. Woodruff and S. Shimabukuro, *Studies on Individual Differences Related to Performance on Programed Instruction,* Cooperative Research Project No. 3129, Northern Illinois University, DeKalb, 1967, pp. 53-54.
[27] Garner, *Programed Instruction,* p. 97.

TEAM TEACHING

Like programed instruction, team teaching in current educational theory and practice is of recent origin and is conceived by some of its proponents as an ideal form of instruction. Hence it behooves teachers in secondary education to weigh thoughtfully the features and functions assigned to this pattern of teaching. Is it essential for the production of high-quality learning? Could efficient use of traditionally organized classroom procedure result in educational outcomes equal or superior to those of team teaching? As of the present, does research seem to support the theoretical claims made for this form of instruction?

Distinguishing Features and Functions

As an aid to perception of the characteristics of team teaching, one may recognize that there always has been some degree and kind of such teaching in schools. Teachers have occasionally chosen to cooperate in pursuit of their individual goals. Specifically, it is not uncommon for those of a department to work together and to visit in the others' classrooms. Furthermore, in the early part of this century a few schools designed unique organizations of cooperative instruction, for example, the Platoon System of Gary, Indiana; the Dalton Plan of Dalton, Massachusetts; and the Winnetka Plan of Winnetka, Illinois. Significantly, all such efforts to improve working relationships of teachers involved retention of a relatively independent teacher in the classroom.

An essential of current team teaching is the assumption of responsibility by two or more teachers for the instruction of the same students, the number often being about 100. The teacher ceases to be solely responsible for the teaching of a class but, rather, plans and executes plans in cooperation with one or more teachers. This requires regularly scheduled conferences in which the team considers such items as the nature and needs of the students, sets up specific educational objectives, and assigns particular tasks to each member. The form and the function of team teaching vary in some respects among schools, but it is not orthodox team teaching unless there is elimination of the independent classroom and inclusion of joint action by a group of teachers in the instruction of a group of students.

Implicit, if not explicit, in this working relationship is the assumption that the team teachers will share instructional tasks and goals; plan together; assign appropriate tasks to individual team members; see each other teach; have access to each other's classrooms; join together in evaluation of instruction; share information about the students for whom they are jointly responsible; and hold discussions, based upon common observations, of teaching and the effects of teaching.[28]

[28] J. T. Shaplin and H. F. Olds, Jr., *Team Teaching*, Harper and Row, New York, 1964, p. 9.

Each day the team assumes responsibility for providing appropriate learning experiences for different groups of students within the group assigned to the team. About two periods a week the whole group may be taught by one member of the team by lecture. In other periods small groups of 25 or less are scheduled for interaction of the students in discussion and for individualized instruction. The grouping and the scheduling involve considerable flexibility. In the words of Trump:

[Team teaching is] an arrangement whereby two or more teachers and their aids, in order to take advantage of their respective competencies, plan, instruct, and evaluate, in one or more subject areas, a group of elementary or secondary students equivalent in size to two or more conventional classes, making use of a variety of technical aids to teaching in large group instruction, small group discussion, and independent study.[29]

Large group instruction is a prominent feature of team teaching. It often seems to be the chief reason for that form of instruction. Typically, the lecture to all the team's students is given by the teacher having special interest and versatility in the particular area of subject matter being introduced to the class. The other member or members of the team usually attend to aid promotion of cooperation and continuity of the teaching process. This large group instruction, which usually includes use of audiovisual equipment, provides for efficient presentation of information. However, it has been found that a lecture, even one well prepared and delivered, may not meet the needs of all kinds of students, particularly the poor ones. Quite a percentage of the team's students may need individualized instruction within small group procedure more than a lecture to a large group.[30] Yet, "according to testimony and observations of university people associated with a number of team teaching projects, the teams have thus far failed to develop any usual or promising techniques for instructing small groups."[31]

The Teacher and Team Teaching

Although the general, ultimate function of team teaching is improvement of the student's learning, its special, intermediary function is promotion of the teacher's efficiency. An important purpose of this form of teaching is to make a contribution to the professional growth of the teacher. Of course experienced and inexperienced teachers have at hand opportunities and means of growth in nonteam situations, and the resourceful, interested teacher makes use of opportunities. However, teachers as well

[29] J. L. Trump, "What Is Team Teaching?" *Education* (February, 1965), 85, p. 327.
[30] For suggestions about provision of small-group and individualized instruction without use of team teaching see the section on individualized instruction in Chap. 5 and section on teaching English in Chap. 7.
[31] Trump, "What Is Team Teaching?" p. 208.

as students may be significantly stimulated and directed in learning through interactions within a group in pursuit of common goals. Team teachers exchange ideas in planning and evaluating tasks for themselves and for the students, and they give each other needed information and constructive criticism. The team teacher almost invariably testifies to the beneficial effects of team teaching in professional understandings and attitudes.

The actuality of those potential benefits to the teacher is enhanced by good teacher relationship. A satisfactory relationship depends partly on the team's organization. There is the hierarchical form in which a chairman or leader for the team is appointed on the basis of experience and ability by an administrator. The other type of organization provides for selection of a leader by the team. Although some proponents of team teaching favor the hierarchical organization, most of the teachers seem to prefer the other form, which seems to be conducive to promotion of unity in spirit and action.[32]

It is important to note incidentally that some teachers lack the personal qualities required in real team activity. The insecure, intolerant, or opinionated person is unlikely to be happy and efficient and may be even a troublemaker. Although such characteristics may be a handicap also in the one-teacher classroom, the teacher in this environment may experience little threat from colleagues and considerable success in working with the same relatively small groups of youngsters each day. From a survey of teachers, the investigators concluded that among the essential traits of the team teacher are flexibility, ability to work cooperatively with other adults, consideration for one's peers, ability to accept criticism, and organizational skill.[33]

Educational Objectives and Team Teaching

Unfortunately, some team teaching projects seem to have focused more on an organization for improvement and utilization of teachers than on the aims of education and their use for provision of suitable education for different students. Some educators recognize, however, that the fundamental weaknesses in American education are not faults in organization for instruction but faults in courses, methods, tests, teaching materials, and the teachers' education. No doubt some schools in shifting to team teaching prefer continuation of the status quo in content and method of courses. Others retain traditional practices apparently in fear of change, especially as it requires considerable study and work. The fact remains, however, that team teaching by itself does not ensure improvement of instruction. High quality learning may be expected from that form of teaching only

---

32 C. H. Peterson, "Team Teaching in the High School," Education (February, 1965), 85, pp. 343-347.
33 W. R. Borg and L. R. Brite, "Teachers' Perceptions of Team Teaching," California Journal of Educational Research (March, 1967), 18, pp. 71-81+.

when it is oriented by a sound psychology of learning and democratic objectives of education, such as presented in Chapters 2 and 3, respectively.

If team teaching is to improve the quality of instruction, it will do so by helping students attain the basic goals of education. It is reasonable to expect that all team teaching projects would be planned with this fact in mind and would make explicit how team-work can foster the attainment of certain educational aims. In point of fact, most projects have lacked this feature. . . . The implication is that, whatever the educational goal one has in mind, team teaching will contribute toward its attainment. This implication merits examination.[34]

Another look at unity of action, a key feature of team organization, may help here. There is nothing in teacher cooperation that guarantees learning in accord with any list of educational goals. Teachers may co-operate toward promotion of learning that has either little or much meaning or is conducive to students' living either democratically or undemocratically. Whatever educational objective the team understands and accepts, the team situation provides a setting for unified action in the advancement of learning toward the goal.[35]

Likewise, the use of the lecture to the whole group of students requires reexamination at this point. As was noted, preparation of a lecture or a demonstration for a large group challenges the teacher to present interesting and useful materials in an effective manner. Also, many students prefer mere reception of information to an active search for it. However, many educators over the years have questioned the quality of learning often resulting from reception of "ready-made" thoughts. With their aim on development of a mature, self-directing student and citizen, they have advocated a teaching-learning process that emphasizes assistance of students to investigate and find out for themselves. As seen in Chapters 7–9, both the aim and method of student discovery in learning have been advocated by leaders on the teaching of each subject of the high-school curriculum. For such instruction adequate provision of small classes is required. Yet, according to reports, the focus in team teaching sometimes seems to be more on large than on small group instruction. For example, one high school reported that the teachers are usually enthusiastic about the success of the large group instruction but have not found improved ways of making small group instruction effective.[36] Thus in providing for small-group instruction, team teaching organization may not have surpassed conventional classroom organization.

Too often reports of team teaching indicate a deductive process in which

34 Shaplin and Olds, *Team Teaching*, p. 347-348. See also F. T. Arone, "Toward Greater Success in Team Teaching," *Clearing House* (April, 1971), 45, pp. 501-502.
35 H. Ohme, "Steps toward Relevance: An Interest-Centered Curriculum," *Journal of Secondary Education* (November, 1970), 45, pp. 299-304.
36 R. W. Joly, "Observations on Team Teaching at Monroe," *High Points* (May, 1964), 46, pp. 41-46.

the teachers concentrate on telling and demonstrating facts, ideas, or thoughts with insufficient provision for students to recognize and formulate problems and investigate and devise means of solving the problems. For example, this seems to be true in a report of team teaching in chemistry in a high school in a large city. The teaching pattern there provided for the lecture approach to the unit of study. A team teacher initiated the learning activity by a lecture to the entire class. On completion of the lecture, the group was divided into sections for work in laboratory or classroom. In the laboratory experimentation stemmed from the lecture and was of the demonstration type. During the presentation of a demonstration, one instructor performed the mechanisms of the demonstration while another instructor gave the explanations. In the classrooms there were "recitation-lecture-demonstration sessions" for small groups. Thus the report indicates focus on teacher activity toward informing and showing without active involvement of chemistry students in an inductive process of learning. Yet it stated as a conclusion that the school had found an ideal form of teaching.[37]

That team teaching may be used to involve students in initiation and solution of problems and in learning through inquiring, discovering, relating, and reflecting may be seen in a report of team teaching at Baldwin High School in Pittsburgh. In the Pittsburgh school, curriculum revision led in the initiation of team teaching. The initial step was to improve the content and method of courses in line with the new courses in mathematics and science. For instance, in the social studies there was extended study of world cultures which "dealt with the eight cultural universals of all civilizations: reproduction, biological aspects, maintenance of order, economics, meaning and motivation, geography, history, and socialization." Instead of deductive procedure initiated by a lecture that explained those universals and was followed by discussion of the presentation, an inductive approach was employed. First the students were divided into small groups and, through discussion, constructed expressions of what they considered to be the major needs and problems of human beings, which were classified and considered for study. Pertinent questions were raised about the nature of the needs and how they could probably be met. Obviously, this is a problem-raising approach. In this somewhat unorthodox team teaching, there is a place for the lecture, but it does not have the prominent role it seems to have in typical team teaching. Primacy apparently is given to small group instruction so that students may have opportunities to share in formulating and pursuing goals in learning activities.[38]

[37] R. L. Watson, "Team Teaching of Chemistry at the High School Level," *School Science and Mathematics* (June, 1965), 65, pp. 556-562. See also R. K. Atwood, "Team Teaching: New Models Are Needed," *Science Teacher* (January, 1970), 37, pp. 59-60.
[38] A. Jeffries and others, "Team Teaching Brings New Kinds of Learning," *Pennsylvania School Journal* (May, 1966), 114, pp. 420-422+.

The necessity of meeting the needs of different students also requires special consideration in relation to team teaching. As is well known, use of this aim in any form of instruction involves securing knowledge of each student's nature and needs. Although study of the student by the whole team is advantageous, the extensive experiences of the teacher with every student in the self-contained classroom do not exist to the same extent in a team-teaching situation. It takes longer for a team to become acquainted with the students than for the teacher of the traditional classroom.[39] At any rate it seems to be recognized that team teaching, as it is sometimes practiced, is more suitable for the strong than for the weak student. Reports indicate that it is found most often in suburban schools consisting of a large percentage of college-bound students or in special classes of superior students. Yet it can be used effectively in inner-city schools.

Research on Results

As in appraisal of content and method in team-teaching organization, an appraisal of the outcome requires consideration of education goals. A common weakness in experimentation on results of that form of teaching consists of a comparison of outcomes with those of the ordinary self-contained classroom. In this there is lack of specific reference to the outcomes of high quality education, such as growth in critical or creative thinking and rational self-direction. Usually the academic achievement of the students has been discovered solely by standardized achievement tests, which have been designed primarily for measurement of acquisition of information. How well may team teaching promote learning toward important objectives of modern educational theory and practice?

Results from experiments on team teaching fail to show that it has produced significant changes in either the quantity or the quality of learning in high school. The findings do not reveal convincingly that it is a superior form of instruction for teaching the knowledge of subject matter. Almost invariably the reports do not even mention the extent of any results such as development in scientific and social attitudes and in inclination and ability to engage in investigative and creative activities. A review of research on the team pattern of instruction thus far leads one to conclude that those who seek guidance for its adoption toward advancement of purposeful, relevant learning will receive little help from the research findings.[40]

An example of the investigations is in a report of an efficiently conducted experimental team-teaching project of the biology staff in Wausau Senior High School, Wausau, Wisconsin. Students of the sophomore biology

[39] Shaplin and Olds, *Team Teaching*, p. 214.
[40] Ibid., pp. 322-341.

class were divided into two equal groups, one being the control and the other the experimental group. Those in the former group were taught by the traditional pattern of instruction; those of the latter group, by a pattern containing the common characteristics of team teaching. From results of tests the conclusion was reached that students of the experimental group learned as much of the subject matter of biology as those of the control group. Also, in response to a questionnaire, the former group indicated a positive liking for team teaching. There was no mention in the report, however, of any attempt in the experiment to discover how well each group may have developed in the spirit and mind of the scientist. This omission in an otherwise well-planned and executed study of team teaching is typical of other studies of this teaching procedure. A sound conclusion seems to be that research on the results of team teaching has failed to show broad superiority of this form of instruction over the traditional form.[41]

Two other investigators studied team teaching in five junior high schools of Racine, Wisconsin. In view of their findings, along with those of other investigators, they questioned whether any seeming advantages of team organization over nonteam organization are sufficient to justify the rearrangements, reassignments, and readjustments required for adoption of that form of teaching.[42]

Suggestions on Adoption of Team Teaching

As has been indicated, a school considering adoption of team teaching may wisely ask two questions: (1) "For improvement of learning in our school, will team teaching be more efficient than our present form of instruction?" and (2) "Are conditions in our school conducive to use of the team organization?" As previously seen, teachers of a team need to possess both favorable attitudes and special personal and professional qualifications. Certainly the administrators, especially the principal, must have strong interest in that form of teaching. It is essential further that the school building contain some large and some small rooms equipped with adequate appropriate learning materials. The nature of the community also requires some consideration, at least with reference to its inclination to accept change in the school.[43]

The initiation of the team pattern of instruction demands thorough planning and preparation. "Most team teaching projects have been established without the substantial planning period required, without a prior learning period for participants, and without allowing sufficient time for on-the-job

41 R. W. White, "How Successful Is Team Teaching?" *Science Teacher* (October, 1964), 31, pp. 34-37.
42 H. J. Klausmeier and W. Wiersma, "Team Teaching and Achievement," *Education* (December, 1965), 86, pp. 238-242.
43 G. A. Poirier, "Isn't It Time to Change from Linear Teaching to Team Teaching?" *Journal of Secondary Education* (October, 1969), 44, pp. 243-251.

planning."[44] The staff, especially the team, needs to study the literature on that form of teaching, and some may find it helpful to visit one or more schools engaged in such teaching.

In all the initiatory activities, the real, functional objectives of the school have strong bearing on the points of emphasis. The dominating goals of a school will affect the pattern of team teaching. This could involve, for example, alteration and reduction of the large group instruction, accompanied by increased amount and improved quality of small group instruction. After giving a review of research on the role of class size in promotion of learning, Hollingsworth concluded that teachers' goals, particularly as these affect their interest in individualized instruction, determine whether they consider class size to be irrelevant.[45] Thus team teaching can exist in different forms and for various reasons. "Each community will have its own specific reasons for undertaking team teaching and must work out an essentially unique solution to its recognized problems."[46]

Unfortunately, some schools seem to have as the purpose and pattern of team teaching a form of instruction directed toward learning characterized more by passivity, receptivity, and memorization than by activity, goal seeking, and reflection. This is evident in the focus on the large group lecture for initiation and subsequent guidance of a teaching-learning activity. There are, however, some schools that reveal a function and form of team teaching aimed at assistance of students to pose and work on problems. Toward this end, small group and individual work appear to be basic or primary, and the large group lecture, to be supplementary or secondary.[47]

Apparently because team teaching often has not been appraised thoughtfully in advance of its adoption, some schools have abandoned it. In a study of this form of teaching in 4,000 accredited high schools of the North Central Association of Colleges and Secondary Schools, this innovation had the fourth highest abandonment rate. It is thought that the two leading reasons for this is that team teaching, as it has been practiced, tends to reduce teacher-pupil relationship and to emphasize unduly acquisition of information, thereby neglecting other important outcomes of instruction.[48]

Our conclusion is that team teaching possesses potential usefulness for improvement of learning in high school. Some schools have conditions indicating the possibility of efficient, successful use of this form of instruction in some classes, but few if any schools have the staff, facilities, and other required factors for adoption of team teaching in every class. In

[44] Shaplin and Olds, Team Teaching, p. 7.
[45] P. M. Hollingsworth, "The Issue of Class Size," Education (March, 1964), 84, pp. 433-436.
[46] Shaplin and Olds, Team Teaching, p. 181.
[47] D. E. Shawver, "Team Teaching: How Successful Is It?" Clearing House (September, 1968), 43, pp. 21-26.
[48] J. A. Meyer, "Salvaging Team Teaching," Clearing House (December, 1969), 44, pp. 203-205.

fact, conditions in some high schools make adoption of any orthodox team teaching inadvisable. For promotion of useful, relevant learning, some schools would do well to continue reliance largely on nonteam organization of instruction. For example, a reporter of team teaching in a department of English concluded that changing the complete English program to team teaching would not be feasible and that a class under a traditional plan and an excellent teacher could be very successful. In either form of teaching, the key to improvement of instruction in a school seems to be improvement of the teachers' objectives and skills and provision of adequate facilities for their use toward implementation of the school's program.

QUESTIONS AND ACTIVITIES

1. Debate which of the two principal theories of learning, the Gestalt theory or the stimulus-response theory, seems to supply best a rationale for programed instruction.
2. Construct a sample program using some content from your subject field. Have some classmates "take" your program and evaluate it against a psychological rationale.
3. Our major objectives of education include development of the student in rational self-guidance, critical and creative thinking, and social and scientific attitudes. In line with our educational objectives, evaluate programed instruction. Discuss or debate this topic as a class activity.
4. Point out how programed instruction may be an aid to a teacher of a foreign language, math, or science. How can this principle be applied to other subjects?
5. Consider individually, and then discuss openly, three conditions that are essential in a school for it to adopt team teaching with the likelihood that it will improve the quality of learning.
6. How may a school improve the cooperative action of teachers without including all the features of orthodox team teaching?
7. Leading educators in each subject of the high-school curriculum have advocated classroom procedures to meet the needs of youth in the modern world. How may team teaching be a means to that end?
8. Point out ways by which the teaching-learning process of the one-teacher classroom may function to produce results equal or superior to those of team teaching.
9. Observe team teaching in a high school as a means of evaluating its strengths and weaknesses. Discuss this appraisal in class.

10. Invite a teaching team of experienced high-school teachers to your class to discuss their perceptions of team teaching. How do their experiences correlate with the research literature?
11. Devise a questionnaire on team teaching, and then survey a sample population for its reactions to your questions. Analyze and summarize your findings; share them with the class.
12. Arrange to team teach with a classmate some segment of content so as to experience firsthand the stages of planning, teaching, and evaluating the lesson that was team taught.

SELECTED REFERENCES

Programed Instruction

Bigge, M. L., *Learning Theories for Teachers*, 2nd ed., paper, Harper and Row, New York, 1971, Chap. 5.

Bigge, M. L., and M. P. Hunt, *Psychological Foundations of Education*, 2nd ed., Harper and Row, New York, 1968, Chaps. 15, 21.

Calvin, A. D., *Programmed Instruction: Bold New Venture*, Indiana University Press, Bloomington, 1969.

Garner, W. L., *Programmed Instruction*, The Center for Applied Research in Education, New York, 1966.

Holland, J. G., and B. F. Skinner, *The Analysis of Behavior: A Program for Self Instruction*, McGraw-Hill, New York, 1961.

National Education Association, *Programmed Instruction in Large School Systems*, paper, National Education Association, Washington, D. C., 1966.

National Society for the Study of Education, *Programmed Instruction*, Sixty-sixth Yearbook, Part II, University of Chicago, Chicago, 1967, Chaps. 6-10, 16.

O'Day, E. F., and others, *Programmed Instruction: Techniques and Trends*, Appleton-Century-Crofts, New York, 1970.

Skinner, B. F., *Beyond Freedom and Dignity*, Alfred A. Knopf, New York, 1971.

Skinner, B. F., *The Technology of Teaching*, Appleton-Century-Crofts, New York, 1968.

Taber, J. I., and others, *Learning and Programmed Instruction*, Addison-Wesley, Reading, Massachusetts, 1965.

Von Haden, H. I., and J. M. King, *Innovations in Education: Their Pros and Cons*, paper, Charles A. Jones, Worthington, Ohio, 1971, Chap. 4.

Wyrwicka, W., *The Mechanisms of Conditioned Behavior: A Critical Look at the Phenomena of Conditioning*, Charles C Thomas, Springfield, Ill., 1972.

Team Teaching

Beggs, D. W., *Team Teaching,* Indiana University Press, Bloomington, 1965.

Chamberlin, L. J., *Team Teaching: Organization and Administration,* Charles E. Merrill, Columbus, Ohio, 1969.

Davis, H. S., *How to Organize an Effective Team Teaching Program,* Prentice-Hall, Englewood Cliffs, New Jersey, 1966.

Hanslovsky, G., and others, *Why Team Teaching,* paper, Charles E. Merrill, Columbus, Ohio, 1970.

National Society for the Study of Education, *Educational Evaluation: New Roles, New Means,* Sixty-eighth Yearbook, Part II, University of Chicago, Chicago, 1969, Chap. 12.

Peterson, C. H., *Effective Team Teaching: The Easton Area High School Program,* Prentice-Hall, Englewood Cliffs, New Jersey, 1966.

Polos, N. C., *The Dynamics of Team Teaching,* William C. Brown, Dubuque, Iowa, 1965.

Von Haden, H. I., and J. M. King, *Innovations in Education: Their Pros and Cons,* paper, Charles A. Jones, Worthington, Ohio, 1971, Chap. 27.

CHAPTER 12

Like programed instruction and team teaching, some other special means of instruction have been advocated with few, if any, reservations by proponents, claiming phenomenal results. Accordingly, teachers need help toward gaining a comprehensive, balanced view of these special innovational means of instruction. In viewing each means, the teacher needs to ask the question "For production of what kind of learning was this means designed?" Another helpful question is "Does this means contribute well toward meeting the needs of students for education that enables them to become useful, democratic citizens in a changing, technological society?"

INDEPENDENT STUDY AND FLEXIBLE SCHEDULING

Independent study has evoked little controversy. In fact, we have always had some independent study in our high schools, and teachers have welcomed it. Yet apparently because students have been requesting increased involvement in the process of learning and teachers have been recognizing the growing need for responsible, self-directed individuals to confront group pressure and propaganda, some schools have been making special provisions for students to experience independent study. How well does this form of study help all students acquire suitable learnings?

Independent study exists in any learning situation in which students experience minimal teacher direction and maximal self-direction. In this situation the students work not on a dictated, uniform assignment, but on their chosen assignments. Consequently, students' own objectives motivate and direct their study, and success in reaching objectives is an intrinsic value which rewards all of their work. They are relatively free to study what meets their own interests and needs, to set up goals, and to discover means

OTHER SPECIAL MEANS
OF TEACHING

of reaching goals. In using this independence in study, individual students obtain help from various sources, including the teacher as a counselor and critic.

We may clarify our conception of independent study further by recognizing the contrast between it and another form of individualized instruction, tutoring. In tutoring the subject matter is prescribed and structured for the student. The teacher assumes the role of continuously telling and directing. In contrast, independent study involves the student in the initiation of a learning activity, the determination of specific objectives, and the finding of materials and methods to reach individual objectives.

Expressed in outline form, independent study includes the following features:

1. Study beyond the uniform assignment made to all or a majority of students in a class.
2. Placement of emphasis on the student's responsibility for learning.
3. Freedom of the student from constant direction by the teacher.
4. Motivation to study by the learner's own aims.
5. Independence of the study from conventional instructional practices.
6. Utilization of teachers and counselors primarily as resources by the learner.
7. Provision of decision making opportunities for the student.[1]

The reason for independent study is to enhance learning characterized by intrinsic motivation and meaning. This is the type of learning presented in Chapter 2, which is advocated by most of our educational psychologists and supported by extensive experimentation. Independent study helps the student to learn how to learn well. It contributes to development of attitudes and habits essential for continuous intellectual growth, particularly interests and abilities in investigative and creative activities.

More than just skill is involved in becoming an independent learner. Perhaps even of greater importance is the development of an interest in learning. The learner who continues to pursue intelligently the answers to his own questions will do so because he finds learning satisfying. Schooling must make learning activity attractive rather than make it something to be avoided. Independent study has to be rewarding if it is to become a way of life for the adult.

Thus, education aiming to develop the self-directing learner is education of the highest order involving both the affective and cognitive areas. It is education which seeks a type of personal development that enables the student to behave ultimately as an independent learner. Independent study aims to develop the specific behaviors required. These may be listed as follows:

1. The independent learner undertakes on his own initiative learning tasks that are important to him.

1 Adapted from G. Beltz and D. A. Kohn, "Independent Study in Five Missouri High Schools," *Clearing House* (February, 1970), 44, p. 334.

2. He uses sources of information efficiently.
3. He tests out reflectively possible answers, solutions, ideas, to see whether they are adequate.
4. He seeks to apply generalizations from former to new situations.
5. He is not easily discouraged by the difficulty of the learning task nor by forces which would have him accept inadequate answers, solutions, and ideas.
6. He enjoys learning and seeks opportunities to learn.[2]

High schools professing to promote independent study have designed several slightly different forms of procedure. Among these forms, two significant differences are (1) the focus of some schools solely on superior students, and of the other schools on all students, weak as well as strong, and (2) the reliance of some schools on all the regular courses, and of the other schools on special, independent courses or activities.[3]

Those different practices have clear implications. Apparently, some high schools need to consider further (1) the task of developing potential failures toward independent study and (2) that it is both economically and pedagogically sound to provide independent study through group-individual instruction in regular courses. As has been seen in preceding chapters, the dependent student can learn how to be independent through the example and assistance of other students and the teacher. It is especially important to develop all freshmen and sophomores in independent study to increase the probability that they will continue in high school until graduation and to enable them to study well all through high school. In considering the promotion of independent study apart from regular courses, some high schools have stated that they are financially unable to provide for independent study. All that they may need are efficient teachers, dedicated to the idea of independent study experiences for all students, and a media center well supplied with instructional materials.[4]

As an aid to independent study, some writers have included programed instruction, which they recommend for students of all levels of achievement except those who are poor in reading. Of course, a student engaged independently in a project on insects, for example, could turn voluntarily to a programed book on that subject for some particular information needed to complete the project; but probably the student would prefer going to a conventional book. It is true that there would be freedom to choose when, how fast, and how far to go through the program. The program is so rigidly structured, however, that it would furnish the student with scarcely any aid toward devising and pursuing objectives and toward

2 W. M. Alexander and V. A. Hines, *Independent Study in Secondary Schools*, paper, Holt, Rinehart and Winston, New York, 1967, pp. 3-4.
3 G. G. Unruh and W. M. Alexander, *Innovations in Secondary Education*, Holt, Rinehart and Winston, New York, 1970, p. 113.
4 J. P. Casey, "Independent Study: A Plan for All Pupils," *English Journal* (November, 1971), 60, pp. 173-177; and L. D. Newton, "Independent Study Programs—Reasons for Failure," *English Journal* (May, 1972), 61, pp. 711-714.

developing in self-directed study. In programed instruction in ninth-grade algebra, for example, experimentation indicates that the program does not provide for the student to discover and generalize and that it relies too much on the rather purposeless and meaningless "rule-example" approach, which contributes little to learning through inquiry. Consequently, the students' motivation may be mainly external, consisting of success in passing tests and making satisfactory grades. A student's performance can be rather high on tests without ever having developed sufficient purpose, understanding, and self-direction to develop significantly in independent study of the subject.[5]

Adequate promotion of independent study in a high school dedicated to democratic values requires that every teacher develop in all students this approach to study, the inferior as well as the superior students. Teachers can accomplish this to a significant extent without reorganization of the curriculum, extensive rescheduling of classes, or use of any sensational, difficult to adopt form of instruction. The efficient, committed teacher has always used group and individual instruction in regular classes to provide all students with experiences that require them to assume responsibility and self-direction in the process of learning. Such a teacher does not spoon-feed them by sole use of the lecture-demonstration method and the factual, question and short answer recitation. Instead, a suitable method of teaching helps them to learn through investigating, discovering, and thinking. Such a teaching procedure requires that all students develop responsibility for self-direction of study and learning. An important result from all effective teaching is development of the learner in independent study.

How every high-school teacher can contribute to development of all students in independent study has been indicated in preceding chapters, particularly Chapters 4 through 9. In the teacher-student assignment, the teacher questions the students about personal and societal problems and leads them to ask questions, informing them about how they can find answers to their questions in the library, laboratory, the media center, or the community. In the study period, the students receive individual counseling or guidance when it is needed while they search for answers to their questions. In the process they are helped to develop the essential skills of independent study in the four areas of reading, research, writing, and reflection.

This procedure has been explained and demonstrated in accounts of teaching the new subjects in Chapters 7 and 8. These chapters give examples of how students are led to confront social or scientific problems and then go to the library or laboratory to find solutions to their problems.

---

[5] See the section on programed instruction in the preceding chapter. See also E. Kornhaber and D. Kappus, "Designing an Algebra I Performance Curriculum for a Heterogeneous Student Population," *School Science and Mathematics* (June, 1970), 70, pp. 493-500.

Reports have stated that through such experiences in *active* participation in the process of learning, even poor students have significantly improved in independent study. In both group and individual instruction they learned how to learn—to be responsible, self-directing students. They learned by observing and receiving help from one another as well as from the teacher.

It should go without saying that for teachers of a high school to approach development of all students toward independent study, including the potential dropouts, they must make a concerted effort to help every student be able to read successfully in all of the courses. The basic importance of this is indicated later in this chapter and in the section on teaching students how to study in Chapter 5. High-school teachers must continuously recognize their responsibility to improve their students in reading, especially the large percentage of them who read a grade or more below the required levels for their grades.

What we have endeavored to emphasize is that to educate all students for reflective, democratic living in a rapidly changing society, teachers in every high school should earnestly work toward enabling every student, weak or strong, to have suitable study experiences to enable development in independent study. This requires that the average and the below-average student have these experiences in the usual courses, with helpful guidance by the teacher. As stated by a high-school teacher of English:

Independent study can be made a dynamic part of any secondary school program without fear of disrupting the system or turning students loose to do nothing. Moreover, it can include all kinds of interested young people, not just the academically talented. If a program in independent study cannot be geared to the needs of the reluctant, the disenchanted, and the potential dropout, as well as to those of the brilliant and creative, then it is probably not worth having anyway. . . .

Since the average high school student is without prior experience in independent study his involvement with it should be viewed as transitional, a period of training and development in self-teaching. But he cannot do it all himself; he needs advice, guidance, information, and supervision. He needs a teacher.[6]

Expressing further how group-individual instruction may be directed toward development of poor learners in independent study, Alexander and Hines add:

Each of the approaches just described, individualized assignments and task-oriented small group work, if it is effective in developing independence in learning, sooner or later involves some teacher guidance of the individual student. Today the third approach to guiding independent learning is to develop some specific pattern for actual individualization of instruction, a pattern in which there is clear provision at times for a one-to-one relation of teacher and pupil. The essence of this newer approach is a very old principle: that the learner under-

[6] Casey, "Independent Study," p. 174.

takes his learning tasks most efficiently and enthusiastically when he has frequent, at times continued, access to advice from someone who cares about him and can help him in his task. This help is more in the form of a counseling session than of a tutorial lesson. The learner is helped both to raise and answer his own questions.

This individualized instruction approach to independent study is not seen as a revival of the project method nor as another form of supervised study. Both of these terms were associated with learning activities that merely prepared for or supplemented group instruction. The present reference is to a plan of instruction which deliberately aims to guide the individual learner in his own independent study. This study may but need not be an extension of work under way in some class. Nor is it just a plan for able students. In fact the able, motivated student usually requires little help in his independent study. The poor and the reluctant learners are those most in need of the teacher's patience and skill to get them started on their own.[7]

Flexible Scheduling

For assisting teachers and students to vary their activities, particularly in relation to team teaching and independent study, some schools have adopted flexible scheduling. In contrast to the typical conventional schedule, consisting almost uniformly of hour periods throughout each day, the flexible schedule consists of periods of distinctly different lengths throughout the week. Of course some traditional schedules have been made somewhat flexible, for example, in block time, double periods, and rotating periods. This degree of flexibility provides teachers and students with some increased choice of action but not enough to satisfy educators who are proponents of flexible scheduling.

Flexible scheduling constitutes a distinct break from traditional scheduling. This new form of scheduling has as its unit not the hour but a fraction of the hour, usually between 10 and 30 minutes, called a "module." For example, in a school using a 30-minute module, 15 modules constitute the school day, which corresponds to the traditional seven-period day with a half-hour for lunch. Another school, using a 15-minute module, needs at least 27 of this unit to make a school day. Each period is designated in terms of the number of modules, and the periods vary extensively. In fact, this type of schedule has been called the "variable schedule," and it is so complicated that for its construction a computer is a necessity.

All of these periods of variable sizes are suitable especially for team teaching, but they can be helpful in other forms of instruction. The designation of time for independent study is a prominent characteristic of this type of schedule. In some schools there is an effort to schedule an independent study period for every student; but, in others, only for the honor students. For some control of students, some schools provide them with a pass card but others require them to register their study activity with the homeroom teacher.[8]

Are there indications that the modular schedule is a valuable means for production of high quality learning? In seeking an answer to this question, we need to keep in mind that like a conventional schedule, a modular schedule may or may not be structured toward that kind of learning. As already noted, this type of schedule is especially suitable for team teaching, a form of teaching that a school with a modular schedule probably uses. Furthermore, as we noted in the preceding chapter, team teaching can be used to improve the quality of learning, provided the school has suitable equipment and efficient teachers who are committed to that kind of learning. The common practice in team teaching, however, seems to be the introduction of a topic, unit, or problem to a large group by lecture and demonstration, without active involvement of the students. This is followed by students meeting in small discussion groups called "inquiry" groups, the discussion stemming from the lecture-demonstration. Moreover, reports on the results of team teaching have focused on factual learning, often without any reference to improvement of intellectual and social attitudes and habits. A conclusion from a study of team teaching in 4,000 accredited high schools of the North Central Association of Colleges and Secondary Schools is that this form of teaching tends not only to overemphasize acquisition of information but also to reduce teacher-student relationship. These characteristics and results of team teaching have clear implications for the nature and use of the modular schedule.

Reports from schools using the flexible schedule indicate that several of the teachers are concerned about their role in small group discussion. Examples of questions that they ask are "What is the purpose of the small group?" and "What shall I do?" They also seem to believe that they have only two choices—either extreme permissiveness or teacher domination. Apparently, in the self-contained classrooms of their former conventional schedule, they did not practice helping students learn by initiating and solving problems, and their schools had not provided them with adequate in-service education immediately before adoption of the flexible schedule. Hence they lacked the attitudes and skills required for successful, satisfying direction of students in small group learning situations.

Other teachers reported being disturbed about infrequent person-to-person relationships with some of their students. This unsatisfactory relationship with students probably was because of faults in the teachers as well as because the schedule did not provide adequately for that relationship. Yet the conventional schedule may be potentially more suitable for

8 See H. I. Von Haden and J. M. King, Innovations in Education: Their Pros and Cons, Charles A. Jones, Worthington, Ohio, 1971, pp. 127-132; and Unruh and Alexander, Innovations in Secondary Education, pp. 117-121.

continuous, helpful person-to-person relationships between teachers and students than the modular schedule now is.[9]

In the few schools that provide special periods of independent study for all students, some teachers and parents have been quite concerned about the behavior of some students. At any time of the day about 25 percent of the students are free from classroom supervision, some of them studying in the library or laboratory or away from the campus. Others are wandering in the halls or loitering in the parking lot or in nearby stores. The result has been increased disturbance, confusion, petty theft, and vandalism.[10] Significantly, this condition has caused some of these schools to revert to traditional schedules.

Teachers need to realize that students do not become independent in study merely by being relieved of direct supervision by the classroom teacher. Like persons who are too immature or crippled to walk independently, poor students probably are too unhealthy, physically and mentally, to undertake studying independently without quite a degree of help. To begin learning how to study independently, they need frequent encouragement and guidance from an understanding, sympathetic teacher. As was pointed out in our appraisal of independent study in the preceding section, schools would do well to rely on regular classroom procedure, particularly during the directed study period, to help all students learn how to study independently. If the students have been experiencing too much irrelevant instruction and extreme teacher domination within the classroom, the remedy is not extreme permissiveness or laissez-faire procedure, which lets students flounder, become discouraged, and drop out of school. As noted previously, particularly in Chapter 6, the weak student needs to observe and work with the strong student, by which procedure both will be strengthened as students. Both students also can gain much from a teacher who understands when to commend and when to criticize.[11]

Whatever may be said about some features of the flexible schedule and about the unpreparedness of some teachers to follow it well, reports indicate that the kind of instruction resulting from adoptions of this schedule has not been very encouraging. A study of several high schools using it led to the conclusion that not much change in instruction had occurred except that traditional teaching was done for different lengths of time and in different sizes of groups.[12]

Although the modular schedule has not looked as good in practice as in theory, there are reasons to believe that improvement in its use would

---

[9] J. Wilmoth and W. Ehn, "The Inflexibility of Modular Flexible Scheduling," *Educational Leadership* (April, 1970), 27, pp. 727-730.

[10] R. R. Gard, "A Realistic Look at the Flexible Schedule," *Clearing House* (March, 1970), 44, pp. 425-429.

[11] For further expression of this view see M. Fallers, "Choice Is Not Enough," *School Review* (February, 1970), 78, pp. 229-239. See also H. C. Sun, "The Open Classroom: A Critique," *High School Journal* (December, 1972), 55, pp. 134-141.

[12] Wilmoth and Ehn, "The Inflexibility of Modular Flexible Scheduling," p. 130.

make it helpful in providing education relevant to the needs of different high-school students. However, it is important to recognize that a conventional schedule can be reconstructed so that it possesses quite a degree of flexibility. For example, the schedule could consist of the traditional hour periods during parts of each school day, but at different times on some school days it could include periods of two or three hours for work in the laboratory and for other lengthy individual and group activities. Accordingly, some schools having a conventional schedule may wisely choose to reconstruct it by incorporating within it some features of the modular schedule.[13]

Instructional Materials Center

Obviously, a basic requirement for employment of a flexible schedule, team teaching, or indepedent study to produce effective learning is an adequate suitable supply of instructional media, printed and audio visual. Of course this is also true of the new subjects of the curriculum, which we considered in Chapters 7-8 as providing for learning through discovery. During several years there has been consensus among educators that a school should have a library well stocked with a variety of books and periodicals to provide for self-directed study and purposeful, useful learning. With the advancement of technology for production of audio-visual materials and with continued emphasis of educational psychologists on the need of sensory experiences for perceptual learning, there was increased demand for and use of audio-visual materials in high schools. Accordingly, in 1956 the American Association of School Libraries expressed a policy decision stating that in addition to providing printed materials the school library should provide audio-visual materials and equipment, films, recordings, and other technical aids and should serve the school as an instructional materials center. This center—sometimes called a multimedia center, media laboratory, or learning-resource center—has been established in several high schools in different parts of our country.

The instructional materials center contains a modern school library, well stocked with a variety of printed materials including periodicals, many paperbacks, and microfilms. It also stores audio-visual supplies: radio, television, films, film strips, slides, tapes, overhead transparencies, and the like. There is a large reading room and smaller rooms for seminars and carrels for individuals to view and listen. Another important feature consists of the work room, where teachers and students may join workers of the center in the construction of audio-visual materials.[14]

---

13 E. T. Kelly and J. P. Turano, "Variable Scheduling," *Clearing House* (February, 1971), 45, pp. 365-368.

14 Unruh and Alexander, *Innovations in Secondary Education*, pp. 162-163; Von Haden and King, *Innovations in Education*, pp. 7-11; and J. Powell, "From Library to Media Center: There Is a Difference," *National Association of Secondary School Principals Bulletin* (March, 1971), 55, pp. 79-85.

A list of the center's instructional media goals is as follows:

1. Provision should be made for both teachers and pupils to use all varieties of instructional materials. This includes activities involving reading, viewing, and listening.
2. Instruction should be provided to enable students to acquire the skills necessary to identify and locate appropriate instructional materials.
3. A continuing program should be developed, designed to keep pupils, faculty, and community appraised of available materials and services.
4. Teachers should be encouraged to construct instructional aids and to explore new techniques of media utilization.
5. A system of effective distribution and materials and equipment maintenance should be devised.
6. Complete reference services should be made available to students, teachers, and community.
7. Reading guidance should be made available to individuals relating to both curriculum activities and personal interests.
8. Appropriate materials should be stocked and made available for the slow learner, the academically talented, and the average learner in order that the needs of all pupils may be accommodated.
9. Adequate opportunities should be provided for pupils to engage in independent study and research activities.
10. An up-to-date compilation of community resources should be made available to teachers and pupils.[15]

Rendering of such services to teachers and students requires an efficient, committed staff in the instructional materials center. The librarians need about the same kind of professional education as they have been receiving; but the workers of the audio-visual department, who provide instruction and counsel to teachers and students about use of audio-visual materials and equipment, need to be not only technicians but also professionally prepared teachers. Furthermore, classroom teachers have the responsibility of using preservice and in-service professional education to prepare themselves to help students acquire both the technical skills and the techniques that they need to engage successfully in seeking answers to their questions.

Capable teachers working cooperatively with an efficient staff of a well-supplied instructional materials center probably will gain improved attitudes and skills in research, which they can pass on to their students. At least the teachers and students will have instructional media when needed, and this will incline teachers toward an inquiry approach. Teachers will be encouraged further to promote learning through investigation and discovery when they observe that students who were bored by the restric-

15 J. D. DiSanto, "The Media Laboratory," Education (April, 1970), 90, p. 343.

tions of the classroom, the textbook, and the telling and showing are now intrigued with finding for themselves vital, relevant information.

BEHAVIORAL OBJECTIVES, ACCOUNTABILITY, AND PERFORMANCE CONTRACTING

A rational approach to an appraisal of behavioral objectives may require us to clarify our perception of the essential elements or the points of emphasis of the behavioral objective. This type of objective, far from being ambiguous, is a demonstrable and observable goal that is precisely expressed in terms of doing or performing. It is unlike general objectives, stated by use of such words as enjoy, understand, and appreciate. For instance, a teacher who has the general aim of teaching the students to enjoy poetry may also have as a behavioral objective the development of the students' skills in identifying a specified percentage of the authors of selections from sixteen poems, the authors to be identified being, say, Longfellow, Whittier, Tennyson, and Wordsworth. Similarly, an arithmetic teacher having as a general objective the promotion of the students' understanding of square measure may also set up the two behavioral objectives of drawing a parallelogram and of stating the rule for finding the area of a triangle.[16] Further description of these objectives, sometimes called "instructional objectives," is given by an original proponent of the objectives.

1. A statement of instructional objectives is a collection of words or symbols describing one of your educational *intents*.
2. An objective will communicate your intent to the degree you have described what the learner will be DOING when demonstrating his achievement and how you will know when he is doing it.
3. To describe terminal behavior (what the learner will be DOING):
   a. Identify and name the over-all behavior act.
   b. Define the important conditions under which the behavior is to occur (givens or restrictions, or both).
   c. Define the criterion of acceptable performance.
4. Write a separate statement for each objective; the more statements you have, the better chance you have of making clear your intent.
5. If you give each learner a copy of your objectives, you may not have to do much else.[17]

The behaviorist focuses not only on behavior but also on specificity and objectivity in objectives for both instruction and determination of results. For instance, an expression that students will learn to sew, to read maps, or to solve equations does not constitute the statement of a behavioral

---

16 Von Haden and King, *Innovations in Education*, pp. 43-47.
17 R. F. Mager, *Preparing Instructional Objectives*, Fearon, Palo Alto, California, 1962, p. 53.

objective because it does not include precise specification of the nature of the performance required to demonstrate reaching the objective. In the words of Newport:

Behavioral objectives are statements which describe some type of learner behavior, or a product of his behavior, which is desired following instruction. Behavioral objectives accurately convey the meaning intended, and permit precise evaluation.

The following are behavioral objectives:

1. Given addition problems with two addends whose sums are not more than 20, write the sums.
2. Distinguish between mixtures that are solutions and those that are not.
3. Identify and state the meaning of five symbols on a given map.

These are not behavioral objectives:

1. The student will learn to add.
2. Have an understanding of mixtures and solutions.
3. Be able to use maps.

In the first set of examples almost all persons would agree upon the intended meaning and we could evaluate to determine which students have mastered the objectives and which need more instruction. In the second set of examples, many different meanings could be inferred, and precise evaluation would be impossible.

Behavioral objectives are clear, precise, or explicit statements which serve as instructional intents.[18]

Further analysis of this plan of precise construction and rigid use of behavioral objectives indicates that it constitutes a way of programing instruction. Significantly, in writing on preparation of educational objectives, Mager points out that he uses the words *instructor and programmer* interchangeably.[19] Furthermore, writers on construction of instructional programs present as the first step the construction of behavioral objectives.[20] Obviously students can be required to learn through programed instruction whether the teacher uses a teaching machine, a programed textbook, or a programed course. In the process of programing a course, the programmer expresses the behavioral terminal objectives of the course and then several interim behavioral objectives considered to be useful for the teacher to advance the students toward each terminal objective. The role

18 J. F. Newport, "Behavioral Objectives, Ready or Not, Here They Come!" *School and Community* (May, 1971), 57, p. 22.
19 Mager, *Preparing Instructional Objectives*, p. 2.
20 R. Glaser, ed., *Teaching Machines and Programed Learning*, National Education Association, Washington, D. C., 1965, Chap. 2.

of behavioral objectives in the programing of instruction is indicated in the following statement:

Why is it considered an important step in the design of instruction to describe and analyze instructional objectives? Many writers have simply stated that this must be done before a program can be constructed—and left it at that. Some, however, either clearly state their reasons for considering this an essential step or else imply them in more or less unmistakable fashion. . . .

At the very least, the reason for knowing the nature of the terminal behavior is so that the instructional designer can plan properly the final sequences of his program. While such learning may have taken place in an instructional program, there will be no proof of this unless the designer and the user are agreed upon what the learner will be able to do after he has been through the instruction. "What the learner is expected to be able to do" is the key phrase. The latter parts of a program can be designed to go in any of several directions, i.e., to aim at any of several forms of terminal behavior. Accordingly, they can be designed to establish in the learner some particular capability which is agreed upon as an instructional objective. Since the designer wants to choose the acceptable course for arriving at this terminal behavior, he must have a statement about the sort of human performance which is overtly observable.[21]

A point of basic importance to realize is that the current movement for behavioral objectives is supported by the atomistic, associationist, behavioristic psychology of learning and the deterministic philosophy. In contrast, the goal-insight, field psychology of learning and the democratic ideal support the practice of letting the teacher and the student set up definitely stated principal objectives and then leaving the freedom to them to choose the many subordinate objectives as they need them in progressing through the course toward each principal objective. This has been the view of the nature and use of objectives in instruction described, illustrated, and supported in all sections of this book including those on modern mathematics, the new natural sciences, and the new social sciences. It is a conception of objectives directed toward involvement of students in choice and pursuit of relevant objectives for their development in self-direction for life in a changing, confused society.

It also may help to note that in arguing for the use of behavioral objectives the proponent typically presents the either-or choice of having clear (behavioral) objectives or having "vague," "ambiguous," "indefinite" objectives. The teacher needs to see that the only alternative to the use of behavioral objectives is not to use objectives so "fuzzy" that they are meaningless and nondirective. Instead, there is also the alternative of having objectives set up and used in cooperative action of teacher and students. In the use of this alternative the teacher and the students exercise freedom and responsibility in the choice of objectives that are definitely relevant to the students' personal and societal needs, and they

21 Ibid., pp. 23-24.

thoughtfully choose the specific objectives required for their advancement toward each terminal objective. Since these objectives, which may be either behavioral or nonbehavioral, are formulated by the teacher and the students in cooperative classroom procedure, they are not vague or ambiguous but are *clear, purposeful, and useful to them, whatever they may be to other persons.*[22]

Some critics of behavioral objectives have been concerned about some of the learnings produced by the extensive, rigid programs of those objectives. "In the perception of those critics, promotion of behavioral objectives has prompted undue attention to the insignificant, the trivial and the simpler operations in education."[23] The students are so occupied with "passive" mechanical learning that they have little time or incentive for involvement emotionally and intellectually in self-directed, investigative, creative, and reflective learning and toward the development of concepts, and generalizations. As expressed further by Ebel:

. . . The situations in which such behavioral objectives are appropriate appear to be limited to instruction which aims at the cultivation of particular skills. Behavioral objectives seem quite inappropriate to instructional efforts whose aim is to enable the student to respond adaptively and effectively to unique future problem situations; to equip him to make, independently but responsibly, the kind of individual choices and decisions which are the essence of human freedom.

A useful distinction can be made between training, for which behavioral objectives are often quite appropriate, and education, for which they are seldom appropriate. Educational development is little concerned with the establishment of predetermined responses to recurring problem situations. Rather, it is concerned with the student's understanding, his resources of useful and available knowledge, his intellectual self-sufficiency. It sees him not as a puppet on strings controlled by his teachers, but as one who needs and wants the help of his teachers and others as he tackles the difficult problems of designing and building a life of his own. . . .

Teaching is purposeful activity. Part of a teacher's effectiveness depends on his having the right purposes. Hence it is important for the curriculum builder, the textbook writer, the teacher, and the student to think hard about their purposes, about the objectives they seek to achieve.[24]

Other educators are disturbed about the educational values apparently disregarded by some in their insistence on objectivity as the primary criterion for judging the value of an objective. It is not by chance that among the chief proponents of behavioral objectives are professionals in educational measurement. They know that use of these objectives in instruction prepares students specifically for objective testing and makes it

22 For explanations, demonstrations, and experimentations of how this alternative is better for the student than either of the two other alternatives, see other chapters of this book, particularly Chaps. 4-9.

23 C. B. Cox, "Behavior as Objective in Education," *Social Education* (May, 1971), 35, p. 440.

24 R. L. Ebel, "Behavioral Objectives: A Close Look," *Phi Delta Kappan* (November, 1970), 52, pp. 172-173. See also J. M. Fishbein, "The Father of Behavioral Objectives Criticizes Them: An Interview with Ralph Tyler," *Phi Delta Kappan* (September, 1973), 55, pp. 55-57.

logical and less difficult for the teacher and the researcher to use only the objective test in measurement of all the student's achievements. "But worthwhile goals come first, not our methods for assessing progress toward those goals. Goals are derived from our needs and from our philosophies. They are not and should not be derived primarily from our measures."[25]

Referring particularly to the slogan, "Down with all nonbehavioral objectives," and its effect on instruction and educational measurement in our country, Broudy states:

When I say that this slogan dominates educational research, I do not mean to convey the idea that this is all that it dominates. It is also at the heart of the objective-teaching movement, which, in turn, has great influence upon curriculum design and teaching method. This is so because if it is argued that only that can be tested which can be stated objectively, and if one conjoins thereto the injunction that only that shall be taught which can be tested, then the curriculum maker's task and the teacher's duty are clearly delimited if not prescribed. Willy-nilly this requirement has put a premium on the teaching of information, the rote recall of definitions, rules and principles, particular operations, and the solution of problems that have only one correct solution. In other words, the slogan when embodied in testing programs puts a high premium on the replicative use of learning which asks the learner to reinstate that original learning pretty much as learned in response to definite cues.[26]

What these and other educators have been pointing out is that there are very important outcomes of instruction that are neglected or prevented by extensive, rigid use of behavioral objectives in teaching a course and that are evaluated better by subjective means than by objective tests. Examples are development of democratic and scientific attitudes and habits, intrinsic interest in the activities of the course, appreciation of "good" literature or music, social cohesiveness of the class, individual initiative and self-direction, painting a picture, writing a poem, singing a song, participation in an individual or a group project, and participation in free discussion of and attacks on current personal and societal problems. Such outcomes of instruction do not require prescribed in advance behavioral objectives, which tend to direct the attention of teachers and students away from such outcomes. Furthermore, to judge how well the instruction has resulted in production of these outcomes, teachers, as educational critics and artists must use evaluation of the student's behavior in the process of producing as well as evaluation of the finished product. "And I would add that what is most educationally valuable is the development of that mode of curiosity, inventiveness, and insight that is capable of being

[25] J. M. Atkin, "Behavioral Objectives in Curriculum Design: A Cautionary Note," *Science Teacher* (May, 1968), 35, p. 30. For appraisal of the objective test for measurement of some important outcomes of education, see Chap. 15.
[26] H. S. Broudy, "Can Research Escape the Dogma of Behavioral Objectives?" *School Review* (November, 1970), 79, pp. 43-44.

described only in metaphoric or poetic terms. Indeed, the image of the educated man that has been held in highest esteem for the longest period of time in Western civilization is one which is not amenable to standard measurement."[27]

Obviously, the task of constructing behavioral objectives for every course of the curriculum is a tremendous undertaking. Certainly teachers should not be burdened with the task of designing behavioral objectives for each course in advance of teaching the course. Accordingly, some schools or school districts are engaged in mass production of those objectives and are establishing "banks" of objectives. Furthermore, the objectives for many courses are available for purchase.[28] There are questionable aspects about providing teachers with a long list of objectives that they are expected by administrators to follow rigidly. For many years democratically oriented educators, in focusing on the needs of the student and the demands of modern society, have condemned the slavishness of some teachers to the textbook. Now some educators seem to propose holding teachers strictly to objectives that they obtain from the school "bank" or from a publishing company. This would restrict the teachers' freedom to set up and pursue objectives that they and the teachers and students deem to be important to meet the current educational needs of the class. An expression from a teacher of tests and measurements, addressed to teachers of English, is significant here.

It is commonly recognized that objectives are value judgments made by the instructor based upon the needs of students in his classes. I cannot tell you what objectives are appropriate for your English classes, since I know neither the entering competencies of your students nor your views on the place of English in your students' later activities. I can, however, envision some classes where the needs of the students dictate emphasis on grammar and paragraph organization. Similarly, I can envision some classes where the emphasis is on reading and interpreting varied literary works. Clearly, objectives are not a means of standardizing English teaching, and they should not, without ample consideration of the consequences, be used as such. Objectives ought to permit each instructor to define the outcomes which are most relevant, given the needs of his students.[29]

Teachers need to view behavioral objectives in a flexible, pragmatic manner. They should not feel required to choose between sole use of behavioral objectives and sole use of nonbehavioral objectives. They ought not to take an absolute, unalterable either-or position. In a given instructional situation, not all of the possible behavioral objectives are of

---

27 E. W. Eisner, "Behavioral Objectives: Help or Hindrance?" *School Review* (Autumn, 1967), 75, p. 257.

28 One source is Instructional Objectives Exchange, Box 24095, Los Angeles, California, 90024.

29 P. W. Airasian, "Behavioral Objectives and the Teaching of English," *English Journal* (April, 1971), 60, pp. 495-496. See also L. B. Strain, "Behavioral Objectives: A Needed Perspective," *Journal of Secondary Education* (April, 1970), 45, pp. 182-184; and C. Helwig, "Innovation: What's It All About?" *Clearing House* (October, 1971), 46, pp. 82-85.

superior value and not all of the other objectives are of inferior value. Significantly, behavioral objectives appear to be of absolute importance to some educators, who consider objectivity to be a prime requirement in all steps of instruction. But they are of relative importance to educators who prize highly freedom in the classroom for teacher and students to work cooperatively to construct instructional objectives that are clear, purposeful, and meaningful to them and also to develop in students self-directing, independent study.

Thus some behavioral objectives can be made helpful toward provision of education that is significant and relevant to different high-school students. Evidence of this position abounds throughout this book. For example, in Chapter 3 teachers are urged to adopt instructional objectives that lead students to practice democratic behavior in the process of learning within any subject. Also, in Part II, there is insistence that teachers stimulate students to become actively involved in setting up and pursuing purposeful and useful behavioral objectives through each step of the teaching cycle. Similarly, in Chapter 7 the teacher is advised to help students improve their oral and written expression by having them focus not on study of prescribed, specific behavioral objectives but on oral and written expression, possessing purpose, meaning, and usefulness for the students. This requires that the student with the guidance of the teacher set up and use behavioral objectives to reach objectives in speaking and writing.

Educational Accountability

One of the most recent innovations in high-school teaching is the current demand for strict accountability of the school. Among the causes of this are the unrest and the antisocial conduct inside and outside the school. Also, there seems to be a growing awareness that some graduates as well as many dropouts of the school are deficient in the basic skills of reading and arithmetic. The taxpayers, therefore, are saying that the schools must approach the balancing of "input" with "output." Certainly, citizens must hold their public schools accountable for the results of instruction. In doing this, however, the schools and the public should agree (1) on the quality of learning they want and (2) on the necessary equipment, materials, and methods needed to produce that kind of learning.

Unfortunately, proponents of the current accountability movement have demonstrated more interest in the quantity of atomistic, mechanical learning of bits of information and isolated skills than in high quality learning, consisting of students' involvement in complete acts of problem solving, investigation, experimentation, and creativity. They have stated that before their plan can be adopted successfully by the public schools many people must change. This is true, but they may find it to be much more

difficult than they expect. There are fundamental psychological, sociological, and philosophical differences between those of the accountability
group and nearly all of our educational psychologists, sociologists, and
philosophers. The basic educational views of this latter group are unlikely
to be changed to the point where they can accept the current theory and
practice of the accountability innovation. During several decades this
group of educators has advocated accountability of our public high
schools for quality education suggested by educational research; the
wholistic, goal-insight conception of learning; the democratic ideal; and
the needs of youth in their present world.

Another objectionable feature of the accountability program is that the
school is held accountable for setting up in advance and later reaching
only the behavioral type of objectives, which are specific, observable,
and measurable. We recall that the proponents of behavioral objectives
have given as their chief reason for those objectives their use in enabling
the teacher and others to check precisely on the results of instruction.
Furthermore, school boards in particular have been warned that they must
provide "measurable instructionable objectives" to be able to determine
the deficiencies and failures of the instructional program. Not only must
they rely solely on objective tests for measurement, but the tests also
must be standardized with national norms.[30] Since we do not have
standardized tests that adequately measure appreciations and patterns
of performance in school, must we conclude that the school cannot be
held accountable in these outcomes of instruction? Let us ask the same
question about development of students in scientific and social attitudes.
Apparently the accountability program is not inclusive enough to provide
for the school to be accountable for some of the most important areas
or aspects of the students' education.

Every high school is obligated to students to meet their needs for development in worthwhile *behavior patterns*. These patterns of behavior
consist of more than specific, explicit, observable behaviors. They also include the causes of those behaviors, and often the causes cannot be observed directly or measured objectively. A person's numerous specific
ways of behaving are determined by his or her own self-perceptions in
relation to physical and social environments. To improve students' behaviors in various areas of instruction, the teacher needs to focus on improvement of their understandings, interests, attitudes, ideals, and the
like. Obviously this is recognized by proponents of each of the new sciences who make the laboratory the center of instruction so that the

30 K. E. Underwood. "Before You Decide to be 'Accountable,' Make Sure You Know for What,"
   American School Board Journal (September, 1970), 158, p. 32: W. A. Deterline, "Applied Ac-
   countability," *Educational Technology* (January, 1971), 11, p. 19; A. M. Cohen, "Objectives,
   Accountability, and Other Unpleasantries," *English Journal* (April, 1972), 61, pp. 565-570; A. W.
   Combs, *Educational Accountability Beyond Behavioral Objectives*, Association for Supervision
   and Curriculum Development, Washington, D. C., 1972, pp. 1-11.

students develop in understandings, interests, purposes, and activities of the scientist. "Thus, to attempt to change behavior by concentrating on the behavior itself is to deal with symptoms, and is likely to be no more satisfying than going to a doctor who might mistakenly do nothing but deal with symptoms while ignoring the causes of illness."[31]

The school must be held responsible for assistance of students toward solution of their personal-social, vocational, and educational problems so that they may become useful, democratic citizens. This includes helping them to improve not only in scholastic achievement but also in mental hygiene, self-esteem, and social outlook and sensitivity. To accomplish this teachers need *freedom, encouragement, and assistance toward involvement of students* in the study of relevant problems *through choice and pursuit of suitable group and individual objectives.* Teachers and students must not be handicapped with a long list of prescribed, specific behavioral objectives. Furthermore, it is unfair to hold only the teachers accountable for the quantity and quality of the students' learnings. The local citizens and school board and the school's administrators also must be held accountable. For example, teachers have limited responsibility for having an instructional media center containing an adequate supply of audio-visual and reading materials. Proper use of those materials contributes much toward retention of students in high school and improvement of their conduct and scholastic achievement.

Performance Contracting

The current focus on accountability has led some schools to relieve themselves of some direct responsibility for effective instruction by the employment of private corporations to teach retarded students, particularly in the basic skills of reading and arithmetic. In October 1969 Texarkana became the first city in which a school board engaged a private corporation to "train" teachers and direct the instruction of students. The contract bound the company to bring retarded and failing students of grades 7-12 up to specified levels of achievement in reading and mathematics. All of these students were about two grades behind in these two subjects. The immediate report was that students made "phenomenal progress."[32] A report one year later stated that the company's program was a "qualified success" but "impressive."[33]

Through Federal aid, additional cities have experimented with performance contracting, usually in reading and mathematics. The companies

31 Combs, *Educational Accountability Beyond Behavioral Objectives,* p. 7. See also J. Landers, "Accountability and Progress by Nomenclature: Old Ideas in New Bottles," *Phi Delta Kappan* (April, 1973), 54, pp. 539-541.
32 D. Bratten and others, "Performance Contracting: How It Works in Texarkana," *School Management* (August, 1970), 14, p. 8.
33 J. D. Reynolds, "Performance Contracting: Proceed with Caution," *English Journal* (January, 1971), 60, p. 102.

promise in the contract to bring low-achieving students up to or above the national norms in these areas of the curriculum.

These adoptions of performance contracting do not mean that it has been approved by a majority of educators. Both the National Education Association and the American Federation of Teachers have taken stands against performance contracting.[34] The legislative head of the National Education Association, John M. Lumley, said to a Senate subcommittee that performance contracting weakens the structure of the public school system and discredits it. The American Federation of Teachers announced a national campaign against what it designated as "educational gimmickry" involving "exploitation of children for profit."[35] At least one state group of teachers, the Massachusetts Education Association, took a strong stand against performance contracting.[36]

There are some obvious defects in the program of performance contracting. Since it uses the scores of students on a standardized test to determine the amount of money received by the company and the teachers involved, one has reason to assume that the emphasis in instruction is on preparation of students to take that type of test. In fact, it was discovered in one city that the company was helping students to score well on tests by "teaching the test." This company did not receive a renewal of its contract.[37] Another practice especially disturbing to educational psychologists and many educators is the extensive use of external, financial incentives—candy, toys, trading stamps, etc.—to motivate students to raise their scores. These practices in teaching reading, for example, are very different from those in some remedial reading classes of our public schools, where an efficient, dedicated teacher improves the students in reading merely to meet one of their basic educational needs and, in the process, motivates them solely through their success and satisfaction in reading.[38]

Thus performance contracting is both objectionable and unnecessary. The public school can and should hold itself directly accountable for results from all of its instruction. This has been shown throughout this book. In Chapters 2, 7, and 10, for example, there are reports of experiments revealing how some teachers have improved their students significantly in reading. In their method, students are placed in situations that lead them to read because of the direct usefulness of reading. They learn to

---

34 J. H. Porter, "Performance Contracts: A Challenge for Teachers," *Clearing House* (February, 1972), 46, pp. 339-342.

35 L. Lessinger, "Engineering Accountability for Results in Public Education," *Phi Delta Kappan* (December, 1970), 52, p. 225.

36 G. D. Hottleman, "Performance Contracting Is a Hoax," *Education Digest* (September, 1971), 37, p. 1.

37 K. Gehret, "Performance Contracting: How Does It Score?" *Christian Science Monitor* (January 3, 1972), 64, p. 7.

38 Hottleman, "Performance Contracting Is a Hoax," pp. 1-4; and E. J. Farrell, "Performance Contracting: Some Reservations," *English Journal* (April, 1972), 61, pp. 560-564; and E. B. Page, "How We All Failed at Performance Contracting," *Phi Delta Kappan* (October, 1972), 54, pp. 115-117.

read by reading to satisfy their curiosity and get help toward the solutions of their problems. Thus the developmental, functional method of teaching reading, unlike the method in performance contracting, provides for motivation of the students through their intrinsic interest in reading. Furthermore, the teacher, the student, and the student's parents know when reading has so improved that the student enjoys it and can read sufficiently well to do satisfactory work in high school. An objective test is used only to verify this further to themselves and especially to others.[39]

As is true of reading, some teachers in high school have significantly improved learning in mathematics. It is shown in the section on mathematics in Chapter 8 that these teachers use the method of inquiry, discovery, and conceptionalization, which results in motivation of the students through their developing interest in the subject itself. This method does not require any kind of external reward or reinforcement but has a built-in motivation factor, and it is intriguing to watch it operate under the guidance of a qualified teacher.

Examples of schools that have demonstrated accountability to the students and the public without a program of behavioral objectives or performance contracting are described in the concluding paragraphs of Chapters 13 and 14. These schools succeeded in improving the students not only in reading and mathematics but also in the other subjects. The teachers and counselors of these schools made an all-out, concerted effort to meet the real educational needs of potential failures, underachievers, and troublemakers. In doing this they used adequate, suitable instructional materials; thorough, comprehensive guidance; and personalized instruction. In two schools there was an unusual percentage of graduates going to college, and in all the schools there ceased to be a problem of dropouts or incorrigibles because the students were quite absorbed in their schoolwork. By adoption of these and similar practices all other high schools can approach meeting all the important items of their accountability to the students and the public. Thus a school can raise its level of accountability not by performance contracting but by comprehensive, cooperative work of administrators, counselors, and teachers toward improvement of instruction within the school.

From our look at the special means of instruction in this and the preceding chapter, a valid conclusion seems to be that nearly all of them have some potentiality for improvement of learning but that their adoption should be preceded by thorough evaluation and preparation. In judging the value of an innovational means of instruction the teacher needs to consider whether it is in harmony with a sound psychology of

[39] For further explanation of how well this developmental, functional method of teaching reading works, see two yearbooks of the National Society for the Study of Education: *Development in and Through Reading*, Sixtieth Yearbook, Part I, 1961, especially Chaps. 3, 8, 11, 17-18; and *Innovations and Change in Reading Instruction*, Sixty-seventh Yearbook, Part II, 1968, especially Chaps. 4-5 (both published by University of Chicago, Chicago).

learning and how well it contributes to the real needs of different students toward their becoming useful democratic citizens in a turbulent, troubled world. A second conclusion is that an innovation may be suitable for some purposes in some schools but may be quite inappropriate for other schools. Accordingly, in advance of deciding to adopt an innovation it is necessary to consider the nature of the school's faculty, budget, building, educational objectives, and other relevant items. The faculty, of course, is of supreme importance. The attitudes and habits of the teachers largely determine the success or failure of any means or form of instruction, "new" or "old." In the words of the editor of *Phi Delta Kappan:* "The differences of school structure and organization, of course offerings and scheduling, seem still not to be nearly as important as the quality of the teacher."[40]

QUESTIONS AND ACTIVITIES

1. Survey a high-school faculty, a school administration, a school board, and students to discover reasons why schools traditionally are reluctant to adopt innovations. Share your findings with all concerned.
2. Evaluate two or more of the innovations cited in this chapter against democratic ideals and sound learning theory.
3. Select a "new" teaching technique and plan a lesson using this technique. Evaluate it for effectiveness. You may want to video tape your lesson for playback to the class.
4. Arrange a field trip to a school noted for some innovation. Spend the day observing and talking with students, faculty, and administrators about the innovation's advantages and disadvantages.
5. What are some reasons teachers might be afraid of some innovations that are designed to improve instruction?
6. Gather additional information on accountability applied to education. Discuss this trend and its relationships to student learning, teachers, instruction, and school financing.
7. Explain how some schools could improve student achievement by "making the most of what they have" rather than through employment of some innovations.

40 D. W. Robinson, "Alternative Schools: Do They Promise System Reform?" *Phi Delta Kappan* (March, 1973), 54, p. 443.

SELECTED REFERENCES

Alexander, W. M., and V. A. Hines, *Independent Study in Secondary Schools*, paper, Holt, Rinehart, and Winston, New York, 1967.

American Association of School Librarians, *Standards for School Media Programs*, paper, American Library Association, Chicago, 1969.

Berg, Lyle L., and others, *Individualization of Instruction: The Role of the Learning/Resource Center*, Division of Educational Research and Services, University of Montana, Missoula, 1972.

Combs, A. W., *Educational Accountability Beyond Behavioral Objectives*, Association for Supervision and Curriculum Development, Washington, D. C., 1972.

Eurich, A. C., *Reforming American Education: The Innovation Approach to Improving Our Schools*, Harper and Row, New York, 1969.

Gorman, B. W., *Secondary Education: The High School America Needs*, Random House, New York, 1971, Chaps. 9-10.

Horton, Lowell, and Phyllis Horton, *The Learning Center: Heart of the School*, T. S. Denison, Minneapolis, 1973.

Inlow, G. M., *Maturity in High School Teaching*, 2nd ed., Prentice-Hall, Englewood Cliffs, New Jersey, 1970.

Kibler, R. J., and others, *Behavioral Objectives and Instruction*, Allyn and Bacon, Boston, 1970.

McGinnis, D. A., ed., *Standards for School Media Programs: Their Significance for All Libraries*, Syracuse University Press, Syracuse, New York, 1970.

Merrill, M. D., ed., *Instructional Design: Readings*, Prentice-Hall, Englewood Cliffs, New Jersey, 1971.

Overly, D. E., and others, *The Middle School: Humanizing Education for Youth*, Charles A. Jones, Worthington, Ohio, 1972, Chap. 15.

Popham, W. J., and E. L. Baker, *Establishing Instructional Goals*, Prentice-Hall, Englewood Cliffs, New Jersey, 1970.

Sarason, S., *Culture of the School and the Problem of Change*, Allyn and Bacon, Boston, 1971.

Silberman, C. E., *Crisis in the Classroom*, Random House, New York, 1970.

Unruh, G. G., and W. M. Alexander, *Innovations in Secondary Education*, Holt, Rinehart and Winston, New York, 1970.

Von Haden, H. I., and J. M. King, *Innovations in Education: Their Pros and Cons*, Charles A. Jones, Worthington, Ohio, 1971.

Weisgerber, R. A., ed., *Instructional Process and Media Innovation*, Rand McNally, New York, 1968.

CHAPTER 13

All classroom instruction involves some kind of guidance. Consciously or unconsciously, the teacher guides by appearance, action, and word. The guidance may lead toward anarchy, autocracy, or democracy, depending on the teacher's philosophy and skill. In line with our democratic ends and means in education, good guidance focuses on provision for the chief educational needs of different youths, especially on development of the individual in self-perception and self-direction and in social outlook and sensitivity. Every teacher is responsible for promotion of such guidance in all instruction. In addition, some teachers may well devote at least part of their time as special workers in the guidance program of the school.

THE NEED FOR AN ADEQUATE GUIDANCE PROGRAM

Guidance in school has become increasingly necessary because of life in an interdependent, fluid society. Adults along with adolescents are having difficulty living intelligently, trying to adjust in traditional ways to continuous, complicated changes. Many blindly depend on custom or caprice for direction in confrontation with choices between the old and the new conduct. They need to understand how to deal rationally with their problems in relation to the present as well as the past. There is extensive, disturbing evidence of the alienation and revolt of many young people in and outside of schools.[1]

[1] R. W. Carey, "Student Protest and the Counselor," *Personnel and Guidance Journal* (November, 1969), 48, pp. 185-191; R. W. Warner, Jr., and J. C. Hansen, "Alienated Youth: The Counselor's Task," *Personnel and Guidance Journal* (February, 1970), 48, pp. 443-448; J. B. Zack, "Restless Youth: What's the Message?" *National Association of Secondary School Principals Bulletin* (May, 1970), 54, pp. 146-158.

GUIDANCE IN TEACHING

Increasing necessity of guidance appears further in the changing composition of the school population. Many youths still leave high school before graduation. Sufficient, appropriate guidance would result in retention of a large percentage of them through school. However, it is well known that a larger percentage of young people between the ages of fourteen and seventeen are in school than formerly. Consequently, secondary school students today are less homogeneous in intelligence and in educational, vocational, and avocational interests than students of the past, those selected few who could survive unsuitable, nonpersonalized instruction. Moreover, many of those who graduate do not attend college but seek employment at once in a technological society of change, conflict, and confusion.[2]

The growing need of guidance is evident particularly in the nature and needs of underachievers and potential dropouts. As noted in Chapter 1, about 22 percent of youths entering high school leave before graduation. More than one investigation has revealed that those young people leave school chiefly because the school is not providing adequate help for them toward the solution of their problems. Of the students who continue to graduation, many are underachievers. Their level of achievement seems to be determined almost entirely by avoidance of trouble with teachers and parents and by minimum requirements for a diploma. Many of those two groups of students have poor mental health, feelings of inadequacy and unacceptance, and vague vocational and educational goals. Nearly all are handicapped by low interest and ability in reading. Experimentation shows that proper guidance improves such students in self-confidence, self-value, vocational information, and interest in formal education.[3]

Many such youths in high school desire guidance. They worry about failure, low grades, relationships with their teachers and peers, study habits, inability to read well, and choice of and preparation for a vocation. Some have more concern about getting along in school than they are willing to reveal. They may develop a "don't care" attitude to relieve their minds and to thwart the teacher's efforts to impose unsuitable subject matter upon them. Moreover, many of them believe they do not receive helpful guidance in school. There is some evidence in support of this belief. For example, it is known that an unsatisfactory relationship exists between the educational programs of some students and their vocational aspirations.

The gifted, high achievers also may be helped by some personalized guidance. They may gain from experiences that afford direction toward the best possible development and use of their talents. Moreover, they

---

[2] D. H. Mills, "Counseling in the Culture Cycle: Feeling or Reason?" *Personnel and Guidance Journal* (March, 1971), 49, pp. 515-522; L. O. Eckerson, "The White House Conference: Tips or Taps for Counselors?" *Personnel and Guidance Journal* (November, 1971), 50, pp. 167-174.

[3] W. L. Camp, "A Successful Classroom Program for Potential High School Dropouts," *Vocational Guidance Quarterly* (Spring, 1966), 14, pp. 187-191.

may be assisted to acquire additional information about traits and skills required for success in occupations and for leadership in community activities.

In light of the foregoing facts, the purpose of this chapter is to encourage high-school teachers to undertake an important role in the guidance of students. The chapter's focus is on helping teachers to develop attitudes and skills that will prepare them to grasp many opportunities in the classroom to guide students toward improvement in (1) their personal traits and (2) their academic achievements. The humanistic teacher may have begun development of these attitudes and skills for student guidance while taking professional courses, especially in educational psychology, methods, and student teaching, and thus will continue to develop them while teaching. Although not required to duplicate the skills of the school counselor, all teachers, whatever may have been their past training in guidance skills, should join the school counselor and the principal to form a team that works toward providing suitable guidance for every student.[4]

Sufficient and appropriate guidance for all kinds of students is both group and individual. It occurs in instruction as well as counseling. The program may be used to help different kinds of students to learn how best to direct themselves in three major areas of their interests and problems: education, vocation, and human relationships. Thus guidance may be classified as educational, occupational, and personal-social. These three areas of life and of guidance are interrelated but for discussion may be considered separately.

EDUCATIONAL GUIDANCE

The function of educational guidance is to assist students toward directing themselves in the choice and pursuit of worthwhile objectives in education. In a country dedicated to democracy as a way of life, at least in theory, the objectives of education should stem from the democratic ideal. These objectives emphasize enlargement and refinement of students' interests and their development in social and scientific mindedness. They apply in guidance of the individual toward viewing educational problems in relation to occupational and personal-social problems existing in home, community, and nation.

The objectives of educational guidance suggest procedure characterized by regard for the individual, self-direction, finding out, sharing ideas, and cooperative activity. There is provision for students to participate in determination of specific objectives, in discovery of alternate ways of acting,

---

[4] For examples of how a teacher may provide valuable individual guidance in many learning situations, see especially Chaps. 5, 7, and 9.

and in evaluation of the process and product. The teacher avoids dictating to youngsters or leaving them to flounder aimlessly. Endeavors are made to furnish guidance as needed by the individual or the group—by raising questions, directing discussions, recommending appropriate activities, and providing suitable learning materials. This was seen in earlier considerations of procedures in the major steps of teaching and in each area of the curriculum, including the new mathematics, the new sciences, and the new social studies.

VOCATIONAL GUIDANCE

The foregoing discussion indicates that educational guidance may contribute to and stem from vocational guidance. Educational goals and vocational goals are interwoven. This is not to say that a young person's chosen occupation is or should be the sole determinant of an educational program. But it is well known that one of the chief interests of nearly every youth in high school is choice of and preparation for a vocation. The occupational objective gives purpose and meaning to educational experiences bearing even remotely on preparation for an occupation. In fact, vocational guidance raises the morale of students as it helps them to recognize and begin basic education toward one or more suitable occupations.

While directing students in the study of subject matter, the teacher guides them vocationally as well as educationally. Strict adherence to a college preparatory curriculum may influence significantly both the gifted and the retarded student—one toward entering college and the other toward leaving high school. Obviously, the individual educational attainment of these students will affect their vocational careers. Similarly, the development of an intense dislike of mathematics or a strong commitment to it will affect a boy's or girl's future in education and vocation. Likewise, level of interest and skill in reading is a determining factor in one's educational and vocational planning. "Whatever a pupil experiences or fails to experience has some effect upon his career development; consequently, the curriculum and how it is implemented by teachers is a very important consideration."[5]

Opportunities for occupational guidance appear in all courses as teachers relate instruction to modern society. In the social studies, for example, study may center on the occupations of the people of a country. This could occur in history or geography but especially in a course on current economic, social, and political problems. The teacher could well direct the students in study of occupations in a broad setting of time

[5] E. C. Roeber, "The School Curriculum and Vocational Development," *Vocational Guidance Quarterly* (Winter, 1965-1966), 14, p. 88. See also H. E. Nelson, "The Vocational Curriculum: Patterns of Experimentation," *National Association of Secondary School Principals Bulletin* (November, 1969), 53, pp. 108-119.

and space. Occupations of other countries and times may be studied in relation to occupations in the United States today.

Of course, sufficient vocational guidance of adolescents in high school depends not only on group and individual instruction but also on group and individual counseling. In the counseling, improvement of the students' occupational understandings and attitudes is essential. Findings from investigations of occupational choices of high-school students indicate that (1) some have not chosen a vocation, (2) among those who have made a selection, there is a tendency to select from a narrow range, (3) many choices are unrealistic in view of the individual's present level of development, and (4) many choices do not correspond closely to job opportunities. Thus the occupational preferences of students are often a poor basis for decision-making in education. Furthermore, a study of 400,000 students in grades 9 through 12 indicates that a majority of the boys change their vocational choices during their years in high school. Accordingly, teachers and counselors have reasons to work together to promote continuous comprehensive guidance.[6]

Improvement of youths in their insights and feelings concerning occupations requires provision for them to find sufficient information for satisfactory reflection on choice of and preparation for a vocation. The information may be obtained from an outside speaker, a picture, a field trip, and library reading. It includes such items about occupations as the following: description of the work performed, education and training required, hiring practices, working conditions, opportunities for and limitations on special groups, employment outlook, wages, hours of work, and possibilities of promotion.[7] Opportunities to study and evaluate several vocations may be given to students in a special course or a unit on occupations. Furthermore, as mentioned above, opportunities appear incidentally in teaching each subject of the curriculum.

In the process of guidance, the teacher helps the student to reflect, to gain knowledge, and to draw conclusions. No member of the staff should try to impose an occupation on a boy or girl. For satisfactory adjustment in the vocational area of life, as in other areas, the young per-

[6] G. B. Jones and D. E. Nelson, "Approaching a Vocational Education Problem Through Project TALENT-Related Guidance System Components," *Vocational Guidance Journal* (March, 1970), 18, pp. 187-193. See also H. L. Munson, *Foundations of Developmental Guidance*, Allyn and Bacon, Boston, 1971, Chap. 14.

[7] Sources on which counselors and teachers may draw for information for students on occupations are B'nai B'rith, Vocational Service, 1640 Rhode Island Avenue, Northwest, Washington, D. C.; Chronicle Guidance Publications, Moravia, New York; U. S. Government Printing Office, Washington, D. C.; Harcourt, Brace and World, New York, New York; National Education Association, 1201 Sixteenth Street, Northwest, Washington, D. C.; Prentice-Hall, Englewood Cliffs, New Jersey; Science Research Associates, 259 East Erie Street, Chicago, Illinois; U. S. Department of Commerce, Washington, D. C.; U. S. Department of Labor, Washington, D. C.; and U. S. Office of Education, Washington, D. C. See also issues of *Vocational Guidance Quarterly*, American Personnel and Guidance Association, Twentieth and Northampton Streets, Easton, Pennsylvania. Of particular value are the vocational guides prepared by each state and information from the state employment services of each state.

son needs help in choosing and planning. This is clearly evident in view of the sudden appearance and disappearance of occupations. For example, nearly all occupations in electronics have arisen since World War II. Moreover, many students have poorly developed personality traits and self-concepts for successful vocational adjustment in a changing, technological society.[8] Accordingly, vocational guidance is directed more toward vocational education than toward vocational training—education for future as well as present changes and complexities.

PERSONAL-SOCIAL GUIDANCE

It may be seen that as teachers concentrate on educational and vocational guidance they become involved in personal-social guidance. This is because the personal-social qualities of students strongly affect selection and attainment of their educational and vocational goals. In turn, progress toward these goals significantly determines their growth in personality and social adjustment. Furthermore, they need traits enabling them to live intelligently in free association with others not only in vocation but also in leisure. These are reasons why guidance may appropriately be focused on the personal-social problems of youth.

As in educational and vocational guidance, personal-social guidance involves study of the student by the teacher as well as the counselor. Many students have inadequate understanding of themselves. When they say that they do not know why they feel and act as they do toward others they are often sincere. Moreover, they frequently perceive in themselves characteristics that do not actually exist and so are not perceived by others. The kind of person one considers oneself to be affects one's ambitions and attainments in all areas of life. The teacher who knows about individual students' school, home, and community life can help them to view themselves realistically in relation to their environment. This help may be rendered through rich, fitting experiences in group and individual counseling in instruction. These experiences contribute not only to mental health and social adjustment but also to aspiration and achievement in education and vocation.

Learning About the Student

Ideally, each high school acquires adequate, pertinent information about the educational, vocational, and personal-social status of each student. The information may be obtained (1) directly, as in observation of the student's behavior in various instructional and counseling situations,

8 C. E. Bare, "Personality and Self Concept Correlates of Occupational Aspirations," *Vocational Guidance Quarterly* (June, 1970), 18, pp. 297-305. See the section on vocational problems of youth in Chap. 1. See also the section on industrial arts in Chap. 9.

and (2) indirectly, as through tests, inventories, and papers. Obviously, the teacher may gain knowledge of each student in the classroom and from the counselor's and the principal's office.

Observation has always been a common, effective means of studying the student. A member of a class may be observed unawares while reacting to a variety of situations. When actively involved in pursuit of intrinsic goals in learning, students tend to project their real selves and thereby reveal the kinds of persons they are. Activities conducive to absorption of students in learning are those that engage them in choosing, planning, investigating, discussing, constructing, generalizing, applying, and the like. Careful observation of their level and kind of involvement in various learning situations discloses some significant values, understandings, and abilities.

Effective use of observation to acquire information about the student rests chiefly on the teacher. This is true even in instruction characterized by narrowness of subject matter and passivity in learning. The teacher is the only member of the guidance team in daily contact with the student and thereby in a position to perceive early symptoms of the need for counseling. An astute teacher can detect not only the maladjusted underachiever but also one with special, high-level interests and achievements.[9] Of course, the school counselor has a unique opportunity to observe the behavior of the young person as the two exchange ideas in the privacy of an interview. Yet the counselor's observation is usually restricted to the interview situation, whereas the teacher may observe in a variety of situations, including that of the interview.

Among the indirect means of understanding the boy or girl are tests and inventories. The intelligence test, which is frequently used by counselors and teachers, provides some insight into the person's mentality. However, psychologists recognize that it is more valid for measuring academic intelligence than social or mechanical intelligence. It also indicates both acquired and inherited ability, not native ability alone. Similarly, standardized achievement tests are limited in validity, being more helpful in checking the acquisition of facts than the use of facts in logical self-expression and thinking. This type of test, however, has distinct assets: a high degree of objectivity, norms of achievement, and ease of administration. Likewise, published personality and interest inventories are useful but have limitations. Since they are constructed by experts, they are likely to be superior, at least in form, to those that could be designed by the usual classroom teacher. Yet the person studied by an inventory may make some inaccurate responses, which are undetected by the examiner. In fact, the individual examined by any standardized instruments mentioned above is in such restricted and unusual situations that he or she

9 L. N. Downing, *Guidance and Counseling Services: An Introduction*, McGraw-Hill, New York, 1968, Chap. 3.

is unlikely to reveal accurate reactions to many ordinary life situations. Thus standardized tests and inventories are helpful but inadequate means of studying the student.[10]

A related indirect means of learning about the student is through written expression. This may be in the form of a real, well-constructed essay examination, requiring the examinee to attack problems, relate ideas, and form and apply generalizations. This examination is a projective means of measurement because it places the examinee in a situation causing self-projection through organization and expression of thoughts. In this respect it has a function comparable to dramatic and constructive activities. Within the limits of the assigned task, students have freedom to express their own thoughts, thereby revealing incidentally their ideas, interests, and values. The same is likely to be true in another form of written expression, the student paper. As was seen in Chapter 7, this paper usually should be written in class under the observation of the teacher. Through questioning the student in the process of writing, the teacher may discover some traits for not only writing but also other activities.

Guidance by Group Procedure

As has been indicated, group procedure is an effective means of guidance. Certainly individual guidance by the interview is also essential. It has been found, however, that group guidance helps toward detection of the student in need of special individual counseling; and, of course, it also may function in guidance subsequent to the interview. There is some evidence that it is especially forceful in changing basic attitudes and habits. Free exchange of ideas in the give and take of discussion on common problems is conducive to development of social mindedness—a sense of responsibility to and acceptance by the group and of regard for the right and responsibility of free expression by the individual.[11]

The subject matter of group guidance may be in any course of the curriculum or in special units on guidance. Examples of the latter, particularly for the junior high school, are orientation in school, how to study, knowing ourselves, getting along with others, choosing a vocation,

[10] Among the sources from which the teacher may purchase tests and inventories are Bureau of Educational Measurements, Kansas State Teachers College, Emporia, Kansas; Bureau of Educational Research and Service, University of Iowa, Iowa City, Iowa; Bureau of Publications, Teachers College, Columbia University, New York, New York; California Test Bureau, Del Monte Research Park, Monterey, California; Division of Education Reference, Purdue University, Lafayette, Indiana; Center for Psychological Service, George Washington University, Washington D. C.; Educational Test Bureau, 720 Washington Avenue, Minneapolis, Minnesota; Harcourt, Brace and World, New York, New York; Harvard University Press, Cambridge, Massachusetts; Houghton Mifflin, Boston, Massachusetts; Psychological Corporation, 304 East 45 Street, New York, New York; Public School Publishing Company, Bloomington, Illinois; Science Research Associates, 259 East Erie Street, Chicago, Illinois; Stanford University Press, Stanford, California; University of Chicago, Chicago, Illinois; Educational Testing Service, Rosedale Road, Princeton, New Jersey.
[11] Downing, *Guidance and Counseling Services*, Chap. 11.

and planning for senior high school. The method of instruction in either a common course or a special unit is essentially that recommended by leading educators on teaching procedure in each area of the curriculum. The class is led to adopt common goals and is assisted in planning and carrying out plans toward reaching the objectives. In this kind of learning situation each individual demonstrates characteristics to others of the class. When youths are in pursuit of group objectives, they are strongly affected by their peers.

Referring specifically to content and procedure in group guidance, Blocher writes:

Content, of course, refers to the topics, materials, or ideas that are being discussed by groups. Most individuals in our society are conditioned to be aware of the content inherent in group interactions. Often, however, these same people are very insensitive to the *process* of group interactions. By process we mean the roles being played by group members, the ways in which the group meets the needs of its members, the degree to which members are free to express their feelings and attitudes, the extent to which members experience feelings of belonging or rejection, and so forth.[12]

A teacher or counselor strongly committed to involvement of youths in improvement of their attitudes and habits, needs to provide for group dynamics in group guidance. In what is sometimes practiced as group guidance or counseling the class constitutes a "group" marked by passivity and receptivity of nearly all its members. Efficient, effective group guidance is promoted by a group characterized by active participation of its members in pursuit of common interests or objectives. This kind of group is cohesive and dynamic, whatever its major goal may be. Examples are youth groups and especially all democratic groups. It was seen in preceding chapters that some classes in high schools have been so organized and instructed that the class constitutes a group, possessing a high degree of unification of interests and activities. The sharing of interests and the exchange of ideas by members of such a class may be expected to have a significant effect on beliefs and actions of each of its members.

Guidance by Interview

Extensive, efficient use of group guidance does not reduce the necessity of good individual guidance through interviews. In fact, as high schools and classes increase in size, there is growing need of individual counseling because the student is likely to be lost in the group and become little more than a number. The staff and the program, particularly of the large school, must be organized for adequate, effective individual counseling

---

12 D. H. Blocher, *Developmental Counseling*, Ronald, New York, 1966, p. 171. See also H. W. Bernard and D. W. Fullmer, *Principles of Guidance: A Basic Text*, International Textbook, Scranton, Pennsylvania, 1969, Chap. 14.

for all kinds of students. Unfortunately, some teachers lack the necessary understanding of and attitude toward adolescents for conducting satisfactory interviews. Specifically, research indicates that some teachers are inclined to be more attentive to students in a high economic group than to those in a low one.[13] The latter group, of course, is in special need of help. Adequate in-service education of those teachers on individual counseling is necessary.

In practice, the interview has typically inclined toward autocracy or democracy. In an autocratic interview the counselor dominates—lecturing, advising, and dictating—and thus affords the counselee little freedom of expression. The alternative for such an interview, however, is not the other extreme of provision for no direction. Some recent writers on counseling state that nondirection in counseling is a myth and, therefore, should no longer be made an issue. The counselor cannot and should not avoid some direction of the student. Accordingly, the issue hinges on the kind and degree of direction, that is, whether it is for life in a democratic or an undemocratic society.[14]

The democratic interview consists of a free exchange of ideas between two individuals, the counselee doing a considerable portion of the talking. The teacher and the student question and inform each other, each gaining insight into the student's nature and needs and the alternative courses of action. As the two share ideas rather freely, the student may be helped toward self-understanding in relation to the particular environment and toward working out his or her own salvation. All the while the teacher shows sincere regard for the counselee as an individual and a real desire to assist that person to learn ways for self-help. This kind of interview may be expected to assist the students to improve in directing themselves toward worthwhile goals—personal-social, vocational, and educational.

Such counseling may be termed "developmental counseling" in that it is focused on development of the individual toward production of changes in dependable behavior. As stated by an advocate of this type of counseling:

A considerable degree of client responsibility in the counseling process is necessary if the client is to remain an active and involved learner and if the counseling process is to be a model through which he can grow in responsible independence. The exercise of counselor responsibility is neither good nor bad in itself, but must be used with judgment and discretion by the counselor in terms of his immediate and long-term goals. . . .

The purpose of the developmental interview is to help the client find and try

---

13 J. W. Hart, "Socially Mobile Teachers and Classroom Atmosphere," *Journal of Educational Research* (December, 1965), 59, pp. 166-168; and S. Charnofsky, "Counseling for Power," *Personnel and Guidance Journal* (January, 1971), 49, pp. 351-357.

14 D. H. Blocher, "Issues in Counseling: Elusive and Illusional," *Personnel and Guidance Journal* (April, 1965), 43, pp. 796-800.

out new and alternative ways of behaving that will be goal-oriented for him. The interview must provide maximum communication between counselor and client and must lead to plans, tasks, and actions that can provide a basis for changes in behavior. The developmental interview, therefore, is characterized by *communication, openness,* and *action.*[15]

Of basic importance in the process of an interview is the counselor's point of view. Attention to choice of techniques is necessary. However, the counselor employs techniques in accordance with what he or she aims to communicate to the counselee. An effective interview begins with the purposes and plans of the counselor and the needs of the counselee, but its progress and results are altered by the continuous interaction of the two personalities. Too much emphasis on a list of techniques for the interview may lead to a mechanical and superficial type of counseling.

Another essential in the interviewing process is the relationship between the counselor and the counselee. This relationship may help or harm the counseled individual. The relationship is determined more by the counselor's personality than by the technique. The helpful personality reveals genuine interest, sympathetic understanding, intelligent adjustment, constructive feedback, self-control, a sense of humor, sincerity, and comprehension of the problem. A good counseling relationship is obtained not by putting on a professional cloak or pulling out a bag of tricks but by real regard and concern for the counselee. The successful teacher in either individual or group guidance is democratically oriented, being emotionally, socially, and mentally mature and having strong interest in the development of every student, regardless of economic or social status.[16]

Thus not only professional counselors but also many classroom teachers possess essential qualifications for an effective student-centered interview. These teachers have winsome personal qualities, and their relationships with students show mutual respect. Furthermore, many unique occasions for interviews occur in the classroom. As previously mentioned, the teacher observes the student in action more than the school counselor or other members of the staff. Often the student needs guidance immediately, at the time this is evident in the teaching-learning process. Some teachers have scheduled periods for individual instruction and counseling. The interview in these periods assists them to discover the needs of each student in close relation to classroom situations. Moreover, many boys and girls in secondary school, especially the junior high school, desire and seek counseling from a teacher whom they like and trust. Accordingly, free and effective use of the interview is a concern of the classroom teacher as well as of the school counselor.

15 Blocher, *Developmental Counseling,* pp. 160-161, 166.
16 D. S. Arbuckle, "The Alienated Counselor," *Personnel and Guidance Journal* (September, 1969), 48, pp. 18-23, and D. H. Blocher and others, *Guidance Systems: An Introduction to Student Personnel Work,* Ronald, New York, 1971, Chap. 11.

The qualified teacher can have an effective interview which improves the teacher-student relationship and thereby the student's learning. In school, as in the community, two persons may not get along well simply because communication between them does not exist. A good talk between teacher and student usually helps each to interpret the other's behavior and thus improves attitudes one toward the other. Furthermore, the student, as every other person, wants to be treated as a real individual, not as a statistic in mass instruction. Each youngster has particular interests and needs. By using the conference to provide individualized help understandingly and sympathetically, the teacher may lead the counselee to feel that genuine interest is being shown in his or her welfare. No doubt the impressive effectiveness of individualized instruction in reading, as shown by research, is largely a result of the individual conference in the teaching procedure.

An illustration of using the conference in instruction may be seen in the section on teaching literature in Chapter 7. The teacher of this subject may use a conference to learn about the young person's attitudes and skills in reading and the kind of reading materials of special interest, use, and meaning to that student. Some leaders on the teaching of English insist that frequently every member of a class should not be held to the reading of the same material. There is a trend toward considerable reliance on individualized reading of literature. During the reading period the teacher may spend much time holding conferences. In the interview the student is encouraged to express freely particular reading abilities and interests, while stating personal reactions to books and periodicals being read at the time. In view of the information thus received, the teacher may suggest to the student ways of improving in both the selection and process of reading. A classic may be suggested to one individual but a modern detective story to another. In either case the reader is directed toward reading to enrich his or her life and to gain insight into personal and societal problems.

The good interview, conducted by either the specialist in guidance or the classroom teacher, incorporates the essential elements of sound group procedure. It provides a learning situation in which the learner takes the steps of problem solving in an effort to find a solution to a problem. In many cases the counselor must lead the counselee to recognize and analyze one or more disturbing problems. Often the adolescent realizes that all is not running smoothly but has only a vague conception of the obstacles. After being led to confront the problem with some understanding, he or she may be helped to perceive possible solutions and use reason to choose a wise course of action. In frequent instances the student may be directed to attack further a problem through reading and other means of acquiring pertinent information. The interview is thus employed to assist the young person not only to deal with a particular problem but also to develop inclination and ability to deal with subsequent problems.

Within the school organization, the teacher is the person charged with the greatest responsibility for helping the individual understand himself and his way of life.

The size of the school need not affect the atmosphere within the classroom if the teacher is creative and guidance-minded. In each class the student can be taught as a unique individual. Differences of talents and needs can be met if the classroom is developed and used as an experience gaining laboratory for vitalized learning activities.

In order to create a laboratory "feel" in the classroom and actually to guide a student according to his ability and interest needs, the teacher works through cooperatively developed group activities, teaching how to think and work increasingly independent of the teacher, as well as with each other on equal terms. This teacher-guidance approach helps the student learn how to organize his work, plan his activities, apply facts, visualize possible solutions, and come to his own conclusions in solving his problems. As a result of this kind of learning experience, the student gains confidence in his ability to plan and execute a unit of work as in a social group. Each individual retains his individuality, but contributes his talent or ability to the others and becomes enriched through the experiences of the others. Teacher direction decreases as the student's skills and abilities improve in cooperative planning, sharing ideas, executing responsibilities, organizing materials, coming to conclusions, and applying his information to problem situations.[17]

The Role of Environment in Guidance

In both individual and group guidance provided by the classroom teacher or the school counselor, it is essential to recognize the role of the environment. The environment is a basis of the student's present needs and is the means of meeting those needs. It was shown in Chapter 2 how modern psychologists agree that learning occurs as the learner interacts with the environment.

The interview, consisting of free communication between the counselor and the counselee in a favorable physical and social environment, has been found to improve the student, particularly in educational and vocational interests and applications. However, there is some evidence that the interview alone has little observable effect on the individual's basic personality traits. Likewise, group guidance alone does not suffice. Yet it, along with the interview, can be made a potent means of using the environment to produce fundamental changes in a student's personality. An adequate program of guidance in high school includes use of the environment of the school and, as far as possible, the home and the community. Recognizing this, a specialist in guidance of adolescents empha-

[17] H. L. Blanchard and L. S. Flaum, *Guidance: A Longitudinal Approach*, 2nd ed., paper, Burgess, Minneapolis, 1968, p. 20.

sizes that study of and help for a student in isolation does not suffice. To meet the individual's personal and educational needs, the staff must work through the student's environment in and outside the school. Recognition of the essential role of the student's environment in the guidance program is well expressed below.

The counselor does believe in individual freedom and individual responsibility as vital human values. He is not, however, naive enough to deny that great amounts of human behavior are directly determined by the environment, and that very often the most effective and productive way to change behavior is by intervention with the environment as well as with the individual. This concept has great relevance to the formation of counselor role. . . .

The developmental counselor is interested in modifying environmental situations both within and without the institutional settings in which he operates. He intervenes in ways that make it possible for clients to relate themselves to the environment and react to it in maximally growth-producing fashions.

A student may be confronted with a family or school situation in which he is rejected for being himself, where he is consistently expected to be something other than that which he feels he is, wants to be, or can be. . . . In such situations, the most significant intervention of the counselor may well be to change the social situation in school or family or community so that the client may relate to it in more positive and growth-inducing ways.[18]

For a high school to function well in providing a rich, suitable environment for guidance of different youths, concerted effort by every member of the staff is required. It is well known that some teachers concentrate on "spoon-feeding" and conditioning students, training them to follow directions blindly and to accept unquestioningly all statements of the textbook. Such instruction counteracts somewhat that of other teachers focused on involvement of the student in reflective thinking and self-direction. Likewise, efficient counseling by the school counselor avails little without a curriculum and a method of teaching that provides a variety of vital experiences conducive to developing the student in scientific and social mindedness toward satisfactory handling of personal problems. This suggests the need for counselors, teachers, librarians, and administrators to work cooperatively toward having an integrated program of counseling and instruction.[19]

The opportunities and corresponding responsibilities of the librarian in guidance are of significance here. Among the ways the librarian may function as a guide to students are insistence on appropriate conduct, encouragement of good habits of study, instruction in use of reference tools,

18 Blocher, *Developmental Counseling*, p. 184. See also Blocher and others, *Guidance Systems*, Chap. 4.
19 R. W. Graff and R. W. Warner, Jr., "Attitude Toward a School's Counseling Services as Seen by Administrators, Teachers, and Counselors," *Journal of Secondary Education* (November, 1968), 43, pp. 320-323; A. B. Clark, "The Counselor: A New Role in Instructional Services," *Journal of Secondary Education* (December, 1969), 44, pp. 366-368.

stimulation and direction of reading, and introduction of new reading materials. In such contributions to guidance the librarian may use brief group or individual conferences and extensive displays on the bulletin board. The fact is that the good librarian is much more than a person who knows the technicalities of library science. If he or she has thorough knowledge of young people and the modern world, along with professional information and an attractive personality, this key individual may make the library an effective agency in guidance of youth.

Guidance in the Urban High School

The nature and need of the teacher's extended role in guidance is forcefully demonstrated in inner city high schools. Most of the students belong to the lower class of society and come from poor, culturally deprived homes, located in deteriorating, depressing environments. Unfortunately, the typical local high school has a program mainly for middle and upper-class students. In addition, the school lacks essential equipment and audio-visual and reading materials. Accordingly, many of the students begin attendance in high school with a negative attitude toward the school's program and the teacher. Few of them see any relevancy in the school's program toward meeting their needs. Some of them are apathetic, but more of them express open rebellion by word and action.

In confrontation with an unfavorable classroom situation, every teacher needs to begin on the first day and continue each day to provide group-individual instruction, focused on guidance of the student. This can best be done by employing the teaching procedure described and demonstrated in preceding chapters, especially Chapters 4-9, and mentioned earlier in this chapter. With support from the city superintendent of schools, the school principal, and the school counselor, the teachers of a school must work as a team to provide adequate guidance for those underprivileged students. This may well include visitation in the students' homes by teachers or other representatives of the school. It certainly will require revision of the curriculum according to needs of the majority of those students and provision of freedom to the teacher and the students to select from the curriculum the content most suitable for the individual. The team also should place proper pressure on the board of education to provide each school with an instructional media center, well stocked with learning materials, so that students may enlarge and enrich their cultural and scholastic backgrounds.

In preparation for this all-out guidance program geared to meet the needs of every urban high-school student, prospective teachers should have some special preparation, and some teachers could benefit from some in-service work. Teachers also should be encouraged to request help from and give help to one another. To make education relevant to the students so that they will become useful, happy citizens, a comprehensive, student-centered guidance program is a must in every urban high school.[20]

A Model Demonstration of a Successful Urban Program

An example of the processes and results of a comprehensive and intensive program of guidance is in the Demonstration Guidance Project of the City of New York. The project was conducted in Junior High School 43 and George Washington High School in the years 1957-1962. School counselors and classroom teachers worked cooperatively to provide guidance through individual and group instruction and counseling. Students with limited cultural backgrounds were chosen for the project. They were potentially able students whose cultural deprivation was interfering with their success in high school and their likelihood of attending colleges.[21]

The project was a result of concern by the New York City Board of Education about the deterioration of some pupils in scholastic ability between the primary grades and high school, particularly those of minority groups. Relatively few of these children were completing academic high-school courses, and fewer still were admitted to college.[22]

The program of guidance involved dealing with the whole individual in a total environment. For instance, counselors were especially alert to health needs. The schools took all possible steps to help young people toward improvement of their physical condition. Further, counselors consulted with parents in educational and vocational guidance of their children. A specialist in guidance visited the homes of students with acute emotional disturbances. For some it was possible to arrange part-time jobs, monetary help, and improved sleeping and study conditions. The counselor also aided by bringing about a better relationship between student and parent or parents. Such counseling often included use of social workers and other community agents.

In instruction, a major program of cultural enrichment was provided. The school drew on community resources and other instructional aids to provide students with background in each course. The content and the method of instruction were directed toward meeting individual needs. Toward this end counselor and teacher worked in close, continuous cooperation. "During the term, there was a steady flow of information about the students between teachers and counselors. At the end of every term, the teachers furnished the counselors with evaluative reports on the progress of the students, their attitudes and relationships in class and their academic achievement."[23]

[20] See Blocher and others, Guidance Systems, Chap. 10.
[21] H. T. Hillson and F. C. Myers, The Demonstration Guidance Project, 1957-1962, New York City Board of Education, New York, 1963.
[22] Ibid., p. v.
[23] Ibid., p. 8.

The effects of this guidance project on the educational attainments of young people of a depressed area were impressive. The teachers and the students were almost unanimous in an expression of enthusiasm about the results. The teachers thought they could observe marked improvements in the personalities of many of the young people, for example, growth in poise, self-confidence, and a sense of worth. There were still some dropouts, but in most cases they were the results of sickness, poor home conditions, or a move from the community. The dropout rate was one-third lower than that of the rest of the city. In comparison with students prior to the project, two and a half times as many project students earned academic diplomas and at least three and a half times as many went to college. Also of special significance is that in each graduating class the project students took highest honors.[24]

An important conclusion from this experiment is that a large percentage of deprived youths may be helped to raise their academic achievement through adequate, suitable guidance in both instructional and counseling programs. The instruction must be enriched to provide for deficiencies in backgrounds and be directed toward development of intrinsic interests and meanings for self-direction in study. The counseling must be continuous and tailored to the individual. Without such guidance the transfer of underprivileged students to a "good" school may avail little toward upgrading their academic attainments.

An analysis of this and similar experiments, showing how deprived students may be helped by both counseling and instructional experiences to up-grade their self-esteem and academic achievements, leads to the conclusion that such students have the capacity to engage in advanced learning. Research indicates that, whenever schools provide adequately for culturally deprived students to obtain high quality education, these students can obtain it.[25]

A valid generalization seems to be that, for guidance in high school to result in significant improvement of different young people in rational direction of themselves toward worthwhile goals, it must permeate the whole program of education. The educative process is a process of guidance, and guidance is educative. Hence it is unreasonable to state that a teacher is good in instruction but poor in guidance. Furthermore, investigations indicate that counseling alone does not produce basic changes in the individual. Improvement of the student in solving educational, vocational, and personal-social problems requires counseling plus instruction—both focused on provision of environments conducive to development of the individual in self-direction for democratic living in a pulsating, perplex-

24 Ibid., p. 27. For further analysis and appraisal of comprehensive, developmental guidance see Munson, *Foundations of Developmental Guidance*, Chap. 4.
25 P. A. Zirkel, "Enhancing the Self-Concept of Disadvantaged Students," *California Journal of Educational Research* (May, 1972), 23, pp. 125-137.

ing world. Dedicated, efficient teachers are finding ways of promoting such guidance.[26]

QUESTIONS AND ACTIVITIES

1. Arrange to visit the guidance department of a high school. Inquire as to its function, services, and personnel.
2. Analyze the guidance department's procedure to determine how extensive guidance is provided for all students.
3. Discuss with a group of high-school teachers the concept of the teacher as a counselor. Be concerned with such topics as time for counseling, opportunities for counseling within the teaching stages, and who is responsible for counseling.
4. Consider how both academic achievement and classroom discipline may be improved by frequent individual counseling.
5. Why do some leaders in guidance hold that flexibility in technique is of primary importance in counseling rather than adherence to any particular technique?
6. Apply your concept of democracy to the process of individual counseling. Demonstrate this conceptual approach in a mini-counseling session before the class.
7. State relationships between guidance practices and classroom discipline in a modern educational program.
8. As a class, brainstorm ways by which the ordinary high school may so improve its program of guidance that each student is well counseled.
9. To what extent should the teacher rely on the school counselor in matters relating to discipline? Under what circumstances should the teacher rightfully "refer" a student to the counselor?

SELECTED REFERENCES

Amos, W. E., and J. D. Grambs, eds., *Counseling the Disadvantaged Youth,* Prentice-Hall, Englewood Cliffs, New Jersey, 1968.

Benjamin, A., *The Helping Interview,* Houghton Mifflin, Boston, 1969.

[26] W. Phillips, "Guidance Services: Range and Scope," *High School Journal* (January, 1971), 54, pp. 243-250; and D. S. Arbuckle, "The Counselor: Relevant or Irrelevant?" *High School Journal* (January, 1971), 54, pp. 265-275.

Blanchard, H. L., and L. S. Flaum, *Guidance: A Longitudinal Approach,* 2nd ed., Burgess, Minneapolis, 1968.

Blocher, D. H., and others, *Guidance Systems: An Introduction to Student Personnel Work,* Ronald, New York, 1971.

Gilchrist, R., and others, *Curriculum Development: A Humanized Systems Approach,* Fearon Publishers, Belmont, California, 1974.

Hansen, D. A., ed., *Explorations in Sociology and Counseling,* Houghton Mifflin, Boston, 1969.

Holland, J. L., *Making Vocational Choices: A Theory of Careers,* Prentice-Hall, Englewood Cliffs, New Jersey, 1973.

Johnson, D. E., and M. J. Vestermark, *Barriers and Hazards in Counseling,* Houghton Mifflin, Boston, 1970.

Kell, B. L., and J. M. Burow, *Developmental Counseling and Therapy,* Houghton Mifflin, Boston, 1970.

Lee, J. M., and N. J. Pallone, *Guidance and Counseling in Schools: Foundations and Processes,* McGraw-Hill, New York, 1966.

Mink, O. G., and B. A. Kaplan, eds., *America's Problem Youth: Education and Guidance of the Disadvantaged,* International Textbook, Scranton, Pennsylvania, 1970.

Munson, H. L., *Foundations of Developmental Guidance,* Allyn and Bacon, Boston, 1971.

National Society for the Study of Education, *The Changing American School,* Sixty-fifth Yearbook, Part II, University of Chicago, Chicago, 1966, Chap. 3.

Ohlsen, M. M., *Group Counseling,* Holt, Rinehart and Winston, New York, 1970.

Osipow, S. H., and W. B. Walsh, *Strategies in Counseling for Behavior Change,* Appleton-Century-Crofts, Boston, 1970.

Patterson, C. H., ed., *The Counselor in the School,* McGraw-Hill, New York, 1967.

Peters, H. J., and J. C. Hansen, *Vocational Guidance and Career Development,* Macmillan, New York, 1966.

Roeber, E. C., and others, *A Strategy for Guidance: A Point of View and Its Implications,* Macmillan, New York, 1969.

Sachs, B., *The Student, The Interview, and The Curriculum: Dynamics of Counseling in the School,* Houghton Mifflin, Boston, 1966.

Traxler, A. E., and R. D. North, *Techniques of Guidance,* 3rd ed., Harper and Row, New York, 1966.

Weinberg, C., and others, *Social Foundations of Educational Guidance,* Free Press, New York, 1969.

CHAPTER 14

That discipline is an essential aspect of an educational program has been recognized by educators of various beliefs. Contrary to assertions of some "instant critics" of modern educational theory and practice, no prominent, reputable educator has advocated disregarding discipline in schools. Although there seems to be a consensus on the importance of discipline, there are significant differences of opinion about what it is and how it may best be provided.

AN INCLUSIVE CONCEPTION OF DISCIPLINE

Discipline in school has been conceived typically as only keeping order or preventing misbehavior. If nearly all the students refrain from doing what is forbidden, the discipline is said to be good. This conception excludes recognition of how well students may be engaged in educative activities as they abstain from misconduct. Moreover, it seems to rely largely on punishment as a means of reducing misbehavior. It is focused on securing outward conformity to standards of conduct whatever the student's inner reactions may be. Those who express such a limited view apparently perceive the youngster's conduct in school with little understanding of its relationship to present or future conduct in the home, community, and nation. Thus comprehended, discipline is restricted in time, place, and purpose.

Discipline adequately viewed is as broad as education. Its aims and procedures are those of education. In discipline as in education, the curriculum, the teaching-learning process, counseling, and all the school environment are involved. In all instruction every student receives some kind of discipline. A person cannot be good as a teacher but poor as a disciplinarian. In fact, the general objective of education may be stated

DISCIPLINE IN TEACHING

as discipline of students for useful, democratic living in a world of change and confusion.

The question may be raised whether or not one can discuss discipline *per se,* isolated from the main stream. Admittedly, it does appear to be anathema to the teaching function, but this is deceptive. There must be a direct and cohesive correlation between teaching and discipline as a functioning unity of any classroom situation. For neglect of one begets defeat of the other. To give greater showmanship to one usually means to render less than satisfactory performance to the other. In a word, to teach is to discipline—to discipline is to teach. The technique employed is singularly personal, developing as it does from and within the teacher-student relationship.[1]

Adequate understanding of discipline in school requires consideration of it as (1) positive and negative, (2) permissive, autocratic or democratic, and (3) within and external to the individual. By recognition of these characteristics of discipline as they may appear in the classroom, teachers may evaluate the kind and amount of disciplinary experiences they are affording different students.

In the education of any person, both positive discipline and negative discipline are required, but positive discipline is of fundamental importance. Discipline is positive as a person deliberately and persistently pursues a goal and negative as one avoids such pursuit of a goal. In the classroom positive discipline centers on improvement of the student's objectives and ways of moving toward the objectives, while negative discipline centers on direction of the student away from harmful objectives and ways of advancing toward the objectives. Positive discipline is essential for the youth's mental health and achievement within and outside the high school. It is well known that the student who is absorbed in educative ends is unlikely to misbehave. However, the primary reason for concentration on positive discipline in school is not for reduction or elimination of misconduct and punishment but for promotion of desires, understandings, and skills directed toward worthwhile ends. This is because a person may be "good" but "good for nothing."

Either positive or negative discipline may be predominately permissive, autocratic, or democratic. While many laymen and some educators have deplored extreme permissiveness and the resulting disorder in schools, they have not called for increased adoption of democratic discipline but for a shift to autocratic discipline, a dictatorial "get tough" policy. Likewise, some teachers in trying to avoid letting students do as they please apparently believe that the only alternative is that teachers do as they please with little regard for the interests and needs of different students. Other teachers, in an effort to steer free of autocratic discipline, have drifted toward laissez faire and anarchy. Encouragingly, many turn to the

---

[1] J. E. Winkler, "Reflections on Discipline," *Clearing House* (October, 1964), 39, p. 113.

third alternative, democracy, using democratic ends and means in direction of discipline.[2]

In addition, complete comprehension of discipline requires viewing it as involving both inner and external forces, those within the individual and those within the environment. Discipline results from learning, and learning occurs through interaction between the learner and a particular environment. In the classroom, as elsewhere, the environment is both physical and social. It consists of such factors as size, appearance, temperature, and light of the room; appearance, speech, and action of teacher and classmates; and subject matter, teaching process, and class management. All such aspects of a classroom environment may function toward positive or negative discipline and democratic or undemocratic discipline. The interaction of students with forces in the school environment affects their ideals, values, understandings, and habits. Properly oriented, these resulting forces within the individual lead to the adoption of a reasonable, democratic relationship between self-authority and external authority, between self-centered desires and requirements of the environment.

Discipline in Relation to Objectives of Education

For direction in implementation of a concept of discipline in school, one needs to refer to the general objectives of education. These objectives, as expressed in Chapter 3, designate three essential factors of the individual's development for life in a democratic society—shared interests, social outlook and sensitivity, and intelligent conduct.

Discipline includes interest; the two are not in opposition. The well-disciplined person does not act against self-interests through a will devoid of interests. A person's will to act includes interest in the act. A man wills to work hard because he wants comfort and happiness in his home, a boy practices diligently on the piano because he desires to play well, and a girl works hard in science because she wishes to prepare herself for medicine or engineering. Likewise, a sense of duty is composed of interests. In a decision making situation, the person faces competing interests. For instance, one may be required to choose between work and play, between being on time and helping a person in distress, and between individual freedom and the rights of others. It is the person's duty to consider all the competing interests in the situation and to choose an intelligent course of action. As stated by Dewey:

It is hardly necessary to press the point that interest and discipline are connected, not opposed. Even the more purely intellectual phase of trained power—apprehension of what one is doing as exhibited in consequences—is not possible with-

2 S. S. Shermis and K. S. Kenny, "Discipline—Platitudes and Possibilities," *Education* (December, 1965), 86, pp. 216-220.

out interest. . . . That interest is requisite for executive persistence is even more obvious. Employers do not advertise for workmen who are not interested in what they are doing. If one were engaging a lawyer or a doctor, it would never occur to one to reason that the person engaged would stick to his work more conscientiously if it was so uncongenial to him that he did it merely from a sense of obligation. Interest measures—or rather is—the depth of the grip which the foreseen end has upon one in moving one to act for its realization.[3]

It is important to note the relationship of interest and intelligence in discipline. People do not engage persistently in tasks unless they can see some kind of reason for doing so. Interest functions in a person's will to act to the extent that there is *foresight* of acceptable goals. A person persists in holding to a difficult and extended task only as far as a result is within view that appears to be worthwhile. Even when a person follows a rule or an ideal without weighing carefully all the factors in the moral situation, there is comfort in anticipating the reward for living a good life. Certainly one who follows a sense of duty through giving due recognition to every competing interest in the situation must use intelligence to a high degree. This view was succinctly expressed by Bode, who with Dewey was a leading expositor of democratic discipline a few decades ago. He stated that duty involves adjustment of "various interests or values, and this adjustment is an act of intelligence and a sign of growth. . . . Duty is just the obligation to be intelligent, to cultivate that responsiveness to values which is necessary for the conservation of past achievements and for further progress."[4]

Dewey adds:

The really executive man is a man who ponders his ends, who makes his ideas of the results of his actions as clear and full as possible. The people we called weak-willed or self-indulgent always deceive themselves as to the consequences of their acts. They pick out some feature which is agreeable and neglect all attendant circumstances. When they begin to act, the disagreeable results they ignored begin to show themselves. They are discouraged, or complain of being thwarted in their good purpose by hard fate, and shift to some other line of action. That the primary difference between strong and feeble volition is intellectual, consisting in the degree of persistent firmness and fullness with which consequences are thought out, cannot be overemphasized.[5]

A person who is trained to consider his actions, to undertake them deliberately, is in so far forth disciplined. Add to this ability a power to endure in an intelligently chosen course in face of distraction, confusion, and difficulty, and you have the essence of discipline. Discipline means power at command; mastery of the resources available for carrying through the action undertaken. To know what one is to do and to move to do it promptly and by use of the requisite means is to be disciplined, whether we are thinking of an army or a mind.[6]

---

3 J. Dewey, *Democracy and Education,* Macmillan, New York, 1916, p. 152.
4 B. H. Bode, *Fundamentals of Education,* Macmillan, New York, 1921, pp. 94, 104.
5 Dewey, *Democracy and Education,* pp. 150-151.
6 Ibid., pp. 151-152. See also the discussion of interest and thinking in Chapter 3.

How instruction in high school may be directed toward disciplining students through interest and reflection is given by two educators as follows:

Even junior-high-school students can have their interest in ideological questions developed. We may promote such interest by raising questions about matters of belief. For example, it is common in the United States to require study of the Federal Constitution in the seventh or eighth grade, as part of either civics or American history. Teachers have difficulty making study of the constitution meaningful at this grade level. Learning is often mechanical and lifeless.

But suppose a teacher opens discussion of the First Amendment with a description of attempts to have comic books censored, or of present policies with regard to television or movie censorship, or perhaps of restrictions placed upon freedom of students to study controversial topics. Then suppose he asks, "Do you feel that comic-book censorship violates the First Amendment?" or are restrictions on the freedom of students to study certain topics unconstitutional? or, in the case of the Fifth Amendment, "What is meant by the expression, Fifth-Amendment Communist?" Even among junior-high-school students, approaches of this type are likely to generate interest in conflicts in beliefs and attitudes.

For students of junior and senior high school, we recommend that, in as far as possible, social studies learning be approached through the medium of mutually contradictory beliefs, attitudes, and values. With ingenuity of teaching, probably all socially important issues confronting Americans may be approached through reflective analysis of the beliefs and attitudes students have acquired from out-of-school environments.[7]

Especially in a democracy, the individual develops in rational choice and pursuit of interests by adoption of social ends and means, developing for and by life in the group. Concern for freedom of the individual is accompanied by concern for responsibility of each individual. This includes all individuals, whatever may be their race or religion and economic, political, or social status. Ideally, the democratically disciplined person reveals through word and deed little of extreme self-centeredness or of unquestioning obedience to authority. Instead, such a person expresses a spirit of fellowship or goodwill, which leads to sharing with others in the acquisition and enjoyment of material and spiritual blessings. Students may be disciplined in social outlook and sensitivity as they have various purposeful and insightful group experiences in the classroom and on the playground. *This is positive, socially oriented discipline.*

Thus democratic discipline in school centers on development in shared interests and reflective or scientific thinking. It is essential to see the reasonableness of conduct as it is viewed in a broad setting of a democratic frame of reference. For example, since the welfare of all persons in a democratic society depends on the educational, economic, social, and political status of every individual, it is an intelligent act to assist every

7 M. P. Hunt and L. E. Metcalf, *Teaching High School Social Studies,* 2nd ed., Harper and Row, New York, 1968, pp. 59-60.

person to reach the highest possible level of all-around development. This is especially important in that a democratic society has marked characteristics of change, interdependence, and complexity. Students receive positive discipline toward desire and ability to think reflectively on socially oriented problems as the school repeatedly places them in situations requiring them to think.[8]

This kind of discipline may be promoted in a positive manner by instruction in each subject of the curriculum. In the instruction the student learns through intrinsic interest and meaning—a purposive-cognitive process. It is well known that boredom is one of the chief causes of poor learning and behavior problems in the classroom. It should be kept in mind that the youngster who does not share in making an assignment is likely to work only to the point of getting by the teacher and of making a passing grade. In contrast, aiming at an objective he or she has shared in choosing, that same student usually persists in warding off distractions and overcoming difficulties until the goal is reached. This is valuable discipline for students, not only in the classroom but also in the modern world.

Such instruction disciplines boys and girls in thinking reflectively in confrontation with personal and societal problems of today. Along with truth, much propaganda is spread by various agencies. Misrepresentations are common in political speeches and commercial advertisements. Technology has provided the means of presenting more falsehoods more often to more people than ever before. The result is that the person who has not learned to suspend judgment until an extensive search for the truth has led to a seemingly valid conclusion is a victim of continuous bombardment by propaganda. This suggests that the teacher of any subject is obligated to discipline the student in expression and defense of beliefs in the light of reliable information. Teaching procedure that presents only packaged, "ready-to-eat" beliefs to youngsters contributes to disciplining them for life in an undemocratic society. The secondary school student in the United States needs a variety of experiences in many situations that afford opportunities to study all sides of a question and thereby to reach and support conclusions.

Finally, the teacher should so direct instruction that students are disciplined in responsibility to the group. The democratically minded teacher does not advocate absolute freedom for the student, whatever any irresponsible critics may assert. Rather, freedom is thought to be relative. In democratic classroom procedure the teacher recognizes as important the obligations of each individual to work actively with the group on problems of common concern. Indeed, effective steps are taken to elicit expressions from the intellectual misers of the class who hoard ideas

---

[8] For further discussion of the characteristics of the democratically disciplined person, see Chap. 3.

instead of exchanging them with others. At the same time efforts are made to provide learning situations to change the prejudicial, negativistic attitudes held by some toward expressions of others in the class. Thus, different members of the class may be led to see that the most useful and happy people are those who have learned to share rationally their thoughts and acts in school, home, and community.

Through direction of young people in group undertakings, the democratic type of teacher may lead the individual to practice thinking with the group without blindly following the thinking of the group. It is thus that the individual may receive not only positive discipline of sharing mentally and emotionally in working with others but also negative discipline of refraining from infringing on the rights of others. The individual who may thoughtlessly or momentarily cause disturbance and may thereby interfere with the work is likely to be corrected by other members of the class. At least the teacher is in a good position to assist individuals to view their behavior as it effects the rest of the class as well as the teacher.

KEEPING ORDER IN THE CLASSROOM

The Situation Confronting the Classroom Teacher

In the foregoing discussion we implied and stated that discipline in the classroom is more than keeping order or controlling the overt behavior of boys and girls. It also includes improving their characters, attitudes, and habits for useful and happy living in and outside the school. Indeed, the extent to which the teacher succeeds in developing youths in socially desirable interests, in a sense of responsibility to others, and in ability to direct themselves affects the necessity of giving special attention to correcting and controlling their observable behavior. The positive discipline from good teaching may almost eliminate the necessity for negative discipline, particularly by punishment. However, the best teachers, working under almost ideal conditions, must occasionally take direct and immediate steps to stop misbehavior. In almost every classroom there are a few youngsters who are so emotionally unstable, socially maladjusted, or intellectually immature that they are problem cases in academic achievement and in conduct. Also, the school grounds, building, and equipment may be unsatisfactory for good order. In addition, if the teacher has a poor personality and has little inclination or ability to adjust instruction to the needs of all kinds of youngsters, there are certain to be problems of misconduct. Whatever may be the causes of disorder in the classroom, observations and reports of teachers indicate that keeping order is a major problem, especially for beginning teachers.

How well beginning teachers may be expected to cope with classroom discipline has been indicated by research. In one study student teachers of more than 300 lessons in English, social studies, and science in three junior high schools were observed during a period of four years by the college supervisor who had taught them methods. The categories in which they were rated in student teaching were (1) teaching techniques and procedures, (2) classroom discipline, (3) projection of teaching personality, (4) planning of lessons, and (5) demonstration of sound academic background. The ratings of the group in discipline were 14 percent, excellent; 37 percent, good; 38 percent, fair; and 11 percent, poor. In this area of rating the group was next to the highest with respect to need for improvement. Significantly, the teachers who rated poor in maintenance of classroom discipline also rated poor in the teaching process. One clear implication stated by the investigator is: "Maintaining classroom discipline and control is a many-faced problem reflecting influences from all other categories in the study."[9]

A few years ago a questionnaire was sent to classroom teachers in several high schools in representative areas of the United States. The questionnaire requested responses bearing on the prevalence of different kinds of disorderly conduct in the schools and on the apparent causes of the disorders. The teachers indicated the belief that only about 3 students in 100 are real trouble makers. Several reported complete absence of any violent or rebellious conduct in their schools. Furthermore, other surveys showed that teen-agers seem to be increasingly active in community enterprises. The teachers of the study, however, expressed the belief that every high school was challenged by the behavior problems of adolescents.

The causes of the disciplinary problems, as designated in the study, lie largely in the home and the school. Causal factors in the home are low wages, broken families, inadequate housing, and irresponsible parents. Among the contributing conditions in the school are inadequate attention to the special needs of students, particularly the academically retarded, an unsuitable curriculum, weakness or absence of guidance, poor teachers, and overcrowded classes.[10]

More recent writers on student conduct report that some main causes of student unrest and protests are within the school. Drawing on an investigation by the U.S. Department of Health, Education, and Welfare, Anrig stated that students' complaints are directed against cafeteria procedures, the rigid rules on length of hair and manner of dress, and poor relationships between teachers and students and between races. The chief

9 E. J. Swineford, "An Analysis of Teaching-Improvement Suggestions to Student Teachers," *Journal of Experimental Education* (Spring, 1964), 32, pp. 299-303.

10 D. Iwamoto, "Student Violence and Rebellion—How Big a Problem?" *NEA Journal* (December, 1965), 54, pp. 10-13; National Education Association, Research Division, *Students Behavior in Secondary Schools,* 1964, Research Report 1965-R12, National Education Association, Washington, D.C., 1965.

object of protest, however, was found to be poor instruction.[11] According to McKenna, schools marked by unrest and protests are likely to have "dull and irrelevant curriculum content and non-motivating teaching methods" with little involvement of students in decision making.

Where the school itself contributes to the causes of disorder, teachers urged self-examination and correction. Troublemakers, they found, were usually deeply troubled by frustrating problems. Specifically, about half of the high-school students in cities read below their grade level and are handicapped further by poor physical and mental health. When teachers and administrators seek to help students get to the root of their problems, they also help them to stay out of trouble in school—and in the community.[12]

Personal Qualities of the Teacher in Classroom Discipline

Toward maintenance of good order in the classroom, teachers need to consider thoughtfully all parts of the disciplinary situation. In doing this they would do well to direct special attention to themselves. This is fully as important as that they study the boy or girl. In fact, they are likely to improve their understanding of the student through improving their understanding of themselves. That some teachers are insecure, emotionally unstable, and socially maladjusted is well known. They lack social maturity; they are timid, fearful, and tactless in dealing with people. They may never have experienced functioning as group leaders. In addition, some show plainly that they have either an autocratic or a permissive point of view about discipline. They antagonize some youngsters to open rebellion or to repressed resentment, or they let some develop poor study habits and disregard for the rights of others. Thus it seems reasonable that every teacher should undergo a self-examination to discover whether or not the cause of misconduct in the classroom may lie partly in his or her personality.

Some teachers contribute to nervous tension and disorder in the classroom through a show of irritation and frustration in loud remarks addressed to individuals and the whole class. Typical expressions are "Must I tell you again?" "Some people can't follow directions." "No! No! That's not the way I told you to do it." "Don't you ever listen?" "When is this class going to get over this terrible habit?" Such comments are of no positive assistance to the students toward being studious and orderly.

[11] G. R. Anrig, "Student Unrest: High Schools Brace," *American School Board Journal* (October, 1969), 157, pp. 20-22+; B. McKenna, "Student Unrest: Some Causes and Cures," *National Association of Secondary School Principals Bulletin* (February, 1971), 55, pp. 54-60. See also S. S. Brodbelt, "The Problem of Growing Dissension in the High Schools," *High School Journal* (March, 1970), 53, pp. 363-371; R. J. Havighurst and others, "Part A. A Profile of the Large-City School," *National Association of Secondary Schools Bulletin* (January, 1971), 55, p. 80.
[12] A. B. Briggs, "Crisis in Control," *Adolescence* (Spring, 1971), 6, pp. 107-115.

Instead, they reveal a frustrated, irritable teacher and make the issue of behavior a personal one, antagonizing the whole class.

It is encouraging to note that many teachers seem to have all the characteristics necessary to maintain proper classroom discipline. Their bodily movement, facial expression, tone of voice, attitude, and efficiency promote good order. They understand people as well as the subject matter, and they are well-informed, self-confident, calm, alert, tactful, sensible, fair, firm, and friendly. A teacher who has such qualities succeeds in having an orderly class in which another kind of teacher would fail.[13]

An illustration of how the teacher's personality may be the determining factor in student behavior is in the case of two student teachers who did their teaching in the same class—one during the first half of the semester and the other during the second half. The class consisted of 35 sixth-grade pupils taking arithmetic at 2 o'clock in the afternoon. The first teacher was the valedictorian of her high-school graduating class of 175 students. She had a studious expression, apparently being more interested in books than in people. Her knowledge of arithmetic was quite satisfactory, but she had difficulty teaching it and managing the class, and so she had poor order. There was considerable idleness, confusion, and unnecessary whispering and walking in the room. Her urging the youngsters to be quiet and to keep busy usually went unheeded. The second teacher likewise had a high scholastic record, but she noticed people, had a ready smile, and revealed strength in action. After she began to teach the class, behavior improved markedly. Without continuously reprimanding or occasionally punishing, she confidently walked about the room, assisting those who needed help. In fact, the response the students gave her was better than what they would have given to many experienced teachers.

The successful teacher in classroom discipline manages the class with understanding and foresight. The writers often observed teachers trying to teach at the beginning of the period before they secured the necessary order and attention from all in the class. After repeatedly reprimanding a class for disorder, those teachers continued trying to teach, finally yelling desperately at the class or punishing one or two of the students. Keen discernment would have enabled them to see that their effort to teach above noise and confusion at the beginning of the period would lead students to expect them to continue the admonishments. In the meantime they could have fun.

As another illustration, a teacher of 30 seventh-grade students in music attempted to teach them square dancing by first having the whole class take positions in groups. Then he began an explanation of the procedures

<hr/>

[13] A. W. Howard, "Discipline: Three F's for the Teacher," Clearing House (May, 1965), 39, pp. 526-529; D. Hamachek, "Characteristics of Good Teachers and Implications for Teacher Education," Phi Delta Kappan (February, 1969), 50, pp. 341-344.

and requested all the groups to engage in each performance simultaneously. The result was clowning, confusion, and chaos. Adequate foresight could have enabled him to see that as a first step the use of one group of dancers to demonstrate to others in the class would contribute to both efficiency in learning and order in the classroom. Only after each group had experiences in observation and demonstration was it feasible to undertake having the whole class perform.

Further, to maintain good order the teacher needs self-control. It is unintelligent to give way to a fit of temper, for example. Aside from the fact that it is impossible to think clearly when angry, an irate teacher does not frighten many adolescents but is disgusting or amusing to most of them. Thus the teacher who loses temper control is likely to lose self-control and control of the class, in that order. Although few teachers show lack of self-control through a display of anger, many of them show it through too much reckless, unnecessary talking. The nervous, fearful teacher seems to feel obligated to react to every distracting act, even to the accidental dropping of a book. The almost continuous talking of this kind of teacher causes more disturbance than the talking of all the students. For example, a boy was doing a little clowning before the class. The teacher said, "You don't need to think that is smart." The boy and at least some of his classmates obviously enjoyed the remark. Another boy sitting in a back seat was combing his hair. The teacher told him to put his comb into his pocket and get to work. Seemingly, this emotionally disturbed teacher was unable to see that it was much better for the boy to be combing his own hair than to be combing or pulling the hair of the girl seated in front of him. The teacher who has difficulty controlling the class may need to consider personal controls, especially tongue control, in the classroom.

The teacher who earnestly desires to improve teen-agers in personality and conduct will aim toward becoming a model of personality and conduct. There are still too many teachers who move restlessly about the room while they tell children to be still and quiet. Other teachers frequently fail to regard the feelings of young people, humiliating them unnecessarily before their classmates. Yet they do not hesitate to punish the youngster who may become disrespectful to them. It should be unnecessary to point out that these teachers do more to promote misconduct through bad examples than they do to check it through reprimands and punishments. They are like the father who used profane language while he was in the process of correcting his boy for using it, or like the mother who shook her daughter and said, "How many times have I told you to have poise?"

To have traits essential for satisfactory classroom discipline, teachers need to develop these traits in themselves. Some students of education apparently believe that they can have the necessary traits for a successful disciplinarian by "putting on" the traits as they enter the classroom. A common question that they ask is "Shall I be stern or lax the first week?" Seemingly, they believe that they can make a favorable impression on the class through acting the part of Dr. Jekyll in the classroom and living the life of Mr. Hyde outside it. What they need to see is that what a teacher genuinely is in the classroom is what that same person is elsewhere and that youngsters are very keen in detecting a lack of sincerity. The person who lacks freedom, ease, self-confidence, warmth, and common sense in dealing with people outside the classroom will lack the same qualities in dealing with them in it.

A person can best develop a strong personality for influencing and directing young people by having many experiences in working and playing with them. For instance, there are opportunities to lead and direct young people in the Girl or Boy Scouts and in other youth organizations sponsored by the church or community. These experiences help one to discover strong and weak points and to improve oneself accordingly.[14]

Dealing with Additional Causes of the Student's Misconduct

Studying oneself as part of a disciplinary situation must be accompanied by study of the student. The two most important factors in the situation are the teacher and the student—the two in process of interaction. In fact, the student's behavior can be only partially understood by the teacher unless it is viewed in relation to the teacher's own personality and behavior. Holding this interactive relationship with the misbehaving student in mind, the teacher may trace a chain of events leading to the incident of misconduct. This may involve consideration of the student's whole environment, in the school, home, and community.

The need for complete understanding of causes of a student's misconduct can be illustrated by many cases. One boy made so much trouble by his misconduct that the teacher sent him to the principal, unfortunately, without taking the proper steps to discover the causes of the misbehavior. The principal did not scold or punish the student but asked him to state why he persisted in annoying his teacher and disturbing the class. The boy replied, "You would misbehave also if you had to look all day at a book you could not read." As a result, the principal investigated the boy's level of reading and instructed the teacher to provide him with much suitable reading material. His misbehavior ceased. A girl who stole at school lacked money to buy sufficient food. There was definite evidence that she was suffering from malnutrition. She was not punished but was first counseled and then directed to the proper agency to secure financial aid for herself and her family. A boy who was slightly crippled came to

14 D. E. Hamachek, *Human Dynamics in Psychology and Education: Selected Readings,* Allyn and Bacon, Boston, 1968, pp. 187–203.

school tired from delivering papers. His school work was so unsatisfactory that he was sent to the detention room a few times. Later a counselor discovered his plight, and the school took steps to secure an operation for him to improve his physical condition. The principal stated that he felt conscience stricken in having sent this boy even a few times to the detention room.

To understand problem students in the class, the teacher needs to study the interests and problems of adolescents in present-day society. Suggestions toward doing this are given in Chapters 1 and 13. It should suffice to mention here that the study of outside causes of student misconduct points to increase of such facets of modern society as mobility of families, slum areas, and examples of violent protests by adult groups. Some teachers need in-service education involving a functional study of adolescent psychology and its application to the current behavior of young people. Those who have insight into current teen-age behavior are thereby helped to gain understanding of different members of their classes and can provide for rational, effective individualized instruction.[15]

From observation of and conversation with quite a number of teachers who have problem students, it has been discovered that most of these teachers rarely use a good individual conference as a beginning step toward the solution of a disciplinary problem. Usually they either ignore the student's frequent misbehavior—apparently in hopes the problem will go away—or they reprimand or punish the person promptly in class. A teacher may assert emphatically that every effort has been made to improve a student's conduct. Yet asked about an individual conference, that same teacher may readily admit to not trying, adding that there is a lack of time or opportunity or that it would do no good anyway.

Encouragingly, some teachers are realizing the possible value of a well-conducted interview. If a conference provides for a free exchange of ideas between the teacher and the student, each may gain understanding of the motives of the other. This may assist the discerning, sympathetic teacher to work effectively with the young person to remove the causes of disorderly conduct. There is also the likelihood that as youngsters express themselves freely to the teacher, they may gain a sense of relief and begin to view their conduct in a new light. They may be led to see that their present way of behaving will not produce as much future satisfaction as another way. If as a result these young persons do not choose to change their behavior and the teacher has no alternative but to insist firmly on change, they are more likely to respond favorably to the teacher's insistence in a conference than in the presence of the class. As shown in the preceding chapter, interviews in which the teacher shows genuine interest in, and sympathetic understanding of, the student's welfare and

15 J. F. X. Carroll, "Understanding Student Rebellion," *Adolescence* (Summer, 1969), 4, pp. 163-180.

personal problems may be expected to improve student's attitudes and habits. The result is likely to be such promotion of positive discipline that negative discipline, especially through punishment, is unnecessary. As stated by a writer on positive corrective measures:

The individual conference between the pupil and the teacher is by far the most desirable, single, major corrective measure to be employed by the teacher. A serious and frank talk would appear to be the logical first step in the understanding of behavior problems. . . . Conferences are helpful techniques if they are designed to understand the causes of misbehavior, to learn the problems the pupil faces, and to interpret school or class regulations to the pupil as desirable for individual and group welfare.[16]

In the use of counseling for maintenance of order in the classroom, even the efficient, dedicated teacher needs help from the school counselor. This raises the question of whether the school counselor should participate in discipline. Of course, if discipline is made to consist solely of reprimand and punishment, the counselor along with the teacher will have a poor counseling and instructional relationship with the student. When discipline is positive and is focused on improvement of the individual's values, attitudes, and insights, the school counselor in cooperation with the teacher may markedly contribute to both orderly conduct and academic achievement. When a teacher needs help in dealing with a behavior problem, the counselor can provide assistance by helping the teacher discover the cause or causes of the misbehavior and by recommending instruction relevant to the needs of the misbehaving student.

The concerned counselor, aware of the kinds of regulations needed by the staff in fulfilling their educational function and cognizant of the concerns of the students, can knowledgeably cite areas for reconsideration and possible modification. He is also in a position to initiate dialogue between students and staff as a means for maintaining acceptable standards. . . . Working together, the teacher and counselor could devise and evaluate specific strategies designed to help the unruly student while enabling the teacher to perform his job with minimum distraction and disruption of the class. In addition, methods for identifying and subsequently reinforcing student strengths might be uncovered, which represents a positive approach to discipline.[17]

Students should not be blamed for lack of good school discipline until we examine the challenge of programs, competence of staff members, and the factors that develop good school citizenship. If you have good school discipline, make every effort to keep it; and if your school lacks it, study the causes and don't spend so much time dealing with symptoms.[18]

16 H. H. Batchelder, "Corrective Measures, Punishment and Discipline," *Journal of Secondary Education* (February, 1964), 39, pp. 86-87.
17 R. A. Atherley, "The Counselor and Discipline: An Expanded Viewpoint," *Journal of Secondary Education* (January, 1971), 46, p. 37.
18 L. E. Vredevoe, "School Discipline," *National Association of Secondary School Principals Bulletin* (March, 1965), 49, p. 226.

Group Procedure and Order in the Classroom

A fundamental way of maintaining order in the classroom is through good instruction in the course. The instruction provides for learning through inquiry as students work toward individual and group objectives. It leads learners to share among themselves and with the teacher in comprehension and direction of learning activities. As nearly all members of a class are absorbed in their work they are likely to correct a disturbing member in an impressive manner. The ideal way to prevent misbehavior in the classroom is to direct the class in continuously planning and carrying out plans. Of course this ideal cannot always be followed fully, but it works toward promotion of positive discipline and thereby toward prevention of negative discipline, including punishment.

One way of destroying group spirit for discipline is the occasional practice of reprimanding and even punishing the whole class for the disturbance of a few members. The teacher may let the order drift until the noise and confusion becomes unbearable. Then, not knowing all the individuals who have been misbehaving, the frustrated teacher condemns all members of the class, apparently without recognizing that failure to make a distinction between those behaving and those misbehaving may discourage and antagonize the former and have no corrective effect on the latter. The likely result is that the whole class will turn against that teacher. In contrast, the resourceful teacher soon discovers the person or persons causing the disturbance, and deals with them quietly, reasonably, and promptly.

In good group discipline in the classroom, the teacher leads and assists the members of the class to take part in classroom management from the first day they meet, perhaps asking them to express their beliefs about how the class work should be conducted and about what constitutes good order. Some teachers organize each of their classes into committees that function in instruction as well as classroom management.[19]

For further assistance to the teacher toward having good order in the classroom, a list of specific practices are suggested.

1. Consider whether your own behavior demonstrates a high degree of self-control directed toward democratic ends.
2. From the beginning, aim toward development of a class spirit conducive to intelligent pursuit of shared interests.
3. Plan well before each class period toward having the students plan with you.
4. Use your freedom and responsibility to make all instruction relevant to the needs of the students.

[19] F. T. Wilhelms, "Discipline in a Quicksand World," *Arizona Teacher* (January, 1968), 56, pp. 14-18.

5. Involve the students each day in setting up goals and in designing possible ways of reaching the goals.

6. Begin work immediately after the gong sounds, but do not attempt to teach while there is disorder.

7. Be considerate, respectful, patient, friendly, and firm in dealing with each student, whatever the economic, social, and educational status may be.

8. Take an individual interest in each student, but avoid a "buddy-buddy" relationship.

9. Avoid sarcastic or uncomplimentary references to an individual or the group.

10. Avoid arguing with a student in class. Arrange for a meeting after class, and remind the student at the end of the period about the conference.

11. Provide for each individual to succeed as often as possible in class-room activities.

12. At intervals, go about the room to observe and assist individuals in their work and to check on their behavior.

13. Usually avoid having more than one student at your desk, because you need to be in position to observe every student at all times.

14. Never reprimand or punish the whole class for what a few are doing. Deal with the individual quietly and privately if possible. Thus you may avoid alienating the entire class and destroying group pressure against disorderly students.

15. Make wise use of group and individual conferences to develop understandings and attitudes necessary for good class conduct.

16. Praise the students as often as you can do so sincerely, because young people as well as others tend to act according to other people's opinions of them.

17. If you have done all you can to have order, and it is still deteriorating, seek help at once from your counselor or principal.

Use of Punishment

That punishment is sometimes necessary in a school or classroom no one except the unrealistic will deny. Only if it were always possible to have ideal conditions in the school could teachers dispense entirely with punishment. If the teacher, the students, the parents, the subject matter, the teaching procedure, the school plant, and every other factor in the situation were all that they should be, the teacher would never need to resort to punishment. However, it is observable that some teachers have such weak personalities and poor mental health and are so ineffective in instruction that they contribute to disorder. These teachers, in particular, may need to use punishment temporarily at least to check misconduct. Furthermore, many boys and girls have been spoiled in the home, are suffering from poor health or physical defects, and are emotionally disturbed and socially maladjusted. Some of the worst cases may not respond satisfactorily to individual conferences by teacher and counselor or to other means of providing them with suitable educative experiences. As a final resort the teacher may need to turn to some form of punishment. This is especially likely to be true if the school is without an adequate counseling program; if the building lacks a proper library, a laboratory, or other essential facilities; and if the classes are too large. A teacher should not expect to be completely successful with every student, and it may not necessarily be a defeat to find that some do not respond to every effort the teacher makes to help them succeed.

It may help to mention here that leading proponents of modern, democratic education do not rule out punishment entirely as a means of discipline. According to them, some individuals who do not respond satisfactorily to persuasion and reason may be improved by punishment. Appropriate punishment, intelligently and impassionately administered, may be a means of assisting a person to reconsider personal conduct and to realize how others view it. The value of punishment depends on whether the person reflects on the undesirable act and thereby improves future aims. Thus we do not reject all kinds of punishment under any circumstances but hold that its effect should improve the individual's insight into undesirable personal behavior. The fact is that all persons reflect to some extent and in some direction upon their acts. If they cannot be led to choose socially desirable conduct without punishment, maybe they can be directed to choose this conduct through punishment. To say the least, they must not be allowed to conclude that they are privileged characters —who can get by with behavior that is injurious to themselves as well as others.

An example of a young person who may require punishment is the leading disturber of the class. If the teacher has done everything possible to provide this student with suitable instruction, if both the teacher and the school counselor have had one or more individual conferences with the student, the teacher may be forced to turn to punishment. If seating the disturber in another part of the room does not work, the teacher may need to send the person from the room with the understanding that readmittance to class will not be allowed until assurance of improved behavior is given. If such a case is not handled promptly, there is an extended period when the disturber gains pleasure from the misconduct, hinders some classmates in their work, and encourages others to follow the bad example. It is much more easy and effective to deal with one disturbing student than with several followers.

It must be recognized that punishment is best used only to supplement and support positive means of discipline. Punishment should not be considered as the first or principal way of correcting misbehavior. Only after the teacher has earnestly tried to promote good conduct through constructive means may resorting to punishment be justified. It can easily be seen that some teachers turn at once to punishment to check misconduct. If they do not actually punish the youngsters, they frequently threaten them with it. Recklessness in punishing or threatening students is ineffective. They may be temporarily restrained in class, but they are unlikely to develop favorable attitudes toward orderly conduct or academic achievement.

Any use of corporal punishment in high school is of questionable value. Some administrators and teachers believe that if a youth cannot be helped to behave in high school without corporal punishment, he or she should be sent to a reform institution. But few high schools resort to any corporal punishment. Unfortunately, however, some teachers advocate its use.

There is evidence that corporal punishment is unlikely to be found in a secondary school with a good educational program. It has not been shown that schools using corporal punishment surpass other schools in orderly conduct and academic achievement. There is reason to believe that this kind of punishment is likely to be more harmful than helpful to the recipient. As mentioned before, problem students have personal and academic problems with which they are unable to cope. In their frustration they typically become negative and antagonistic toward the school and community. They need positive help toward the solutions of their problems. The severity of corporal punishment is likely to increase their rebellious spirit against the school's personnel and program. What problem students basically need is a school environment in which they may discover by precept, example, and actual experience how best to cope with their environment. Too often a high school that resorts to corporal punishment of problem students has not provided them with adequate, wise, and sympathetic counseling and with instruction in accordance with their personal and academic needs.[20]

It is recognized here that even in a rich, suitable environment a student may engage in intolerable conduct. If positive, constructive means of correction fail, negative means, including brief dismissal from school, may be employed. In extreme cases a final step may be transference to a state institution for delinquents. Thus corporal punishment is not required for maintenance of good order in school. The slowness of some teachers and even a few administrators to recognize this suggests that they may advocate this form of punishment partly to relieve their own tensions and frustrations.

Another form of punishment requiring special consideration is detention after school. Several schools have a detention room, but there are differences of opinion about the advisability of having such a room. Nearly all the detained students have useless or harmful experiences, particu-

20 R. B. Wright, "Discipline or Corporal Punishment," *Education* (September, 1969), 90, pp. 69-71+.

larly on an afternoon when a weak teacher is supervising. The hour of the day and the composition of the group are not conducive to study. Consequently, many of those detained continue to develop habits of wasting time and disturbing others. Accordingly, time spent in detention of students should be spent removing the basic causes of their assignment to detention.[21]

INVOLVING STUDENTS IN THE DISCIPLINARY PROCESS

There is consensus among educators that the democratic individual possesses freedom with responsibility. Also, a principle of educational psychology is that a person effectively acquires a functioning trait chiefly through its actual use. Thus a school may contribute to discipline of students for democratic living as it allows them some opportunities to share in decision making concerning behavior in the school, especially in the classroom.

To involve students in decision making in the classroom, a teacher may well spend some time during the first week of class in discussion of proper classroom procedure. In the discussion the teacher is careful to encourage free participation and to demonstrate and request evidence of a sense of responsibility along with the exercise of freedom. The result may be the students' sharing in formation of a list of regulations or principles of classroom procedure such as those reported in Chapters 4 and 6. In addition, some teachers provide for organization of the class, including selection of individuals and committees who assume particular responsibilities in both class instruction and management.

How well some schools have assisted students to practice freedom of choice has been indicated by the way they have dealt with clothes and hair styles of teen-agers. As reported in the press, some schools have made the appearance of boys and girls a major issue and have resorted to extreme means of resolving what they consider to be a serious problem. Specifically, the staffs of these schools have prescribed as a basis for continuation in school the length of the student's hair specified in terms of inches. (This rule has been a "law of the Medes and Persians, which altereth not.")

Expressed reasons for such drastic action are (1) that obligation of the school to educate for life includes improvement of a sense of appropriateness in dress and (2) that inappropriateness in dress impedes the process of education. What some administrators and teachers seem to ignore is that real improvement of a person in a sense of values is more likely to occur through rich and rewarding experiences than through the force of punishment. Further, they appear not to recognize that long hair and

21 T. Gnagey, "Let's Individualize Discipline," *Adolescence* (Spring, 1970), 5, pp. 101-108.

"inappropriateness" of dress are unlikely to be two major problems for a teacher who feels secure and is engaged in providing suitable instruction for each youth. Of course the requirement of decency in dress is necessary. Of special importance, however, is the realization that extreme concern for a teen-ager's appearance may hinder adequate concern for more basic needs. Thus schools may well reexamine their ends and means of discipline.[22]

Other schools have employed a positive, student-involvement approach to the improvement of student appearance. They have accepted as a responsibility the guidance of teen-agers in grooming, including cleanliness and modesty. By instruction, counseling, and example, the staff makes a concerted effort to produce a social climate conducive to proper personal appearance. In some schools there is an organized provision for the student council to share in both the formulation and the application of the dress code. Some schools do not have a written code, but nearly all have established policies and practices. The ideal toward which some schools seem to be moving includes freedom of the individual to make decisions about dress but also emphasizes responsibility to others, including peers, in the use of this freedom. All schools need to move toward this ideal of including decision making by students as they receive instruction in accord with their personal and educational needs.[23]

Finally, we need to realize that some high schools have markedly improved discipline by meeting several basic needs of misbehaving students. For example, the Sacramento Unified School District began to concentrate on the provision of personalized instruction for its problem students.[24] Each individual of this group was studied. A psychologist or a social worker visited the student's home to learn about the environment there and to improve the relationship between the school and the home. Students who were deficient in the skills of reading and arithmetic were given individualized instruction in these skills. In "opportunity" classes, each student was assisted toward the solution of personal, social, and academic problems. The teachers were instructed to keep "cool heads" and "warm hearts" and to enable the student to experience success toward pursuit of personal goals. Thus counselors and teachers cooperated toward making instruction relevant to the student's needs. Soon nearly all these students became intrinsically interested in their schoolwork; they ceased their mis-

[22] M. A. Raywid, "The Great Haircut Crisis of Our Time," Phi Delta Kappan (December, 1966), 48, pp. 151-155.

[23] D. L. Pucker, "A Secondary School District Looks at Its Dress Code," Journal of Secondary Education (November, 1970), 45, pp. 293-298; N. W. Fink and B. Cullers, "Student Unrest: Structure of the Public Schools a Major Factor," Clearing House (March, 1970), 44, pp. 415-419; E. G. Scriven and A. Harrison, Jr., "Student Dress Codes—Repressive Regulations of Questionable Legality," Journal of Secondary Education (November, 1970), 45, pp. 291-292.

[24] H. K. Parker, "On Making Incorrigible Youths Corrigible," Journal of Secondary Education (February, 1970), 45, pp. 57-60.

conduct; and they applied themselves diligently to useful, meaningful activities. Parents as well as teachers observed significant changes.

In summary, there have been many nationwide efforts to lead underachieving, frustrated, belligerent young people on the path to becoming decent citizens. There have been few successes in spite of all the efforts and the millions of dollars spent. Many of the programs are so complicated and so costly that it simply isn't practical to put them into effect on a general basis. The Opportunity School Program as envisioned by the Sacramento City Board of Education is a practical one that is working. The program personnel already know what is good and what is bad. They know what yields success with the students and what doesn't. They are demonstrating in the classroom and in the homes that such a program can be successful—that defeated children and families can be rescued. The general public must be made aware of the financial and human saving involved for every student who returns to the regular classroom and becomes a decent citizen.[25]

The conclusion seems to be that discipline in the high school is improved as teachers, like physicians, come to grips with fundamental conditions and causes. They then employ classroom procedures in accord with the real educational needs of youths. Dealing with symptoms through correction and punishment does not suffice. For proper discipline of the student and order in the classroom it is imperative that teachers and administrators draw on objectives and means of education such as have been presented in this and preceding chapters. Each student needs to be disciplined for democratic, reflective living in a world of changing, interdependent problems.

QUESTIONS AND ACTIVITIES

1. Describe the characteristics of the democratically disciplined person.
2. How does the program of education in some high schools reduce the necessity of negative discipline?
3. Explain the role of interest and of thinking in the positive discipline of a person.
4. Interview, survey, or have as guests on a panel a group of experienced educators concerned with discipline in the schools and how best to improve it.
5. Visit a school, an institution, or a home where behavior modification is practiced as a means of dealing with discipline. Evaluate how you might use this in your own teaching.
6. How may the teacher's personality and teaching procedure contribute to disorder in the classroom?

[25] Ibid., p. 60.

7. Evaluate the use of punishment as a means of producing an inner discipline in the pupil for both present and future living.
8. Visit a classroom and analyze the situation to determine why the teacher may or may not be a good disciplinarian.
9. How much should student councils be involved in the formulation and supervision of school dress codes, standards of personal conduct, smoking regulations, and the like?

SELECTED REFERENCES

Alcorn, M. D., and others, *Better Teaching in Secondary Schools,* 3rd ed., Holt, Rinehart and Winston, New York, 1970, Chaps. 12-14.

Dreikurs, R., and L. Grey, *Logical Consequences: A Handbook of Discipline,* Meredith, New York, 1968.

Erlich, J., and S. Erlich, eds., *Student Power, Participation and Revolution,* Association Press, New York, 1970.

Eson, M. E., *Psychological Foundations of Education,* 2nd ed., Holt, Rinehart and Winston, New York, 1972, Chap. 15.

Frey, S. H., ed., *Adolescent Behavior in School: Determinants and Outcomes,* Rand McNally, Chicago, 1970.

Gnagey, W. J., *The Psychology of Discipline in the Classroom,* Macmillan, New York, 1968.

Gorman, B. W., *Secondary Education: The High School America Needs,* Random House, New York, 1971, Chap. 8.

Hendrick, I. G., and R. L. Jones, eds., *Student Dissent in the Schools,* paper, Houghton Mifflin, Boston, 1972.

Kujoth, J. S., *The Teacher and School Discipline,* Scarecrow, Metuchen, New Jersey, 1970.

LaGrand, L. E., *Discipline in the Secondary School,* Parker, West Nyack, New York, 1969.

Larson, K. G., and M. R. Karpas, *Effective Secondary School Discipline,* Prentice-Hall, Englewood Cliffs, New Jersey, 1969.

Ornstein, Allan C., *Urban Education: Student Unrest, Teacher Behaviors, and Black Power,* Merrill, Columbus, Ohio, 1972.

Silberman, C. E., *Crisis in the Classroom,* Random House, New York, 1970.

Strom, R. D., *Psychology for the Classroom,* Prentice-Hall, Englewood Cliffs, New Jersey, 1969, Chap. 3.

Wilson, J. A. R., and others, *Psychological Foundations of Learning and Teaching,* McGraw-Hill, New York, 1969, Chap. 19.

Wittenberg, R. M., *The Troubled Generation: Toward Understanding and Helping the Young Adult,* Association Press, New York, 1967.

CHAPTER 15

We have considered how aspects of an instructional program in high school may be consistently directed toward objectives suggested by the different needs of youth for self-directing, democratic living in the modern world. Our remaining task is concentration on how teachers may efficiently evaluate the student's learning. The problem is essentially one of devising and using means of evaluation in line with sound objectives and other facets of a good educational program. Our aim is assistance to the teacher in appraising procedures that both reveal and advance the progress of students in high quality learning.

SOME BASIC UNDERSTANDINGS ABOUT EVALUATION

The process of evaluation involves perception of something in relation to a standard or value. It occurs in the classroom as teachers use their educational goals to judge the quality and the quantity of students' achievements. This means that a teacher's real, functional objectives are determiners of how the results of the instruction will be appraised.

Adequate, efficient evaluation of a student's progress toward educational objectives depends largely on means of measurement.[1] For information about quantity of learning, teachers commonly employ (1) observational procedures and (2) teacher-made tests. Observational procedures consist of viewing both the process and the product of learning activities. They exist in all the nontesting situations of the classroom, for example, in student involvement in class discussion or in individualized creative activities. The tests are the well-known objective test and the essay examination, each of which has a special function in relation to the teacher's ends and means of teaching.

[1] Writers on measurement in education typically view measurement broadly to include the rating of students on degrees of attainments.

EVALUATION OF THE STUDENT'S ACHIEVEMENT

Of fundamental importance also are the purposes or functions of evaluation. These may be stated as (1) guidance and stimulation of the students in learning, (2) direction of the teacher in improvement of instruction, and (3) provision of the teacher with a sound basis for grading the students. Obviously, the first purpose is of chief importance; it is the reason for the other two. In the process of evaluating the student's achievements, the question teachers need to raise continuously is: "How well do my ends and means of evaluation contribute to improvement of each student's attitudes and habits of study?" The importance of this question is indicated by the common question of students: "What and how should I study for the test?"

Role of Educational Objectives

In the measurement of achievement, no less than in teaching procedure, every teacher aims toward at least one objective, even though it may be only "covering the ground" of the textbook. If the aim of instruction is centered on acquisition of information, the teacher consistently limits measurement to that outcome. Similarly, if the goal of instruction is broad, including not only a gain in knowledge but also development in interests, ideals, and higher mental processes, the teacher rightly employs means of measuring all such achievements. Thus the objectives teachers set up in instruction determine their goals and processes in measurement. In turn, the true objectives of instructional procedure are revealed by the methods of measurement used.

Two leaders in educational measurement collected and examined hundreds of teacher-made tests from many school systems. In view of their study and of published studies by others, they concluded that teacher-made tests are usually quite deficient means of measurement. The tests do not cover the range of objectives that many teachers profess to follow. Instead, nearly all of the test items require only specific, factual answers, and they often lean toward the trivial. There is little or no provision for students to relate, organize, apply, or express their knowledge.[2] This situation suggests that many teachers need to reexamine and improve their real objectives in both teaching and testing.

Adequate objectives in instruction and measurement include both the gain of knowledge and the development of attitudes, appreciations, and intellectual skills. We have observed that leading educators in each subject of the high-school curriculum have proposed aims involving acquisition of course content through such mental processes as investigating, relating, and conceptualizing. This is especially true of those who have produced and used the new courses in science, mathematics, and social

---

[2] R. L. Thorndike and E. Hagen, *Measurement and Evaluation in Psychology and Education*, 3rd ed., John Wiley, New York, 1969, pp. 33-35.

studies. These educators have directed their efforts toward the modernization of course content and the use of a teaching-learning process characterized by reflecting, discovering, and creating. Teachers who actually instruct classes with such ends in mind are obligated to the students and themselves to employ appropriate means of measurement. On the other hand, unless teachers work toward such outcomes they will not prepare their students or even themselves for measurement of the outcomes. As stated by some writers:

Objectives should refer not only to the subject matter of a course but also, and especially, to the mental processes of remembering, reasoning, appreciating, and being interested. And particularly for the higher mental processes, statements of objectives should be comprehensive. The higher mental processes are those to which the individual makes a large contribution through his own conscious effort. Such processes as sensation or mere memory are considered to be lower in the intellectual hierarchy because the individual makes less contribution; he is more "active" when he compares, infers, and abstracts. Deductive and inductive reasoning is more powerful in solving most human problems than is mere recall of facts or the mechanical application of rules to familiar problems.[3]

Referring particularly to the aims of the educators who produced the new courses, Heath notes that their concern has been toward intellectual processes, understanding of basic ideas, and the like, with reduced emphasis on memorization of terms and facts.

The problem of assessing student-progress toward the distinctive goals of the new curricula is not a simple one. . . . It seems necessary to approach the problem from a frame of reference which is different in the conception of achievement and therefore different in method of measurement. The interest is not in whether the student can identify correct and incorrect information but rather in what he is likely to do with information intellectually. If a goal of instruction is to change the student's intellectual style within some academic subject, a test of such "achievement" must permit him to demonstrate differing styles. The test items should allow the student to exhibit some preference in cognition.[4]

As is true of teaching toward high quality learning, time, effort, and skill are required to measure that kind of learning. It is comparatively easy to teach and test for memorization of generalizations, facts, and terms of a textbook. Dedicated effective teachers, however, are willing to overcome the difficulties and employ the necessary means of teaching and measuring in accord with important objectives of education:

---

[3] H. H. Remmers and others, *A Practical Introduction to Measurement and Evaluation*, Harper and Row, New York, 1960, pp. 175-176. See also N. E. Gronlund, *Measurement and Evaluation in Teaching*, 2nd ed., Macmillan, New York, 1971, pp. 30-31.

[4] R. W. Heath, "Curriculum, Cognition, and Educational Measurement," *Educational and Psychological Measurement* (Summer, 1964), 24, pp. 240-241. See also W. Georgiades, "Evaluating New Strategies in Teaching and Learning," *Journal of Secondary Education* (November, 1970), 45, pp. 320-325.

We have accomplished little in our schools if we produce only verbalization of knowledge. Such verbalization is comparatively easy to measure, but it demonstrates little more than that the learner can recite what he has been taught or has read. Formulation of objectives can be very useful to the evaluation process if they emphasize the functions of knowledge as well as knowledge itself, and if the objectives are expressed in terms of the learner's performance and behavior rather than in terms of the facts he has learned.[5]

Observational Procedures

As a means toward adequate measurement and evaluation of students' achievements, observation is essential. Observation occurs in rather informal, lifelike situations, often while the students are unaware of being observed. It provides a view of both the process and the product of learning—of how students learn as well as what they learn. This has been recognized by teachers of English who often turn the classroom into a workshop in which individuals receive directions as they actively read to learn and speak and write to communicate. The same is true of teachers of industrial arts and home economics, who insist that each student must work on projects under the teacher's observation and guidance. While youngsters are involved in shop or laboratory work, they reveal interests, habits, and intellectual processes that they do not reveal in any testing situation.

For discovery of students' knowledge, feelings, and skills in performance, an observational situation is often superior to that of testing. An examination may reveal the extent of the learners' information and how well they apply it in the setting of a test, but it may not show how they may act when relatively free to pursue an individual or group goal. In an examination, a student who responds that "good citizens meet their social obligations to the community" may often fail to meet those obligations in the classroom. Similarly, a student may indicate on a test a preference for a particular type of reading but may never select that type to read. Again, student expressions of understanding and disapproval of propaganda in a testing situation may be followed by the practice of propaganda in class discussion.

Opportunities for observance of students' behavior in various activities are possible in all classrooms. While the class engages in the give and take of discussion, a teacher may note that a student is inclined to remain calm or become excited, to make assertions recklessly or to accompany them with support, and to talk unhesitatingly or with reserve. Likewise, in a study period the teacher can see that some students work intermittently and "blindly" while others work steadily and thoughtfully. Also, as individuals report on special projects they show various degrees of interest, application, and understanding.

[5] V. H. Noll, *Introduction to Educational Measurement*, 2nd ed., Houghton Mifflin, Boston, 1965, p. 107.

Situations for observation of the characteristics of students in action vary among classrooms. Where formal and informal lectures and drill on isolated facts and terms constitute the chief means of teaching and receptivity and passivity characterize the learning process, opportunities for observation of student interests and skills for self-direction in accomplishment of tasks are quite limited. The opposite is true in classes where teacher and students jointly plan and execute plans. In such classes individuals and small groups frequently investigate, construct, report, and perform. This is common practice in the new courses. Significantly, some writers, in reporting results from such courses, have drawn somewhat on observation of the student's reactions when challenged to work understandingly toward goals.

Some effective, behavioral outcomes of instruction that may be discovered better in observation than in testing situations are listed below:

1. Performance and construction skills: speaking, writing, reading, investigating, experimenting, reporting, drawing, creating, singing, dancing, and playing games or an instrument.
2. Attitudes and habits of work: enthusiasm, promptness in beginning, diligence in application, efficiency in planning, skill in use of materials, ability to relate and organize ideas, and evaluation of the results.
3. Scientific attitudes and habits: an inquiring mind, skill in recognition and formulation of problems, appraisal of possible solutions, suspension of conclusions, use of reliable data, and provision of support for generalizations.
4. Social attitudes and habits: regard for the feeling of classmates, assumption of obligations to classmates, reactions of students to one another, concern for people of community, contributions to welfare of community.
5. Interests and appreciations: vocal and other expressions of enjoyment of experiences in various areas of education—scientific, mechanical, aesthetic, social, vocational and recreational.[6]

An observational procedure of special value is individualized instruction. We have seen that in some subjects, notably English, science, home economics, art, and industrial arts, some teachers provide in their schedules for individual conferences and assignments. This way of teaching involves studying individuals in conference and guiding them in work adjusted to their interests and needs. The teacher learns about the youngsters' interests and abilities while in the process of providing them with suitable instruction, often consisting of individualized reading or a construction project. Since the individual students want help, they are inclined to express their interests and understandings freely. Through this person-to-person relationship in the teaching-learning process, a teacher may discover learnings of a student not revealed by any pencil and paper test.

[6] Adapted from N. E. Gronlund, *Measurement and Evaluation in Teaching*, p. 410. See also D. G. Kurfman, "Evaluating Thinking in Secondary Schools," *High School Journal* (March, 1972), 55, pp. 297-307.

A valuable nontesting procedure used by some teachers for discovery of organization, integration, and self-expression of the student's knowledge is the written report. During or at the end of individual or group projects, students are requested to write reports of their investigative or creative activities. The paper may be written in class under the guidance of the teacher. Such a written report assists students to relate ideas, construct and support generalizations, and express their thoughts coherently.

The report paper has some distinct advantages over a test, including a thought-provoking essay examination. The situation in which the students write enables them to produce the equivalent of an essay—an extended, integrated presentation of their knowledge. They are not hindered by insufficient time or short answer questions. Moreover, the teacher has favorable opportunities to observe the attitudes, habits, and skills of the students in the process of writing. In addition, the written productions may approximate an expression of the real feelings and thoughts of the learners.

As an aid to the use of any observational procedure, some teachers keep brief, daily records. They use a code of signs to record the performance or nonperformance of each student during the class period. They have found that this requires only a few minutes at the end of the class period or the school day. The use of an abbreviated account of a student's expressions of learnings over a period of weeks can be helpful to a teacher in evaluating, improving, and reporting each student's achievements.

Achievement Tests

Although observation is essential for adequate evaluation of a student's attainments, a useful role for achievement tests remains. It is well known that these tests may be classified as teacher-made and standardized. Since standardized tests contain norms of achievement, they are of unique value in educational research and for teachers and administrators to check on some of the outcomes from particular methods of instruction. However, teachers necessarily use their own tests more often than standardized tests. Furthermore, the basic suggestions for efficient use of each test are essentially the same. Hence consideration of achievement tests for ordinary classroom use may well focus on teacher-made tests.

In an appraisal of achievement tests, one confronts at once the controversy over the comparative usefulness of the objective test and the essay examination. Writers on measurement and evaluation typically present the advantages and disadvantages of each of the two tests and then conclude that both have special functions, each being superior to the other in measurement of one or more kinds of results. Our aim here is a look at the two in the light of educational objectives and the findings of research. In the process we will apply the three commonly accepted criteria of a good test: validity, reliability, and usability.

Validity of Teacher-Made Tests

A test is valid to the extent that it measures what it is intended to measure. In achievement testing a test is valid insofar as it measures the outcomes stemming from the teacher's objectives and instructional procedures. Validity in testing is a matter of degree; it does not exist on an all-or-none basis but may be rated as high, moderate, or low. Also, it is always specific, never general. It functions in consideration of how far a test goes toward adequate measurement of particular outcomes. For a classroom teacher, validity is specific to a particular way of teaching.

Applying the concept of validity to the objective test and the essay test, we see that the two have different degrees of validity for measurement of particular achievements. There is consensus among writers that the objective test is uniquely suitable in testing for recall or recognition of small units of information—terms, facts, and generalizations—and that it can be constructed to measure understanding and skills in problem solving. There also seems to be a common belief among writers that a well-constructed essay examination is especially appropriate for measurement of integrated learnings, complex achievement, problem solving, and self-expression. In this test a student may be required to have breadth of knowledge and be able to recall and apply facts bearing on the solution of a problem. Within the limits of each task in the test, examinees are free and responsible for recollection, organization, and expression of their knowledge.

The validity of the two teacher-made tests is determined partly by the inherent structure of the test. The objective test is designed to measure the specifics or parts of learnings, and the response to each item is by a word or a sign. The pattern of this test gives it priority for testing elements of knowledge. In contrast, the essay examination, consisting of a few definite but broad questions and permitting rather extended answers, has a form especially adapted to measurement of organization and expression of related ideas.

It is important to recognize that objective tests can be constructed to test understanding and thinking. However, the exercises in this kind of test have as a limitation the measurement of only the separate, specific abilities of problem solving—not ability to attack a whole problem. Also, since the exercises contain muliple-choice items, students need only a recognition level of learning. They check the correctness of thoughts listed in the test without the necessity of recalling some pertinent facts needed in the process. Information for the examinee's use in recognition of the correct test items is provided in each test exercise. An example of this interpretive kind of objective test for a class in United States history is given below:

Salmon P. Chase was Secretary of the Treasury during the first three years of Lincoln's administration, and became Chief Justice of the Supreme Court in 1864. While he was a young lawyer, he missed no opportunity to combat slavery, providing free aid to run away slaves and to the harborers of the fugitives. In 1855, he and other political leaders met to form an anti-slavery party. In the National Republican Convention of 1856, and in the succeeding nominating conventions of the next twelve years, he sought the presidential nomination. As a member of Lincoln's cabinet, he was often in conflict with the President, considering him deficient in force and efficiency. In presiding at the impeachment trial of President Johnson, he conducted the proceedings with dignity and control, thwarting attempts to end the trial without inclusion of pertinent testimony. In addition, he refused to restrain the President from enforcement of reconstruction legislation.

( )   1. Chase was a political opportunist.
( )   2. Throughout his career, he was concerned about promotion of justice for the accused.
( )   3. He was an ambitious, power-seeking politician.
( )   4. At every opportunity he worked against what he believed to be wrong.
( )   5. His actions were governed more by passion than by reason.
( )   6. In confrontation with the issues of that stormy period, his sympathy seemed to be more with the South than with the North.[7]

An analysis of the preceding test exercise reveals that it is essentially the same as those commonly seen in standardized reading tests. It examines students' abilities to understand and interpret what is read. In fact, a qualified reader in a class in United States history could make satisfactory responses to the multiple-choice items without previously reading or hearing about Salmon P. Chase. Thus, as a means of testing in history, it is deficient in requiring of all the students (1) possession of the necessary information prior to the examination and (2) construction and expression of ideas during the examination.

In an appraisal of interpretive exercises as means of measuring skills of problem solving, Gronlund states:

In comparison to the essay test, the interpretive exercise has two shortcomings as a measure of complex achievement. First, it cannot measure a pupil's over-all approach to problem solving. It is efficient for measuring specific aspects of the problem-solving process but it does not indicate whether the pupil can integrate and use these specific skills when faced with a particular problem. Thus, it provides a diagnostic view of the pupils' problem-solving abilities, in contrast to the wholistic view that can be obtained with essay questions. Second, since the interpretive exercise usually uses selection items, it is limited to learning outcomes

[7] For further discussion and illustration of the interpretive exercise, see Gronlund, *Measurement and Evaluation in Teaching,* Chapter 9.

of the recognition level. To measure the ability to *define* problems, to *formulate* hypotheses, to *organize* data, and to *draw* conclusions, supply procedures such as the essay test must be used.[8]

Furthermore, the teacher's construction of either type of test affects its validity. Specifically, if an objective test is designed to measure understandings and skills of problem solving, it must include items especially designed toward those ends. It is an observable fact, however, that nearly all teacher-made objective tests are not so constructed. Likewise, an essay examination does not test for organization of thoughts and logical self-expression unless its composition requires expression of such intellectual processes. It is disturbing to observe that too many "essay" tests consist mainly of short answer, factual questions. Thus within the structural essentials of either test, a teacher may alter the validity of the test for measurement of a particular outcome.

A general, summarizing statement on the validity of a test is succinctly given by Ebel:

The validity of any test is clearly a matter of degree, not an all-or-none quality. Tests are not valid or invalid. They are more or less valid. Further, the validity of a test is not completely determined by the test itself. It depends on the purpose for which the test is used, the group with which it is used, and the way it is administered and scored. . . . Most classroom tests are constructed with a very specific group and purpose in mind.[9]

Reliability of Teacher-Made Tests

Consideration of how appropriate a test is in a particular situation must be accompanied by consideration of how reliably it does the job. Writers commonly express the meaning of reliability in terms of consistency in the test's scores. For example, a test is said to possess high reliability if the reading of the set of papers at two separate times by a teacher results in little difference between the two lists of scores. Likewise, satisfactory reliability is indicated if two or more readers obtain approximately the same scores.

In any teacher-made test there is some reliability, and no test is completely reliable. The difference between the objective test and the essay test in reliability is of degree. It is known that subjectivity in testing contributes to unreliability. The objective test involves scarcely any subjectivity in scoring but a significant amount in construction. The essay examination is significantly subjective in both construction and scoring.

It is commonly stated by teachers as well as writers that in scoring

---

[8] Ibid., p. 211. Incidentally, it should be noted that the inherent structure of the multiple-choice test limits it to measurement of the recognition level of learning in factual as well as interpretive testing. Only the completion test of the forms of the objective test requires a recall level.
[9] R. L. Ebel, *Measuring Educational Achievement*, Prentice-Hall, Englewood Cliffs, New Jersey, 1965, p. 392.

the objective test is "foolproof" but the essay test is scored partly according to the attractiveness of the student and of the paper, the physical and emotional condition of the teacher, and the like. What seems not always to be grasped, however, is that in construction and administration of the objective test as well as of the essay test, quite a degree of subjectivity exists. Variableness in the scores may result from such factors as the following: content, form, number, variety, and clarity of the items; the teacher's personality and the choice of environmental conditions for the test.

That quite a degree of subjectivity is involved in constructing and administering objective tests is not only a sound inference but also has some support from experimentation. About three decades ago Pullias investigated the extent to which nonscoring factors may produce variability in the scores of tests that are objective in scoring. He attempted to find an answer to the question: "If *two competent teachers* construct objective tests designed to measure the acquaintance of a group of pupils with a given section of text material, and if both of these tests are given to the same group of pupils, how will the results of the measurement secured by the application of one test compare with the results when the other test is used?"[10] The investigator secured scores from over 3,000 students in the vicinity of Durham, North Carolina, who were studying social studies and were distributed in upper grades of the elementary school and in high school. Thirty-five competent teachers participated in teaching and testing. Near the end of the teaching period, each teacher independently constructed an objective test for the subject matter the students had covered. Two tests, one produced by the teacher of the class and one by another teacher, were given to each class.

The results from the study indicate that, outside of scoring, objective tests are subjective and the scores are significantly variable. As stated by Pullias, "The relationship between paired objective tests which are constructed to measure identical bodies of text matter expressed in terms of a coefficient of correlation is approximately .50." In terms of letter marks, about 8 percent of the students varied three mark intervals; 23 percent, two mark intervals; and 36 percent, one mark interval.[11] The findings from this investigation seem to show that because of the teacher's judgments in various aspects of the testing situation, objective tests are somewhat subjective and unreliable.

The reliability of the essay test may be raised by improvement of its composition. Rather frequently one may observe on a chalkboard vague, indefinite, all-inclusive questions containing such expressions as "Tell what you know about grasshoppers" or "Discuss the Fugitive Slave Law."

10 E. V. Pullias, *Variability in Results from New-Type Achievement Tests,* Duke University Press, Durham, North Carolina, 1937, p. 13.
11 Ibid., pp. 42, 79.

Real essay questions are not short answer questions but, to be reliable, they must restrict the student clearly and definitely to a prescribed task. The teacher who presents distinctly to the students a suitable problem is in a position to hold them to the problem in the process of scoring the papers. Furthermore, the teacher thereby mentally clarifies the objective toward which the students should aim as they write the papers. By thus improving both the students' and the teacher's own view of the goals of the essay test, the teacher increases reliability in both taking and scoring the test. Reliability of the test may be enhanced further by the use of short tests distributed throughout the semester. Long tests may so tire students and teachers that efficiency in their respective performances is lowered.

Thus construction of the essay examination is of basic importance for reliability in scoring the papers. Vague objectives and poorly phrased questions, especially of a long essay test, contribute significantly to unreliability of scores. Skill in any techniques in the process of scoring an essay test cannot compensate for previous inefficiency in the process of composing it.

In the process of grading papers, each paper may be rated with the other papers of the class. In classification of student achievement in perception of related ideas and reorganization of thoughts, the precision of the classification may be restricted to about five categories. The writers have found it helpful to record tentative scores for the first papers read, giving them final scores after about five levels of performance appear for classification of all the students in the examination.

Only as teachers endeavor to meet all the requirements for reliability in a testing situation may they expect a satisfactory degree of reliability in the use of an essay test. Unfortunately, some writers seem not to have recognized this as they have cited research reported as indicating disturbingly low reliability of the essay test. Some of the investigations reported include no reference to an agreement by the scorers on the chief outcomes they will consider in determination of the scores. In addition, there is often no recognition that the scoring of one paper by those who had no part in construction of the test is quite different from the scoring of several papers by the teacher who both taught the class and constructed the test.

During several decades there have been references to the studies of Starch and Elliott as evidence of low reliability of the essay examination. In one study, these two investigators sent an essay type of geometry paper to several teachers of mathematics in high schools in different localities. The teachers were requested to grade the paper according to the way they ordinarily graded geometry papers; no guidelines were given. The form and appearance of the paper were of poor quality. Some teachers disregarded the make-up of the paper, but others reacted to it by reducing the score markedly. Furthermore, the teachers were reading the paper outside a classroom setting. It is not surprising, therefore, that the scores assigned to the paper showed a range between a low of 28 and a high of 92. However, of the marks assigned the paper, nearly all clustered between 53 and 85, this range being only about 30 instead of 64. It is also worthy of note that in the school from which the paper was obtained, the five teachers of geometry graded the paper independently as follows: 70, 70, 65, 60, and 59, with obviously small variations. Such pertinent factors in this and other investigations of reliability of the essay test are often disregarded by those who cite studies reported as showing very low reliability in that test.[12]

About forty years ago, an experiment was conducted by Bolton in a rather normal classroom setting. He requested a group of teachers of the sixth grade in some schools of Seattle to construct cooperatively a set of essay examination questions that would fairly test their pupils on the work done. After the examination was given to all the pupils, 24 papers were selected to be scored by 22 teachers. According to Bolton, the papers showed great uniformity of rating by the 22 teachers. This finding suggests that when an experiment on reliability of grading essay papers is conducted in a situation closely approaching that of teachers in a school, close agreement of their grading can be obtained.[13]

In another significant study, Traxler and Anderson requested two graduate students in English at the University of Chicago to grade two sets of composition papers written in the University high school. The experimenters and the two students conferred on the standards that would be used in the grading of the papers. The result was a correlation of .94 between the grades the readers assigned to the first batch of compositions and of .85 to the second batch. This correlation is high, especially in view of the fact that reading of compositions is expected to yield more variability in scores than reading of responses to essay test questions.[14]

After referring to investigations commonly presented as showing rather low reliability of the essay examination, one writer commented:

In all fairness, however, it should be pointed out that in most studies reporting on the reliability of scoring essay questions the learning outcomes being measured were not clearly identified. Evaluating essay questions without adequate attention to the learning outcomes being measured is comparable to the "three blind men appraising the elephant." One teacher stresses factual content, one organization of ideas, and another writing skill. With each teacher evaluating the degree to

[12] D. Starch and E. C. Elliott, "Reliability of Grading Work in Mathematics," *School Review* (April, 1913), 21, pp. 254-259.

[13] F. E. Bolton, "Do Teachers' Marks Vary as Much as Supposed?" *Education* (September, 1927), 48, pp. 23-39.

[14] A. E. Traxler and H. A. Anderson, "The Reliability of an Essay Test in English," *School Review* (September, 1935), 43, pp. 534-539.

which different learning outcomes are achieved, it is not surprising that they disagree so widely in their scoring. Even variations in scoring by the same teacher can probably be accounted for to a large extent by inadequate attention to learning outcomes.[15]

A look at one more experiment may help here. This experiment was performed in the departments of English and social science of a state university to discover the degree of reliability of essay questions. It was reported in a magazine article in 1938 and was later recommended by about twenty experts in educational measurement for publication in a book of readings. In the experiment, students of the university were given an examination of essay questions, and three professors read the papers. The findings showed wide disparity of scores. However, analysis of the questions reveals that the neglect of the investigator to follow closely the rules for construction of essay questions was probably a chief cause of the extensive disagreement of the readers on the scores. Most of the questions required students merely to discuss assigned topics; they did not consist of precisely stated problems. There was also some provision for students to choose a question from two or more options. In addition, the report of the experiment did not mention any consensus of the readers on guide posts or standards for scoring.[16]

Thus research has not provided evidence that the essay examination is too unreliable to be a valuable means of measuring educational achievement. Yet, as noted by Freeman more than two decades ago, the notion that marks based on the essay examination are almost entirely arbitrary has persisted many years despite the findings from investigations showing that this test can be made sufficiently reliable to be of service in the measurement of important results of education.[17] Present leaders in educational measurement have not revealed recent experimentation on the reliability of achievement tests that significantly alters procedures and findings of experiments produced a few years ago when the controversy on reliability of achievement tests was at its height.

In testing we teachers need to balance our concern for reliability with due regard for validity. A high degree of reliability is desirable, and it must exist to some extent for validity to exist. Yet in some testing situations, we may face the likelihood of lowering the validity of a test for measuring high-level learnings as we raise the test's reliability. Thus in some instances we may be required to choose between degrees of reliability and of validity. For instance, a teacher who actually aims in teaching toward the outcome of developing the students in problem solving and

---

15 Gronlund, *Measurement and Evaluation in Teaching*, p. 224.

16 C. I. Chase and H. G. Ludlow, eds., *Readings in Educational and Psychological Measurement*, Houghton Mifflin, Boston, 1966, "Preface" and Chap. 34.

17 F. N. Freeman, "The Monopoly of Objective Tests," *Educational Forum* (May, 1946), 10, p. 391.

reflective thinking may consistently use essay tests having superior validity for measurement of that result, even though the scores of the test may
be less reliable than those of an objective test having inferior validity for
measurement of that result.

Usability of Teacher-Made Tests

However accurate a test may be in the measurement of what it is supposed to measure, it must be usable. This third criterion of a good test
refers to its practicality in the use of time, energy, skill, and money. The
practical features of testing require realistic consideration. There can be
false economy in educational measurement as elsewhere.

In usability, there are advantages and disadvantages of both the objective and the essay test. Adequate preparation of items for the objective
test is difficult and time consuming, but the scoring is quick and easy.
The construction of questions for the essay test is relatively easy, but it
requires more work than is usually assumed. The scoring of this test is
slow and tiring. Thus if the two tests are appraised solely on the basis of
usability, the objective test may have an advantage, but not as large as
some may believe.

The usability of a test varies with its purpose and structure. Although
it is not easy for the classroom teacher to do a good job of constructing
any objective test, it is particularly difficult and time consuming and is
somewhat costly to construct that test for measurement of skills in problem solving. Only a few books on educational measurement present sam-
ples of objective test exercises constructed to measure aspects of reflective thinking. Each interpretive exercise, designed to test only one
aspect of an act of thought, covers a large part of a page. It typically
consists of information to the student in the form of a paragraph, map,
graph, or chart, followed by about six multiple-choice questions. Significantly, this kind of objective test is rare in teacher-made tests, apparently
because the process of finding and revising new information and of
devising good test items requires much work and skill. This long and
difficult process of construction makes this test low in usability.[18]

Likewise, the usability of the essay examination must be viewed in relation to its structure and function. This test in any form is unsuitable and
too time consuming and tiring for use in obtaining a wide sampling of a
student's factual learnings in an entire month or semester. This is the
special function of the objective test. The essay examination can be
structured so that it is quite workable in discovery of the student's abilities to recall, interpret, relate, and express ideas in complex responses.

---

[18] Gronlund, *Measurement and Evaluation in Teaching,* Chap. 9; R. L. Thorndike and others, *Educational Measurement,* 2nd ed., American Council on Education, Washington, D. C., 1971, pp.
124-128, 273-275.

The measurement of such outcomes is of sufficient importance to justify the expenditure of time and energy required in scoring the test. Moreover, there are ways to reduce the burdensomeness of this task.

Teachers have found that the difficulty of grading an essay examination can be reduced by stating the questions in the form of clearly structured problems. It is quite wearisome to grade the answer to a question that permits a student to ramble, presenting unrelated bits of information in an area. Some teachers have made the grading less demanding at a particular time by prescribing the maximum number of words for the test being given. This practice incidentally may encourage an increase in thinking by the reduction of writing. It can prevent writing long, wordy discourses. Others distribute relatively short essay tests throughout the semester. Teachers may use the assignment period to introduce a few thought questions for guidance of the class in study. Occasionally, on the following day they may use one or more of these questions in an announced or unannounced test for part or all of the class period. Teachers who believe strongly in the necessity of the essay test for measurement of important results have found ways to reduce limitations on its usability.

Effect of Tests on Habits of Study

An adequate appraisal of a test's value in measurement should include recognition of its effect on habits of study. A teacher tends to teach and students to study in accord with the tests used. Students soon discover the kind of preparation required for success in taking the tests of each of their teachers. If tests are the chief means of determining students' grades in a course, they furnish them direction in when, what, and how to study. In preparation for the objective test, students may be expected to focus on details, exact wording, names, dates, and the like, but for the essay examination, on main ideas, perception of relationships, organization of information, and personal reactions. Accordingly, a question teachers may well ask themselves repeatedly is "How effectively am I using tests to direct students toward high quality learning?"

It follows that teachers are obligated to assist students to study in line with the tests they give. Unless teachers feel that they must apologize for the kind of examination they design and administer, they may well consider assistance of students in preparation for their type of examination as one of their chief goals. In teaching procedure consisting almost entirely of factual questions and short answers in recitation and a repetition of the same in reviews, the class is provided with experiences in preparation for tests designed to measure bits of information. On the other hand, classroom procedure in which students share in the formulation of problematic questions and subsequently use these questions for direction in study and discussion, furnishes opportunities for them to prepare for tests composed for breadth of view, reflection, and self-expression.[19]

Construction of Objective Tests

The construction of a good objective test requires more time and work than are often given. A test on subject matter taught during a month or a semester cannot be well constructed in an hour. Teachers can improve the test by writing items at times throughout the whole month or semester. Of course they need considerable creativity and skill in writing and a willingness to apply themselves diligently to repeated revision of the items in both content and form.

Some suggestions for the construction of any form of objective test may be helpful:

1. Avoid ambiguous items and those that call for obvious or trivial responses.
2. Be certain that you observe the rules of grammar and rhetoric.
3. Include items the "correct" answer to which all experts will accept.
4. Avoid "trick" or catch items, that is, those so phrased that the right answer depends on obscure key words to which even good students are unlikely to give sufficient attention.
5. Do not include items that furnish answers to other items.
6. Statements usually should not be taken verbatim from the reading material or the lecture.
7. Words that provide irrelevant clues which enable students to respond correctly without knowledge or understanding should be excluded.
8. For sake of objectivity, each item should test for only one idea.
9. Of supreme importance is clearness in the statement of each item.[20]

Composing a particular form of the objective test can be improved by the practice of a few observable requirements. For example, it is easily seen that to avoid enabling students to perceive right responses through the process of elimination of other responses, a matching test must contain more responses than stimuli and a multiple-choice test must not include such obviously incorrect alternatives that the correct one is thereby revealed. Teachers may improve further the different forms of the objective test by references to lists of rules in books on measurement in education and by occasionally requesting a colleague to read and criticize their test items with respect to both content and form.

---

[19] Thorndike and others, *Educational Measurement*, pp. 275-276; and J. Eulie, "Meaningful Tests in Social Studies," *Clearing House* (February, 1971), 45, pp. 333-336.
[20] Thorndike and Hagen, *Measurement and Evaluation in Psychology and Education*, Chap. 4.

Construction of the Essay Examination

Skill in the construction of objective tests does not suffice for teachers whose aims and practices are focused on complex learnings. In fact, in the process of teaching for those results, their experiences assist them toward designing real, suitable essay questions. As they direct students in recalling, relating, and expressing ideas in problematic situations, they develop ability to compose different types of thought questions for that particular class. They can draw on these questions for patterns when constructing new questions for the test.

An effective essay question is relatively broad, but it restricts the student to a definite, clearly stated problem. As previously noted, observation of essay questions in classrooms reveals that many are only loosely constructed, factual questions. Examples are: "Tell what you know about the boll weevil," "List the principal results of the War of 1812," and "Discuss John Brown's raid on Harpers Ferry." Such questions constitute a poor gesture toward use of the essay examination. What they measure could be more efficiently measured by objective test items. An essay examination that involves students in reflective expression requires them to express a comparison of two things, cause-and-effect relationships, support or application of generalizations, criticism of the adequacy or correctness of statements, how to accomplish a task, and the like. This kind of examination consists of one or more precisely expressed problems.

Whatever the phraseology or form of a question may be, it is not a thought question for a particular group of students unless it provides some degree of novelty. For instance, the use of *why* or *how* in a question may or may not require students of a specific class to think. That requirement depends on whether the answer to the question can be expressed merely in ready-made form from the textbook without understanding and thinking. A real thought question presents students with a new, problematic situation—a changed setting and a demand for different facts and a different relationship of the facts. Of course the question must not be so new as to be completely frustrating.

A few examples of suitable essay questions for some classes may help:

---

1. Write a paragraph on a topic of your choice. Explain how you followed two rules of good paragraphing.
2. Give and support two generalizations from your reading of *Ivanhoe*.
3. Compare the writing of Mark Twain with that of O. Henry, particularly with respect to picturing characters.
4. Explain application of principles of the lever to provision in the bicycle for relatively easy and swift movement.

5. How does an aviator adjust the wings of an airplane on takeoff? Why?
6. Explain why cutting a second hole in the top of a can results in speeding the flow of liquid from the can.
7. Geographical conditions in Argentina are like and unlike those in the United States. Point out how a similarity and a dissimilarity of these conditions between the two countries have a bearing on their commercial relations.
8. Drawing on your knowledge of propaganda and the scientific method, evaluate arguments for and against open housing.
9. Point out how economic conditions in our country have effected increased control of management and labor by the federal government.

Thus evaluation of the student's achievements is a broad and vital concept. It is an integral part of the whole instructional process. It affects and is affected by the teacher's aims and practices—the choices of course content and the methods of teaching, guiding, and disciplining. It occurs as he observes the processes and the products of learning and as he uses tests to examine the learnings. Moreover, it includes achievements not only in knowledge of subject matter but also in development of attitudes, abilities, and habits of a good student and citizen. These achievements of adolescents in today's high school assist them to develop in thinking toward democratic ends and to live useful, happy lives. A teacher committed to meeting the real educational needs of different youths endeavors to direct evaluation no less than instruction toward all these ends.

QUESTIONS AND ACTIVITIES

1. Discuss how the observational method of evaluating results is superior to the examination method for evaluation of some outcomes.
2. Give examples of the many good opportunities for evaluating results incidentally in the modern high school.
3. Organize a panel of high-school students to discuss their experiences with "testing." Can they suggest any additional ways of evaluating learning?
4. How might a teacher encourage subjective student self-evaluations as a defensible part of a total evaluation?
5. State whether the essay examination or the objective test has high

validity for measurement in "new" courses of the high-school curriculum. Support your statement.

6. Invite a specialist in tests and measurement to your class to discuss various phases of evaluation at such levels as the classroom, the school, the district, the state and the nation.

7. Construct a list of objective test questions and a list of essay examination questions, and defend each construction.

8. How would you improve current practices of evaluating results in high school?

SELECTED REFERENCES

Alcorn, M. D., and others, *Better Teaching in Secondary Schools*, 3rd ed., Holt, Rinehart and Winston, New York, 1970, Chap. 16.

Bayles, E. E., *Democratic Educational Theory*, Harper and Row, New York, 1960, Chap. 14.

Brown, F. G., *Principles of Educational and Psychological Testing*, Holt, Rinehart and Winston, New York, 1970.

Dizney, H. F., *Classroom Evaluation for Teachers*, William C. Brown, Dubuque, Iowa, 1971.

Green, J. A., *Introduction to Measurement and Evaluation*, Dodd, Mead, New York, 1970.

Gronlund, N. E., *Constructing Achievement Tests*, paper, Prentice-Hall, Englewood Cliffs, New Jersey, 1968.

Gronlund, N. E., *Measurement and Evaluation in Teaching*, 2nd ed., Macmillan, New York, 1971.

Gronlund, N. E., *Readings in Measurement and Evaluation: Education and Psychology*, paper, Macmillan, New York, 1968.

Horrocks, J. E., and Thelma I. Schoonover, *Measurement for Teachers*, Charles E. Merrill, Columbus, Ohio, 1968, Chaps. 5, 21.

Karmel, L. J., *Measurement and Evaluation in the Schools*, Macmillan, New York, 1970.

Nelson, C. H., *Measurement and Evaluation in the Classroom*, Macmillan, New York, 1970.

Remmers, H. H., and others, *A Practical Introduction to Measurement and Evaluation*, 2nd ed., Harper and Row, New York, 1965.

Strom, R. D., *Psychology for the Classroom*, Prentice-Hall, Englewood Cliffs, New Jersey, 1969, Chap. 6.

Strom, R. D., ed., *Teachers and the Learning Process*, Prentice-Hall, Englewood Cliffs, New Jersey, 1971, Chap. 6.

Thorndike, R. L., and E. Hagen, *Measurement and Evaluation in Psychology and Education*, 3rd ed., John Wiley, New York, 1969.

Thorndike, R. L., and others, *Educational Measurement*, American Council on Education, 2nd ed., Washington, D. C., 1971.

Wilson, J. A. R., and others, *Psychological Foundations of Learning and Teaching*, McGraw-Hill, New York, 1969, Chap. 23.

SUBJECT INDEX

Committees, of students, 84–85, 331. *See also* Group activities

Community

  effect on students, 4–5, 33–34, 310–311

  as laboratory for learning, 16, 94, 109–110, 200, 209, 227–228, 313

Concept

  acquired through concrete experiences, 25, 70–72, 75–76, 124, 139, 147–149, 164–165, 172, 212–216, 225–226, 239–241

  as element of thinking, 54, 84, 148, 239. *See also* Generalization

Concerns of students, a basis of instruction, 6–16, 38, 128–129, 150, 208–209

Concrete experiences

  toward generalizing, 37, 62–63, 65, 71–72, 76–77, 83–84, 95, 102, 116, 259

  in specific subjects, 124, 142–143, 177–181, 184–185, 189, 195–196, 207–208, 214–215, 217

Conditioning

  basis of programed instruction, 32, 255–257

  inadequacy of, 31–32, 256–257, 311

Conference

  features of, 306–308

  for improvement of learning, 63, 86, 97–99, 126, 134–135, 313

  in order of classroom, 329–330

  in personalized reading, 90, 125–126, 128–129, 309

  in practical arts, 201–202, 207, 212

  in writing of compositions, 133–135, 141

Construction activities, 32–33, 210–211, 343. *See also* Creative learning

Controversial matters, 15, 150–155. *See also* Problems

Cookbook procedure, 167, 200, 210

Counselor, 300, 308–313, 330

Creative learning, 200–201, 210, 216, 259, 269, 276, 288, 291. *See also* Construction activities

Creative writing, 132–136. *See also* Creative learning

Culminating activities

  barriers to reflective procedure, 117–118

  dynamic discussion, 110–113

  facts through thinking, 103–106

  final steps in problem solving, 103–104

  group spirit, 106–108

  guidance of, 112–113

  practices, specified, 109

  questioning procedure, 114–117

  reporting of experiences, 109–110

  standards constructed, 113–114

Cultural backgrounds, 9–10, 17, 33–35, 37, 188, 206

Cultures, focal area in new social studies, 144–145, 148–149

Current events, 145–148. *See also* Problems

Curriculum

  relevancy of, 8, 10–11, 38, 44, 124, 217, 289, 312, 322, 324–325

  in revised subjects, 144–149, 164–174, 198–199, 215–216, 263

Delinquents

  changing attitudes of, 5–6, 96–97, 336–337

  production of, 3–5, 10

Democracy

  erroneous views of, 41–42

  frame of reference for educational objectives, 46–55

  an ideal way of life, 42–43, 205, 259

Democratic objectives

  challenge to all types of teachers, 54–55, 112–113

  implementations of specified, 62–66, 103–108, 150–154, 204–206, 266–267, 295–296, 319–323, 340–342

  reflective thinking, 309–312, 320–321

  shared interests, 46–48, 319–321

  social outlook and sensitivity, 48–51, 321–323. *See also* Objectives

Determinism

  basis of programed instruction, 257–259

  in conflict with democracy, 258–259

Discipline

  democratic objectives and, 47, 319–322

  features of, 46–55, 317–320

  through teaching, 102–108, 118–119, 321–323, 325–327, 329, 331–332, 335–336. *See also* Order, in classroom

Discovery learning

  toward conceptualizing and generalizing, 72–77, 102–106, 111, 159–160, 180–188

  experimental support of, 28–30

  in independent study, 276–279

  in initiation of problem solving, 65–72, 208–210, 215–216, 268

  in new subjects, 147–149, 161–175, 178–179, 182–188, 214–216, 259

  provisions for, 62–63, 67–78, 180–188, 200–201, 207–212, 259, 283–284

Discussion

  democratic climate, 112–114, 117, 150–154

  extensive participation, 78–79, 110–112, 129–130

  guidance, 19, 63–64, 111–114, 207–208

  from vital experiences, 71–72, 109–111, 127–130, 145, 150–152, 207–209, 215–216, 306

Disk records, important uses of, 236–238

Dress code, 335–336

Drill

  on meaningless performance, 25–26, 38, 139, 177–178

  on significant performance, 139, 177–178, 196–197

Dropouts

  causes of, 3–5, 8, 17

  instruction for, 63, 119, 164, 167, 206, 279

  retention of, 298–299, 313–314

Duty

  and intelligence, 47

and interest, 47, 319–320. *See also* Discipline

Ecological problems, for study, 146, 164–165, 168–170

English composition
evaluation of, 140–141
group experiences, 84–85, 133–134
independent creative writing, 135–136
individualized experiences, 133–136
through thinking, 84–85, 132–136
workshop situation, 98, 133–135

English literature. *See* Literature

Environment
and discipline, 319, 328–329, 336
an educational force, 3–6, 17, 34–35, 51, 64, 94, 97–98, 106, 125, 127, 258, 336
in guidance, 303, 310–314
interaction with learners, 24, 31, 258–259, 310, 319, 328–329

Essay examination
in literature, 132
in new science, 169
in studying students, 305. *See also* Tests

Evaluation of achievements
and educational objectives, 132, 140–141, 340–341
functions of, 339–340
nontesting procedures, 133–135, 140–141, 169, 342–344
testing procedures, 344–356. *See also* Tests

Evaluation of activities, 31, 85–86, 102–106, 132–135, 150–152, 211. *See also* Activities

Experiences, past, 33–34, 62–65, 70–71, 78–79, 83, 137, 256–258. *See also* Background

Extracurricular activities, 8. *See also* Curriculum

Facts
learned through thinking, 38, 95, 103–106, 162–163, 208–209
measurement of, 132, 340–342
memorized from textbook, 103, 143, 170

Factual examination
effect on study, 97, 154, 353–354
prevalence of, 53, 70, 95, 340. *See also* Tests

Failing, of students, 17, 47–48

Family, students' study of, 149, 205–209.

Field theory. *See* Gestalt theory

Field trips, thoughtful use of, 228–229

Film strips, in new subjects, 235

Films, for new courses, 161, 186

Flexible scheduling
characteristics of, 280–283
use of, 281–283

Foreign languages, modern, 141–143. *See also* Grammar

Freedom
a relative concept, 41–42, 257–258, 322
and responsibility, 105, 259, 312, 321–323, 335–336

General Science
inquiry procedure, 166–167

new organization of, 164–165. *See also* Science

Generalizations
formation of, 69–70, 73–76, 102–105, 145–146, 148, 153–154, 173–174, 183, 210, 277–278
memorized from textbook, 37, 143, 159–160, 179
providing support for, 102–106, 111, 115, 151

Geometry
former recommendations for, 72–75, 179–183
inductive-deductive procedure, 72–76, 180–183
nature of proof, 181–182
toward transference of learning, 179–182. *See also* Mathematics

Gestalt learning
demonstrations of, 35–37, 131–132, 150–152, 173–174, 196–198
general implications of, 37–38
goal in, 24–25, 31, 34–35, 150, 259
insight in, 24–25, 33–34, 150, 259
pattern in, 32–33, 147–149, 196–197, 199–200. *See also* Learning

Goals
group, 83–85, 106–107, 110–114, 268, 305–306
intrinsic, 25–27, 34–35, 70–71, 88, 124, 133–134, 136–137, 177–178, 216–218, 257, 304
personal-societal, 37, 48–49, 51, 70, 83–85, 104, 106–107, 110–114, 128–131, 268, 303, 305–306
in relation to results, 106–108, 132, 140–141, 305–306. *See also* Intrinsic objectives

Goal seeking, in ideal learning, 26–27, 34, 38, 70–71, 76–77, 96, 130, 218, 271. *See also* Independent study

Grammar
formal, appraised by research, 138–139
functional, effectiveness of, 67–70, 139, 142. *See also* Linguistic grammar

Graphical materials, 231–233

Ground covering, 61–62, 66, 70, 146, 340. *See also* Textbook

Ground rules, 77–78, 113–114

Group activities, cohesiveness and thinking, 63–64, 83–85, 106–108, 131–135, 211–213. *See also* Individual activities

Grouping, through interests and needs, 84, 131, 133, 211–212

Guidance
toward academic success, 7–9, 83–92, 98–99, 123–127, 300–301
through environment, 97–98, 310–312
in group procedure, 106–107, 133–135, 305–306, 328–330
in interviews, 98–99, 306–310, 329–330
need of, 8–9, 54–55, 282, 298–300

Guidance *(continued)*
    toward personal-social development, 8–16,
      300, 303
    teacher's role, 9–11, 55, 62–64, 91–92, 98,
      103, 111–112, 275–280, 300
    through understanding students, 206–207,
      303–305
    in urban schools, 312–314
    toward a vocation, 12–14, 202–203, 301–303
Guides, for teachers, 148, 161, 165–168, 171,
    186

Haircut crises. *See* Dress code
Health problems, instruction on, 9–10, 209–
    210
Home
    effects on students, 3–4, 10–11, 17, 312,
      324, 329
    visitation in, 206–207, 312, 336
Home economics
    broad objectives, 204–205
    investigative, democratic procedure, 207–212
    personalized instruction, 206–207
    problems in home and community, 205–207
    suggestions for written-composition instruc-
      tion, 98, 133–134
Homogeneous grouping, nature of, 84, 89–90
Humanistic teaching
    some features of, v
    representative practices of, 17–20, 35–38,
      61–66, 90–92, 109–114, 306–310, 336–
      337. *See also* Democratic objectives

Incorrigibles
    guidance for, 298
    positive discipline for, 119, 321–323, 331–
      332, 336–337. *See also* Delinquents
Independent study
    characteristics of, 275–277
    in modular scheduling, 280–282
    through reflective learning, 34–37, 70, 75–76,
      97–99, 129–131, 135–136, 196–198, 261,
      271, 275–279
    for all students, 92–99, 109–114, 133–136,
      265, 277–280, 291. *See also* Study
Individual activities, 51, 72, 83, 85–86, 90–92,
    109–110, 167, 174, 197–198, 201–202
Individual differences, nature of, 88–90. *See
    also* Individualized instruction
Individualized instruction
    in English, 127–128, 133–136
    group-individual procedure, 90–92, 278–280,
      306–310
    in home economics, 133, 206–207, 210–212
    in independent study, 276–280
    toward positive discipline, 322–323
    in reading, 19–20, 35–37, 90–92, 126–127
    in science, 167, 174
    in team teaching, 265, 268–269
    in typewriting, 196–198
Inductive-deductive procedure, 69–70, 75–76,
    146–149, 175, 177–178, 181–188, 268

Industrial arts, career education, 202–203
    implications for English composition instruc-
      tion, 98, 133
    objectives and program, 198–199
    problem solving, 199–201
    student planning, 200–201
Insight, an essential of learning, 24–26, 30, 33–
    34, 37, 76. *See also* Meaning
Intelligence
    in ability grouping, 88–89
    in discipline, 320–322
Intelligence test, use of, 90, 304–305
Interest
    in discipline, 319–322, 336
    for retention and transfer of learning, 88, 108
Interests, shared
    a democratic objective, 46–48
    in duty, 47
    in personal qualities and scholastic achieve-
      ment, 47–48, 63, 84, 106–108, 123, 130–
      135, 178–179, 188–189, 207–209, 305–
      306, 310
    in thinking, 48. *See also* Goals
Interview, 306–310. *See also* Conference
Intrinsic objectives, in self-directed learning,
    62–63, 93, 111, 125–136, 275–276. *See
    also* Goals
Inventory, 90, 304–305

Laboratory, for student research, 77, 94–95,
    102, 109–110, 161, 166–168, 171–175,
    199–201, 211, 259, 278. *See also* Materials
    center
Laboratory manual, in new sciences, 87–88,
    166, 168, 171–172
Laissez faire, 37, 111. *See also* Permissiveness
Learners
    high achievers, 88, 90–92, 131, 174, 202,
      206, 262, 269, 277–278
    low achievers, 16–20, 88, 90–92, 131, 174,
      188–189, 203, 206, 213–214, 262–263,
      277–278, 313–314. *See also* Individualized
      instruction
Learning
    demonstrated in reading instruction, 35–36,
      124–127, 244–245
    effective features of, 24–27
    experimentation on, 28–30, 245
    focal points of, 32–35
    implications for humanistic teaching, 37–38
    retention and transfer of, 88, 108, 177, 180–
      183
    supported by educational psychologists, 30–
      32
    theories of, 31–35. *See also* Study
Lecture, 98, 103, 128, 265–268, 271
Lecture-demonstration, 210, 265–268, 271,
    281
Lesson plan
    essentials of, 67
    necessity of, 55, 66–67. *See also* Planning
Librarian, functions of, 36, 129, 311–312

362

Personal problems *(continued)*
    154, 207–210, 278, 322. *See also* Problems
    of students
Personal traits, developed through guidance,
    300, 303, 314, 322–323. *See also* Students
Personalized instruction, 8–9, 19–20, 336–337.
    See also Individualized instruction
Physical sciences, integration of physics and
    chemistry, 169–170
Physics, laboratory approach, 172–173
    origin of new course, 172
    report of adoption, 173
    teacher-student assignment in, 77
Pictures, still, 230–231
Planning, of activities, 55, 62, 64, 66–67, 108,
    123, 133, 201, 208, 210–211, 213–214,
    306, 310, 331. *See also* Reporting experi-
    ences
Prejudice, practices and preventions of, 107,
    112, 114, 144, 151–152, 155. *See also*
    Propaganda
Principal, in improving teaching, 17–18, 270,
    300, 312
Problem solving
    demonstrated, 67–70, 104, 150–151
    in guidance, 8–13, 309–310
    in specific subjects, 70–77, 129–130, 153–
    154, 208
    steps of, 65–66, 71, 95, 103, 195, 200–201,
    208–209, 309
Problems of students
    educational, 7–9, 300, 336
    personal-societal, 6–16, 70–71, 104, 128–
    131, 148, 205–207, 278, 303, 309, 322,
    336
    vocational, 12–14, 301–303. *See also* Goals
Programed instruction, features of, 253–254
    modern education and, 259
    philosophical basis of, 257–258
    psychological basis of, 255–257
    usefulness of, 254–255, 277–278
Programed textbook, 255, 261, 277–278. *See*
    also Textbook
Projects, 200–201, 210–211. *See also* Activities
Propaganda, means of combatting, 5, 104, 152,
    275, 322. *See also* Prejudice
Punishment
    corporal, banned, 334
    used with reservation, 18, 332–335. *See also*
    Order in classroom

Questioning
    in culminating period, 103–104, 107, 110–
    111, 114–117
    in particular subjects, 127, 129, 150–151,
    170, 178, 182, 186, 194–195, 213
    by students, 55, 62, 78, 103, 107, 110–111,
    115, 129, 182, 215, 278
    toward thinking, in assignment period, 62,
    65–67, 71, 75–77, 79, 115, 178, 194–195
Questions, thought, lists of, 66, 71, 116, 129,
    146, 153. *See also* Questioning

Radio. *See* Television
Reading instruction
    in content courses, 94, 124, 244–245
    demonstrations of, 19–20, 35–37, 126–127
    individualized procedures, 35–37, 125–127,
    336
    special programs, 93–94, 124–127, 244–245
Reading materials
    for "content" subjects, 173, 244–245
    distributors of, 246–250. *See also* Materials
    of instruction
Reading skills, deficiency of, in underachievers,
    8, 17, 93, 124, 279, 325, 336. *See also*
    Reading instruction
Reflective thinking
    an antidote to prejudice and propaganda, 144
    a democratic objective, 42, 51–55
    implementation of, 28–30, 52–55, 65–66,
    103–106, 109–117, 129–132, 145–154,
    160, 166–169, 171–172, 200–201, 210–
    212
    importance of, 51–52, 94–96, 132–133,
    143–144, 320–322
    instructional barriers to, 117–118. *See also*
    Discovery learning
Reinforcement
    in behavioristic psychology, 31
    key feature of programed instruction, 253,
    256, 262
Relevancy, of instruction. *See* Needs
Religion
    in new social studies, 144
    a student concern, 14–15
Report paper
    in evaluation of achievement, 344
    as means of learning, 95, 97, 109–110, 133–
    136, 229
    in study of students, 305
Reporting experiences, 34, 64–65, 85–86, 95,
    97, 102, 109–110, 133–134. *See also*
    Report paper
Research, in effective study, 71–72, 94–95,
    110, 150–151, 166–167, 170–172, 210–
    212, 229. *See also* Discovery learning
Retention of learning, 30, 177, 255. *See also*
    Learning
Rule approach
    in English instruction, 68, 139
    in mathematics, 29, 76, 178, 260

Science
    biology, 167–169
    general science, 164–167
    as a method, 160
    new chemistry, 170–172
    new physics, 172–173
    new science, 161–175
    objectives of, 162–164
    physical sciences, 169–173
    satisfactory results, 169, 173–174
Scientific thinking, a focal point in all subjects,
    75–78, 107, 143–144, 149–151, 159–175,

199–201, 210–212. *See also* Reflective thinking

Self-direction, 278–280, 287–291, 298. *See also* Independent study

Self-esteem
effect on reading ability, 9, 20, 96
improvement of, 8–9, 20, 106–107, 132, 292–293, 303, 314
low in underachievers, 7–9, 14, 20, 89, 97

Sensory experiences
as a basis for reading, 127, 225–226
in initiation of student activities, 236
for perceptual-conceptual background, 30, 34–35, 200, 225–226, 239–240. *See also* Materials of instruction

Sets, a focal point in modern mathematics, 183–184

Seven Cardinal Principles, 43–44

Sex education, 11–12

Skills acquired
through insight, 13, 25, 142–143, 183–184, 196–197
through use, 37, 132–139, 210–212. *See also* Reading skills

Social groups, affecting students, 3–6

Socialmindedness, 63–65, 83–85, 106–107, 118–119, 143, 305–306. *See also* Social outlook

Social outlook
analysis and implementation of, 5–6, 15–16, 50–51, 61–65, 106–107
a democratic objective, 42, 48–51
extensive advocacy of, 48–50. *See also* Social studies

Social studies
current problems studied, 70–71, 146–148, 151
Indiana experiment, 153–154
objectives and courses, 143–144
problem solving illustrated, 150–154
Project Social Studies, 146–149
revisions of, 144–150
scientific thinking in democratic climate, 143–144, 148–153
Secondary School History Committee, 145–146

Societal problems. *See* Problems of students

Society, a basic point of reference
in appraisal of learning, 24, 27, 32
in culminating activities, 106–107
in guidance and discipline, 314, 317, 329
in initiation of activities, 65, 70
in practical arts, 196, 198–200, 202, 204–205
in provision for student needs, 3, 6–7, 12, 14–16
in relation to educational objectives, 42, 44, 49–50
in science instruction, 159, 161, 165
in social studies, 147–148
in special procedures, 259, 275, 290

Sociogram, 207

Specimen, as a visual aid, 229–230

Speech instruction, 136–138

Spelling, effective learning of, 25–26

Standardized tests, use of, 154, 292, 304–305. *See also* Tests

Student council, 336. *See also* Committees

Students
cultural backgrounds of, 3–6, 17, 188, 206–207, 213, 312
freedom of, 275–280, 282, 287–288, 290–291, 293
mental health, 8, 17, 91, 299, 318, 325, 332
negative attitudes, 8, 16–18
physical condition, 9–10, 17, 313, 325, 329, 333
self-esteem, 7–8, 14, 20, 91, 97
teacher's understanding of, 6, 37, 63, 88, 206–207, 303–305, 328–330. *See also* Needs

Study
essential student abilities, 93–95
improvement of, 92–99
mental health and motivation, 96–97
whole student in total environment, 97–98. *See also* Independent study

Study period, group activities, 83–85
homogeneous grouping, 88–90
improvement of study, 92–99
individual activities, 85–92
individualized reading, 90–91. *See also* Study

Success
affected by home, 3–4, 8, 17
in future attainments, 8, 19–20, 96, 189

Tape recordings, 217, 236–237

Teachers
attitudes toward students, 18–20, 89, 152–153, 307–309
freedom of, 287–288, 290–291, 312
importance of, 88, 106, 117–118, 149–150, 155, 162, 175, 184, 217, 260, 271–272, 278–279, 282, 284, 296, 308–309, 323–328
in-service education of, 162, 173–175, 185, 199, 271–272, 284, 312
knowledge and skills of, 18–19, 76, 170, 184, 199, 217, 266–267, 270–272, 277–278, 282, 284, 300
mental health and philosophy of, 37, 67, 149–150, 154–155, 175, 203, 266, 272, 325–328, 332, 334–335
as models for students, 94, 98, 111, 162, 327–328

Team teaching
appraisal of, 267–269
characteristics of, 264–265
effect on teachers, 265–266
research findings about, 269–270
and school's goals, 266–267
suggestions for adoption, 270–272

Technological products, as bases of instruction, 163, 174, 200

Television, 238–239
Tests, teacher made
  construction of, 354–356
  effect on study, 353
  reliability of, 347–352
  usability of, 352–353
  validity of, 132, 140–141, 169, 345–347.
    See also Factual examination
Textbook, conventional uses, 66, 70, 87, 95,
    98, 103–104, 127, 145, 147, 167, 170,
    217, 262, 311, 340
  programed, 261, 277
  reflective uses, 77, 95, 127, 147, 150–153,
    165–166, 168–169, 171, 186, 194, 217
Transfer of learning
  in English composition, 138
  through interest and meaning, 88, 108, 255,
    262–263
  in mathematics, 72–74, 177, 180–182
  in social studies, 147

Underachievers
  concerns of, 7–16
  environments of, 3–6, 63, 312
  guidance for, 299–300, 312–314
  implications for teaching, 6, 16–20, 312–313
  improvement of, 17–20, 186–189
  mental health of, 3–4, 7–8, 17, 299
  reading skills of, 7–8, 17. *See also* Students
Understanding, in learning, 177, 180–181, 184–
    185, 187–188, 196–197, 200, 203, 209–210,
    213–216, 255, 263. *See also* Insight
Units
  in business, 194

toward development of concepts, 37
  in home economics, 211–212
  in literature, 127
  in modern mathematics, 183–184, 186
  in new industrial arts, 199
  in new social studies, 145–149
  in science, 165, 170, 186
Unrest, of students, 6, 119, 312, 325, 336
Urban education, comprehensive program
    demonstrated, 336–337
  guidance in, 312–314
  improvement of instruction in, 17–20,
    312–314
  unfavorable conditions, 16–17, 312

Verbalization
  premature, 70, 76, 185, 225–226, 259
  reduced by meaningful experiences, 114–117,
    147, 225–226
Visitation, in home, 206–207, 312–313
Vocational education
  guidance in, 301–303, 313
  need and quality of, 12–14, 193–196,
    202–204, 212

Will and interest, 319–320. *See also* Interest
Workbook, a questionable means of instruction,
    52, 98, 108, 141, 173
Workshop environment, 84, 86, 98, 134
Work-study experiences, 14, 203, 313

Youth groups
  effect on students, 4–5, 106–107, 129–132
  production of, 3–5. *See also* Peer groups

NAME INDEX

Deterline, W. A., 292
Dewey, J., 49, 65, 81, 99, 150, 153, 160, 163, 319, 320
DiSanto, J. D., 284
Dizney, H. F., 357
Doll, R. C., 18
Dorney, W. P., 96
Douglas, H. R., 49, 50
Douglas, L. V., 196, 197, 219
Dover, N. B., 196
Downing, L. N., 304, 305
Dreikurs, R., 338
Duker, S., 100, 157
Dumas, W., 57
Duncan, C. H., 198
Dunn, K. J., 243, 252
Dyrli, O. E., 90, 165

Easterday, K. E., 189
Ebel, R. L., 288, 347
Eckerson, L. O., 299
Edelson, E., 221
Ehn, W., 282
Ehrenhaft, G., 132
Ehrenwerth, B. J., 126
Eisner, E. W., 290
Elliott, E. C., 349, 350
Emmer, E. T., 82
Erickson, C. W. H., 234, 242, 243, 251
Erickson, E. L., 5, 64
Erlich, J., 338
Erlich, S., 338
Esler, W. K., 191
Eson, M. E., 39, 120, 338
Estvan, F. J., 158
Eulie, J., 147
Eurich, A. C., 297

Fabiano, E., 169
Fagan, E. R., 140
Fallers, M., 282
Farrell, E. J., 294
Farwell, G. H., 11
Fawcett, H. P., 181, 184, 188, 191
Feins, D., 261
Feirer, J. L., 202
Feldman, M. E., 262
Fenton, E., 57, 72, 105, 147, 158
Ferguson, W. E., 76, 186
Findley, W. G., 89
Fink, N. W., 336
Fishbein, J. M., 288
Flaum, L. S., 310, 316
Fleck, H. C., 205, 208, 211, 212, 220
Fleming, C. M., 22
Folk, H., 13
Folstrom, R. J., 221
Foster, B. J., 8
Freeman, F. N., 176, 351
Fremont, H., 191
French, J. L., 8
Frerichs, A. H., 22, 91, 92

Frey, S. H., 39, 260, 338
Fullmer, D. W., 306
Furukawa, J. M., 262
Fussel, R., 194

Gabor, G. M., 34
Gallup, G., 11
Gard, R. R., 282
Gardner, W. E., 158
Garner, W. L., 253, 254, 262, 263, 273
Garrison, K. C., 15, 30
Garrison, L. L., 194
Gehret, K., 294
Georgiades, W., 341
Gilchrist, R., 316
Glaser, R., 256, 286, 287
Glass, B., 161, 191
Glenn, N. E., 221
Gnagey, T., 335
Gnagey, W. J., 39, 338
Goldberg, M. H., 262
Good, J. M., 147
Gordon, E., 221
Gordon, G. N., 251
Gordon, I. J., 22
Gorman, B. W., 50, 57, 82, 297, 338
Graff, R. W., 311
Graham, G., 4, 16, 42, 50, 57
Grambs, J. D., 315
Green, E. A., 221
Green, J. A., 357
Grinder, R. E., 22
Grittner, F. M., 157
Grobman, A. B., 167, 169, 191
Groff, P., 127
Gronlund, N. E., 341, 343, 346, 347, 351, 352, 357
Gunderson, D. V., 128
Gunn, M. A., 124, 125, 129
Guthrie, M. R., 198

Hackett, D. F., 198
Hackney, Jr., B. H., 9
Hagen, E., 340, 354, 358
Halchin, L. C., 220
Hall, I. N., 9, 21
Hall, M. M., 89
Hall, O. A., 205, 207, 220
Hallahan, D. P., 100
Halsey, Jr., V. R., 145
Hamachek, D. E., 39, 326, 328
Haney, J., 251
Haney, R. E., 163
Hanna, C. C., 8
Hansen, D. A., 316
Hansen, J. C., 298, 316
Hanslovsky, G., 274
Hardy, C. A., 80
Hardy, L. L., 100
Harmin, M., 165
Harris, L. A., 100
Harrison, Jr., A., 336

1 2 3 4 5 6 7 8 9 0